AMERICAN
BUSINESS HISTORY

HERMAN E. KROOSS
Graduate School of Business Administration
New York University

CHARLES GILBERT
Graduate School of Business
Hofstra University

PRENTICE-HALL, INC., *Englewood Cliffs, New Jersey*

ISBN: P 0–13–024083–4

C 0–13–024091–5

Library of Congress Number: 71–172403

10 9 8 7 6 5 4 3 2 1

Printed in the United States of America

PRENTICE-HALL INTERNATIONAL, INC., *London*
PRENTICE-HALL OF AUSTRALIA, PTY. LTD., *Sydney*
PRENTICE-HALL OF CANADA, LTD., *Toronto*
PRENTICE-HALL OF INDIA PRIVATE LIMITED, *New Delhi*
PRENTICE-HALL OF JAPAN, INC., *Tokyo*

CONTENTS

iii

THE TRANSITION FROM THE MERCHANT
TO THE MANUFACTURER, 1780–1850

BUSINESS PROBLEMS IN THE EARLY
NINETEENTH CENTURY

DISTRIBUTION AND OTHER EARLY
NINETEENTH-CENTURY PROBLEMS

THE APPEARANCE OF BIG BUSINESS, 1850–1900

TABLES

PREFACE

The purpose of this book is to tell the story of American business in terms of its changing problems, changing environment, and its changing attempts at solutions. It is an endeavor to fill a gap in understanding the development of the United States, a gap caused by historical emphasis on political, military, social, and (much later) economic affairs which perhaps seemed much more fascinating but were not, in our opinion, more important.

Although the entrepreneur has long been accepted as the fourth factor of production, combining the others in machine-like fashion, his function has more or less been taken for granted with little thought and less analysis of the implications of his decisions and their effect on society—or, on the other hand, the effect of societal institutions on his decisions.

However, business has not been completely neglected. Many are the laudatory works commemorating anniversaries of "our founder," and many are the diatribes that have depicted business as a monstrous institution. Unfortunately, these have contributed little to our knowledge and less to our understanding. Of greater value have been more recent company histories and scholarly articles with less biased views and more analytical insight. To the authors of these works we owe a debt of gratitude.

We are not attempting "to set the record straight" but to describe without pride or prejudice on our part what has occurred in the business life of the United States. We are concerned with the problems that businessmen have faced and their attempts at solutions, with their successes and the reasons for success, and with their contribution to American life.

Over a period of years our students at the Graduate School of Business of New York University and at Hofstra University have provided a receptive and, at times, critical audience for much of the material in this book. For this we thank them. We are also indebted to those two stalwarts of the typewriter, Lee Silman and Diane Gilbert, who somehow managed to decipher the scrawls we set on paper.

HERMAN E. KROOSS
CHARLES GILBERT

1

INTRODUCTION

Since this is a book about business history, it seems reasonable to begin with a brief explanation of what we mean by business history.

History is the study of how things came to be as they are. Business is the branch of economic activity that combines the other factors of production—land, labor, and capital—in the production and exchange of goods in order to make a profit. The history of business, therefore, is the story of how the business system and the businessman came to be what they are today. In this book we are concerned with the obstacles and problems that businessmen faced, the solutions that were tried, the successes that were attained, the institutions that were built, and the interrelationships between business and society's other blocs—government, labor, and the public in general.

BUSINESS AND BUSINESSMEN

By definition, anyone who is engaged in producing or exchanging goods and services in order to make a profit is a businessman. But businessmen as well as business firms come in all sizes and shapes. There is no such thing as a typical businessman. Some are big businessmen spending their working time in offices with a Bigelow on the floor. Others are medium-size executives superintending the operation of a factory. There are businessmen in large stores, and there are others in small shops. The men who make business decisions run the whole gamut of standards and types.

Nor are all businessmen of equal importance or equal influence. There are at least 5 million business firms in the United States today. The Census

Bureau counts approximately $3\frac{1}{2}$ million firms that are included in the social security program. Of these, approximately one-third are in retailing, and another one-quarter provide services. Table 1 tells us that one-tenth do constructing and building, another one-tenth handle finance, one-twelfth are in manufacturing, and another one-twelfth are wholesalers. Of the $3\frac{1}{2}$ million firms under social security, almost 90 percent employ fewer than 20 people each (see Table 2). They account for only one-quarter of the employed who are covered by social security. On the other hand, firms employing 250 or more constitute only $\frac{3}{4}$ of 1 percent of all firms, but they employ $\frac{2}{3}$ of all the workers. Quite clearly, there are only a small number of big business firms, but these firms are very big indeed. Just how big can be gathered from a cursory look at the General Motors Corporation. GM employs more people than the entire population of Boston. Its annual income is larger than the total tax revenue of the twenty-two states and one territory covering the East and the South.

Given the vast diversity of the business population, it is patently impossible to talk about business history in terms of the total business population. We must be concerned with those firms and those businessmen who by their decisions have a significant effect on the business system and through the business system on society in general. Small businesses such as the corner drugstore, the green grocer, and the haberdasher have no such power. Their proprietors may be, and often are, worthy members of the community. Hard working and sometimes successful, they may be the backbone of America. Certainly, they are the most numerous group in business, but their influence on the totality of society is infinitesimal.

On the other hand the large business firms are in a strategic position to influence the business environment. But a great many of these firms, either because of lack of interest or courage, never exert their influence. It is only a small fraction of all business firms and all businessmen who exercise their latent power. It is with this small fraction that we are concerned. They are entrepreneurs in the true sense of the word. They are the businessmen who make significant decisions regarding the conduct of a business enterprise.

TABLE 1   Industrial Distribution of Firms Reporting Under Social Security, 1966

Retail	30.3%	Manufacturing	8.3%
Service	26.7	Transportation	3.8
Finance	9.2	Agriculture, forestry,	
Construction	9.1	fishing	1.7
Wholesale	8.4	Other	2.4

Source: Bureau of the Census, *County Business Patterns.*

THE BUSINESSMAN AS ENTREPRENEUR

One noted business historian, Professor Fritz Redlich, has defined the entrepreneur as "a man who (alone or with others) shapes and reshapes business enterprise, establishes its relations with other enterprises and fits it into the market . . . the man who directs and determines its spirit and its strategy by making the major decisions." A synonym for the word entrepreneur as it is used here would be top decision or policy maker. The difference between the executive and the manager, that is, between top decision making and administration was once explained as follows:

By "administration" is meant the daily conduct of the Corporation's affairs. By "formation of policy" is meant both the establishment of the broad principles by which administration is to be guided and the determination of the fundamental concepts of the business. The prime objectives of the business; the scope of its operations, both as to products and markets; the desirability of expansion, horizontally or vertically or both; the provision of the essential capital for its operations; and the question of distribution of its profits as between the amount paid in dividends and the amount retained in the business—all are problems involving "formulation of policies" and illustrate the principle involved.[1]

TABLE 2   Number of Firms by Share of Employment, 1966

Firms Employing	Percent of all Firms	Share of Employment
1–3	54.66%	6.35%
4–7	19.37	7.00
8–19	15.27	12.69
20–49	6.59	13.84
50–99	2.19	10.46
100–249	1.24	13.20
250–499	0.39	9.55
500 and over	0.28	26.91

Source: Bureau of the Census, *County Business Patterns.*

How important is the entrepreneur to business history? The answer is that, like another famous institution, he is so important that if he didn't exist, he would have to be invented. Scholars who believe that the economic environment accounts for everything and the individual human be-

[1]Annual Report of the General Motors Corporation for the year ending December 1937.

ing for nothing argue that individual entrepreneurs do not matter because if they did not exist, some one else would take their place. As one recent writer expresses it, the play is the thing and not the star.[2] But this beating a tired horse has nothing to do with the fundamental question. The fact of the matter is that the entrepreneur did exist and does exist. It happened to be Henry Ford, Andrew Carnegie, et al, and not John Doe or Richard Roe, To be sure, emphasis on the human being in history, whether it be business history, political history, intellectual history, or any other kind of history, does tend to underestimate the importance of the environment. It therefore has the danger of becoming a personality cult. Entrepreneurship is a function, not a person, but functions are performed by entrepreneurs.

The entrepreneur has four basic functions. He must determine the organization's objectives. He must build an organization by obtaining the necessary managerial personnel and by securing adequate financial resources. Third, he must determine the organization's strategy. That is, he must decide on the firm's rate of expansion; he must build markets, create new products, be aware of the technological environment, and create and anticipate demand. Then finally, and this should not be minimized, he must maintain the organization, a function that includes labor relations, public relations, government relations, and the replacement of capital goods.

It is evident that the entrepreneur who accomplishes the above is a successful entrepreneur. But the entrepreneur who makes history goes a step further. He is the entrepreneur who innovates, the one who does new things or does old things in a new way so that his actions significantly affect the business system and economic life in general. But note that his actions must *significantly affect* the business system. It is this that distinguishes the innovator from the pioneer. The pioneer, it may be said, is the unsuccessful innovator. He also does new things, but he has no significant effect; his actions do not catch on. Perhaps they are too far ahead of his time or they do not get enough publicity. By contrast, what the innovator does and what seems novel at the time is quickly picked up by adaptive entrepreneurs and eventually becomes the customary way of doing things.

Yet innovation is seldom spectacular. It is one piece in a jig-saw puzzle or one section of a vast tapestry. The puzzle when completed may be impressive, and the tapestry may be magnificent, but the individual pieces are not. The automobile, the railroad, the steamship, and so on, were inventions. None of them was a single innovation, but rather a collection of numerous innovations.

One more aspect of innovation's importance to business history must be mentioned. Innovation is not limited to what happens in production in

---

[2]"Individual entrepreneurs, whether alone or as archetypes, *don't matter!*" Robert Paul Thomas, 'The Automobile Industry and Its Tycoon,' *Explorations in Entrepreneurial History*, Second Series, Vol. 6, No. 2, Winter 1969.

the everyday meaning of that word. It includes what goes on in the office as well as in the factory. It includes new techniques in marketing, in management, in personnel relations, in public relations, and in every other aspect of business.

TYPES OF ENTREPRENEURS

Business history, which goes back as far as ancient Sumeria, has produced four basic types of entrepreneurs. First, there is the specialized owner-manager, who owns his business and directs it. His primary interest is production, and his primary objective is profit. Then there is the financial entrepreneur, who is also sometimes called the promoter or the finance capitalist. As the name implies, the promoter's function is to create a new firm, usually by an amalgamation of a number of existing firms. Once having done this, he may drop out of the picture entirely, or he may remain in a superintending capacity, holding himself aloof from managerial details and confining his activities to overall planning. The third type is the career executive or professional manager, with no significant ownership stake in the company he manages. To him, prestige, salary, and security may be more important than the profits in which he has no direct share. Finally, there is the professional manager who gathers most of his wealth through ownership in the firm either by stock options, bonuses, or profit sharing. His share in the ownership of the firm may be small in proportion to the firm's total shares outstanding, but as a proportion of his own wealth and income it is large. A 2 percent share in the ownership of a large corporation is a very small share from the firm's view, but it may represent millions of dollars to the owner himself.

This seldom emphasized distinction between different kinds of career executives is of more than usual importance. It is plausible to assume that businessmen who do not share directly in profits will not be tempted to make profits their primary objective. It is equally plausible to assume that businessmen who share in profits will put profits high on the list of primary objectives.

THE STATUS OF BUSINESS IN THE
AMERICAN CULTURE

Entrepreneurs do not live and work in a vacuum. What the entrepreneur does and how he does it have always been greatly affected by what is going on in society in general and among the different social and economic groups in particular. The structure of a society—its culture—will determine the nature of that society's entrepreneurship. Business' economic importance and its influence will vary with the degree of prestige and freedom of action allowed to it by society. If other occupations have more prestige than business, the ablest members of society will gravitate to those occupations. If the culture puts more importance on nonentrepreneurial values than on entrepreneurial values, business behavior will have to be modified. The result will usually be a lower scale of economic accomplishment.

Business will also be considerably shaped and influenced by what is happening in the external economy. Consider the impact of population growth on manufacturing and trade, the effect of geographical expansion on transportation, and the influence of technology on manufacturing, marketing, and all the other facets of business. There are few better examples of the importance of exogenous factors in business than the cotton textile industry, for its rise was the result of an increased demand more than anything else. And its early growth was more a matter of technology than anything else.

Entrepreneurs will, of course, have a reciprocal effect on the external economy. They are the ingredient X in economic growth.[3] We know that economic growth cannot be explained solely in terms of additions to the supply of capital and labor. In fact, added inputs of these two factors account for less than half of economic growth. The rest is due to what for want of a better name we call "efficiency" or "technology." This includes, to be sure, engineering and better (i.e., more efficient) workers, but certainly a good share is the result of entrepreneurial ability.

The importance of an efficiently operating business system to economic growth and well being has long been known in this country. The American culture has historically been imbued with the entrepreneurial spirit, which may be defined as an attitude that emphasizes working hard and productively, making money, and plowing it back into the business. From its beginnings, the United States has been devoted to the business ideal. Success in our culture has been measured by counting the material rewards; in other words, by the amount of money acquired. But money-making is not quite enough. Historically, Americans did not approve of spending one's substance on riotous living. Money was to be made and then used productively, that is, to make more money. This Calvanistic streak had its twin in the great respect that was paid to work. General Robert E. Lee once said, "Duty is the sublimest word in the English language." Such a sentiment was more in accord with *middle-age* feudalism than with nineteenth-century

---

[3]Some noted economic historians have cautioned business historians that the importance of the entrepreneur may be overemphasized. See Alexander Gerschenkron's provocative article "Social Attitudes, Entrepreneurship, and Economic Development," *Explorations in Entrepreneurial History*, Vol. VI, 1953, p. 1. See also the comments by Cochran, Landes, and Sawyer in the same volume.

capitalism. Henry Ford was much more in tune with America's historical culture and beliefs when he said, "Work is the salvation of the race." Yet, ironically, Lee the military man is probably more admired in the United States than Ford the businessman.

The explanation for this lies in the oft-repeated maxim that those who like the whole often dislike the parts. It has been said of more than one person that he liked humanity, but not human beings. Americans have admired and valued the business system and the businessman in the abstract, but the mass of the people have rarely demonstrated any love or overt admiration for the great business success, the "captain of industry." The tycoon in the business novel, perhaps more because of envy than for any other reason, has been mostly regarded with hostility.

Henry Seidel Canby, the critic and essayist, in recalling the pecking order of his youth in Wilmington, Delaware, wrote:

> If there had been an ABC marking system, the awards would have gone something like this: a good parent, B; a brilliant conversationalist, C; a lover of the arts, D; an honest man, B; a public-spirited citizen, C; a shrewd trader, A; a good lover (married or unmarried) C; a really kind man, B; a deeply religious person, C; an inventor, scientist, or journalist, C; a radical thinker, E; an expert in handling debts, i.e., a banker, A; a good salesman, retail, B; wholesale, A; a successful producer who was also a good trader, A; a contented idler, D; a first rate business man with all that implied, A+.
>
> Business was much more than an occupation—it was a philosophy, a morality, and an atmosphere.[4]

Because of the great value that the American culture has placed on the business system, it has become commonplace to say that America is a business civilization. The cliché rests on a solid foundation. American culture and mores have been shaped more by business than by any other institution, and business has done more to shape growth in America than in any other nation. Historically, our best talent went into business, whereas in other nations it went into the land, the government, the military, or the church.

Statesmen and ward politicians, intellectuals and run-of-the-mill publicists, raconteurs and memoir writers have always known that in the words attributed to Calvin Coolidge, "America's business is business." It was Woodrow Wilson, liberal and intellectual, who said, "Business underlies everything in our national life." Richard Croker impressed Lincoln Steffens by telling him, "Ever heard that business is business? Well, so is politics business, and reporting—journalism, doctoring—all professions, arts,

[4]Henry Seidel Canby, *The Age of Confidence* (New York: Farrar & Rinehart, 1934), p. 241.

sports—everything is business."[5] Even the frontier very quickly exhibited the characteristics of a business society.

It may be contended, and probably correctly, that business no longer has the aura of prestige that it once possessed. In his anecdotal, *The Old Merchants of New York City*, Joseph Scoville wrote:

> Where are your Clintons—Your Burrs, Hamiltons, and the names that adorn history—mere politicians or so-called statesmen, when compared with the creators of wealth and the glory of the great commercial city. The merchants were the bees that made the honey—the drones were the statesmen that made the noise.

No one today would write as Scoville did. But the business system still claims an ultimate respect. Two-thirds of those who participate in public-opinion polls approve of business and what business does. This may not be as many as in past generations, but it still constitutes a majority voting its recognition of the business system's importance.

But if all we have been saying is true, it has not been widely recognized by academic historians or even by the businessmen themselves. Nor is it apparent from the nation's intellectual artifacts. There are no statues of businessmen in the big cities, although there are monuments to their fame in museums, hospitals, libraries, and colleges and universities. Of the approximately 100 distinguished Americans in the Hall of Fame, ranging from Daniel Boone to William Thomas Green Morton, eight had some connection, slight or great, with business,[6] but five were admitted as inventors, and one as an engineer. Two were given the honor because they were merchants and philanthropists with the emphasis more on the latter than the former. Forty-one other businessmen and philanthropists have been nominated, but twenty-nine of these failed to get a single vote, and four received only one vote. Of the entire forty-one, only Andrew Carnegie, Cyrus Field, Stephen Girard, Johns Hopkins, and Cornelius Vanderbilt received votes in more than one year.

Evidence of the fleeting fame of businessmen can also be gathered from the standard biographical references. Of the 1,217 biographies contained in the two supplementary volumes of the authoritative *Dictionary of American Biography*, only 78, or 6.5 percent, are on businessmen. Businessmen loom larger in *Who Was Who*. In the volumes covering those who died between 1897 and 1960, there are almost 50,000 listings. Over 6,000 or 13 percent are biographies of businessmen.[7] A more popularly oriented

---

[5]Lincoln Steffens, *The Autobiography of Lincoln Steffens* (New York: Harcourt, Brace & World, Inc., 1931), p. 237.

[6]Alexander Graham Bell, Peter Cooper, James B. Eads, Thomas A. Edison, Robert Fulton, George Peabody, Eli Whitney, and George Westinghouse.

[7]The more recent history texts and biographical references are, the greater the at-

reference work, *Current Biographical Index*, lists thirteen as "in business," but only three of these are really businessmen. The others are professors of business, dress designers, and so forth. By contrast, the index includes eleven sports figures.

Anonymity is endemic to the business world. It has been pointed out that Charles E. Wilson during his tenure as Secretary of Defense got ten times as much coverage in the press as he had received when president of General Motors. The *Readers Guide to Periodical Literature*, covering the years 1925–28, surely the halcyon years of business prestige, had 76 lines on ten leading businessmen, and 1,503 lines on ten governmental and political figures.[8]

Businessmen themselves demonstrate an astonishing lack of familiarity with their illustrious predecessors, and what is even more shocking, they seem to know very little about their successful contemporaries. According to a 1967 poll of some 400 corporate executives, the ten greatest living businessmen were Robert S. McNamara, George Romney, James C. Penney, J. Paul Getty, Henry Ford II, Henry J. Kaiser, Roger M. Blough, David Sarnoff, Conrad N. Hilton, and Howard Hughes. Two of these had long since abandoned business for government, two more were retired, and one was so anonymous that his success or failure was altogether clouded in mystery and legend.

The way the same executives voted on the great businessmen of the past was also a matter for eyebrow raising. Eight men received 1,000 or more votes. They were Henry Ford, Andrew Carnegie, Thomas A. Edison, John D. Rockefeller, Alfred P. Sloan, Bernard Baruch, Alexander Graham Bell, and E. I. du Pont.[9] There would be little argument about the first five, but of the last three, one was a speculator whose claim to a business career is dubious; another was a much more successful inventor than businessman; and the third, although very able, probably polled most of his votes because he was the founder of a successful and venerable business and business dynasty.

---

tention they pay to businessmen. In *Who Was Who*, for example, the breakdown is as follows:

Date	Total No. of Biogs.	No. of Businessmen	Percent Businessmen
1897–1942	27,458	3,049	11.1%
1943–50	8,500	1,131	13.3
1951–60	12,829	2,166	16.9
Total	48,787	6,346	13.0

[8]This count did not include Henry Ford, nor did it include the President or the candidates for the presidency.

[9]David L. Lewis, "America's Heritage: The Entrepreneur," *The MBA*, Vol. 11, No. 7, April 1968.

WHY THE ANONYMITY?

It is not too difficult to explain the paradox of the business system's prestige in the culture and the simultaneous anonymity of the businessman. Much of it is the responsibility of the businessman himself. For the most part he hasn't been interested in becoming a recognized category. It is the rare businessman, indeed, who has a flair for articulation and publicity. He cannot afford to be involved in abstractions, for making business decisions is a practical, not a philosophic matter. The businessman has, in addition, regarded most other occupations and avocations patronizingly. But then too, some of the other blocs have regarded him not only patronizingly but with hostility. This has been especially true of those in the upper intellectual level who regard him as a villainous Philistine.

Above all, however, the businessman could not possibly emerge as a folk hero because the simple truth is that business is dull. Business success, no matter how stupendous, is dull reading unless surrounded by brass, chicanery, or some high order of mystery. As Miriam Beard once put it, "Businessmen have not sacrificed others like tyrants or themselves like saints. . . . They were the representatives of thrift, temperance, reticence, hard work, domesticity and other qualities which wearied instead of thrilling."[10] The public is much more interested in villainy than in the homely virtues. Choreographers may create ballets about Billy the Kid and Jesse James, but a ballet called *John D. Rockefeller* is too absurd to contemplate. As Crawford H. Greenewalt of DuPont once wrote:

> The American businessman has not been too skillful in merchandising his professional qualifications. He has been neglected by the historian, scorned by the litterateur, and snubbed by the social critic. In the stuff of which heroes are fashioned, he is well down the list, less romantic than the cowboy, less spectacular than the soldier, less portentous than the statesman. There is apparently nothing in the business suit quite so glamorous as epaulets or cutaway.[11]

THE HEREDITY AND ENVIRONMENT OF THE
AMERICAN ENTREPRENEUR

Popular opinion has believed that America was once a land of almost unlimited opportunity for boys to rise to the top in riches and prestige. The Horatio Alger story was not considered one of Grimm's fairy tales, and reputable historians assumed that most of the country's business successes came from poverty-stricken parents who were either immigrants or farmers.

---

[10]Miriam Beard, *A History of the Businessman* (New York: The Macmillan Co., 1938), p. 23.

[11]Crawford H. Greenewalt, *The Uncommon Man* (New York: McGraw-Hill Book Co., 1959), p. 7.

Tied to these two assumptions was a belief that America was a classless society with far greater occupational mobility than existed in the Old World. Many studies have shown that all of these assumptions and beliefs are wrong. There is little difference in the backgrounds of businessmen in Sweden, Britain, Holland, and the United States.[12] Relatively few of the business class were immigrants or farm boys. It was never easy for a poor boy to achieve business success, but it is a little less difficult today than it was in the days of "unlimited opportunity."

Whether the survey was made about businessmen of the 1870's or of the 1950's, the results were much the same. The model business executive was the son of a businessman, born in the East or Middle West, Anglo-Saxon in national origin, Episcopalian or Presbyterian by religion, of middle-class urban parents, ordinarily college educated, and Republican by political affiliation.[13] Perhaps the results would not be the same if the sample of businessmen were taken from only the very top echelons of success. In one study of a wide group of nineteenth-century businessmen, 51 percent came from business families and 25 percent from farm families. But in another study of only 43 outstanding businessmen of the same time, 43 percent were from the farm and 43 percent from business.[14]

To carry this a step further, the business publicist B. C. Forbes put together a list of fifty foremost business leaders in 1917 and again in 1957. Of the 1917 leaders, 38 percent had been to college in contrast to 96 percent of the 1957 group. Asked about their ancestry, the fifty executives of 1917 cited a businessman or banker somewhere in the background sixty-three times, but the executives of 1957 only mentioned such ancestry fifty-one times.

THEORETICAL DESCRIPTIONS OF BUSINESS EVOLUTION

Every discipline, if it is to have any significant meaning, must develop a set of generalizations. Business history is no exception. Although the subject is new, generalizations about it go back to the beginning of the century

[12]Seymour Martin Lipset and Reinhard Bendix, *Social Mobility in Industrial Society* (Berkeley, Cal.: University of California Press, 1959), Ch. 5.

[13]Of the 6,346 businessmen listed in *Who Was Who*, approximately half attended college, 2,259 claimed to be Republicans and 494 Democrats; 10 percent were Episcopalian, another 10 percent Presbyterian; 2 percent were Catholic and 2 percent Jewish.

[14]See William Miller, "American Historians and the Business Elite," *Journal of Economic History*, Nov. 1949; *Men in Business* (Cambridge, Mass.: Harvard University Press, 1952); Frank W. Taussig and Carl S. Joslyn, *American Business Leaders* (New York: The Macmillan Company, 1932); Mabel Newcomer, *The Big Business Executive* (New York: Columbia University Press, 1955); W. Lloyd Warner and J. C. Abegglen, *Big Business Leaders in America* (New York: Harper and Row, 1955); Chester McArthur Destler, "Entrepreneurial Leadership among the Robber Barons," *Journal of Economic History*, Supplement, 1946.

when the eminent German economic historian, Werner Sombart, constructed a theoretical framework of business evolution. Sombart used the word "capitalism" instead of "business," but this is of no importance. What Sombart wrote about capitalism applied equally well to business.[15]

WERNER SOMBART: THE QUINTESSENCE OF CAPITALISM

Sombart insisted that capitalism did not grow impersonally or collectively, but was the product of outstanding individuals (entrepreneurs) who possessed a talent for calculation plus the qualities of restlessness, persistence, and perseverance. In other words, they were at home with numbers and they had drive and enterprise.

Sombart saw business evolving through three periods that he labeled early, full, and late capitalism. In the first period, business was small, primitive, and medieval. It had a decidedly personal cast. Buyers and sellers, employers and employees confronted each other and bargained in person. In the structure and organization of business, traditional rule of thumb prevailed.

In the period of full capitalism, mechanistic technology invaded and permeated the business world. The things with which business dealt became fixed and standardized. Thus, fixed prices replaced haggling in the market place, standardized goods replaced the hand-made, labor contracts became standardized, and impersonal credit relations through such documents as bills of exchange, security certificates, and so on, superseded direct financing.

The third period, "late capitalism," was characterized by a severe diminution of the "genuinely entrepreneurial spirit." Intuition and inspiration became less important as the number of determinable factors in the business system constantly increased. The entrepreneur was more and more disposed to build his business upon the foundation of systematized knowledge. The striving for profit grew less intense. The firm became more like a government enterprise with a thoroughly systematized and externally regulated management. The freedom of action that characterized the period of high capitalism was gradually eliminated by an increase in the number of restrictions until the system became regulated rather than free. Some of these restrictions were self-imposed, others were prescribed by the government, and still others were enforced by labor. In this bureaucracy, the manager came to resemble a "minister of finance who had to act within a framework imposed on him from the outside." The worker in turn became more like a civil service employee.

---

[15]Werner Sombart, "Capitalism," *Encyclopedia of Social Sciences*; see also J. W. Gough, *The Rise of the Entrepreneur* (New York: Schocken Books, Inc., 1969), Ch. 1.

Sombart's description of the evolution of business forms and organization had a counterpart in his description of the evolution of the businessman. He distinguished among three different types of entrepreneurs: the *expert*, the *merchant* or businessman, and the *financier*, but he was careful to point out that these ideal types were seldom encountered in real life, and all of them existed simultaneously rather than that one replaced the other.

The expert concentrated his interest on the product. He was primarily interested in the labor market rather than in the capital or the commodity market. If he had to compete, he preferred to compete in service rather than in price. The second type of businessman, the merchant, focussed his attention on market demand. The commodity market was his main field of activity, and his contribution to the business system was through improving the sales mechanism rather than the organization of the plant. The financier's activity was the creation and the accumulation of capital. He became important only after the process of concentration succeeded the process of expansion.

N. S. B. GRAS: BUSINESS AND CAPITALISM

Taking off from Sombart's pioneering work, the late Professor N. S. B. Gras formulated in the 1930's what is probably the most widely known theory of business history. Gras presented a stages theory in which each stage was dominated by a different, distinctive form of "capitalism" and a different type of businessman.[16] The metamorphosis from one stage to the next resulted primarily from forces in the external economic environment, such as wars, long-wave price movements, and the competition set in motion by market forces. The entrepreneur or businessman in all of this is a somewhat passive figure with a greater resemblance to a mechanical abstraction than to a human personality. Although Gras would have been shocked by the judgment, his theory was heavily deterministic and resembled the models built by Karl Marx and, more especially, by Sombart. His description also had a Hegelian twist in that the pendulum of business evolution swung back and forth between specialization and diversification.

According to Gras, early business was dominated by the "petty capitalist" by whom Gras meant small businessmen, shopkeepers, storekeepers, and traveling merchants. Although they dealt in a wide variety of goods, they were really specialists because they followed only one line of business

---

[16]N. S. B. Gras and Henrietta M. Larson, *Casebook in American Business History* (New York: Appleton-Century-Crofts, 1939), pp. 3–15; N. S. B. Gras, "Capitalism," reprinted in Frederic C. Lane and Jelle C. Riemersma, eds., *Enterprise and Secular Change* (Homewood, Ill.: Richard D. Irwin, Inc., 1953); N. S. B. Gras, *Business and Capitalism* (New York: Appleton-Century-Crofts, 1939).

activity—trade or hand manufacture—and dealt in a very limited market. They resisted controls, and Gras labeled their public policy "democratic economic equality."

The shopkeepers were small artisans—weavers, shoemakers, black-smiths, and so forth—who made goods usually on order. The second group of petty capitalists were the keepers of the general stores. Finally, there were the traveling merchants, who were really peddlers, hawking their wares from one end of the country to another. The whole panorama of petty capi-talism can be seen in historical restorations such as that at Williamsburg, Virginia.

In time, economic expansion bypassed the petty capitalist. He was not able to take care of a market larger than the town area, and although he has never disappeared, his position of dominance was taken over by the "sedentary merchant" in an era of "mercantile capitalism," which ran in this country from about 1750 to about 1830.

The sedentary merchant differed from the petty capitalist in a number of ways. To begin with, his business was diversified. The merchant prince had his fingers in every economic pie, and the more diversified he was, the greater his success. He was first and foremost an importer, exporter, and wholesaler, but he also retailed goods, built and bought ships, did some business as a common carrier for other merchants, insured cargoes, engaged in banking through dealing in bills of exchange, carried the mails, provided warehouse facilities, and dabbled or engaged in such manufacturing as candles, whale oil, iron, and distilling.

The petty capitalist was often a man on the move, whereas the seden-tary merchant, as his name indicated, was at home in his countinghouse. He delegated some of his powers and spent much of his time thinking and planning and scheming, whereas the petty capitalist took care of everything himself and lived and planned for the day, not for the morrow. What this meant was that big business had appeared, and the democratic economic equality of the petty capitalist had passed away. As Gras expressed it, "The rise of the sedentary merchant meant the dominance of commercial capital, the supremacy of well-considered business policy, the victory of careful management, and the triumph of metropolitan economy."

Just as petty capitalism gave place to mercantile capitalism, so mer-cantile capitalism gave place to industrial capitalism. The old order, ac-cording to Gras, was killed by "specialization from within and by the Indus-trial Revolution from without." The latter event brought into existence heavy machinery and the factory system, and so changed business that the institutional arrangements that had been eminently satisfactory for the trad-ing operations that featured mercantile capitalism did not meet the needs of the new system. What was required was not a jack-of-all-trades, but a specialized entrepreneur who could put together a working force to handle the new techniques of machine production. The highly diversified sedentary merchant simply did not fill the bill. If he was to survive, the merchant capitalist had to change his outlook, philosophy, occupation, and mode of behavior. Some sedentary merchants were able to accomplish this difficult task, and they emerged as industrial capitalists. Most industrial capitalists, however, were petty capitalists grown large.

Gras' industrial capitalist was the same person whom other writers called "the heroic entrepreneur" and "the robber baron." He was the empire builder of the late nineteenth century. He excelled in production and was therefore ideally suited to the needs of a virgin market. He was adequate in marketing, for in his day and age extraordinary sophistication in marketing was hardly necessary. Judged by today's standards, however, his financial policies were weak. He lacked adequate reserves. He did not draw any distinction between fixed and working capital, and he had no clear-cut vision of long-run policy.

In the virgin market in which the industrial capitalist operated, it could be expected that a reduction in price would result in a more than proportionate increase in sales. Demand was, in the economist's language, price elastic, and firms competed in terms of price rather than by offering more services or a more attractively differentiated product. This, as Gras saw it, was the root of the industrial capitalist's downfall. Extreme price competition was the order of the day, and this in the long run spelled disaster, for, according to Gras, it had to lead to bankruptcy or reorganization. The reorganizers were the bankers—investment bankers and the giants among commercial bankers. Thus was ushered in the fourth stage, "finance capitalism."

Finance capitalism, which according to Gras dominated American business in the period 1879–1933, performed three functions: it eased the flow of capital funds into business; it influenced the conduct of business; and in the case of the far-sighted, it did so in the interest of investors.

Finance capitalism marked the final triumph of diversification over specialization in business life, for bankers were interested in every variety of business—banking, insurance, manufacturing, service industries, such as utilities, and eventually even retailing.[17] Because they were so diverse in their interests, they could not devote much time to the administration of any one firm. They made only the broadest decisions and left much discretionary power to hired managers.

[17]The progression is easy to trace. In the late eighteenth and early nineteenth century, Thomas Willing, the Coster Brothers, William Phillips, John Pintard, and Condy Raguet, and others were involved in commercial banking, savings banks, and insurance. In the late nineteenth and early twentieth century, the House of Morgan and Kuhn Loeb were active in railroads, manufacturing, and utilities. In the 1920s, Goldman Sachs and Lehman Brothers were recapitalizing large retailers.

In other respects too the bankers' outlook differed fundamentally and completely from their "ruggedly individualistic" predecessors. They were horrified by the chaos and competition that industrialism had spawned. They preferred law and order to the anarchy of individualism, and they preferred cooperation to competition.

Professor Gras carried his schema a number of steps further than the state of finance capitalism. "National capitalism," a kind of state socialism, and "security capitalism" were to succeed finance capitalism, but much of this was conjecture rather than history and is therefore beyond the scope of this book.

Like all stages theories, the Gras thesis has been severely criticized. It is much too neat. As with all generalizations, there were many exceptions to the rule and many of these exceptions were too significant to pass unnoticed. It is questionable, for example, whether the bankers whose influence was always more passive than active really dominated the business community. Then too, the so-called industrial capitalist was not so much a product of the calendar of time as he was a product of the condition of his industry. He was a product of a virgin market, not of the period 1830–1879. Thus Henry Ford and the entrepreneurs of the electronics industry fitted Gras' specifications of the industrial capitalist, but one had his great day in the 1920's, and the others were a sensation in the 1950's long after the supposed capitulation of industrial capitalism.

But Gras was not describing all businessmen or even the model businessman. He was attempting to isolate the dominant businessman at different periods of time. It could be said that what he was describing were the arithmetic means of a series of standard deviations. As such, his model is a handy tool of description.

ARTHUR H. COLE: FROM EMPIRICAL TO COGNITIVE ENTREPRENEURSHIP

In contrast to the Sombart-Gras approach, Arthur H. Cole has suggested a theory of business history in which the entrepreneur rather than the external economy dominated the process of change. Cole suggested that entrepreneurship had traveled through a series of categories: empirical, or rule-of-thumb, entrepreneurship; rational, or informed, entrepreneurship; and cognitive, or sophisticated, entrepreneurship; twenty years after his original statement, Cole added a fourth category: mathematically advised entrepreneurship. The differences among the four were largely a matter of the breadth of knowledge a businessman could gain, and the span of operations he had to oversee. "The business leader of modern decades," wrote Cole, "not only must know more facts about more subjects . . . synthesize more appraisals of experts and advisors, and be cognizant of more services from more service institutions, but he must relate his decisions to a longer time space of past and future."[18]

ALFRED D. CHANDLER, JR.: STRATEGY AND STRUCTURE

Gras viewed business history as the history of the subjects taught in schools of business, and Cole thought in terms of the businessman's expanding range of knowledge and information. Alfred D. Chandler, who in recent years has written extensively on business history, concentrates almost exclusively on business administration or, more accurately, on the decision making process.

Chandler's objective was to describe analytically how business administration evolved in a quite logical fashion from the single-product, single-function firm of a century ago to the multiproduct, multifunction, multidivisional, decentralized organization of today.[19]

His initial proposition is that administration is an identifiable activity differing from buying, selling, processing, and other necessary parts of the business process. His second proposition is that administration encompasses two tasks: long-run coordinating, planning, and appraising the effective use of vast and varied assortments of men and materials; and short-run day-to-day operation.

The first is the territory of the entrepreneur; the other, the task of the manager. Another way of expressing the difference is to say that the entrepreneur is concerned with keeping the organization alive whereas the manager is concerned with keeping the mechanism in working order. Whenever entrepreneurs act like managers, they fail to carry out their goals effectively.

Chandler's thesis is that in the successful firm, structure must follow strategy. Strategy is defined as "the determination of long-term goals and

[18]Arthur H. Cole, "An Approach to the Study of Entrepreneurship," *Supplement to the Journal of Economic History*, Vol. VI (1946); "The Entrepreneur," *American Economic Review*, "Papers and Proceedings," May 1968, p. 60. The entrepreneur is also emphasized in Joseph A. Schumpeter, "The Creative Response in Economic History," *Journal of Economic History*, Vol. VII (1947) and Thomas C. Cochran, "Role and Sanction in American Entrepreneurial History," in *Change and the Entrepreneur* (Cambridge, Mass.: Harvard University Press, 1949).

[19]Alfred D. Chandler, Jr., *Strategy and Structure* (Cambridge, Mass.: The M.I.T. Press, 1962). See also "Management Decentralization," *Business History Review*, Vol. XXX, 1956; "The Beginnings of 'Big Business' in American Industry," *ibid.*, Vol. XXXIII, 1959; "Development, Diversification and Decentralization," in *Postwar Economic Trends in the United States*, ed. by Ralph E. Freeman (Cambridge, Mass.: Massachusetts Institute of Technology, 1960); Alfred D. Chandler, Jr. and Fritz Redlich, "Recent Developments in Business Administration and Their Conceptualization," *Business History Review*, Vol. XXV, 1961.

objectives and the adoption of courses of action and the allocation of resources for carrying out these goals." Structure is "the design of organization through which the enterprise is administered."

Strategy, which has to do with the allocation of a firm's resources
clearly existed as long as business existed, but structure is something else
again. In early industry, there was no such thing as a full-time administrator. The "boss" was a little bit of all the factors of production. He was at
one and the same time decision maker, manager, capitalist, laborer, and
probably land owner. The firm was too small for occupational specialization. It handled a single product and a single function, ordinarily manufacturing. It marketed its products through a selling agent or commission
merchant, and it bought its raw materials from an independent producer.
To be sure, the phrase "single function" should not be taken too literally.
It really meant that the firm concentrated on one function and as far as
possible left the others to independent enterprises.

Population growth, urbanization, economic crises, and technological
development, especially the railroad and new types of power, put great
pressure on industrial firms and their executives. If they were to keep their
resources fully employed, they had no choice but to adopt a new strategy.
The successful firm was forced to adopt a strategy of expansion in order to
assure more satisfying marketing facilities or to have more certain supplies
in order to employ more fully existing plant and personnel. Control of
competition loomed large, and marketing was of overwhelming importance.
But although technological and market requirements set a limit on growth,
the extent to which this limit was reached depended upon the ability of the
firm's executives. Thus external economic forces combined with entrepreneurial talents produced big business.

In the last part of the nineteenth century, aggressive entrepreneurs,
dissatisfied with the ways in which outsiders were marketing their goods and
encouraged to expand because of external influences, began to integrate
vertically. They changed from single-product, single-function companies to
single-product, multifunction companies. In the process they freed themselves from dependence on wholesalers and raw material producers. At the
same time they began to spread out geographically by creating field offices
to take care of the widening market area. Administration now had to be
carried on at two levels instead of one—at general headquarters and in the
field offices. The structure or organization had to be changed to fit the new
strategy if the firm was to continue to be successful.

In reshuffling the organization, manufacturing industry had an excellent model to follow in the railroads, which as the first really big businesses
had long since altered their structure to fit the strategy of expansion.

Structural reform began in the 1850's in the Erie, the Baltimore &
Ohio, and the Pennsylvania. By the 1880's, the Pennsylvania, "in every re-

spect the standard railroad in America," had worked out a highly complex managerial structure with a general headquarters and a full line-and-staff departmental organization. The executives at the top echelons were concerned with broad decision-making and not with day-to-day operations. As time passed, however, there was some backsliding from this ideal arrangement, and senior executives again became involved in operational duties. There was little room left for strategic decision making after major expansion had been completed, after rate making had become more a matter of government regulation than of executive decision, and after systems had through habit become routinized.

Far-sighted industrialists, like the railroad executives, soon learned that a departmentalized structure best fitted the multifunction company that strategy had produced. In the last of the nineteenth century, most large industrial firms were operating under such a structure. The tendency was also toward a more centralized organization, either in individual top executives or in centrally located committees. Chandler points out that these changes were not adopted universally, and when they were adopted, it was gradually and under considerable pressure. It was faltering demand, for example, that forced firms into adopting centralized inventory control, coordination of production to demand, and budget and capital appropriation procedures. All of this in turn tended to confine the top executives to overall planning and to separate them from day-to-day operations.

Yet there were glaring weaknesses in the departmentalized, centralized structure. The empire builders who had created the firm were unable to mind their own business. Instead of concentrating on entrepreneurial activities, they constantly interfered in day-to-day operations. Decision making was very often a matter of negotiation between departments, each supporting its own interest instead of the interest of the firm itself.

These weaknesses were not crippling so long as business did not expand in new ways and forms. But business growth is a continuous process. Firms continued to be forced to expand under the pressure of external economic forces and the drive of the aggressive entrepreneur. Strategy had to change in order that resources might continue to be used to the fullest extent. In the twentieth century, as firms reached the limit of the existing market, some of their executives began to reach out to new and entirely different markets or to new and entirely different products. Thus the basic change in strategy was toward diversification of product and toward the extension of the market area internationally.

The change in strategy made obsolete the departmentalized structure that had been successful in the multifunction, single-product company. How were resources to be allotted among different products? How could existing departments meet the needs of a set of fundamentally different markets? DuPont, for example, found that selling paints was quite different from selling explosives. The strategy of diversification required a new structure. The multifunction, multiproduct company required a divisionalized, decentralized administration, rather than a departmentalized, centralized administration. To be sure, it took an economic crisis to persuade even the innovators to adopt the change, but it was done. What emerged was a four-tier structure. A general office decided upon long-range goals and policies. A central office handled divisions. The department headquarters supervised the departments within the divisions. The field units—sales, plant, and so on—took care of nothing but day-to-day operations.

The occupants of the general office located far from the actual plants were truly top decision makers. The wide distance between them and the field units, the continuous growth, diversification, and dispersion of the enterprise, and its increasing complexity clearly required improved communication. The railroads again offered an example. They had constructed complicated channels of communication, and at the same time they had designed a complicated supply of information to flow through the channels. By the end of the nineteenth century, as Chandler points out, the railroads were commonly using the term *control through statistics.*

Chandler's thesis may be summed up by reemphasizing the importance of the market. Those companies that sold semifinished products to a relatively few large customers required a simple structure. Those that sold a larger variety of one major line consistently centralized their activities. Those that made and sold different lines for increasingly differentiated groups of customers turned to multidivisional structures.

But these rules applied to the successful firms, and not all firms were successful. Some were not willing to adopt their structures to their strategy of expansion. The primary reason for this was the inertia of their chief executive or executives. In general, the firms whose control remained within the family were slow to adopt organizational change; individualistic, empire-building entrepreneurs resisted change; and the first professional managers, who were specialists rather than generalists, were not interested in change.

In the Chandler model, technology, the market, and the personality of the entrepreneur were of ultimate importance. Other factors faded into the background. This is especially true of government behavior: "The market, the nature of their resources, and their entrepreneurial talents have, with relatively few exceptions, had far more effect on the history of large industrial firms than have antitrust laws, taxation, labor and welfare legislation, and comparable evidences of public policy."[20]

In the pages that follow, it would be well to keep these various generalizations about business history well in mind and to consider how adequately each explains how business came to be what it is today.

[20]Chandler, *Strategy and Structure*, p. 384.

2

THE BEGINNINGS OF
COLONIAL BUSINESS

Business and businessmen have played a role of much more than passing importance in this country ever since its beginnings. Indeed, the settlement of almost the whole eastern seaboard was based primarily on the search for profits by private entrepreneurs in England. These early entrepreneurs were of two general types: (1) those in the trading companies, who sought gains from the profits of trade, and (2) the proprietary landlords, who hoped to gain their profits from the land. But before discussing these early manifestations of business, let us take a quick look at the colonial economy.

THE COLONIAL ECONOMY

Despite the prominence of business motives, business did not grow large in the 170 years of colonial history—a period almost as long as our history since the signing of the Constitution. There was one important reason for this. The colonial economy was a primitive economy, and even though it grew at an impressive rate in its century and a half, it was still underdeveloped in 1800. It had vast opportunities and vast potential, but it would take years of growth to fulfill both opportunity and potential.

Colonial population multiplied at a very rapid rate. Its growth probably averaged 33⅓ percent a decade. Nevertheless, the total number of persons living in the colonies at the end of the Revolution numbered no more than 5 million. Late in the Colonial Period, Boston, the largest city, had a population of only 15,000. Marblehead, Massachusetts was the sixth largest town. In 1800, there were only 10 cities of over 8,000.

We know very little about what happened to colonial aggregate income, but we do have some impressions. Probably, income grew slowly in a series of ups and downs just as it does in any developing economy. The early colonists were very poor, but by the middle of the eighteenth century, there were at least 100 merchants living in considerable comfort in New York, Philadelphia, and Boston and another 50 each in Newport and Charleston. The Hancock, Bayard, and DeLancey families, among the richest merchants in the colonies, were worth $200,000 to $300,000 each.

Most of the colonists—over 90 percent—were farmers. There were a few merchants, a few professionals, and a relatively large number of artisans. But it was primarily an agricultural society, and like all agricultural societies its income was small and its economic institutions at an embryonic level. Cash was almost nonexistent. It was not a barter economy, but trade, of which there was very little, judged by modern standards, was handled by various complicated processes, such as open-book accounts and country pay. Merchants on occasion obtained foreign money, and the individual colonies minted some coins and issued paper money until stopped by the British Government. Banks were also created to issue money against mortgages on land, but these bore little resemblance to modern banks since they did not do a discount and deposit business.

Business could grow and did grow in such an environment, but it could not grow to gigantic stature. A small population, scattered over a wide area and living mostly off the land, was not conducive to large-scale enterprise.

THE NEW ENGLAND SETTLEMENTS

The story of business in America begins in 1606 when King James I issued the Virginia Charter authorizing settlement in the New World by two groups, the London Company and the Plymouth Company. The Plymouth Company was given the right to start settlement anywhere between the 41st and the 45th parallels (the Potomac River and the present location of Bangor, Maine). A year later the Company established what was to be an unsuccessful settlement at Sagadahoc at the mouth of the Kennebec River. The new colonists constructed a fort, planted crops, and looked forward eagerly to a continuous and profitable trade with the Indians. But their hopes were not fulfilled. A combination of inexperience, inefficiency, and difficulties with the Indians led to failure, and by the following year the disillusioned settlers had abandoned both their hopes and their settlement, and they returned to England.

This initial venture into the New World and its disastrous outcome might well have relegated New England to an unsettled and undeveloped area frequented only by occasional fishing boats and their crews had it not been for a fortuitous visit to the area by Captain John Smith in 1614. Smith, in a widely read pamphlet, *Description of New England*, emphasized the benefits of the New England area and its main staple, fish, and expounded in great detail on the manner in which the judicious management of fisheries could become the mainstay of a thriving economy.

Smith's pamphlet brought a renewed interest and enthusiasm that resulted in the formation of several merchant companies to tap the expected wealth of New England. The most important of these, the Adventurers, the Dorchester, the New England, and the Laconia companies as well as several lesser enterprises were organized along lines suggested by Smith. They were based on an over-simplified concept of sending settlers to New England, where as self-sufficient settlers living off the land, they could catch fish, collect furs, and process other desired commodities for shipment to the English entrepreneurs.

The financial arrangements between the English investors and the settlers varied somewhat from company to company. In some cases the settlers were also shareholders in the companies, combining the functions of both capitalist and laborer. In other companies, they were personal servants or employees of the investors. In a typical arrangement the total assets of the organization were owned in common by the enterprise for a specified period of time (ordinarily seven years), after which the assets were distributed among the shareholders in proportion to their relative interests in the enterprise.

These early colonial endeavors followed a consistent and unfortunate pattern. The profits expected by the investors failed to materialize. It took much longer for the settlers to become self-sufficient than had been originally estimated. Good soil and locations had to be found, after which the ground had to be cleared and crops planted. This meant that food had to be shipped in, and the time-consuming labor of getting started precluded other activities such as fishing and trading. When the Adventurers finally managed to gather and send out a cargo it was captured by the French, and a few years later a similar shipment was captured by the Turks. The settlement was inadequately supplied with trade goods and was too far from the source of the fur supply. At the end of seven years the English investors sold what remained of their original capital of £7,000 to the settlers for the assumption of the accumulated debts of £1,800.

It was into this bleak commercial world of New England that the migration of the Puritans brought the first contingent of permanent settlers. With different social and economic backgrounds, they were anxious to put their talents to work in the New World, agreeing in principle that religious beliefs were highly pertinent to the practice of trade and that commerce was not exempt from the concepts of morality.

AGRICULTURAL PRODUCTION

Agricultural production was by far the most widespread occupation in the colonies. Even those who pursued other occupations depended to some extent on farming as a means of support. John Adams' grandfather, for example, established a brewery as an adjunct to his farm; his father combined farming with shoemaking; and Adams himself, although a successful lawyer, also ran a farm.

Farming was also the most important economic activity in the colonies. It produced the food, clothing, and other necessities for the settlers and their families. Second, it provided small and even large surpluses for sale or barter, thus enabling the small farmer to obtain some of the "luxuries" that made his life a little easier. From the point of view of commerce, the most important function of farming was that it supplied most of the products for the export trade.

The colonists experimented incessantly with crops to determine which ones would be most feasible and most economical to produce. They learned how to raise tobacco, corn, and several vegetables from the Indians. Abortive attempts were made to grow some of the semi-tropical and exotic crops such as silk, sugar, coffee, and olives. Since these products were in great demand in England, much effort was given and wasted in trying to grow them. Bounties and various other forms of subsidies kept these efforts alive throughout the Colonial Period, but although some production did result, these crops never succeeded in making an important agricultural contribution. Silk exports averaged only 400 pounds in the years from 1747 to 1772, and they exceeded 1,000 pounds in only one year (1766). Most of the silk was grown in Georgia, with South Carolina and North Carolina producing a negligible amount of the total.

Gradually each area, with the exception of New England, besides growing a food crop, began to show signs of agricultural specialization. In Virginia, and to a lesser extent in Maryland, tobacco was the main crop. Tobacco exports grew almost consistently throughout the Colonial Period, reaching a peak of 51 million pounds a year during the 1746–1755 decade.

South Carolina and Georgia emphasized the growing of rice, and because of the English bounty, made a concerted effort to grow the indigo plant from which the dye was obtained. Rice production once it got started grew at a prodigious rate, and exports consistently increased. Indigo was introduced into South Carolina about 1741 and exports grew rapidly, reaching almost 900,000 pounds in 1757. From then on, however, production declined and never again reached that total.

In the middle colonies, once the pioneering period was past, wheat became the principal crop, but not to the exclusion of others. Corn, barley, oats, rye, buckwheat, and flax were also important crops along with the usual household staples. The middle colonies also raised their own poultry and livestock and, like New England, were more self-sufficient than the South.

New England was blessed with neither the fertile soil nor the favorable climate of the other regions. Its agriculture was, therefore, far below that of the other colonies. Indeed, except for corn and the usual household crops, what it grew was hardly worth mentioning. If there was a prime crop in New England, it was corn. This, with the usual household crops, was just about the extent of New England agriculture.

THE FUR BUSINESS IN COLONIAL NEW ENGLAND

At the time of the Puritan immigration, the most highly developed business in New England (aside from agriculture) was the export of furs. This trade flourished until about 1637, but it suffered a rapid decline thereafter and never recovered despite attempts at its revival. Plymouth, the center of the fur trade, failed to produce a substitute industry. The fur traders either settled into farming or sought their fortunes in other areas.

The failure of the fur trade resulted from both natural and economic causes. The Pilgrims were not able to meet the costs of maintaining more distant trading posts, nor were they able to keep others from establishing competing posts. The costs of expansion increased steadily as the fur-bearing animals near the seaboard were depleted. New posts had to be built further inland, resulting in heavier equipment needs and increased time and costs for transportation. At the same time competition reduced the exchange value of trading goods, decreasing the margin of profit and increasing the necessary investment. Then too, the fur business was caught in a vicious circle of capital problems. The export of furs had been expected to repay the debt to the English merchants, but new capital was perpetually required to establish and operate the trading posts by means of which the obligations were to be repaid. The new capital came from the same merchants to whom the colony was already indebted, and by charging high prices for trading goods the merchants managed to keep the debt growing at a faster rate than the Pilgrims (caught in an early cost-price squeeze) could increase their remittances in furs.

The deterioration of the fur trade came at a most unpropitious time, for it coincided with the troubles which heralded the outbreak of the Civil War in England between the Puritans and the Crown. This tragic event put a temporary stop to the flow of immigration that had fed the business prosperity of the 1630's. The cash and, more importantly, the credit brought in by the immigrants had been an important factor in making payments to English exporters. Trade was cut off not only by the war itself but by cessation of the flow of this cash and credit. For some months, panic and depression resulted in price declines and a severe deterioration of trade. The sad state of affairs was considerably worsened by the virtual disappearance of the beaver, whose fur had been in great demand. Merchants were now faced with the problem of finding a substitute for both beaver and credit.

Although the government enacted legislation to alleviate the condition of debtors, it could do little to revive the flow of goods from England. This could be accomplished only by finding a trade commodity acceptable to the English exporters. An alternative was the development of an economy based on home production of essential goods.

ATTEMPTS TO REVIVE THE ECONOMY

In June 1641, the General Court embarked on an ambitious effort to revive New England's faltering economy. It fostered legislation aimed at developing the natural resources of the area and providing a modicum of self-sufficient production to replace the imports from England. To foster discovery and development of mineral resources, the Court offered subsidies in the form of control over all minerals found on either private or public lands, and the right to buy land directly from the Indians. During the same year legislation was also passed aimed at reviving the dying fur trade and fostering a native cloth-weaving industry. However, weaving became at best only an occasional occupation of the population of farmers and artisans, and other attempts to generate regional manufactures were equally unsuccessful.

With the failure of the attempts to create a self-sufficient economy based on home manufacturing, it became increasingly evident that the colony was to be permanently dependent, and that some means of payment had to be found if a steady flow of goods from England was to be sustained. Since fur trading had failed and mining and manufacturing had proved abortive, the settlers turned to the sea for the solution and found it there in the fishing industry.

The success of a fishing venture depended on the size of the catch and on the ability of the merchant to get it to its destination at the right time. At the start, the London merchants were the prime movers in the organization of the fishing trade. They arranged for equipment and supplies, purchased the cargo, and resold it at its final destination. Typically an outward-bound cargo of merchandise was prepared in England for shipment to and sale in New England. After the disposal of the goods, a cargo of fish was picked up for the return voyage and eventual sale in Spain or the Wine Islands. This arrangement left the colonial merchants only a minor part of the profit, and they sought continuously to enlarge their interests in the expeditions and their share of the profits. Gradually, they achieved some measure of success. Together with other colonial merchants they financed outgoing cargoes of fish, which they exchanged at southern ports for local wines and produce. They also entered into temporary partnerships with the London merchants on the outgoing voyages. Eventually the colonial merchant replaced the English merchant almost entirely insofar as the export of fish was concerned. However, the import of merchandise from England to the colonies remained invariably the domain of the English merchant until sold.

The increased activity of the New England merchants in the fish trade produced helpful side effects. It made the colonists aware that the islanders had other needs that they could also supply. Barrel staves, hoops, and other timber products found an excellent market in the islands as did provisions other than fish, so that as the fish trade prospered so did the trade in provisions and timber products.

TRADE AND COMMERCE

Some trade with Europe existed from the time the first European arrived in the New World, but it was in the inflationary decade of the 1630's that the Puritan petty merchants first attempted to establish themselves in trade and commerce.

The colonial merchant operated in a world of limitations, which set the patterns of regional development. One of the most frustrating of these limitations was the shortage of a circulating currency. Money in the form of gold and silver was practically nonexistent throughout most of the period. When some did flow in as a result of trade, mostly from the West Indies, it almost immediately flowed out again to pay the debit balances due to British agents. As a result, credit was absolutely essential for the development of a stable and dependable mercantile trade. And since credit was only obtainable in England, it was necessary for a budding merchant to have good connections there. There was, of course, no formal information about the financial capacity and business reputation of strangers more than 3,000 miles from London. Potential English creditors, therefore, could rely only on knowledge obtained through family and friendship ties to their overseas customers. Blood relationships between British suppliers and colonial customers were exceptionally useful bonds for credit purposes. If no blood relationship existed, the New England tradesmen needed previous experience and English reputations and friendships upon which they could base their requests for credit to finance their mercantile ventures.

The early seventeenth-century, or as Bernard Bailyn calls them, the "first generation" merchants, such as Henry Gray, John Cogan, Valentine Hall, Robert Sedgewick, Pelig Sanford, and John Hull, were all related to British merchants. Gray started out on the basis of a loan from his brother, a London merchant. John Cogan dealt with his brother, Humphry Cogan, a tradesman in Exeter. Valentine Hill drew bills of exchange on his brother John, a merchant in London. Joshua Hughes sold cutlery, ironware, and general merchandise shipped to him by his uncle Joshua Foote from London. Henry Shrimpton drew credit from his brother Edward, a London merchant. The Hutchinsons had mercantile connections through William Hutchinson's brothers, Richard, a London ironmonger, and John, a woolen draper. These early merchants had an additional common background—almost all of them came from small tradesmen and shopkeeper families.[1]

THE RETAIL TRADESMAN

The general merchandise store was the most characteristic retail outlet during the Colonial Period as it was to be during the pioneer years on every subsequent frontier. It supplied almost all the goods required by the settlers that were not made in the home or by local artisans. Whenever and wherever pioneer conditions prevailed, the general store was a part of them, and as the population moved inland the general store moved inland with it.

The store itself was usually a wooden structure perhaps some 20 or 30 feet in size. The following description by Mark Twain could fit a general store in any time or place since its character remained fairly unchanged from place to place and time to time:

> It was a small establishment, with a few rolls of "bit" calicoes on half a dozen shelves; a few barrels of salt mackerel, coffee and New Orleans sugar behind the counter; stacks of brooms, shovels, axes, hoes, rakes and such things here and there; a lot of cheap hats, bonnets and tinware strung on strings and suspended from the walls; and at the other end of the room was another counter with bags of shot on it, a cheese or two and a keg of powder; in front of it a row of nail kegs and a few pigs of lead, and behind it a barrel or two of New Orleans molasses and native corn whisky on tap. If a boy bought five or ten cents' worth of anything he was entitled to half a handful of sugar from the barrel; if a woman bought a few yards of calico she was entitled to a spool of thread in addition to the usual gratis trimmin's; if a man bought a

[1] Bernard Bailyn, *The New England Merchants in the Seventeenth Century* (Cambridge, Mass.: Harvard University Press, 1955). Also in paperback by Harper and Row, 1964.

rifle he was at liberty to draw and swallow as big a drink of whisky as he wanted. Everything was cheap: apples, peaches, sweet potatoes, Irish potatoes and corn, ten cents a bushel; chickens, ten cents apiece; butter, six cents a pound; eggs, three cents a dozen; coffee and sugar, five cents a pound; whisky, ten cents a gallon . . . .[2]

Many of the cruder stores had no fixtures at all, and the stocks of merchandise were kept in locked boxes or chests, which were opened only when a customer called. Otherwise the stores were fitted out with rough wooden counters and shelves, with boxes and barrels piled up in a shed or storeroom attached to the building, or piled up on the outside. But some general store proprietors were more ambitious than others. They had more attractive stores, offered more services, took better care of customers, and played an active role in town activities.

The general store, as its name implies, was not a specialized outlet, but dealt in anything and everything. In many communities, Indian trade was carried on at the same time that trade grew with the white settlers. Indeed, many a general store had its origin in the trading post.

As in all developing economies, nonmonetary trade was the rule rather than the exception. The storekeeper on every frontier took from local producers in exchange for credit almost any article for which there might be a customer. The variety of goods accepted in trade included furs, venison, hides, beef, pork, dairy products, grain, lumber, hoop poles and staves for barrels, and firewood.

Frontier conditions prevailed even in the port cities during the early years. Inventory policy at that time was from hand to mouth. To sell goods, an aspiring businessman had first to obtain a desirable stock. For some period of time the goods were obtained by going directly to the side of an arriving ship carrying goods to Boston Harbor and negotiating directly with the captain of the vessel or one of the ship's officers. This system enabled the budding merchant to obtain periodic supplies of merchandise but did not provide for a stable and lasting business relationship. It favored the buyer who had ready cash or its equivalent at the time the ship arrived, but the merchant who had ready cash at one time might not be so fortunate the next time. Restocking of goods on a permanent basis was not a part of this early system.

As the colonial economy progressed, the general store also grew to a great emporium. The vast extent of the working inventory of a general storekeeper can be illustrated from a list of goods taken from the day book (credit sales) of the store run by Hendrick Onderdonk of Hempstead Harbor, New York covering the period from September 2, 1780 through February 7, 1781.

[2]Mark Twain, *Autobiography* (New York: New York University Press, 1961), p. 2.

Goods Sold by Hendrick Onderdonk

Foods
chocolate (chocolet)
sugar
molasses
eggs
butter
fish
Tushong tea
coffee
rice
rye flour (rye flower)
nutmeg
bottled mustard
cheese
vinegar
bacon (gammon)
pepper

Liquors
wine
spirits
rum

Tobacco
pipes
tobacco box
tobacco
snuff

Miscellaneous
fine paper
almanacs (almanack)
spelling books
ink powder
soap
candles and tallow
combs
hay
lottery tickets

Dress Goods
lawn (laun)
shalloon
osnaburg
buckram
linens
corduroy (corderoy)
sheeting
mohair silk (mohere silk)
calico (callico)
coating

satin denim (sattin denim)
flannel
Persian (Pertian)
baize (baze)
broadcloth
dowlas (dowlass)
cambric (cambrick)
taffety
calamanco (calliminco)
moreen
satin (sattin)
muslin
velvet
everlasting

thread
needles
buttons
knee buckles (neebuckles)
hooks and eyes
small gilt buttons
ribbon
buckles (buckels)
binding
leather for boots
lace
whalebone (walebone)
indigo

Hardware
fishhooks
nails
scythes (syth)
shovels (shovell)
gimlets (gimblet)
knives (knifes)
frying pans
window glass
powder
shot (shott)
flints
jugs (jugg)
bellows (bellowes)
irons (smoothing ironds)
brass kettles
handles and blades (axe?)
porringers
baking dishes
files
razors
lather mugs

teapots, with spouts
case, with bottles
mugs (mugg)
tumblers
wine glasses
bath brush
locks

Finished Dress Goods
hats (hatt), including beaver
handkerchiefs, silk and barcelona
womens shoes (womans shoes)
worsted stockings
coarse stockings
pumps
girls gloves
shoes

Just as the town merchant had gone to the harbor to acquire his first stock of goods, so the frontier or country storekeeper would generally obtain his stock by traveling once or twice a year to the nearest market city. Here he would dispose of his trade goods and replenish his stock of merchandise from a wholesale merchant, or he might buy a new stock at the auction markets, which were becoming increasingly common. The new stock of goods was transported back to the store, sold, and again replenished in the same manner. Long-term credit was customary in all phases of the general merchandise business with settlements on account being made annually or semi-annually. Since specie was scarce, and paper money values confusing, the joint use of credit and trading commodity for commodity was an integral part of the business. Without them, the entire operation would have been impossible.

The successful operation of a general store depended to a large extent on the trading ability of the storekeeper and his foresight (or luck) with the goods he obtained for sale to customers and the goods he obtained from them in trade. Business knowledge as such was not one of his major assets, and his accounts were kept, if at all, in a haphazard manner. Most country storekeepers were farmers as well, and many combined storekeeping with other business ventures, notably money lending, land speculation, and real estate. Almost every merchant who achieved success in shipping and foreign trade, including the first families of New England and New York, started as shopkeepers. The general store proprietor was, therefore, a citizen of eminent importance. His store was the center of village life. It was the gathering place for news and gossip. His advice was sought in both business and domestic matters, and his influence was felt in almost all areas of town and village life.

THE PEDDLERS

The general store was a mecca for those in the immediate area, but not for those who lived far out in the country. The peddler performed the function of bringing the store to these outlying communities. He provided a link between the sources of supply, both native and foreign, and the consumer in those areas where goods were unattainable in other ways. The peddler grew up with the country and followed the frontier communities, so that the experience of the early settlements was duplicated time and again as the frontier moved further and further West and the population spread. There were all kinds of peddlers, and in the course of their activities some of them laid the foundations of larger businesses of later times.[3] Others merely served a temporary economic need and disappeared when that need no longer existed.

Despite an unsavory reputation for "sharp dealing," the peddler was a welcome sight to a family that was cut off by distance and the lack of transportation from the excitement and romance of the city and its conveniences. The following apt descripiton of the peddler could apply at any time or place still visited by these traveling storekeepers:

> . . . On his own back, afoot or on horseback, or atop cleverly designed wagons full of ingenious compartments, he carried his wares into the remotest regions. With his stock of tinware, brassware, watches, clocks, pins, woodenware, brooms, baskets, ribbons and laces to set off the faces of pretty young sweethearts and wives, it is no wonder that the peddler's visits were occasions of excitement, long awaited and never to be forgotten. Novelties from the city, necessities, and news arrived at the homestead door together.[4]

In the early days when roads were mere trails cut out of the wilderness, peddling called for strength and endurance. The early peddlers tended to be young men with the adventurous spirit required of a pioneer and the ability to cope with the natural obstacles. Distances between households were considerable, and the turnover of goods was small. The peddler was limited in the quantity and weight of the goods he could carry, whether he went by foot or on horseback. On foot he could travel at best a few miles a day, and even on horseback ten miles a day was about all he could expect. The first peddlers followed Indian trails and could barely manage the pack they carried. Even in well-settled areas, roads were frequently impassable in bad weather and frail bridges and unbridged streams further limited the amount of goods that could be carried. As the trail widened to a path and then to a road, the peddler began to travel on horseback, and eventually used carts, gigs, wagons, and river craft to transport himself and his wares. But even when the roads improved sufficiently to use a wagon, his marketing area remained small.

Not all peddlers ran their business in the same manner. There were

---

[3]The ancestors of some of our best known investment bankers began their business careers as peddlers.

[4]Malcolm Keir, *The Epic of Industry* (New Haven, Conn.: Yale University Press, 1926), p. 27.

the general peddlers who carried a relatively wide assortment of goods—pins, needles, notions, combs, buttons, shoelaces, and other articles. There were those who specialized in one particular type of goods—tinware from Berlin, Connecticut, hosiery and dress goods from Philadelphia, chairs and other furniture, bibles, almanacs, and other printed matter. There were peddlers who traveled locally and built up a steady route of customers, and there were those who traveled great distances whenever and wherever they felt the inclination to wander. Some peddlers acted for others, usually manufacturers, as commission agents or forerunners of the traveling salesmen; some ventured their own funds and went out on their own.

From the city where current prices could be obtained, the peddler set out into more sparsely-settled regions where he would barter his goods for food, lodging, farm produce, and local handicrafts. There were no fixed prices, and every man operated as best he could. He could buy anything from anyone who wished to sell, and sell to anyone who wished to buy. Price was the only subject of bargaining. Since he carried his stock of goods with him the peddler fulfilled the function of seller and transportation agent. If he also manufactured the goods, as he often did, he performed an additional function. Sales were made almost exclusively by barter so that the peddler was able to profit both by the sale of his own goods and by the sale of the goods he had taken in exchange. Still, it was a lonesome and tedious life, and although a few peddlers did become relatively affluent for the times, most did not.

When peddling began to compete seriously with the business of the town storekeepers, there arose an increasing hostility on the part of "organized business" against their itinerant competitors. Petitions by the storekeepers to town and colonial governments resulted in financial and legal restrictions aimed at the business of peddling. In 1717 peddlers entering Connecticut had to pay the first town entered a fee of 20 shillings for each £100 worth of goods carried. A peddler's license was priced at £5 until 1765 when it was increased to £20. In 1770, except for those who dealt in pelts and the products of Connecticut and neighboring colonies, peddlers were forbidden to do any business in the colony. Other colonies were equally restrictive. A tax on peddlers was imposed in Rhode Island in 1700. In 1713 they were forbidden to sell dry goods, and in 1728 they were outlawed entirely. Pennsylvania in 1730 imposed a tax on peddlers selling goods manufactured outside the colony. These restrictions, instigated by the shopkeepers who paid taxes to their communities, were also used to keep "foreign" goods out and protect local manufacturing.

In many cases peddling was an adjunct of manufacturing, and the combination of the two functions built an extensive system of decentralized production and distribution. Such, for example, was the case in the manufacture and sale of tinware. In 1738, William and Edgar Pattison came from County Tyrone in Ireland and settled in Berlin, Connecticut. They were tinsmiths, but since tin was a scarce commodity locally, they had to import the tin from England and manufacture their utensils at home. When they had made up a sufficient amount, they peddled it from door to door in the local area. When local demand was satisfied, the brothers extended their peddling to nearby communities. Their success brought others to the area, and Berlin soon became the center of tinware manufacturing with factories located along the streams, which supplied the water power.

Methods of selling also changed, from foot peddling in the local area to a system that allowed the tinware manufacturers to cover a much wider area. During the early years the Pattisons and the other tinware manufacturers carried their goods on foot or horseback with the utensils packed in large trunks weighing about fifty pounds each. The peddler usually carried two of these trunks. When better roads were built and the use of wagons became possible, a special cart was built and later was increased in size.

The demand for tinware vastly exceeded the ability of the Pattisons to take care of both manufacturing and marketing. Consequently, apprentices and peddlers were added to the business. As the country spread out, the peddlers' wagons went farther and farther from the base of supply. Trips exceeding 1,000 miles were not unusual, and tinware from Berlin became available in almost every settled region. The peddling trips usually began in late summer. As the peddler traveled, his stock of goods diminished, and an intricate method was used to keep him supplied. The tinworks at Berlin would work up an inventory during the spring and summer. The tinsmiths would then be sent to various towns as widely scattered as Charleston, Richmond, Albany, and Montreal, where they would manufacture additional inventory. The peddlers' routes were planned so that they would end up at one of these towns, where they would turn their profits over to an agent, load up their wagons with additional stock, and start off again ending up back in Connecticut.

Peddling, an important aspect of colonial business, remained a part of Americana long after the formation of the Union. The peddler remained the dealer to the countryside, bringing the variety of the town store to the farm family. He also lightened the burden of domestic manufacturing by widening the small existing market and expanding the market for imports.

COLONIAL MANUFACTURING

Colonial manufacturing consisted of two general types. The first, and more typical, was household manufacturing, which supplied the things the colonists could not or would not buy. The second was manufacturing for others performed by artisans or small mills.

Household manufacturing offers vivid testimony to the farmer's skill as a "jack of all trades." Until the embryonic sinews of industry developed in the smaller communities, the pioneer farm was its own community. The farmer's tools were crude and often homemade, but there was little that he could not do for himself, and there was little that was not made from the products of the farm. Aside from the usual food items such as bread, butter, cured meats, and so on, his varied skills were put to use making beer and whiskey, clothes for the family, tools for the farm, and furniture and utensils for the home. The farm family made its own linen and woolen cloth, coonskin caps, candles, soap, and many other items. Although most of the articles produced were also consumed by the household, at times there were surpluses that could be sold or bartered for other goods.

There were probably few families in early America that did not participate to some extent in household manufacturing. For perhaps 90 percent of the families there was little if any choice. Since the small farmer produced at best only a meager agricultural surplus to sell or barter, he was forced by circumstances to make the additional things he wanted. Because farming was a seasonal business, the farmer and his family could devote the long stretches of idle time to productive labor in household manufacturing. The time devoted to these efforts usually had no alternative cost but leisure, and the materials used were typically by-products of the farm itself. It was therefore much more economical for the farm family to manufacture for itself than to buy the imported items even when it was financially possible to do so. Under those conditions, household manufacturing became an important adjunct of colonial economic life.

Manufacturing for others grew very slowly during the Colonial Period and it was to some extent influenced by both British and colonial legislation. But these efforts to help or hinder industrial development had at best only a marginal effect. The external economy had a greater influence than did legislative edict. Legislation or no legislation, the creation of a successful industrial society required a skilled labor force, a plentiful supply of capital goods, a wide domestic market, and a satisfactory money supply, all of which were sorely lacking. The manufacturing that did develop was closely tied to the available resources at hand, and they were distinctly limited. Nevertheless, some manufacturing did take place.

THE ARTISANS OR HANDICRAFT WORKERS

Somewhere between household manufacturing and the mill that represented commercial industry stood the artisan or handicraft worker, that is, the worker skilled in one or more of the many trades carried on in the colonies from the earliest days of settlement. In the sparsely settled communities, he carried his trade to the outlying farms; in the larger communities he set up his shop; in some areas he did both. The town blacksmith, the carpenter, the currier, the cooper, the tanner, the bricklayer, the wheelwright, the glazier, and the many other artisans formed an important part of every large community, and many were found even in the smaller ones.

The itinerant workmen, those who took their skills to the road, included the inevitable vagabonds who preferred the wandering life to the more sedentary town environment. They also included those who found it difficult to raise the necessary funds to open a shop in town and used this method to attain them. Finally among the wanderers were former apprentices who perhaps had not learned their trade too well. Some remained on the road but many traveled only until they found a likely town in which to set up their business. The artisans were usually welcome visitors, for not only did they supply a much needed service, but they also carried a store of news and gossip. While they traveled they carried their tools on their backs or, if not too far from home, on a cart. In the beginning, they carried only their tools, with the farmer supplying the material, but not too much later, they carried the material as well. Payment for labor was usually a fee plus board and lodging.

An artisan just starting out for himself did not necessarily require a large investment, certainly nothing close to that required by a manufacturer. It is estimated that of the hundreds of occupations practiced about the middle of the eighteenth century some could be started with as little as £5, but might range as high as £100. To meet the capital requirement many communities offered financial and other assistance to artisans who would settle and work there. There is no way of knowing the value of handicraft manufacture but records indicate that widely scattered farming areas as well as all towns and settlements had their share of artisans.

The extent of handicraft manufacture can be surmised from the many reports concerning the number of establishments in various communities. In 1647 Boston could boast of "six wood-working trades, seven metal-working trades, three forms of leather manufacture," plus "weavers and ropemakers, felt-makers and furriers, brickmakers and tile-makers, and minor industries." Philadelphia, in 1697, had 51 manufacturing artisans outside of building trades. By the Revolution, 37 of the 130 families in the frontier settlement of Pittsburgh were manufacturers. At about the same time, Lancaster, Pennsylvania, with a population of about 700 families, had 234 "manufacturers" including 36 shoemakers, 30 smiths, 28 weavers, 25 tailors, 17 saddlers, 14 hatters, and 11 coopers. On the basis of the number of trades followed and the number of artisans in each community, it seems reasonable to assume that handicraft workers made an important contribution to the total manufacturing product.

Most of the handicraft shops were on a small scale. They were family businesses using family labor. Journeymen were to be found only in the larger and more successful establishments in the larger cities. Even when available, they were more often than not men of poor character, unreliable, and given to wandering. Those who were dependable worked for others only long enough to save the amount necessary to start out on their own. The early artisans were usually farmers as well as artisans. The craft was carried on in spare time and during the winter months. This condition persisted well into the 1700's, by which time the artisan was able to survive from his craft alone. At the start he opened a small shop and did "bespoke" work, that is, on specific orders for customers who more likely than not would supply the raw materials. As the population increased and trade grew, the craftsman tended to supply the materials as well. Finally, he started to make goods in advance of sale, selling them by display, advertising, and perhaps through peddlers. When newspapers appeared, the artisans were among the principle advertisers. Some present-day techniques of advertising had their start during this period, such as misrepresentation, false claims, threats, testimonials, snob appeals, and surprise techniques.

When the handicraft operation was a family affair the problem of labor was a minor one. The skilled master passed his knowledge and skill to his wife and sons who would work by his side and carry on after him if he should die. His daughters might tend to customers in the shop itself. Because of this, businesswomen were found in many of the colonial trades, carrying on their late husbands' businesses. Where the master was a bachelor or childless, or when the business had grown to the point where sales outgrew the ability of the family to produce, outside labor became necessary, and taking a leaf from the English, the apprenticeship system developed in the colonies as part of business policy.

Under the apprenticeship system young boys were given to a master for a period up to seven years or until they reached the age of twenty-one. During the apprenticeship they lived with the family of the artisan whose duty it became to feed, clothe, and teach his skill to the apprentice. The apprentice was also to receive rudimentary instruction in reading, writing, and arithmetic. Some contracts stipulated that the boy was to be sent to night school at the expense of the parents, or in some cases at the expense of the master. In addition to these "voluntary" apprentices, there were also "involuntary" apprentices. These were orphans and bastards whom the townspeople wished to keep off the "poor rates."

When the apprenticeship was over, the apprentice was to receive new clothing and sometimes a little money to start him off as a journeyman. According to page 130 of Harrington, for his part, the apprentice

shall his said Master ——— faithfully serve, his secrets keep, his lawful Commands gladly every where Obey; he shall do no damage to his said Master, nor see to be done by Others without letting or giving Notice to his said Master; he shall not waste his said Master's Goods, nor lend them unlawfully to any; he shall not Committ fornication nor

Contract Matrimony within the said Term. At Cards, Dice, or any Other unlawful Game he shall not play, whereby his said Master may have Damage; with his Own Goods or the Goods of those during the said Term without Lycence from his said Master he shall neither buy nor sell. He shall not absent himself Day or Night from his Master's service without his leave, nor haunt Alehouses or Playhouses, but in all things as a faithful apprentice he shall behave himself toward his said Master, and all during the said Term.

A great drawback to the artisan, as it was to all other businessmen of the time, was the scarcity of money. Credit and barter were the rule, with barter more popular in the smaller areas and credit in the larger ones. Credit accounts ran on almost endlessly, and buyers who paid cash were indeed rare. These credit transactions often caused extreme hardship to otherwise profitable businesses, with the craftsmen sometimes ending up as bankrupts or as inhabitants of the local debtors' prison. Sometimes, in order to forestall bankruptcy, several artisans would form a partnership, thus enlarging their operations and capital funds, adding skills, and eliminating competition. In many cases this helped the artisans to keep going during times of adversity. On the whole, however, the artisans as a class were successful, "They were spirited essential citizens in any town of importance." As they amassed some monetary wealth they invested the surplus in land, town lots, and real estate, which they would rent as tenements or shops. They also took part in trading ventures and went into the shipping business.

The artisan was also active in community affairs. He belonged, of course, to his craft guild, as well as to church organizations, and was an important member of his community, more so in the smaller communities than the larger ones. According to Atherton,

> The artisan class in the colonial period everywhere represented an unspecialized type of economy. Such workmen furnished their own shops and tools and in that sense were capitalists; by also furnishing part of the labour they might be called a labouring class. They represented both the wholesaling and retailing functions of the system since they delivered their products directly into the hands of the ultimate consumer. Even the term entrepreneur might be attached, as the custom-order worker provided the directive element in his own shop.[5]

GRISTMILLS, FLOURMILLS, AND SAWMILLS

The third kind of colonial manufacturing, the mill, came in two types: (1) those which primarily served the inhabitants of the surrounding community, and (2) those which produced for wider markets, chiefly foreign.

[5]Lewis E. Atherton, *The Southern Country Store* (Baton Rouge, La.: Louisiana State University Press, 1949), p. 166.

Of the first type, the gristmill, the flourmill, and the sawmill were most representative. Their operation started early in the period, at times along with the beginning of the settlement, and they were quickly constructed in almost every settlement that had any water power, even a small stream. The cost of building a mill ran somewhere between $500 and $1,000. Its capacity was not very great. The average sawmill could cut about 1,000 feet of board a day, and the average flour mill could turn out about 10 to 20 barrels a week. Later on in the period, improvements made possible the construction of larger and more efficient plants. Shortly before the Revolutionary War the improvements in the application of power to milling processes and machinery enabled some mills on the Delaware and Chesapeake Rivers to be compared with the finest in the world. These mills, using six men, could convert annually about 100,000 bushels of grain into flour. However, even at this time, a mill that could grind about 100 bushels a day was considered large.

The owner of a gristmill, who was often a farmer, usually operated the mill himself with the assistance of his family and perhaps one or two hired men. It was a seasonal business, and during the off-season the mill was either closed down or, if possible, converted temporarily into a sawmill. It might also be used to grind malt for beer or rags for paper. The mills usually operated on a toll system, with the farmer paying a share of the grain or flour as the milling charge. In most communities milling was regarded by the local governments as vested with a public interest, and the milling charges were strictly regulated. In New England the customary fee was one-twelfth of the corn and one-sixteenth of other grains. In Virginia and Maryland, where there were fewer mills, the fee was customarily one-sixth. Since he was paid in kind, the miller found himself with a supply of grain or flour on his hands. In addition, the miller would also act as agent for the farmers in selling their surplus flour. Thus he was automatically pushed into becoming a trader as well as a miller. In order to sell or barter his grain and flour, he established contacts with merchants in the nearest cities. These contacts with the importers-exporters and the stock of goods he received in exchange for the flour led to the establishment of a store, where he sold goods to the farmers against future deliveries of grain. Almost by destiny, therefore, the mill owner became a diversified entrepreneur, operating a farm, a mill, and a store, and probably dabbling in land speculation as well.

SHIPBUILDING, GLASSMAKING, AND CANDLEMAKING

Shipbuilding became an important industry in New England from the time the first ship of any size (60 tons) was built at Medford, Massachusetts in 1631. More and larger ships were built so that by 1665 Massachusetts had about 80 ships of from 20 to 40 tons, about 40 ships from 40 to 100 tons, and about 12 ships above 100 tons. The industry quickly spread throughout New England and the middle colonies. By the end of the seventeenth century the colonies were constructing 4,000 tons a year. By 1770, 35,000 tons a year were being built, at which time almost one-third of all British ships had been built in the colonies and about 75 percent of all colonial commerce was carried on in home-constructed vessels.

Glass manufacturing was another industry attempted in the colonies. In 1654 a Hollander, Jan Sneeder, operated a glass factory in New York at the present site of William Street. His monopoly was shortlived, for less than a year later his countryman, one Evert Duyckingk, opened a competing factory. These were small endeavors as were the many others that were started during this early period. The first glass factory of any size was started by Casper Wistar on the New Jersey side of the Delaware River near Philadelphia in 1739. The Wistars, father and son, manufactured window glass and bottles, both in several sizes and in several colors.

The most famous of all colonial glass works, the Stiegel works, were operated by Heinrich Wilhelm Stiegel. Stiegel, already a successful ironmaster in Germany, began to produce the finest and most distinctive glass in America in 1765 at Manheim, Pennsylvania. The Stiegel works made window glass, sheet glass, bottles and flasks, retorts, and drinking glasses of all kinds. By 1772 Stiegel glass was sold in most of the larger cities in the North, and there was a Stiegel store in Philadelphia. Despite the artistry and quality of his product Stiegel ran into financial difficulties, became insolvent, and was finally sold out by the sheriff in 1774.

The manufacture of spermaceti candles (i.e., candles made from whale produce) was still another industry of more than passing importance. By 1763, there were probably a dozen manufactories in the colonies. The leader by far was Rhode Island, where the Jewish merchants of Newport and the Browns of Providence became heavily interested in the business. Candle manufacturing in Rhode Island rivaled the slave trade and surpassed distilling, the two occupations with which that colony is usually associated.

THE IRON INDUSTRY

There were still other important mill manufactures. Lynn, Massachusetts was the center for the manufacture of women's shoes. Germantown, Pennsylvania was an important seat of textile and hosiery manufacture. Berlin, Connecticut was the center of tinware manufacture, and Haverhill, Massachusetts had 44 workshops and 19 mills, or one mill for every 15 residences.

But none of these approached in importance the iron industry, which was as old as Jamestown. In 1608, Virginia exported some iron ore to England. In 1620, the British managers of the colony decided to exploit the iron deposits more fully. With this in mind, they sent over a group of skilled workers. But this failed. No iron was ever smelted. Unaccustomed to the climate, the workers came down with fever, and all of them died. A similar fate met all the early Virginia business ventures. They could not survive the climate and they could not overcome the lack of skilled labor and entrepreneurial talent.

The first successful iron works were established in 1643 when the Undertakers of the Iron Works established a forge on the Saugus River near Lynn, Massachusetts. The Leonard family, who were prominent in the New England iron industry and later in New Jersey, operated the Saugus works vigorously until 1671. Production dropped off thereafter and work stopped completely in 1688.

New England was the leading iron producer in the seventeenth century, but in the eighteenth, the industry spread and grew as new resources were discovered in the middle Atlantic and southern colonies. Pennsylvania, which began iron production in 1692, emerged as the new leader, far ahead of its closest rival.

Long before the Revolution, the colonies surpassed Britain both in number of iron works and in volume of iron produced. Starting off slowly, pig iron exports rose to significant levels. By 1729, the amount exceeded 1,100 long tons. It doubled in the next two years, and exceeded 2,000 tons a year in most years thereafter until the Revolution. In one banner year (1771) exports reached the astonishing total of 5,000 long tons.

The largest and most ambitious colonial manufacturer was Peter Hasenclever, a German who had been a partner in a mercantile firm in Cadiz, Spain. In 1764, he induced a group of eminent Englishmen to invest from £10,000 to £40,000 in the production of pig iron, hemp, potash, and other items in North America.

Hasenclever imported 535 people, including miners, farmers, mechanics, and their families. By 1766, he had in operation four furnaces and seven forges in New York and New Jersey. He had constructed 235 stores, workshops, and dwelling houses, dams for 13 mill ponds, 10 bridges, many miles of roads, and was operating at least 7 mines. By that time he had spent almost £55,000, almost £15,000 more than his associates had promised. Unfortunately for Hasenclever, no additional funds were forthcoming, and when his notes became due, they were not honored.

The full extent of Hasenclever's enterprise can be best appreciated from the inventory of the property of The American Iron Company at the time Hasenclever left the country. There were four furnaces capable of producing 100 tons of pig iron a week and seven forges with a total of 23 fires.

The business practices and policies of the larger iron works can be illustrated from the experience of the Baltimore Company, the second largest iron works in Maryland, and the first of any importance to be locally owned and operated.[6] The company was organized as a partnership in 1731 by Daniel Dulany, Dr. Charles Carroll, Benjamin Tasker, Charles Carroll of Annapolis, and his brother Daniel Carroll. The five partners were all prominent men in the colony, with varied business interests and well-established business connections in London. The starting capital was £3,500 sterling, and over the next few years additional capital investment brought the total to £14,835 sterling plus £2,873 in local currency. Although a few items were fabricated, production was concentrated in the manufacture of pig and bar iron.

Since the market for iron in the immediate vicinity was limited, the company was forced to turn its efforts to other colonies and Great Britain to sell its production. With little, and at best sketchy, information on demand and price structures at the various markets, the partners had to rely mainly on guesswork and chance, and the best outlets for their iron were discovered through trial and error. The principal outlet for Baltimore iron was found to be England, and the terms illuminate the typical way in which this sort of business was conducted. Terms of sale involved credit extension by the seller of from three to eight months, in addition to which the seller was required to accept partial payment in ironware fabricated by the buyer, which made additional exchanges necessary. The credit terms, the part-barter method of payment, and the length of the time involved in shipment and ultimate sale resulted in a great deal of operating capital tied up in trade.

Initially the partners tried to operate the company by issuing individual orders to Stephen Onion, the supervisor of the works. Evidently this method of uncoordinated management did not work very well, for within a short time a new arrangement was made whereby the owners met as a board of directors to decide major policies, allowing greater authority to the works manager in the details of the operation. Each partner acted as an individual salesman for the firm, selling whenever possible to local consumers as well as to customers in other colonies and in Great Britain. When the partners met toward the end of 1733, four of them reported sales totaling £1,769 sterling and £1,571 in local currency. Dr. Charles Carroll does not seem to have participated in the selling phase of the business.

In 1734, the company started to ship pig iron to England. Such shipments averaged about 500 tons a year during the following few years. In

[6]Keith Johnson, "The Genesis of the Baltimore Ironworks," *Journal of Southern History*, Vol. XIX, May 1953, pp. 157–79; Aubrey C. Land, "Genesis of a Colonial Fortune: David Dulany of Maryland," *William and Mary Quarterly*, third series, Vol. XXVII, April 1950, pp. 255–68. Both have been reprinted in Stanley Coben and Forest G. Hill, *American Economic History* (Philadelphia: J. B. Lippincott Company, 1966).

1735 an important connection was established between the company and the Crowley Ironworks, a firm that dominated the iron industry in northeastern England. The Crowley firm offered to buy from 400 to 500 tons of iron a year, delivered to their dock at £6/5s a ton or at the market price if it should be higher. One half of the payment was to be made in ironware at the "ready money price." Eventually the Crowley firm purchased more Baltimore iron than any other firm.

Trade was severely disrupted during King George's War (1745–1748) and the slump in the English market that followed it. Of the 130 tons the Baltimore Company consigned to its London agent, John Price, in 1750, only 15 tons were sold, and much of the remaining iron had to be shipped from London to Bristol and Bewdley where it was finally sold. Although shipping directly to Bristol would have been faster as well as less costly, the lack of direct shipping space provided a formidable barrier, and most of the iron sold in Bristol had to be shipped first to London and then reshipped. Sales in England in the 1750's were no higher than they had been in the 1730's, about 500 tons annually, or about one-fifth of total colonial exports of iron.

The profitability of the enterprise is difficult to ascertain, but from the available information it can be concluded that the returns were more than adequate. For the four-month period covering April to August, 1741, each partner received a payment out of profits of £203 sterling, and Charles Carroll estimated the annual net profit per share at £400 sterling during the 1750's, a return in excess of eleven percent on the original invested capital of £17,708. In 1750–51 a consignment of 376 tons to John Price was sold for £2,324. After deducting shipping and selling costs of £545 and production costs of £1,170, the remaining profit of £609 was equal to more than 26 percent of the sales price. By the 1760's, the value of each share had increased from the original £3,540 to about £6,000 sterling.

GOVERNMENT REGULATION AND CONTROL

In the seventeenth and eighteenth centuries, the overwhelming majority of opinion in the colonies, in Britain, and, in fact, wherever men thought about economic matters, was that the government should regulate the economy. This belief, moreover, was held without the slightest skepticism. The dominant economic faith was mercantilism, a policy designed to increase the value of exports, decrease the value of imports, and so augment the financial and economic power of the state. Laissez faire had never been heard of, and Adam Smith would not publish his *Wealth of Nations* until the year of American independence.

Government control over the economy took three forms. The Crown regulated foreign trade and shipping. Both the Crown and the individual colonies regulated manufacturing, and the colonies tried to regulate prices and wages.

England's attempt to mold the American (and other) colonies into the mercantilistic system resulted in the various Navigation Acts, which set forth the basic provisions of British regulation during the colonial period.

The Act of 1660, "An Act For The Encouraging And Increasing of Shipping And Navigation," stipulated that from December 1, 1660 all goods imported into or exported from the colonies were to be carried in ships built and owned by British subjects. The master and three-fourths of the crew were also to be British. Evasion of the law was to carry the penalty of the loss of both the ship and the cargo. Since the colonists already had a decided comparative advantage in shipbuilding, the legislation merely fostered what to them was already an economic reality.

The second part of the Act designated certain commodities that from and after April 1, 1661 could be shipped only to England or other English colonies. These "enumerated commodities" included sugar, tobacco, cotton, wool, indigo, ginger, fustic, and other dyewoods. Ships carrying any of these commodities were to sail under a surety bond in order to ensure that the desired colonial exports were sent only to England for either manufacture, use, or re-export, and to increase English tariff revenue. During the eighteenth century many more products were added to the enumerated list.

A third feature of mercantilistic policy, contained in the Act of 1663, required that all goods (with some enumerated exceptions) shipped to the colonies from non-British Europe be shipped first to England or Wales and from there reshipped in British ships.

While some phases of British mercantilistic policy tended to restrict the economic freedom and well-being of colonial businessmen, there were many concurrent benefits. The inclusion of colonial shipbuilding and ship-ownership within the protective provisions of the Navigation Acts was not popular with the English shipbuilding industry. Colonial shipping on the high seas was made safer through the protection of the British navy. Various products of the colonies were admitted to England free of or at lower tariff rates than were charged on foreign products. Tobacco growing was forbidden in England, thus giving colonial planters a virtual monopoly in the English tobacco market. In addition, in order to foster production of certain desired commodities, generous bounties were paid to the colonists for tar, pitch, hemp, indigo, lumber, and high-grade cooperage materials.

THE CONTROL OF MANUFACTURING

Both the British government and the colonies tried to bend manufacturing to their own ends. The Crown tried to restrict the manufacture of competing goods and encourage those things that the colonies only could produce. The colonies tried to encourage all manufactures.

British legislation concentrated on bounties and tariff reductions to foster the manufacture of lumber products, indigo, tar, pitch, turpentine, and hemp. In 1699 the Crown prohibited the export of colonial woolen goods, and in 1732 the stricture was also placed on hats. To hamper the development of textile manufacturing, laws were passed imposing fines and imprisonment upon persons with textile knowledge emigrating to the colonies or shipping tools used in the manufacture of textiles.

Colonial legislation and other attempts to encourage manufacturing were quite varied. As early as 1618 the shareholders of the Virginia settlement sent to the governor of that colony a directive sponsoring the substitution of manufacturing for farming as a desirable aspect of colonization:

> And for the better Encouragement of all sorts of necessary and laudable traders to be set up and exercised within the said four Cities and Burroughs We do hereby ordain that if any artizans or tradesmen shall be desirous rather to follow his particular Art or trade than to be imployed in husbandry or other rural business It shall be lawful for you the said Governor and Council to alot and set out within any of the precincts aforesaid One dwelling house with four Acres of land adjoining and held in fee simple to every said tradesman his heirs and Assigns for ever upon condition that the said tradesman his heirs and Assigns do continue and exercise his trade in the said house paying only a fee rent of four pence by the year to us the said Treasurer and Company and our Successors at the feast of St. Michael the Archangel for ever.

Taking a page from British law, the colonies commonly granted bounties to promote manufacturing. Massachusetts in 1640, Virginia in 1662, and Maryland in 1682 offered bounties for woolen cloth. Maryland, in 1671, also granted a bounty for the production of hemp and flax in order to provide materials for domestic manufacturing. Bounties on hemp were also granted in the 1700's by Virginia, North Carolina, Pennsylvania, New York, South Carolina, and New Jersey, with the latter two colonies also granting a bounty for the production of flax. Several of the colonies also granted bounties for the production of such things as tar, potash, salt, indigo, wine, linen, canvas, and saltpeter.

Some of the laws made attempts at coercion. In 1665, Massachusetts directed each of its selectmen to determine how many persons in each household were capable of spinning yarn and the amount of time available for this purpose. On the basis of this information, spinners were assigned to each household to produce three pounds of cotton, wool, or linen yarn a week for thirty weeks. A fine of twelve pence was imposed for each one pound shortage. Virginia passed legislation forbidding mechanics to grow tobacco or corn so that they could devote their full time to industry. Virginia also, in 1661, required each of its counties to establish one or more tanneries, and in 1666 directed each county to set up a public loom within a two-year period.

In the northern colonies public land grants and limited monopolies were used extensively as inducements for prospective businessmen. These grants were offered by both the provincial governments and the town authorities. A few examples out of many are sufficient to illustrate the nature of these inducements. In 1664, Massachusetts gave the promoters of the Lynn Iron Works a choice of eighteen square miles of land. John Winthrop, in 1648, was offered 3,000 acres of land by Massachusetts if he would set up a salt works that would produce 100 tons a year. Winthorp also received from Connecticut, in 1651, lands, wood, timber, and water within two or three miles of any mining property he discovered and developed unless these were already occupied. In 1736, Thomas Plaisted received 1,500 acres of land from Massachusetts for the manufacture of potash. In 1733, Joseph Mallinson, an ironmaster at Duxbury, received 200 acres of land for his service to the public in setting up his cast-iron manufactory. In 1698, William Hubblefield received 300 acres for his services in promoting and instructing many persons in clothmaking.

Town aid to business took three forms: direct allotment to craftsmen and manufacturers of a tract of land, water rights, or the right to use common land; direct contribution to a manufacturer by the building of a mill; conferring the economic and social privilege of freemen on qualified mechanics who would settle in the town. In the seventeenth and early eighteenth centuries, town aid to mills was very prevalent. As early as 1635, Watertown donated a lot for a gristmill, and in 1643, Boston granted as much as 300 acres to the builders of a mill to grind corn. Groton also donated land for a gristmill, and in 1713, Rutland offered 900 acres for the first mill to be erected there. Sawmills were induced by grants of land at Keene, New Hampshire and Woodbridge, New Jersey. Woodbridge also donated land for a fulling mill. Ipswich gave a house lot to a clothier along with twelve acres of meadow land, and what is now Lowell, Massachusetts gave twelve acres of upland to William How if he would set up as a weaver and do the town's work. Salem gave several acres of land to the local glass house, and both Roxbury and Haverhill granted land to brickmakers. Similar assistance was given by Ipswich and Gloucester to saltworks. John Winthrop and his associates were also recipients of a land grant of 3,000 acres from Braintree for the construction of an iron works.

Towns and states also donated money to millbuilders, sometimes as loans but at times as outright gifts. Salem, Massachusetts lent £30 to the glass men and £5 to John Wareing to pay his spinners. Newbury gave £20, and Woodbridge, New Jersey £30 for the first gristmills to be built there.

Keene, New Hampshire gave £25 plus land to its first sawmill. In 1725, Rhode Island lent William Borden £500 at interest, and in 1728, £3,000 without interest to establish a sailcloth factory. Massachusetts lent £800 to the previously mentioned Joseph Plaisted in addition to the land grant.

Aside from land grants, loans, and money grants, limited monopolies were also used by the various colonies to attract industry. Monopolies were usually granted to cover a specific area for a limited period of time, sometimes for the introduction of a new process and at times for the use of a more desirable process. In 1641, Massachusetts granted a ten-year monopoly to Samuel Winslow for a salt works, and in 1656, a 21-year monopoly to John Winthrop for the manufacture of salt "after his own way." Connecticut, Virginia, and South Carolina also granted similar protection against competition to new salt works. Salt-making was only one of the protected industries. Rhode Island granted monopoly rights to manufacturers of potash and castile soap. Connecticut gave similar protection to the user of a flax machine, duck factories, linseed oil, potash works, glass works, and a slitting mill. South Carolina offered protection for the first sawmill and the first gristmill to be constructed in the province. New York gave favorable monopoly treatment to a maker of lampblack and to a sugar refiner.

WAGE AND PRICE CONTROLS

Somehow in every developing economy, demand outruns supply, and the prices of both goods and the factors of production are bid up producing a condition known as inflation. The colonial experience was no exception. Prices rose in most of the colonies, but New England offers a prime example of how the problem was dealt with.

The population of the colony (including Plymouth) increased from 896 in 1630 to 9,952 in 1640, and to 15,603 in 1650, and despite its proclivity for planning, the Massachusetts Bay Company was unable to provide the settlers with sufficient necessities. Nor could it control the distribution of the available supply of goods. Skilled labor was also in short supply causing wages to increase far above comparable English rates, and from its first meeting the General Court was involved in setting wage and price ceilings.

In 1633, carpenters, sawers, masons, bricklayers, tilers, joiners, and other skilled workers were limited to 14 pence a day with board and two shillings a day without. Good laborers ("the best sort") were limited to 8 pence a day with board and 18 pence without. Master tailors received 12 pence a day with board and the "inferior sort" not more than 8 pence a day with board. The penalty for paying or receiving more than the ceiling wage was 5 shillings for each daily infraction. Idlers, loafers, and especially "tobacco takers" were to be punished by the Court. Price controls were established by permitting not more than one-third markup[7] in some goods and "moderate prices" in others. Within two years the price and wage legislation was repealed, but the repeal was accompanied by a warning against excesses.

There seems to be no doubt that the regulations laid down by the General Court were not always closely observed. The case of Robert Keayne illustrated the business attitude toward the legislation. Keayne was fined £200 for overcharging for goods. Governor Winthrop denounced Keayne as being notoriously above others in "taking above six-pence in the shilling profit; in some above eight-pence."

Keayne never forgot his experience and always thought he had been treated unjustly. In his will, he wrote:

> Was the selling of 6-penny nails for 8 d per pound and 8-penny nails for 10 d such a crying and oppressive sin? Though as I remember it was above two years before he that bought them paid me for them; and they not paid for, if I forget not, when he made that . . . unrighteous complaint in the court against me . . . as if I had altered and corrupted my book in adding more to the price than I had set down for them at first delivery. . . .[8]

In the church trial that followed the civil trial, the Reverend John Cotton took the opportunity to dictate the rules for trading and some false principles that were not to be followed:

> Rules for trading:
> 1. A man may not sell above the current price, i.e., such a price as is usual in the time and place, and as another (who knows the worth of the commodity) would give for it, if he had occasion to use it; as that is called current money, which every man will take, etc.
> 2. When a man loseth in his commodity for want of skill, etc., he must look at it as his own fault or cross, and therefore must not lay it upon another.
> 3. Where a man loseth by casualty of sea, or, etc., it is a loss cast upon himself by providence, and he may not ease himself of it by casting it upon another; for so a man should seem to provide against all providences, etc., that he should never lose; but where there is a scarcity of the commodity, there men may raise their price; for now it is a hand of God upon the commodity, and not the person.
> 4. A man may not ask any more for his commodity than his selling price, as Ephron to Abraham, the land is worth thus much.

----

[7]Certainly not an extraordinarily high amount when judged by twentieth-century markups.

[8]N. S. B. Gras and Henrietta M. Larson, *Casebook in American Business History* (New York: Appleton-Century-Crofts, 1939), p. 56.

Some false principles of trade:

1. That a man might sell as dear as he can, and buy as cheap as he can.
2. If a man loseth by casualty of sea, etc., in some of his commodities, he may raise the price of the rest.
3. That he may sell as he bought, though he paid too dear, etc., and though the commodity be fallen, etc.
4. That, as a man may take the advantage of his own skill or ability, so he may of another's ignorance or necessity.
5. Where one gives time of payment, he is to take like recompense of one as of another.[9]

By the end of the Colonial Period, these rules had been considerably modified, and it is hardly likely that Keayne would have been prosecuted had he done in 1750 what he did 100 years before.

At the close of the Colonial Period, agriculture was by far the most important economic effort of most of the population. Manufacturing was still a backward industry and the colonies were still dependent on imported goods. But progress had been made, and in a subtle way the future had started to form. The northern colonies had made some advance in manufacturing and were able to compete in the world market with some products based primarily on an abundance of raw materials. Tradesmen and merchants had become a permanent part of the business environment, and some were starting to branch out into small wholesaling ventures in addition to their normal retailing activities. They accepted and made payments in all kinds of foreign currencies and in commodities. They eagerly sought new products and new markets. Shipping, shipbuilding, and iron smelting joined lumbering, fishing, farming, and home production as the mainstays of business life. Although the size of operations was to increase gradually and also impressively, the essential nature of the northern business environment was to remain virtually unchanged for a half a century after the close of the Colonial Era.

In the course of development, the southern colonies had settled into a one-crop agriculture, which was to continue for many years despite the change from tobacco to cotton. In all parts of the country, many types of businessmen had appeared, but by the end of the period, the northern merchant had emerged as the dominant type of entrepreneur.

[9]*Ibid.*, p. 59.

3

THE RISE
OF THE MERCHANT

Since it was evident from the start of colonization that the settlers could not produce all their desired goods locally, overseas trade became the inescapable answer to their problems. It was the merchant, of course, who handled this trade, for a merchant was, in the words of Dr. Johnson, "one who trafficked to remote countries."

In the early part of the Colonial Era, it was, as we have seen, the petty merchant who provided the service of procuring and disposing of imports and exports. Very often he was the captain of a small ship or a shopkeeper. Thus, James Brown, the founder of the influential business dynasty of Providence, Rhode Island, began his business career on the sea. In 1721, he and four other partners invested in a small sloop of about 75 tons. Brown captained the sloop, which must have done well, for in 1723 he left the sea and "opened his ledger as a shopkeeper." Subsequently, he added the activities of money lending, shipowning, and operating a distillery and a slaughterhouse.[1]

THE EMERGENCE OF THE MERCHANT PRINCE

In time, some of the petty merchants prospered exceedingly, expanded their businesses, and emerged as the dominant businessmen of the day. In all the port cities, by the middle of the eighteenth century, groups of merchants had acquired great influence in the social and economic structure,

[1] James B. Hedges, *The Browns of Providence Plantations* (Cambridge, Mass.: Harvard University Press, 1952).

and they would continue to play a major role for almost another century. In New England, the Crowninshields, Derbys, Lees, Higginsons, Lowells, Cabots; in New York, the De Peysters, Rutgers, Livingstons, Beekmans; in Philadelphia, the Binghams, Willings, McCalls, Francises established along with other mercantile families an early moneyed aristocracy.

The transition in the colonies was very similar to the transition that had occurred in medieval Europe when the sedentary merchant emerged to take precedence and control over the traveling merchant. Each transition illustrated an oft-repeated trend in the history of business. As an industry grew, division of labor and specialization also grew, and the effect of this on the entrepreneur was to push him off the production line toward the office. Thus, the successful colonial merchant supervised his affairs from his countinghouse whereas his predecessor had operated on the production line which, in his case, was a ship's bridge.

There were other differences between the sedentary merchant and the petty merchant. The petty merchant had a shop and bought piecemeal while the merchant capitalist had a "store" or a warehouse and imported in bulk rather than buying from someone else. Then too, the petty merchant was more or less a specialist while his successor's activities were extremely diversified. Indeed, of all the businessmen in history, the merchant was involved in the largest number of activities. He was completely unspecialized. One student of the period has described him as "something like the head of an international mail-order house."[2]

The merchants' basic activity was in international or coastwise trade. Ordinarily, they sold their imported goods at wholesale. In many if not in most cases, they were also retailers as well. Some few did no wholesaling but only retailing. The merchants were also shipowners, using their ships for their own freight and at times acting as carriers for others. They operated warehouses in which they also stored for others. They were commission agents and brokers, insurers of marine cargoes, money lenders, dealers in foreign exchange and bills of exchange, and agents for other merchants both domestic and foreign. In addition, they often engaged in manufacturing, such as shipbuilding, iron smelting, distilling, and candle making.

There were numerous reasons both within the business itself and in the external environment for this diversification. For the ambitious man—and many colonists were ambitious—specialization offered no possibility of achieving wealth or even comfort. There were just not enough customers. And adding to the obstacle of a sparse population, primitive transportation and communication, the lack of money, and the difficulty of putting together a return cargo to pay for British imports made specialization impractical.

[2]Robert A. East, "The Business Entrepreneur in a Changing Colonial Economy," *Journal of Economic History*, Vol. VI, Supplement, p. 16.

THE IMPORTANCE OF FAMILY-KINSHIP RELATIONS

Early merchants were almost completely dependent upon English connections. But as the domestic economy prospered and the merchant families began to accumulate some surplus, the ties to English relatives loosened, and a solid family-kinship structure developed domestically. These family structures were strengthened by the not infrequent marriages among the children and grandchildren of the early group of merchants. Sons, sons-in-law, and nephews all became part of the firm and represented it either at home or abroad, so that there grew up a merchant class bound by social and family ties. Although in later years freedom of entry was somewhat less restricted and could be accomplished by fortunate outsiders, family and social relationships remained, if not the only way, certainly the easiest way to become a merchant.[3]

The celebrated Boston merchant, Thomas Handasyd Perkins, was the son and grandson of merchants. When his father died, his mother successfully carried on the family business. After the usual apprenticeship, Thomas joined his brother James, a merchant in St. Domingo. When he returned to Boston to represent the firm there, his position in St. Domingo was taken over by another brother, Samuel G. Perkins. His interest in the China trade was whetted by Captain James Magee, a relative of his wife, and when the firm started a branch there a nephew, John P. Cushing, was sent along. Eventually, Cushing became a partner and resident manager. When Perkins & Co. was dissolved in 1828, and Cushing returned to Boston, the responsibility for closing out the firm's affairs was given to Thomas T. Forbes, who was a nephew of Perkins and a cousin of Cushing. When the firm was later reorganized, it was by Thomas Perkins and his son-in-law Samuel Cabot.

The Hutchinsons of Massachusetts also had an extended family related business. Their Rhode Island cattle farms were run by Peleg Sanford, a nephew of Richard Hutchinson. Peleg, in turn, exported horses and provisions to his brothers, William and Elisha, in Barbados. The Winthrops had family representatives in Rhode Island, Hartford and New London in Connecticut, Antigua in the West Indies, and Teneriffe in the Canary Islands.

In New York Van Cortlandts married Bayards; Beekmans married Van Hornes; Watts married DeLanceys; and the Livingstons married everyone, so many in fact that England was asked to remove Judge Livingston from office because "no cause of any consequence can come before him in which he or the family are not interested."

Colonial foreign trade was spread over a wide geographical area. Al-

---

[3]The importance of family is still discernable in Boston and Philadelphia, but not so much in New York where kinship relations were never so deeply buried in the culture.

THE COMPOSITION AND DESTINATION
OF EXPORTS

though the colonists presented a market for the many manufactured goods that they were unable to provide for themselves, they could export only their surplus products, and not all these were desired in England. The merchants were, therefore, confronted by the problem of finding markets for those products not desired in Britain so as to obtain the necessary specie to pay for the desired imports from Britain.

As regional specialization developed, the pattern of exports started to take shape. In New England, fish and fish oil, lumber, and ships were the important exports as well as livestock and meat. In the middle colonies the outstanding export was wheat and wheat products along with lumber, ships, meat, corn, oats, beans, peas, livestock, skins, and some iron and copper. In Virginia and Maryland the main export was tobacco, along with indigo, ships, iron and copper, beans, peas, corn, and oats. In the Carolinas and Georgia the export mainstay was rice along with flaxseed, indigo, and lumber.

The routes followed by the merchant ships were determined by a combination of supply and demand and the stipulations of the British Navigation Acts. The requirement that all enumerated products be carried directly to England or to another British Colony determined the first trade route. Since the enumerated products were the important staples of the southern colonies, the South, for the most part, traded directly with England. The traffic was regular and of considerable amount. From 1761 through 1765, 83 percent of total exports to England from the colonies came from Virginia, Maryland, Carolina, and Georgia. Out of this trade there developed also two other routes for southern staples. One from the northern colonies directly to England with re-exported southern commodities, and the other from Carolina and Georgia carrying rice to European ports south of Cape Finisterre.

The trade routes followed by the northern merchants were more varied and more complicated. There was, of course, some direct trade with England, but it was much less than trade with the rest of the world. In 1769, New England sent only 26 percent of her exports to Great Britain, New York only 49 percent, Pennsylvania a mere 7 percent, and New Jersey none. In total less than 24 percent of all northern exports went directly to Great Britain. Imports from Great Britain exceeded exports by some £220,337, an amount that had to be made up by credit or goods from other countries since the staples of the northern colonies competed with rather than complemented the trade of England.

Directly to England, the northern merchants shipped fish, furs, hides, lumber, whale-fins and whale-oil, naval stores, wheat, flour, hops, and small amounts of iron. They also re-exported tobacco, sugar, rum, molasses, dyewoods, and other products. They typically carried these goods in their own ships and, in order to balance their accounts, they frequently sold their ships as well. The northern merchants also exported nonenumerated products to European countries other than England. The bulk of northern shipments, however, went to the West Indies and to the other colonies, exporting any and all commodities that were available. The merchants, through their emissaries and agents, "trafficked and bargained as only the New Englander knew how to traffic and bargain. It was a peddling and huckstering business, involving an enormous amount of petty detail, frequent exchanges, and a constant lading and unlading as the captains and masters moved from port to port."[4]

The return routes to some extent duplicated the export routes. With the southern colonies the procedure was a relatively simple one. The British merchant sent a shipload of manufactured goods directly to the colonies where they would be exchanged for southern staples. Occasionally a ship might stop at Guinea to pick up a few slaves for the plantations.

Although the slave trade was carried on to some extent by all the colonies, it seems to have centered in Newport, Rhode Island, perhaps because of a lack of any profitable alternative such as a productive interior region to supply export goods. Rum would be shipped to Africa where the cargo would be exchanged for slaves; the slaves shipped to the West Indies to be exchanged for molasses; the molasses returned to the numerous Rhode Island distilleries to be made into rum. This triangular process was then repeated. The trade was more than ordinarily risky and not as common as other voyages, but when successful its profitability was above average.

The return routes of the northern colonies were as numerous and varied as were the outgoing ones. A vessel could go to several ports in England and return with manufactured goods. It might go out to England, return to Newfoundland for fish, sell or barter the fish in Portugal, sell the barter goods in England, and return home with British manufactures. The ship might go first to the Mediterranean area, from there to England, and then home. It might go directly to the Wine Islands and return with a cargo of Madeira by the same route. All these and numerous variations thereof were followed by the colonial merchant. He went wherever the chance of trade seemed likely and profitable, and he did so well that the colonies handled one-seventh of all the foreign trade in the British Empire.

THE MERCHANT'S OTHER
BUSINESS INTERESTS

Successful merchants were always disposed to combine trade with other endeavors. In addition to exporting and importing and selling their own

[4]Charles M. Andrews, "Colonial Commerce," *American Historical Review*, Vol. XX, October 1914, p. 60.

line of goods, they were importantly involved with three other types of business activity: shipping, manufacturing, and acting as agents.

Most merchants owned in partnerships with other colonials and with Englishmen a share of a ship, usually one-eighth. Virginia D. Harrington in her excellent *The New York Merchant on the Eve of the Revolution* tells us:

> Thomas Pennington & Sons of Bristol owned part of the *Prince George* in company with Greg, Cunningham & Co. of Belfast and New York, part of the *Grace* with Theophylact Bache, Perry, Hayes & Sherbrooke, Cornelia Rutgers, Elias DesBrosses and James Jauncey. The *Betty* was owned jointly by Walter & Samuel Franklin of New York and David Kennion of Liverpool. The ship *Hope* had for owners Christian Jacobsen, Henry Van Vleck of New York and Joseph Borum and William Mackie of London, while the ship *Elizabeth and Catherine* belonged to Moses Franks of London and his father Jacob Franks of New York.

Many of the wealthier and more successful merchants owned several ships as well as shares of others. The shipowner in addition to transporting his own goods, acted as a carrier for others with terms for space arranged directly between the shipper and the merchant-shipowner.

Many merchants also dabbled in manufacturing. Shipbuilding was a natural outlet for the surplus capital and energy of people whose chief occupation was shipping. In the large port cities—Boston, Philadelphia, and New York—it became by far the most important manufacturing industry. The Waltons, Schermerhorns, and Van Dams in New York early had extensive shipyard operations.

For a few merchants, manufacturing became as important, or even more important, than trade. According to Professor Hedges, the Brown family had, before the Revolution, "come to think primarily in terms of manufacture; their commerce was increasingly conditioned by the needs of the candle and iron business."[5] Obadiah Brown began to manufacture spermaceti candles at about 1750. Somewhat later, the family went into iron. Very shortly after he became a candle maker, Brown formed a combination with merchants in Newport who had also become heavily involved in candle manufacture. The purpose of this combine was to control the price of the whale matter that was used in candle manufacture. But we will have more to say about this later.

The third activity with which the merchant was involved was as agent for his customers, for his own foreign agents, and for other merchants in the colonies. As agent for others the merchant received the cargo, attended to the customs duties if the cargo was foreign, and sold it under instructions from his principal. The instructions might involve a specific mini-

[5] James B. Hedges, *The Browns of Providence Plantation: The Nineteenth Century* (Providence, Rhode Island: Brown University Press, 1968), p. XIV.

mum price or the use of his discretion to get the best price he could. Where the principal was a colonial, the merchant often contributed advice as to what and when to ship specific goods. After the cargo was sold, the proceeds less the merchant's commission were either credited to the account of the principal or used to purchase a return cargo according to the instructions given him. When a return cargo was involved, the merchant took care of the freight, insurance, and the necessary documents. Often he was called upon to act as financial agent as well, honoring bills of exchange drawn upon him by his principal.

For his efforts the merchant charged commissions based on the gross value of the goods and agreed to beforehand by both parties. Typical commission rates in New York were:

Inland cargoes:	
Sales	$2\frac{1}{2}$ percent
Return cargoes	$2\frac{1}{2}$ percent
Foreign cargoes:	
Sales	5 percent
Return cargoes	5 percent
Bills of exchange: Indorsing, Selling, or Negotiating	$2\frac{1}{2}$ percent
Making Insurance	$\frac{1}{2}$ percent
Recovering Losses	$2\frac{1}{2}$ percent
Outfit of Vessels	5 percent
Soliciting and Procuring Freight	5 percent
Collecting of Freight	$2\frac{1}{2}$ percent
Receiving or Paying of Money	$2\frac{1}{2}$ percent

THE ORGANIZATIONAL STRUCTURE

Although joint stock companies were well known in England and there were some corporations in the colonies, they were not used by the merchants. There were some 320 corporations in the United States by 1800. Two-thirds of these were divided about equally among inland waterways, turnpikes, and bridges. In addition, there were about 30 corporations each in banks, insurance companies, and water supply. Most of these were formed after the Revolution and accordingly did not exist in colonial times.

The typical merchant was either a sole proprietor or in partnership with one or more other merchants. Most likely he was a partner, for capital funds were scarce, and it required about £2,000 to carry on a respectable business, with many firms having investments of £10,000 or more. In 1775 the members of the New York Chamber of Commerce included 61 partnerships and 43 proprietors.

The basis of a partnership may have been through business association, but more importantly through family relationship. Cousins, brothers, and in-laws were frequently found among partners, and a merchant taking on a new apprentice looked first among his own sons or nephews and, if desperate, among the offspring of his close friends. The life of a partnership could vary from a few months to many years, and could be dissolved by pre-arranged agreement or by joint agreement. At the dissolution, the assets and liabilities were shared among the partners. As in partnerships today, profits were divided according to the partnership agreement.

Partners not infrequently had private accounts or investments outside the sphere of the partnership. To put it another way, a merchant could simultaneously be a partner or proprietor in several ventures. These would usually be temporary ventures that ended when the project was completed. Similarly a proprietor might also be interested in several joint ventures aside from his main business.

Despite the multifarious activities pursued by the colonial merchant, he did not require a large or intricate organizational structure. The general store needed very few employees, and the countinghouse or counting room where the bookwork was done needed few more. A simple line organization was more than adequate to handle the relatively uncomplicated problems that might arise. At most, five or six people occupied the office: a clerk or two to keep the books, wait on customers, and write an occasional letter; an apprentice or two to sweep the floors, tend the fire, run errands, deliver goods, and learn the business; and the owner himself, who made the decisions, both major and minor, including such intricate matters as how much wood would be burned. In addition, he went around town, seeking new business, collecting bills, and gathering information from his customers, his competitors, and the gossip vendors. Such was available in the coffee houses and taverns, and more formally, in the Merchants' Exchange and the Chamber of Commerce. The first Merchants' Exchange was founded in New York in 1670 and the first Chamber of Commerce in New York almost 100 years later in 1768. By the end of the Era, every sizeable city had a similar organization.

No outside advice was available, and indeed he needed none, for he was his own expert. Business activity took place in a leisurely manner. Despite what legend has taught us, the colonial merchant did not work hard, as the word "work" is ordinarily defined. It was the custom of Boston merchants to shut up the store around 1:00 and to go on 'change and return at 4:00. On the average they spent no more than three hours a day in the office. Correspondence was also not a heavy burden. The most active letter writer in a group of typical merchants of the late eighteenth century sent out only twelve letters a week, and the least active fewer than two a month. Thomas Hancock sent only 62 letters a year; John Rowe of Boston, 204;

John Watts of New York, 112; Henry Lloyd of Boston, 618; the Browns of
Providence, 330; James Beekman of New York, 34; and John Norton and
Sons of Yorktown, Virginia, only 19. Letters received were similarly easy to
handle. Hancock received 15 letters a year in the 1730's; 69 a year in the
1740's; 174 a year in the 1750's; and 224 a year in the 1760's, including
domestic, Canadian, and foreign.[6]

The scale of business of even the most prosperous merchant was very
small. Thomas Hancock, for example, averaged only 778 credit sales a year,
and the Browns averaged 28-40 transactions a day. The reasons for this in-
activity are the same reasons that prevented the merchant from specializing:
a small population, an inadequate money supply, and difficulties of transportation. A land-office business was just impossible at a time when the
mail took six weeks from Boston to Philadelphia and back and when a
voyage from Baltimore to the West Indies was "often performed in six to
seven weeks."

Since his business was on a small scale and highly diversified, the merchant's store resembled the country general stores that still exist here and
there today. The materials that went into the making of clothes—notions
and piece goods—were by far the largest selling items, accounting for about
two-thirds of total sales.

The work of the back office was then as now a matter of routine
drudgery, and although necessary had little to do with the merchant's success. That depended on his own decision-making powers and the abilities
of those who handled his foreign trade. Since the merchant could not per-
sonally superintend his shipping ventures, he had to rely on captains to
navigate his vessels, on supercargoes and foreign agents to do the actual
trading and to act for him abroad. Information and intelligence concerning
markets and prices were meager at best, and although specific prices could
be requested for shipments, there was always the danger of pricing oneself
out of the market. This being the case, it was clear that the merchant had
to rely on the ability, honesty, and discretion of his outside employees. One
of his most difficult problems was the selection of trustworthy and efficient
agents, captains, and supercargoes.

The selection of an agent was most important of all, for the merchant
came to be utterly dependent upon him. So long as trade with any one port
was very small, the merchant's supercargo handled the exchange of goods
that constituted foreign trade. But once the volume of trade reached a relatively high level, the foreign agent entered the stage to play a completely
indispensable role.

[6]Arthur H. Cole, "The Tempo of Mercantile Life in Colonial America," *Business
History Review*, Vol. XXXIII, 1959, pp. 277–99.

THE IMPORTANCE OF THE FOREIGN AGENT

There were two basic relationships between the colonial merchant and his foreign representative—that of principal and agent and of debtor and creditor. It was not only important for the British agent or merchant to expedite his agency function, but of equal importance was his role as granter of credit or banker to his colonial counterpart. With imports from Britain exceeding exports, the northern merchants were continuously in debt to their agents. In addition to bills of exchange and specie gathered in other trade, mostly with the West Indies, colonial merchants assigned cargoes to their British correspondents who sold the goods and, after deducting commissions and other charges, credited the colonial merchant with the net proceeds. The next British shipment would probably wipe out what balance, if any, remained, and the process would start all over again.

The merchant bought much of his merchandise without having seen it, and sometimes he also sold it without having seen it. Purchase orders were given to agents, and except for goods purchased at auction or from other importers, he saw his merchandise only after it arrived at his warehouse. This type of trading presented certain problems due to the lack of uniform quality standards as well as misunderstandings over the quantity ordered. One was never sure that the words he was using would be interpreted in the manner intended. A barrel had a different quantity meaning depending on the commodity. The term "merchantable goods" was frequently used, but even the meaning of this term differed from locality to locality. To be sure that the goods would be exactly what was ordered, samples were sometimes sent of textiles, candles, flour, tobacco, and other items, but this method too had its difficulties. Some products did not lend themselves easily to samples, and in many cases the samples could not be matched. Under these circumstances, it was hardly strange that many disputes arose. These disagreements and misunderstandings were generally settled by arbitration, for the courts took too long.

Provincial governments attempted to cope with the problems of quality and packing of goods so as to uphold the reputation of colonial exports in foreign markets. Numerous legislative acts provided for the inspection of goods both before and after sale to ensure adherence to the law. When the reputation of New York flour had fallen so low in the world market that the merchants themselves requested regulation, the Assembly passed a measure "to prevent the Exportation of unmerchantable flour," providing suitable penalties for any infraction. Similar legislation provided for the proper inspection and packing of meat and pork, which were to be packed in the proper ratio of brine and in casks of "London size." No meat could be exported or re-exported until it had undergone inspection. Other acts provided similar standards for fish, lumber products, naval stores, and other commodities.

Prices of consumer goods were also regulated from time to time. In New York the price of bread was based on the price of flour, and every loaf was to be identified with the initials of the baker. Prices were also fixed for beef, pork, veal, butter, and milk for several years in the 1760's. Laws were passed to regulate the operation of public markets and the commodities sold there; to prevent forestalling, regrating, and engrossing;[7] to prevent the misrepresentation of food items; the sale of bad food; and the regulation of sizes and weights of certain specific commodities.

INVESTING THE SURPLUS

Since it was not possible to find enough able and trustworthy captains and agents nor enough goods to supply unlimited exports, merchants could use only a limited amount of capital in their main business. Because of this and also because they sought the security of diversification of interests, they launched their surplus funds into various outside investments and endeavors. By far the most prevalent type of outside investment was real estate and land speculation. A prosperous merchant would first buy or build a city mansion, then a house or a farm in the country. This was what one could expect, for the merchants, having come shortly from England, patterned their methods of business and their way of life after the methods and the ways of the English merchant. Their overriding objective was to live a life similar to that of a British aristocrat.

If additional funds were available he might buy additional houses and finally some tracts of unsettled lands for speculation. Land speculation of any sizable amount seemed to be limited to those who were rich and in political favor. A list of large landholders is replete with the names of well-known and prosperous merchants such as Van Cortlandt, Livingston, Bayard, Watts, Lispenard, Beekman, and Schuyler in New York; Thomas Hancock in Boston; and Thomas Willing, Robert Morris, and William Bingham in Philadelphia. Bingham, at the time of his death in 1804, had extensive landholdings in New York and Pennsylvania, and more than two million acres of land in Maine.

Three forms of purely financial investments, that is, non-real estate investments, were open to the merchants—British bonds, local government securities, and personal loans. British bond issues were available in the col-

---

[7]All of these practices were inter-merchant transactions. Forestalling meant obtaining goods before they got to market by buying them outside the market place or outside market hours. Regrating consisted of buying in bulk to sell at retail. Engrossing was buying in large enough quantities to practically corner the market.

onies either by direct purchase or through British agents but for the most part the vagaries of the market, the distance from England, and the low yields compared with lending opportunities at home worked to make them less desirable than other types of investments with which the merchants were more familiar and which offered a higher yield. Local government issues were somewhat more appealing. New York, between 1750 and 1775, periodically sold short-term bonds carrying 5 and 6 percent coupons. The Commonwealth of Massachusetts also issued notes at 6 percent interest, which were deemed desirable investments by the merchants.

By far the most favorable forms of financial investment were the lending of money to individuals on bond, and the purchase of bills of exchange. All merchants always had a volume of outstanding paper. Investors found that the rate of interest was high and there was also the advantage of personal knowledge of the affairs of the borrower. The bond was a personal obligation, a somewhat cumbersome document stating specifically the amount due and the time when payment was to be made:[8]

> Know all men by these presents that we John Lloyd and Nathanael Hubbard, both of Stamford in Fairfield in the Colony of Connecticut are holders and Stand firmly Bound and obliged unto Mary Ver Planck of the City and Province of New York, Executrix to the last will and testament of Gulian Ver Planck, deceased, in the full and just sum of £200 lawfull money of the Province of New York, to be paid unto the said Mary Ver Planck, Her Heirs, Executors, administrators, or Assigns. To the which Payment well and Truly to be made we bind ourselves, our Heirs Each and every of them jointly and severally firmly by these Presents, sealed with our seals Dated the 18th day of August Anno Domini 1753.
>
> The Condition of this present Obligation is such that if the above Bounden John Lloyd and Nathanael Hubbard, their or either of their Heirs, Executors, administrators or any one of them, shall and do well and truly pay or cause to be Paid unto the said Mary Ver Planck, Her Heirs, Executors, administrators or assigns, the full and just sum of £200 Lawfull Money of the Province of New York with Lawfull Interest for same till paid on or before the 21 day of August Next, which will be in the Year of our Lord 1754, without Fraud, Coven or further delay, then the above written Obligation to be Void and of None Effect or else to be and abide and remain in full Force and Virtue.

The maturity of these personal notes was usually short—six months or a year. But even the longest maturity did not exceed five years, although notes were renewed from time to time. When the note was secured, usually by land or other property, the note became a mortgage. This type of investment, combining liquidity and security, was a popular medium for the mer-

[8]Virginia D. Harrington, *The New York Merchant on the Eve of the Revolution* (New York, Columbia University Press, 1935), p. 130.

chants' surplus funds, and many went so far as to advertise money to be lent out at interest at 5, 6, or 7 percent.

After real estate, land speculation, and money lending, the next important outlet for surplus funds was in manufacturing. Leaving the domestically consumed manufacturing to the artisans, the merchants, as we have seen, favored those manufacturing enterprises that were aligned with their mercantile activities—shipbuilding, lumbering, flour milling, sugar refining, distilling, iron smelting, and candle making. In connection with iron smelting, some investments in mining were made as well. None of these enterprises issued capital stock, so that the merchant's investment was either as a partner or a creditor.

MARINE INSURANCE—AN EARLY
FINANCIAL INTERMEDIARY

The remaining outlet for surplus funds was marine insurance. Many merchants regarded marine insurance as so closely related to their main activity that they were almost continually involved in this activity. Although London marine insurance was highly developed by the end of the eighteenth century, the situation was quite different in the colonies. Merchants desiring insurance on their ships and cargoes wrote their requests to their correspondents in London. But this arrangement was hardly satisfactory. Coverage was not always received before the ship sailed, or between the time of application and receipt of coverage, conditions may have changed so as to invalidate the policy. The obvious solution was the development of marine insurance coverage on the home front.

The arranging of insurance coverage was a relatively simple matter. The merchant or shipper with a vessel and merchandise to be insured went to a broker where the rates were agreed to, and a policy was written. The policy was left with the broker who then arranged with the various merchant-underwriters the percentage of the risk each was willing to underwrite. When the entire amount of insurance had been underwritten, a copy of the policy was given to the insured, and a copy remained with the broker. When the ship arrived safely at its destination, the premium was divided among the insurers. In case of loss, the broker collected each share from the insurers and turned the proceeds over to the insured.

The premium rates depended on the nature of the voyage and the potential hazards involved. Wartime rates were naturally higher than those in peacetime, and indirect routes with several stopovers commanded higher rates than did those for direct voyages. The insurers were liable for all losses above a 5 percent "average loss," and payment was to be made thirty days after proof of loss was established. In 1745, five Boston merchants insured the brigantine *Providence* on a trading voyage from Surinam to Providence for a premium of 14 percent. The total amount of insurance was £1,000 and was shared equally among the five. A year later another group insured the sloop *Ranger* on a trading voyage from Maryland to Surinam for a premium of 17 percent, the total amount of £400 being equally divided among the insurers. Obadiah Brown of Providence in addition to his other activities took part of the insurance of more than 130 voyages between 1753 and 1762.

Ships were not always insured at their home port. New York merchants underwrote voyages for merchants in other colonies, and if premiums seemed too high locally, merchants were not averse to seeking a better rate elsewhere. In addition there was still insurance written on colonial voyages in England and Holland. By the mid-1760's, typical rates for peacetime voyages had to a large extent been stabilized. Between New York and London, the usual premium was 2–3 percent one way, and 5 percent for the round trip voyage. Round trip premiums were 4–4½ percent to the West Indies; 8–9 percent for the triangular trip to Africa, the West Indies, and return; 3½ percent on coastal voyages; and somewhat higher rates on trading voyages.

The usual amount of insurance underwritten by any one merchant on a voyage ranged from £50 to £200. The merchant diversified his insurance risks as he did his other business activities. When a number of policies were underwritten by the merchant, the total premium income tended to offset the occasional losses. After several underwritings, a cash reserve had been built up with the broker that more or less represented permanent insurance capital. Where several merchants worked together for some period of time, they represented a temporary company.

From this practice of a group of merchants banding together to share mutually the risk on each other's voyages came the modern marine insurance industry in the United States. As early as 1721, an attempt was made to start a formal brokerage, and the following notice appeared in the *American Weekly Mercury* on May 25th of that year:[9]

Assurances from losses happening at Sea, &c., being found to be very much for the Ease and Benefit of the Merchants and Traders in general: and whereas the Merchants of this City of Philadelphia and other Parts have been obliged to send to London for such Assurance, which has not only been tedious and troublesome, but even very precarious. For remedying of which, An Office of Publick Insurance on Vessels, Goods and Merchandizes, will, on Monday next, be Opened, and Books kept by John Copson, of this city, at his House in the High Street, where all Persons willing to be Insured may apply.

[9]N. S. B. Gras and Henrietta M. Larson, *Casebook in American Business* (New York: Appleton-Century-Crofts, Inc., 1939), pp. 141–42.

By the 1750's there were many notices similar in content offering insurance coverage in all the port cities, and brokers competed for the available business. Credit is usually given to Thomas Willing for having formed the first marine insurance company in this country. In 1757, he combined a group of partners under the name Thomas Willing & Co. to underwrite marine insurance.

As can be seen, the colonial merchant had his irons in as many fires as possible. No project was too small or obscure to attract his interest if there was the possibility or likelihood of profit in its undertaking. Often he was burned, for many merchants, including the most eminent, came close to disaster, and some actually met with disaster. Most, however, managed not only to survive, but to earn a comfortable living or to accumulate fortunes. The merchant's importance in the economic development of the colonies and of the early United States can not be exaggerated. He was a vital figure in an infant economy, providing initiative and drive and supplying the sole vestige of organizational ability. The surplus he accumulated boosted the national income by providing the seed funds for the development of later industry.

THE BUSINESS PROBLEMS OF THE
COLONIAL ENTREPRENEUR

By and large, the typical businessmen in the pre-Revolutionary years were petty entrepreneurs, deriving their income from their own labor and remaining small businessmen throughout their business lives. This was especially true in the period before 1750, that is, before the sedentary merchant brought "big business" into the colonial world.

As we repeatedly emphasized in the previous chapter, the colonial economy was an underdeveloped economy, and the state of the arts was extremely primitive. This naturally influenced significantly the way in which business was conducted.

The nation was primarily agricultural, producing little surplus above the needs of the family. Agriculture, even in the South, was small-scale and self-sufficient and used the crudest types of implements and tools. Even the manufacturing industries produced little. Markets were widely dispersed, and transportation facilities meager or nonexistent. Business organization, as such, was almost unheard of, and given the scope of operations, unnecessary.

Yet there were businessmen in the colonies. There were manufacturers and artisans, storekeepers and peddlers. Above all, there were the merchants. The decisions the colonial businessmen made and the problems they faced may have been minor in scope compared with those of the twentieth century businessman, but they were nonetheless real, and they were many. After all, the businessmen of this era made the same kinds of decisions and faced the same kinds of problems, if on a smaller scale, that businessmen have met in all ages and all eras. They had to make decisions concerning such things as the purchase of tools and materials, the design of the product, the choice between price and quality, whether or not to produce in advance of sale, and, if so, the quantity of advance production.

The decisions that the colonial merchant made were inextricably bound with the economic problems that beset him from all sides. Each businessman—the manufacturer, the artisan, the storekeeper, and the great sedentary merchant—had his unique problems. The manufacturer, for example, had special problems of technology and special headaches about his labor supply. The merchant had to be always searching for goods to export. Very often the special problems of one were tied to those of another. The merchant's most pressing problem was to keep abreast of his accounts with his English agents. The most persistent problem of many colonial storekeepers, farmers, artisans, and workers was to maintain their accounts with the merchant.

But all of these unique problems, thorny and aggravating though they were, were few in comparison with the many problems that the businessmen had in common. There were the persistent problems of marketing, raising capital, obtaining credit, and finding a labor supply; and there were the sporadic problems of meeting competition and dealing with "overproduction."

Making a profit was the problem of problems for the colonial businessman as it has been for every businessman before and since. Every other problem was related and subordinate to this fundamental one. Clearly, goods were marketed and credit was obtained as a necessary step in the ultimate goal of earning a net income, a goal that was by no means easy to achieve. To be sure, many landowning and merchant families amassed fortunes during the Colonial Era. Merchants sold imported goods at prices to yield them 60 percent or more above their cost from England, including shipping and insurance. With such markups, it would seem evident that profits must have rolled in, and in the long run they did. Jackson and Bromfield of Newburyport, Massachusetts, for example, are said to have cleared £7,591 on a capital of £1,600 between 1766 and 1774. Most New York merchants in the late Colonial Period had at least £2,000 invested in their businesses, and many had as much as £10,000. Oliver DeLancey is said to have possessed £100,000 in addition to his business. William Bayard had £75,000 and John Watts £20,000. Similar fortunes existed in Boston, Philadelphia, Newburyport, and other trading centers. These fortunes were undoubtedly substantial for their time, but two caveats must be entered. It took over a century to produce these fortunes, and during the course of that century every merchant family, including the best situated, came at one time or other close to bankruptcy.

The ever present threat of bankruptcy was a consequence of radical ups and downs in business activity. There was no such thing in colonial times as a business cycle in the modern meaning of the term, for the colonial economy was not a monetary economy, and the vast mass of people made their living in farming. However, there were alternate spasms of high prosperity and low recession, periods of economic euphoria and of desperate despondency.

The gluts and famines of colonial times seem to have been a function of war and peace and of monetary expansion and contraction. Foreign wars brought apparent prosperity and inflation; peace brought recession and deflation.

The French and the British were continually at war with each other during the century before 1760, much to the delight of the American merchants. What these colonial wars did to the economy was well illustrated in the years, 1750–1759. The first half of this decade was spent in peace, following the temporary truce that ended King George's War in 1748. These were years of deflation and money supply contraction. They were also years of depression. "It is not in my power," wrote one merchant, "to describe the leadness of times and scarcity of money." But fortunately for the mercantile state of mind, peace soon came to an end. When the French and Indian War, the last of the One Hundred Years War, broke out, New York merchants "hoped that it would prove as fortunate as the last war did."[10]

Merchants benefited from the wars in three ways. First of all, many of them became sutlers for the royal military, buying and provisioning food and clothing, negotiating money bills, and selling produce. For this they typically received from $2\frac{1}{2}$ to $7\frac{1}{2}$ percent on each transaction. Those merchants who did not succeed in winning the Crown's appointment still benefited by selling goods to the army's suppliers.

Privateering was a second and more lucrative way in which merchants benefited from war. Privateers were outfitted in shares running as low as one thirty-second. They preyed the West Indian waters and captured not only French ships but any ships that were trading with the French colonies. This might and often did mean Dutch ships and American as well.

The profits from privateering were substantial not only by value of prizes captured, but also because privateering encouraged smuggling, a

---

[10]It would be wrong to interpret this as meaning that all wars benefit business and the economy. Colonial businessmen benefited because the wars were being fought by other people. In similar fashion, American businessmen reaped a benefit from the War of 1812, World War I, etc., as long as the United States was neutral. The picture changed when this country became a belligerent.

third means by which merchants enriched themselves through the wars. As they roamed the seas as privateers in search of enemy craft, colonial ships found it very easy to slip into a port and emerge with a contraband cargo.

Peace eventually changed all this, however, and with it the money supply ceased to expand, and the apparently inevitable deflation set in. Famine succeeded the wartime glut, and hardship succeeded prosperity. Some colonists tried to fight back by proposing monetary expansion by the creation of a bank or by printing paper money. These proposals were not, as is usually supposed, designed to assist debtors at the expense of creditors. They were intended to encourage economic growth. But prevalent opinion regarded the idea of increasing the money supply "artificially" as a heresy. Moreover, such a step would have hurt English creditors just as it would supposedly have benefited colonial debtors. Consequently, the English government vetoed each move the colonists made to raise the amount of money in circulation.

GETTING INFORMATION

There were, of course, no business schools in colonial times, and there was no such thing as a management or economic consultant. Nor were there any business advisory services, bank letters, television, or radio. How then did the merchant get the training he needed for his business career, and how did he keep informed about what was going on in the world around him and in his own business?

The merchant's educational career was a time-consuming process as was almost everything in a day of slow transportation and crude communication. Like all skilled workers, the merchant acquired his training through an apprenticeship that usually lasted seven years. Thereafter, he kept informed by whatever methods he could use. In gossip fashion, he picked the brains of his competitors and his clients in the coffee houses, the exchanges, and the chamber of commerce. Occasionally, he received news about the progress of his own shipping ventures from other ships that had passed his vessels going and coming from Europe or the West Indies. At every opportunity he availed himself of whatever intelligence and information his scattered agents were able to supply.

Every merchant used some form of accounting to keep track of his own business. Just how sophisticated these accounts were is a matter of disagreement. We can be sure that there was no such thing as cost accounting, nor was there any such modern institution as the public accounting firm. What is in dispute is the extent of double entry bookkeeping and the precision with which accounts were kept. According to Harrington, double entry was widely practiced by the New York merchants and by most wholesalers. She cites the journals of the Livingstons, which contained records of "adventures, bills of exchange, bonds and notes, merchandize general, vendue account, invoice accounts, bills receivable, bills payable, interest account, suspense account, profit and loss, and also accounts for special articles such as pig iron, sugar and the 'Ship Commerce'." Most authorities on the subject, however, hold the opinion that double entry was rare and that even single entry was primitive and replete with errors. Yet, Boston public schools were teaching bookkeeping as early as 1682. It does not seem that there were any texts on the subject in use in colonial times. There was an American edition of an English bookkeeping book in 1809. It gave 32 of its 236 pages to single entry and 63 to double entry. Another book in 1818 pleaded that "this invaluable branch of education is almost totally neglected."[11]

What seems to have been the case was that as the Colonial Period wore on, more and more merchants adopted double entry bookkeeping. But even by the end of the eighteenth century, the practice was not prevalent. Many of the successful and far-sighted merchants kept sophisticated books, but many other successful merchants did not bother. After all, their business was small enough so that they knew where it had been and where it was going. Then too, there were no external forces, such as government and shareholders, to whom a report had to be submitted. Finally, in a period when non-money sales were so common, precise accounting was difficult if not impossible and in any case many merchants could see little to be gained from it.

Despite the primitive condition of communication and transportation, colonial businessmen did not always make decisions by intuition alone. The oft-painted portrait of the colonial businessman rushing quixotically into decisions was more caricature than reality. Colonial entrepreneurs often gave much thought and painstaking consideration to new ventures. Consider, for example, how the Browns went into the iron manufacturing business in 1765. First, they asked one of their associates for data on the iron business in Pennsylvania. They received in reply the names of all fifteen furnaces in Pennsylvania, their distances from Philadelphia, the cost of transportation—one shilling per ton mile to Philadelphia—the cost of mining the ore, the number and wage of the workers, and the yearly production. Having decided to go into the business, the Browns and their partners interviewed more than 30 landowners. They asked each one how many cords of wood he would contribute if the furnace were located near his farm.

[11]Quoted in Roy J. Sampson, "American Accounting Education Textbooks and Public Practice Prior to 1900," *Business History Review*, Vol. XXXIV, Winter 1960.

RAISING THE CAPITAL

The capital requirements of colonial business were very small by today's standards, but they were not inconsiderable for that day. A merchant could begin with a minimum of $1,500, but $6,000 was much safer. The smaller rural gristmills and sawmills could be established with a relatively small amount of capital, and the building of a small potash plant cost about $20 in addition to the kettles, but here again some of the colonial industries required a much larger investment. As early as 1664, a New York tile-kiln was rented for $1,500 a year and a brick-kiln for $500. The two properties had an estimated value of $25,000 to $30,000. Some small country breweries represented an investment of $1,000 or less, but many of the larger ones sold for amounts up to $3,000. The inventory of a New England tannery in 1653 showed hides alone valued at $2,700, and a typical tannery in Trenton, New Jersey, consisting of 64 vats, 5 limes, 2 water pools, a bark house holding 300 cords, a currying shop, a skin-dresser's shop, and the facilities for making leather breeches, represented a considerable investment for the period.

The small manufactories were financed primarily with local capital, usually from prosperous merchants, but the larger ones, notably the iron works, had to depend on European capital, mostly English. The concept of absentee-ownership of a business and the use of hired managers was therefore introduced quite early. The Saugus iron works raised about $10,000, mostly from English investors. The $20,000 required to start the Virginia iron works that never operated was also financed in Britain. The cost of establishing the Principio iron works and Stiegel's glass and iron works was close to $250,000. The Hasenclever works, the largest industrial effort in America up to that time, involved an investment of more than $250,000, all represented by European capital. The Hasenclever enterprise controlled six blast furnaces, seven forges, twelve hammers with a capacity of sixty tons of bars a week, a stamping mill to stamp the iron, three sawmills, and a gristmill.

CREDIT—THE LIFEBLOOD OF TRADE

Whatever capital the enterprising merchants raised from their own savings and those of their relatives and friends was not sufficient to carry them to success. They needed a constant stream of credit if they were to operate successful growing businesses. Consequently, they became adept at scrounging for funds. They depended chiefly on their British agents, who as merchant bankers performed every variety of business service. In turn, the merchants had to advance credit to their own customers or forego the business.

The English agent ordinarily gave twelve months credit with interest starting sometime after the actual advance. The merchants gave their customers six to twelve months credit and sometimes they were "obliged to give one, two, and more years credit to our country chaps." Interest did not begin immediately, but this sacrifice was compensated for by the higher prices that were charged in credit transactions.

The colonial merchants and their customers were notoriously slow payers. Dunned repeatedly by their agents, the merchants reluctantly met part of their accounts payable by the use of bills of exchange. Similarly, domestic customers made payment on their occasional nonbarter transactions with bills of exchange written in denominations of £50 to £100 at the most and extending over 30 to 40 days. These bills were frequently endorsed and circulated for a much longer period than was written on the face.

Despite periodic settlements, the colonists fell further and further behind on their debts to English banker agents. Adam Smith estimated that the annual return to colonial merchants amounted to not more than one-third of what they owed, so that by the Revolution they had accumulated a very sizable debt and were well on their way to becoming mature debtors —that is, debtors who were paying more in interest than they were borrowing in new credits.

THE PROBLEM OF A LABOR SUPPLY

All the productive resources, except land, were in small supply in early America. There was not enough capital or credit to feed the voracious appetites of colonial entrepreneurs. Nor was there enough labor. A small population scattered over a large area with tempting opportunities for self-employment in farming and handicrafts limited the supply of wage-earning labor and challenged the entrepreneur's resourcefulness.

Merchants in foreign trade resorted to foreigners for a large portion of their seamen. In their countinghouses they employed clerks and apprentices. Manufacturers and artisans for the most part ran family businesses, but they also used apprentices and indentured servants. Iron bloomeries sometimes used Indians and Negro slaves to dig the ore and work the furnaces. But they also imported skilled labor for the more technical work. It would be some time before America's farms began to provide a supply of labor to man the factories.

MARKETING PROBLEMS

Once having produced or procured his goods, the businessman was confronted with the problem of marketing them. The merchant had several avenues open to him. Some of his shipment went to satisfy the demand of the local community. Wholesalers and the shopkeepers of inland areas provided a second market. Most merchants developed a steady trade of this sort. A third possibility was the export market, where the goods were especially desired in Great Britain or the West Indies. Where goods could not be disposed of by any of these three methods, the merchant had three additional possibilities. He could send his goods to his agent on consignment. He could take part in a speculative voyage with other merchants who found themselves in the same position. Or he could put the goods up for sale at public auction. This last seems to have been a method of last resort, used for goods that were damaged or otherwise unsalable, when cash was needed quickly, and to settle estates.

The major obstacle to trade was of course the crude transportation and communication facilities. It took months to send goods to the West Indies and back. It took weeks to transport goods locally. Yet, the colonial merchant was not as isolated as one would think. The technology of the day was the only one he knew, and he had long since adjusted himself to difficulties that we would think intolerable. If it took weeks for a messenger to make a roundtrip between Boston and Philadelphia, it was still better than the months it had taken the Indian.

Colonial merchants managed somehow or other to keep informed of and to take part in what was happening in other colonies. They struck up partnerships and formed relationships with many agents, never just with one. Peter Livingston, a New Yorker with many irons in many fires, had a partnership with a man named Jenkins of Rhode Island in the manufacture of spermaceti candles. Livingston supplied the capital and got two-thirds of the profit; Jenkins supervised the work and got one-third. Even though the competition between New York and Philadelphia was very keen, relationships between the merchants of the two cities were very close.

With slow communication and even slower transportation, inventory turnover averaged about twice a year or less. Manufacturers soon found that it did not pay them to do their own marketing, and they were forced, reluctantly in many cases, to rely on commission agents. Much of the wholesale business, in turn, was on the basis of specific and definite order.

In the eyes of a modern retailer or a modern marketer, colonial methods of distribution were something less than primitive. For most retail merchants, there was no reason why they shouldn't be. They were generally monopolists or duopolists in the small market areas in which they did business. Only the larger towns had populations sufficiently large to support more than one or two general stores. Yet there were some innovations in the selling of goods, especially in advertising. Half the space in newspapers was given to advertising. One newspaper publisher, Benjamin Franklin, introduced varied type and white spaces far ahead of his time, as he was in most things. Another businessman who was far ahead of his time, Gerardus Duyckinck, proprietor of the *Universal Store* or *The Medley of Goods* in New York, advertised widely and frequently.

COMPETITION

Competition was the most frustrating problem that faced every businessman except the country storekeeper. Periodic gluts and famines made price-cutting a common practice and reduced overall profits. Once, when a number of New York merchants advertised their goods at a markup of 1 percent, a competing merchant advertised that he would give his goods away in small quantities.

The businessmen of the day, including both city craftsmen and manufacturers, were not averse to agreements restricting competition, such as price- and wage-fixing, where it suited their purpose. In 1724 the Philadelphia carpenters drew up a uniform scale of wages for employees and workmen. In the same year the Boston barbers acted in concert to increase the prices of shaves and wigs. In 1761 a group of candlemakers led by the Browns formed the United Company of Spermaceti Chandlers to control the business. Each producer was given a quota of the annual supply of raw materials received from the whalers. A fixed price was agreed to with each member promising not to pay any higher to the whalers. Like most gentlemen's agreements, this one quickly broke down as one producer or another outbid his competitors for the whalers' product. A similar lack of success met other efforts of other producers to control supply. A group of Newport carpenters set standard prices on goods to no avail. The tailors in Philadelphia agreed in the recession year of 1771 to a set of minimum prices and maximum wages, but that was as usual short-lived and ineffective.

THE INGREDIENTS FOR SUCCESS

The obstacles in the race for material success in the Colonial Period were formidable, perhaps more formidable than at any other time. Yet, many succeeded. What it took to succeed was a combination of intelligence, luck, planning, and, above all, a drive to succeed. The merchant who got to the top had an ability to gather information, a tenacity of purpose, an underdeveloped sense of ethics, and a willingness to rely where necessary on others. Although he may not have put in too many hours at his counting house, his thoughts were constantly on business. He was always on the lookout for a profitable piece of business—at weddings, funerals, and any other social functions. His choice of agents to represent him in other parts of the world was also immensely important. Indeed, the agent was responsible for a large share of the success of the successful merchant. After all, the prerequisite for continuous business success then as now was the ability to adjust to changing conditions. Here the agent was indispensable because in addition to handling routine matters, he kept the merchant informed about changing business and political conditions, kept him supplied with credit, and enabled him to make short-range plans more rationally than he might have done.

THOMAS HANCOCK (1703–1764)

Thus far, we have talked about the colonial businessman in general. The case of an unusually successful colonial merchant may serve to summarize what we have said. For this purpose, we present a brief sketch of the experiences and business practices of one of the foremost merchants of the era, Thomas Hancock.[12]

Hancock, the son of a Lexington minister, was apprenticed at the age of fourteen to a Boston bookseller, from whom he learned bookbinding and the book business. After his seven-year apprenticeship, he went into the book business on his own. His initial capital was £100. He advertised his business in the Boston papers and evidently prospered, for in a short time he hired an assistant at £50 per annum to do bookbinding. Initially, he bought sermons and other material published in the Boston area and publications imported from London by the local merchants. Within a period of four years he was buying directly from London on the basis of credit granted him by his suppliers.

During these early years, Hancock got to know many of Boston's leading merchants and was able, through their help, to take part in several commercial ventures in addition to running his book business. Important to him in this respect was Daniel Henchman, soon to become his father-in-

---

[12]There are two excellent studies of Thomas Hancock's business operations: W. T. Baxter, *The House of Hancock* (Cambridge, Mass.: Harvard University Press, 1945); Edward Edelman, "Thomas Hancock, Colonial Merchant," *Journal of Economics and Business History*, Vol. I, 1928, pp. 77–104; reprinted in Ross M. Robertson and James L. Pate, *Readings in United States Economic and Business History* (Boston, Mass.: Houghton Mifflin Company, 1966).

law. Henchman was the leader of a group organizing a paper-making factory and invited Hancock to participate. Hancock also used Henchman's credit to supply goods for the Hancock store, and jointly they purchased large amounts of paper and published pamphlets on important matters of the time.

The book business had many drawbacks in terms of growth, and when both local and London competition became too much to handle, Hancock at about 1730 decided to branch out into more diversified lines of merchandise. Books rapidly decreased in importance compared to the other goods he sold. By 1736 he was advertising clothing material, teas, and cutlery, and his store resembled those of other general merchants. He sold both at wholesale and at retail to his customers, who included Bostonians and country storekeepers. What he could not sell through his usual outlets, he often sold to peddlers.

The country storekeepers were especially important to Hancock, for they looked on him as both customer and supplier. Country buyers extended as far away from Boston as Maine, Connecticut, and Long Island. The business was not very exciting, but it was steady and dependable. Most orders were for small quantities of a large variety of goods, and although an order might occasionally reach £100, most were for much smaller amounts. Credit sales, which comprised most of the business, amounted to $40,000 a month at the most. Deliveries were made by using small coasting vessels, which sailed along the New England coast and then up the rivers to their destinations. Payment for the goods was slow as well as uncertain. Hancock, like all other merchants, sold on credit terms of six, eight, and even twelve months, but he sometimes had to wait several years for payment. At times he would receive goods on consignment from the interior without an order for goods in return.

Most of the merchandise stocked and sold by Hancock came from England. Like most other merchants he depended on agents for purchases and sales in foreign markets, and leaned heavily on the credit granted by them. He used at least half a dozen London agents during the period 1730–1740, but his chief agent, Francis Wilks, usually acted as go-between for receipts and payments to them. An account dated May 31, 1734 sent by Wilks to Hancock showed a total charge of £4,660, of which more than £4,000 was for goods. The remainder represented commissions on payments to other suppliers, insurance charges, and fees for cashing bills of exchange. Credited to his account were the receipts from sales of consigned goods, credit for bills of exchange sent by Hancock, and remittances from other agents. The new balance showed Hancock in debt to Wilks for £2,320.

Agents were as important to Hancock as they were to all colonial merchants. Wherever they were located, they assembled the goods for shipment to Boston. In many cases they sent unordered goods that they thought would sell well. Agency relations were bilateral—each serving as agent for the other. In addition, agents on both sides of the Atlantic were requested and did perform many personal favors having no relationship to the usual buying, selling, and financing functions.

The underdeveloped condition of the economy and the inadequate currency and exchange situation made Hancock's business activities more complicated and more extensive geographically than mere buying and selling would indicate. Values were recorded in Massachusetts currency that depreciated rapidly from 2.7–1 in 1722 to 110–1 in 1750 in terms of sterling. Sterling was scarce and, like other merchants, Hancock found it difficult to meet his London obligations. Settlement in goods was equally difficult, since New England had few export products for which there was a demand in England. He turned, therefore, as did others to trading the New England export goods for cargoes that could be sold in England.

The first source of sterling was the whale industry and other fisheries. Country produce would be traded for whalebones and whale oil which in turn would be shipped to Wilks in London. The risks in these ventures were mitigated by taking on partners. Often they could trade only for fish that had to be shipped to markets in Spain, Portugal, and the West Indies.

By 1738 Hancock had built up a large trade. He had invested in mining properties and a paper mill and had built and furnished a mansion on Beacon Hill. But business was declining due to an oversupply of imports and a depression was setting in when news came of the outbreak of war between Britain and Spain in 1739. The war brought an end to the depression and new opportunities for Hancock and the other New England merchants. They received orders for provisioning the army. They took part in privateering (legalized piracy of enemy ships), and they did much wartime trading. At one time Hancock wrote, "Better for me to sink the cost of the vessel than not have my goods, if a load of coal or salt comes early I shall clear [the cost of] the ship."[13]

Although profits from trading with the enemy, privateering, and smuggling were considerable, his largest profits came from war contracts. Hancock, with a partner, Apthorp, had contracts for material for strengthening the British forts at Newfoundland, and at Annapolis Royal in Nova Scotia. In the last years of the war Hancock was busier than ever before, even to the extent of decreasing his trade with the West Indies. By the end of the war he was one of the wealthiest men in the colonies and was in the process of ordering from London a four-horse carriage and a chaise along with coachman and the coat of arms of the Hancock and Henchman families.

When the war ended, depression set in once more. Money became

---

[13]W. T. Baxter, *The House of Hancock*, p. 93.

scarce again, prices declined, and debts were difficult to collect. Inventory was piled high in the Hancock warehouse, and complaints were voiced of the absence of ready cash. Trade continued as before but at a lower level, and some government contracting was performed. In 1755 war broke out again. This time Hancock and Apthorp got government contracts even before the fighting had started. Hancock hired transport and bought £20,000 of homespun, stockings, shoes, and wheat. At the same time he supplied arms and provisions to Massachusetts and Rhode Island. Hancock prospered enormously even though he was forced to take the Governor's son-in-law as a partner, and even though he suffered several cargo losses. When war contracts declined he resumed his European and West Indies trade, but French privateers made these ventures too risky and insurance rates rose to heights of 30 percent. In addition he was in debt to his agent, Kilby, in London. Yet when he died, he left an estate of £70,000.

Throughout his business life, Hancock was extremely diversified. His basic business was importing. But he had to find the produce to pay for his imports. He then provided the ships to carry the imports. He wholesaled what he brought in, and he retailed what he could not wholesale. He did some banking for friends, customers, and military officers. He shared in providing a mail service to Europe. He furthered the local manufacture of paper, potash, and ships, and he played an important role in the whaling industry.

Hancock's success showed that he was an expert in solving the mercantile problems of the times. First, he dealt in diverse quantities and kinds of merchandise. Secondly, he managed to consummate complicated chains of transactions with a minimum of actual cash. Third, he maintained good relationships with many widely scattered people whom he saw rarely or not at all. Fourth, he kept informed about general affairs, adjusted to war and political change, and took advantage of new business opportunities. As W. T. Baxter, biographer of the House of Hancock, put it: "Thomas gave the world precisely what it needed. He spent his life in the task of finding wants and alleviating them. . . . That he won big profits . . . suggests . . . that he had a shrewder eye for detecting needs, and more skill at detecting waste than his rivals."

4

THE TRANSITION FROM
THE MERCHANT TO THE
MANUFACTURER, 1780–1850

Historians tend to shy away from phrases like "The Commercial Revolution" and "The Industrial Revolution," for such phrases lack in truth what they have in drama. Yet, with the help of poetic license and some exaggeration of reality it can be said that the years from the close of the Revolution to the middle of the nineteenth century witnessed the end of the age of mercantilism and the beginning of industrialism—the decline of the merchant and the progress of the manufacturer.

THE ECONOMIC BACKGROUND

The world in which the merchant had his last great moments of triumph was growing rapidly, and internal as well as external changes were taking place at an accelerated pace.

Population, a mere 1.2 million in 1750, grew at a rate of about 33⅓ percent a decade, reaching approximately 5 million in 1800, 10 million in 1820, and 25 million in 1850. In brief, population doubled approximately every twenty years.

Exhibiting an impressively rapid colonization movement, the growing population quickly spread out from just beyond the Appalachians in 1800 to a little beyond the Mississippi in 1860. When the Treaty of Paris was signed in 1783, the country's entire area encompassed a little more than half a billion acres. By 1850, it was almost six times larger.

Most of the population still lived in rural areas, but in the years between 1820 and 1850, city population grew at the fastest rate in history. In

1790, there were only 24 cities in the entire country, that is, places with a population of 2,500 or more. No city had more than 100,000. Indeed, no city had more than 50,000. By 1850, there were almost 250 cities. One city had over 500,000 and 10 had more than 50,000 each.

We have only hazy estimates of what happened to American income in those years. According to one of the estimates, aggregate real income was about nine times as high in 1860 as it had been in 1800, but per capita real income was about the same. But other students of the subject are much more liberal in their estimates of the progress of per capita national income in the early nineteenth century.

If rising income can be associated with technological progress, the American economy did well, for this was a period of substantial progress in technology. Most of the advances in agricultural equipment had been accomplished by 1850. The same could be said for textile machinery and for the machine tool industry. Toward the end of the period, the railroad began its career of great expansion.

The machine tool industry was so important to the development of manufacturing that some additional details are necessary. Machine tools and high precision instruments were essential in merchandising the manufacture of machinery, and without this process, it would have been impossible to achieve mass production and the large business firm.

The industry progressed from its primitive beginnings in a remarkably short period of time. In the latter part of the eighteenth century, the best-equipped machinist possessed little more than a hammer, a chisel, a file, and perhaps a simple lathe. By the 1850's, when Samuel Colt was using 1,400 different tools to make his revolver, the general principles of machine tools and precision instruments had been firmly established. The future was dedicated not so much to new developments but to improvements in size, versatility, speed, and automaticity.

The strategic link in the chain of progress was the steady improvement in lathes, the machines that controlled the operation of machine tools. The Englishman Maudslay added to the rudimentary power-driven lathes in existence at the beginning of the nineteenth century a slide rest, which infinitely improved its accuracy. Later came Christopher Soener's cam control, which made lathe operation automatic. The final stage came in 1854, when Frederick W. Howe and D. D. Stone of Robbins and Lawrence, the Windsor, Vermont gunmakers, built a turret lathe. By that time the lathe had become an early example of automation.

Precision manufacture in the United States owes an everlasting debt to the vernier caliper, produced in 1851 by Joseph Brown of Providence. The new caliper, measuring accurately to the thousandths of an inch, allowed anyone working closely with interchangeable parts to measure the accuracy of his work without going to the expense of costly equipment. Together with his partner, Lucien Sharpe, Brown also produced vernier protractors, a wire gauge and a precision gear-cutter for clock springs, and the very important micrometer. The milling machine, used to produce plane and formed surfaces, was first offered for sale by Robbins and Lawrence, with Brown and Sharpe being credited with the invention of the "universal milling machine" in 1862.

THE PEAK AND DECLINE OF SHIPPING

An environment characterized by multiplying population, urbanization, and technological achievement offered a heady atmosphere for business progress and prosperity. And on the whole, business did progress, but not without its ups and downs and not without major transformations, the chief of which was the decline of foreign trade and shipping and the rise of manufacturing and domestic trade. Shipping, and for that matter foreign commerce, reached its peak in the early 1800's and was declining rapidly by the 1830's. Meanwhile, manufacturing regularly added to its product as it shifted gradually from the home to the factory. By 1860, the Census estimated the value added by manufacturing at almost $1 billion. One large manufacturing business had already appeared in the McCormick reaper firm. But despite the progress that had been achieved and despite its rapid growth, especially after 1820, manufacturing was still not spectacular in 1850. It was still oriented to agriculture, that is, to the processing of farm products, and the day of heavy industry still lay in the future.

The explanation for the last great surge of the shipping industry and the last great triumphs of the merchant in the first quarter of the century rested largely on the fact that most of Europe seemed intent on committing suicide. Starting in 1792 and continuing with one year's interruption until Napoleon's defeat in 1815, Europe was involved in what seemed an interminable conflict. These wars made the United States, until it too became involved in 1812, the most important neutral carrier in the world, creating a considerable stimulus to American shipping and a noticeable increase in the demand for American exports. The range and extent of the American merchants' involvement in world trade during this period has nowhere been described more vividly than by John Bach McMaster:[1]

> Almost the whole carrying trade of Europe was in American hands. . . .
> The merchant flag of every belligerent, save England, disappeared
> from the sea. It was under our flag that the gum trade was carried on
> with Senegal, that the sugar trade was carried on with Cuba, that coffee

[1]John Bach McMaster, *A History of the People of the United States* (New York: D. Appleton and Company, 1906), Vol. III, p. 225.

was exported from Caracas, and hides and indigo from South America. From Vera Cruz, from Carthagena, from La Plata, from the French colonies in the Antilles, from Cayenne, from Dutch Guiana, from the isles of France and Reunion, from Batavia and Manila, great fleets of American merchantmen sailed from the United States, there to neutralize the voyage and then go on to Europe. They filled the warehouses at Cadiz and Antwerp to overflowing. They glutted the markets of Emden and Lisbon, Hamburg and Copenhagen, with the produce of the West Indies and the fabrics of the East.

The other reasons for the merchant's continued prosperity, although of some consequence, were far less important than the Napoleonic wars. The opening of trade with China and the East Indies offered new opportunities. Two things that had given Americans an advantage in colonial days—the superiority of American ships and the entrepreneurial abilities of those who sailed them—would continue to give Americans an advantage until the appearance of a practical steamship ended the day of commercial sails.

One final item must be mentioned in the reasons for American shipping success—the actions of the federal government. Shipping and merchant interests had been strong supporters of the new Constitution, and the new government lost little time in coming to their aid with a series of navigation acts. One of the first laws passed by the new Congress, the Act of July 4, 1789, although ostensibly designed for the "encouragement and protection of manufactures," was a boon to shipping, for it allowed a 10 percent tariff reduction on goods imported in ships built and owned by American citizens. The Act also allowed a tariff reduction on tea brought in directly from the Far East, at the same time imposing a relatively high tariff on tea brought in from Europe, even in American ships. Another act, passed sixteen days later, gave American shippers a virtual monopoly on the coastal trade. A port duty of six cents a ton was imposed on American-built, American-owned ships. Thirty cents a ton was charged on American-built, foreign owned ships, and fifty cents a ton on foreign-built and foreign-owned ships. To tighten further the American shipping grip on the coastal trade, the Act stipulated that American ships need pay the port tax only once a year while foreign ships were to pay at every port entry.

THE POST-REVOLUTION DEPRESSION
IN FOREIGN TRADE

The Revolutionary War and the eventual restoration of peace created both new opportunities and new problems for American merchants. British rule and British restrictions were now things of the past. The merchant of the new nation was free to buy and sell anywhere in the world without fear or favor insofar as England was concerned. But in exchange for this, important colonial advantages were lost. American shipments no longer received the favorable treatment accorded those who belonged to the Empire. The British navy no longer protected American shipping. West Indian trade, previously so important to the colonial merchant, was limited to a handful of specific items, and American ships were forbidden to enter West Indian ports. British shipowners were no longer permitted to enter American-built vessels to British registry, and American imports into England were limited mainly to naval supplies.

As a result of these changed conditions, American exports to Great Britain averaged only $4.5 million during the early 1780's as against an average of $5.4 million before the Revolution, a decline of about 20 percent. Exports to the West Indies showed an even more drastic decline, from $2.2 million a year to $1.4 million a year, dropping still further to $1.2 million by 1793. Imports, however, rose to the point where they far exceeded the citizenry's desire or ability to purchase, so that an avalanche of goods glutted the market and prices dropped accordingly. Americans, especially the merchants, were in the process of discovering that their new-found freedom had for the time being retarded rather than stimulated business growth. The New York Chamber of Commerce noted in 1785 "with concern, that a flourishing and successful commerce has not yet been numbered among the blessings that peace and independence have restored to the State." Almost a decade later Tench Coxe was to write, "Nothwithstanding the actual prosperity of the United States of America at this time, it is a fact which ought not to be concealed that their affairs had fallen into a very disagreeable condition by the year 1786."

THE CHINA TRADE

Conditions began to improve after 1787, and by the time of the ratification of the Constitution, the corner had been turned. The years that followed turned out to be the most prosperous in the history of the American merchant. Exports to Great Britain recovered slightly, averaging $4.9 million annually from 1788 to 1790, but total exports soared to $17.5 million in 1789–90 and $20.8 million in 1791–92. Trade with Holland had increased sufficiently so as to offset the decline in the West Indian trade. New markets were sought and found in Europe, and especially in the Near East and China. As early as 1784, the *Empress of China*, fitted out by a group of New York and Philadelphia merchants, including Robert Morris, and with a supercargo from New England, sailed out of New York with a cargo of ginseng, brandy, wine, tar, turpentine, and $20,000 in hard money. Ginseng, a weed that was supposed to be good for tired blood and other difficulties of advancing age, became a staple of the China trade. The *Em-*

press set the pattern. It carried 440 piculs (a picul was about 140 pounds avoirdupois) of ginseng.

The *Empress* returned in May 1785, after a fifteen-month voyage, with a cargo of tea and silk. This successful establishment of trade with the Far East was followed by other merchants, including the famous Elias Haskett Derby of Salem, who sent his *Grand Turk* and several other vessels. By 1789, there were fifteen American ships at Canton, a number exceeded only by the British.

Philadelphia outshone all the other cities that were engaged in the China trade. Its merchants employed larger ships and used more specie than their rivals in the other cities. Boston shipowners were trading to China chiefly by way of the northwestern coast, but on a relatively small scale, and because they lacked anything else, they relied on sea otter skins to finance their business. Only the Dorrs of Boston had sent more than one vessel to Canton, but the combined tonnage of their two craft was only 320 tons, compared to 700 tons for the *Canton* owned by Willing and Francis of Philadelphia. Philadelphia remained dominant for as long as the China trade flourished, but in time New York did narrow the gap.

Five American houses stood above all the rest in the Far East. Willing and Francis was undoubtedly first. Then came Stephen Girard also of Philadelphia, John Jacob Astor of New York, James and Thomas H. Perkins of Boston, and Brown and Ives of Providence.

Willing and Francis in five visits to Canton brought 438,000 hard dollars. Girard paid three visits, bringing 405,000 Spanish dollars. John Jacob Astor made three calls with 346,000 hard dollars. The Perkins firm made two calls with a total of 510,000 dollars in specie. Brown and Ives made four visits and brought 575,000 Spanish dollars.

The primary source of the dollars, like the principal market for tea and coffee, was in Europe. American ships on occasion sailed directly from the East Indies to Amsterdam. Discharging their cargoes, they procured Spanish dollars and then returned to the Pacific for fresh cargoes of tea and coffee. On other occasions, ships en route from the Indies merely touched in the United States for fresh orders, continuing to Europe without breaking bulk. Brown and Ives, for example, were no longer engaged in the importation of tea and coffee for American consumption. Their chief concern now was the carriage of these products from the countries of origin to markets in northern Europe.

THE TWILIGHT OF THE SHIPPING BUSINESS

Despite interference from British warships, French privateers, and Tripoli pirates, the decade ending in 1807 was one of unprecedented prosperity for American merchants. Registered tonnage engaged in foreign trade grew from 124,000 tons in 1789 to 840,000 tons in 1807. Merchandise imports increased from $23 million in 1790 to $139 million in 1807, and exports increased from $20 million to $108 million during the same period. In the latter year almost 94 percent of imports and 91 percent of exports were carried in American vessels. The shipbuilding industry was equally prosperous, not only increasing its output for American shippers, but also selling in the foreign market.

This happy situation abruptly reversed itself as the United States endeavored unsuccessfully to remain a neutral. Both France and England took steps to put an end to American trade with the opposing belligerent. At home, the Jefferson administration passed, between 1808 and 1810, the Non-Intercourse Act, the Embargo, and the Macon Bill, all designed to keep the United States neutral but at the expense of trade restriction. As a result of this restrictive legislation, trade fell drastically. Merchandise imports and exports declined from $247 million in 1807 to $79 million a year later. They fell still further when the United States went to war with Britain, amounting to only $20 million in 1814, the lowest amount in history.

John Lambert, an English visitor to New York during this period (November 1807) noted that:[2]

> The port was filled with shipping and the wharfs were crowded with commodities of every description. Bales of cotton, wool and merchandise; barrels of pot-ash, rice, flour, and salt provisions; hogsheads of sugar, chests of tea, puncheons of rum, and pipes of wine; boxes, cases, packs and packages of all sizes and denominations, were strewed upon the wharfs and landing-places, or upon the docks of the shipping. All was noise and bustle. . . . The merchants and their clerks were busily engaged in their counting-houses, or upon the piers. The Tontine Coffee House was filled with underwriters, brokers, merchants, traders and politicians, selling, purchasing, trafficking, or insuring, ... Everything was in motion; all was life, bustle and activity. The people were scampering in all directions to trade with each other, and to ship off their purchases for the European, Asian, African and West Indian markets. But on my return to New York the following April (1808) what a contrast was presented to my view!. . . . The Coffee House Slip, the wharfs, the quays along South Street, presented no longer the bustle and activity that had prevailed there five months before. . . . Not a box, bale, cask, barrel or package was to be seen upon the wharfs. Many of the counting-houses were shut-up, or advertised to be let; and the few solitary merchants, clerks, porters, and labourers that were to be seen, were walking about with their hands in their pockets. . . . The Coffee House was almost empty. In fact, everything presented a melancholy appearance.

[2]Richard C. McKay, *South Street: a Maritime History of New York* (New York: G. P. Putnam's Sons, 1934), pp. 54–55.

With the end of the war American merchants were once again eager to reestablish their trade connections, and for a short period they were successful; but the golden era was over. Registered tonnage for foreign trade increased from 675,000 in 1814 to 854,000 in 1815 but declined thereafter. The 1815 tonnage figure would not be exceeded until 1842, almost a generation later. Exports increased from $7 million in 1814 to a peak of $93 million in 1818, while imports rose to $113 million in 1815 and $147 million in 1816, amounts not surpassed until the mid-1830's. The merchants once again had caused a glut of goods on the market, and prices again dropped. Lower profits and frequent losses became increasingly characteristic of the shipping business, and there began an unbroken decline of maritime activities. The Browns were again typical. In the 1820's, they began to withdraw from the business. They sold their last ship in 1838, after having been in the business for 117 years. The Browns, it should be reemphasized, were not the only merchants who left the sea. By 1825, John Jacob Astor had discontinued using his own ships in the China trade and in 1828 he withdrew from the trade completely. Six years later he withdrew from the fur trade as well and devoted his remaining years to his real-estate interests. John P. Cushing, the Perkins' partner in China, returned home in 1828 and except for a few occasional ventures began to transfer his funds into domestic investments. By 1833 his domestic investments exceeded those in foreign trade, and by 1838 very little foreign investment remained. Through his friend William Sturgis, his funds went into government bonds, railroads, insurance companies, banks, manufacturing companies, transportation companies, and real estate. Bryant and Sturgis, also involved in the China trade, started to withdraw in the late 1830's, with the final dissolution of the firm taking place in 1841. Their new partnership was formed primarily for the investment of their own funds. The Olivers of Baltimore had started to leave the field as early as 1810, although they did not retire completely until 1826. However, starting in 1816, their income from interest was always greater than their income from trading voyages.

THE REASONS FOR SHIPPING'S DECLINE

There were as many causes for the decline of American shipping and foreign trade as there had been causes for its earlier brilliant success. The imposition of new duties and new restrictions on trade with Europe and, more importantly, by the Dutch on trade with their islands badly hurt the China and East Indian trade. But there were still more important reasons. The supremacy of American shipping rested on America's superior timber for wooden ships and her superior seamen to sail those ships. Once iron ships and steam replaced wood and sail, America lost both of these advantages and also her supremacy on the seas.

The expansion of the market area that accompanied the westward movement provided still another reason for the relative decline in foreign trade and the relative increase in domestic commerce. And still another factor was the ever-increasing attractiveness of manufacturing. In a young country, such as the United States in the first generation of the nineteenth century, two of the factors of production—labor and capital—were especially limited. Consequently, continued emphasis on commerce tended to starve manufacturing. By the same token, manufacturing grew by taking capital away from commerce. By the middle of the first half of the 1800's, when manufacturing was well on its way to a robust growth, the United States was becoming less dependent on imported goods, and foreign commerce, therefore, dwindled. Per capita imports for consumption purposes fell from almost $10 per capita in 1800 to less than $4 in 1830 and slightly over $5 in 1840.

THE ORGANIZATION OF FOREIGN TRADE

Up to 1818 foreign trade was carried on in ships that either operated along regular trade routes or as "transients," which sailed from an American port and might roam the world before returning home. The brig *Forrester* left Salem in 1826 and did not return for almost three years while visiting New Orleans, New York, Cuba, Genoa, Marseilles, New York, New Orleans, Hamburg, and St. Ubes in that order. Both types of ships served as common carriers in addition to carrying goods for their merchant-owners, and neither type had definite sailing dates. An important innovation to this haphazard shipping system was the inauguration of transatlantic packet lines sailing according to a regular calendar of departures.

Starting in January 1818, the Black Ball line, consisting of four ships, sent out one a month from New York and one a month from Liverpool on a definite day and hour. After several years during which the Black Ball had the packet business to itself, several other lines entered the competition. By 1824 there were four ships sailing from New York to Liverpool, two to Le Havre, and one to London in addition to several in the coastwise trade. By 1845 fifty-two ships were sailing regularly from New York. Although many of the larger merchants depended on their own ships, others, especially auctioneers, smaller merchants, and manufacturers' agents, made increasing use of the packet line services.

Packet lines also plied the coastwise routes with many lines organized to serve the main centers of commerce from Maine to Florida and New Orleans. For the first time, merchants had the dependability of regular sailings by common carriers.

The prime movers in foreign commerce were American and British merchants, who operated chiefly on their own account and between the two countries. Each, most likely, had a branch, a partner, or an agent in the other country. The trade with the Far East was for the most part in the hands of American merchants with branches in Canton or Calcutta. Most trade, roughly two-thirds of imports and exports, took place with Europe; North America was second with 20–25 percent of total trade. Trade with Asia, more romantic than important, never exceeded 10 percent of all trade, and in most years it was considerably less. This was especially true of exports that were only 1–4 percent of this country's total.

The growth of population and the expansion of the domestic marketing area brought about several changes in previous methods of business operation. One notable change that became increasingly evident was the movement toward functional specialization on the part of the merchant. Whereas in the Colonial Period the typical merchant performed as part of his normal operation a host of functions—importer, exporter, wholesaler, retailer—the nineteenth-century merchant performed relatively few. In addition to the merchants who traded for their own account, there were in all trading cities a growing number of merchants who did no direct importing or exporting. They became brokers, wholesalers, jobbers, factors, and commission agents. In addition there was an upsurge in the use of auction markets for the speedy disposal of goods.

Although auction sales had been used prior to the Revolution, they had been used primarily for damaged goods or to settle estates. By the early 1800's auction sales had become important enough to come under the legislative eyes of state governments. New York limited the number of auctioneers and their commission charges, but it taxed auctions more leniently than other states did. Auctioneers were appointed by state or local authority in New York, Massachusetts, Pennsylvania, Maryland, and Ohio, and all but Massachusetts regulated the commission rates as well. The system was most widely used in the distribution of imported goods to retailers who would come to the auction markets about twice a year. It proved to be especially economical for British producers with large volumes of goods to sell, inasmuch as eliminating the importer and the jobber could save as much as 25 percent of the distribution costs.

A second change that gradually took place among merchants during the nineteenth century was the increase in specialization of products and areas of origin. Starting in the first decade of the century there was an increasing tendency for merchants' names to be associated with types of goods or areas of origin. The firm of Henry A. and John G. Coster, wealthy enough to subscribe $100,000 to the 1813 war loan, became widely known as an importer of Dutch and West Indian products. John Jacob Astor became famous for his China enterprises as did Perkins & Co., Bryant & Sturgis, and Russell & Company. George Newbold in New York combined a specialized line of goods and an area of origin, dealing in hardware from English manufacturers.

The nineteenth-century merchant tended to hold his goods for somewhat less time than had his predecessor. He turned them over to a wholesaler or jobber, commission merchant, or to the auction market where they were quickly disposed of. The retailer now dealt almost exclusively with the jobber or wholesale merchant. In addition to the benefit of a greater inventory turnover, the importer was able to operate partly on what amounted to an interest-free government loan. If an import shipment had a value of $50 or more, the government would accept the importer's promissory note for the import duty for a period as long as eighteen months. This allowed the merchant to sell the shipment for cash or discountable notes and use the proceeds for another voyage or two before payment on his own note was due. This type of leverage was extremely risky, and many merchants finally failed because of its use or misuse.

THE RETURN ON FOREIGN TRADE

The driving force behind the activities of the American merchant was the pursuit of profit, and profits were obtainable. *The Empress of China* netted $37,000 on its three-year voyage. Boston merchants thought that trade with the East offered a "moral certainty" of 6 percent, a reasonable expectation of 10 percent, and a chance for 12 percent with very little hazard. Sailing from Massachusetts with a cargo of less than $40,000, it was not impossible for a ship to return with $200,000 or more. True, this might take two or three years, and shipowners fretted and complained about the uncertainties, risks, and aggravations of foreign trade, but the return was often worth it.

Beginning their careers in the family business at an astonishingly early age, New England, New York, and Philadelphia merchants accumulated—even in the low yielding China trade—fortunes that were impressively sizable for that day and age.

Cushing went to China at 16, became a partner in Perkins & Co. at 19, and retired at an early age with a fortune of close to $1 million. John Murray Forbes joined Russell & Co. at 17, became a partner at 20, and left the China trade to become an active promoter and administrator of such western railroads as the Illinois Central, the Hannibal & St. Joe, and the C.B. & Q. In 1827, William Sturgis, whom the Perkins Brothers regarded as a nephew, valued his share of the Bryant & Sturgis partnership at $171,000; in 1847, he estimated it conservatively at half a million. Perkins & Co., which was clearly the New England patriarchal firm in the China trade, was estimated to be worth $3 million in the late 1820's. Russell & Co., not far behind Perkins, netted $100,000 a year in the 1850s. New York and Philadelphia merchants, such as Grinnell & Minturn, Howland & Aspinwall, the Willings, and the Binghams, did equally well if not better. Indeed, New York merchants did so well that they were soon enticing Boston firms to the city just as Boston had drawn some of its merchants out of Salem and New-buryport.

Influenced perhaps by his Puritan heritage, which considered waste sinful, the merchant sought eagerly any chance for income and bemoaned his fate when large profits did not materialize. There was an urgency that forced the man with surplus funds to put them to work anywhere, whether or not conditions were ideal. Nathan Trotter, the Philadelphia merchant and the moving spirit behind the Lancaster Pike, always sought, even in his early years, profitable opportunities for his surplus funds. He was constantly liquidating one transaction and engaging in another. No investment was too small for Trotter's consideration so long as it brought some return. He invested in such things as a cord of wood and a raft of logs. Commercial paper was purchased despite its low yield. A notation in Trotter's account book regarding a 4 percent return on a discount reflected his wry philosophy, "too bad, but had the money idle."[3]

Stephen Girard showed similar signs of agitation at the thought of idle funds, and business was conducted even though the terms of trade were less than desirable. Neither the high price for syrup or the low price of flour discouraged him. His ships had to be kept busy. He noted that "I have at present four of my ships in this port. As I am not in the habit to keep my vessels idle, their sight at our wharves is unpleasant."

During the Embargo the Oliver Brothers complained to their British correspondents, "We have at this Moment a large Sum lying idle in the Bank which we cannot employ."[4] Three months later they wrote "Money is so plenty here that we find it difficult to loan our spare funds to good Men at common Interest . . .," adding that they had "lately purchased Goods to amount of upwards of half a Million of Dollars merely to employ useless funds."

MERCHANT PROFITS—SEED MONEY
FOR MANUFACTURING

The search for profits led the merchants into several outside activities as it had their colonial predecessors, and merchants' surplus funds again found ready outlets in money lending, land and real estate, and manufacturing. The Brown Brothers of Providence, who had as early as the 1760's pioneered in the manufacture of spermaceti candles, launched Samuel Slater in the cotton-textile business in the 1790's. With the money accumulated in the China and West Indian trade, Stephen Girard became a banking

[3]Elva Tooker, *Nathan Trotter: Philadelphia Merchant, 1787–1853* (Cambridge, Mass.: Harvard University Press, 1955).

[4]Stuart Bruchey, *Robert Oliver, Merchant of Baltimore, 1783–1819* (Baltimore: The Johns Hopkins Press, 1956), p. 343.

entrepreneur offering complete banking services under one-man management. The Lowells, Lawrences, Jacksons and Appletons led the Boston Associates into fully integrated textile manufacturing in 1813, and by 1815 had installed power looms. The Jacksons and the Lees were also active in the distillery business. Edmund Dwight in Chicopee and Holyoke, and William Gregg of Graniteville, South Carolina made similar inroads into manufacturing.

Hartford and Springfield merchants provided an important source of capital for the infant industries springing up all over the Connecticut River Valley. By 1829, 36 percent of the shareholders in eight important New England textile mills were merchants. They held 36 percent of the equity holdings. Five years later these figures had increased to 46 percent and 54 percent respectively, and although the proportion of merchant shareholders declined to 39 percent by 1839, their equity holdings remained the same. After 1830, merchant money also made a considerable contribution to railroad finance both in the immediate area and other areas in the growing mid-West.

Land and real estate had always been and continued to be a depository for surplus funds. Astor started his real-estate purchases as early as 1789 and continued them throughout his life. Nathan Trotter's commitments in real estate amounted to $99,777 by 1840 and grew to $135,954 by 1851. By 1819, Robert Oliver had the principal part of his funds invested in lands, house lots, and stocks.

THE MERCHANT'S ETHICS

In their dealings with others the merchants not only took their profits where and when they could, but to some extent by any means they could. Their conduct at times was extremely questionable. In the words of Thomas Jefferson, "Merchants have no country. The mere spot they stand on does not constitute so strong an attachment as that from which they draw their gains." From the beginning when Robert Keayne, the Boston merchant, was convicted in 1639 of charging higher prices for goods than the law permitted, the attitude of the merchant was "business is business." During the Colonial Period the most highly respected merchants were not above a bit of smuggling in defiance of the English law. Later the Jacksons and the Lees were involved in smuggling, bribery, misrepresentation of cargo values to obtain lower tariff rates, trading while the Non-Intercourse Act was in effect, and violating any other laws that would interfere with their profits. According to their biographer, however, "they were angels . . . compared to some of their most respected contemporaries."[5]

[5]Kenneth P. Porter, *The Jacksons and the Lees* (Cambridge, Mass.: Harvard University Press, (1937), Vol. I, pp. 104–106.

The Olivers of Baltimore, during the Embargo, advised one of their captains to violate the law by sailing from New Orleans to Vera Cruz, admonishing him to keep the trip a secret. In addition they falsified invoices and places of origin so as to evade the restrictions against England under the Non-Importation law. A former merchant and agent for the Olivers, Vincent Nolte, noted in 1854 that "integrity and prudence were rather rare in American business circles."[6] John Jacob Astor tricked President Jefferson into lifting the Embargo to permit his ship, the *Beaver*, to sail to China ostensibly to return a Chinese mandarin to his homeland. The *Beaver* carried only 3,000 otter skins and 5 piculs of cochineal. It returned, however, with a cargo estimated at more than $200,000. Astor, along with other fur traders, was an expert at cheating the Indians or, what is worse, feeding them poor whiskey. But the fur business was a peculiarly notorious business. The hunters, trappers, and mountain men on whom it depended were some of the most individualistic and at the same time some of the most vicious human beings this country has produced.

The merchants treated their rivals and competitors with the same disregard they gave to the law. Any means leading to an advantage was regarded as fair business practice. "In matters of business I always endeavor to act like other people," said Robert Oliver. If true he had an extremely poor opinion of other people, for he had no hesitation in selling wormy figs and condemned flour. The Jacksons and the Lees gave specific instructions to their supercargoes and foreign agents to deliberately mislead rival merchants, and to start or stop war rumors in order to manipulate the prices of goods.

"THE INDUSTRIAL REVOLUTION"

Because the population of early America was too small and too dispersed to provide a mass-consumption market, and because efficient transportation facilities were nonexistent, market areas tended to be localized and too limited to permit economic use of specialization and division of labor. Early manufacturing enterprises were, therefore, mostly limited to small-scale production with crude tools. The American businessman who wanted to enter industry rather than trade was further hampered by a small, unskilled labor force and a shortage of both capital funds and capital goods. Before the United States could become an industrial nation, it had to overcome these difficulties, and in time they were overcome. Gradually, the labor force, the market area, and the supply of capital expanded to make possible a steady increase in industrial output.

Although the growth of industrialism was to a large extent a function

[6]Bruchey, *op. cit.*, pp. 368–70.

of growing population, expanding markets, and increasing capital, it was also the result of advancing technology and its adoption and adaptation by industrial entrepreneurs.

From the point of view of the economic historian, any technological innovation was prodigious, for few other things matched technology's mammoth contribution to total production. The view from business history is somewhat different. To the business historian, the importance of a technological development is directly related to the size of the business unit it sets in motion. Thus, an innovation that shakes the economic world may have little *direct* effect on business. A case in point is Eli Whitney's cotton gin. In economic history, few inventions have had so great an influence. The gin broke the bottleneck in cotton growing. Before the gin, an expert field hand could pick 200 pounds a day but could clean only ten pounds a day. The gin made it possible to clean cotton faster than it could be picked. Yet, important as the gin was, it never made any direct impression on business. It gave birth to no major industry and to no major firm.

The technological innovations that contributed significantly to business history were those that made use of mass production and, at a later date, those that resulted in heavy industry. The importance of mass production techniques as a factor in business history can hardly be exaggerated. They not only made big business possible; they made big business inevitable.

Among the first industries to experiment in the techniques of mass production were armaments and consumer goods—textiles, clocks, and food production. These had the benefit of mass demand; in one case, the government and in the other case, an ever increasing and urbanizing population. Later, but not much later, mass-production methods were used in making agricultural machinery.

Mass production would not have been possible without the principle of interchangeable, standardized parts. It was not coincidence that this principle first appeared in the manufacture of muskets, for it was here that the government provided a mass consumer. On June 14, 1798, Eli Whitney received a government contract to manufacture 10,000 stands of arms in a period of slightly more than two years. Whitney set to the task with high, but misplaced, optimism. It took him the entire two years specified in the contract merely to tool up, and it finally took eight years before the arms were delivered. Yet Whitney had proved the value of mass-production techniques and paved the way that others were to follow. As in all such technological landmarks, however, the concept of interchangeable parts caught on slowly. It took Simeon North five years to convince the Navy and obtain an order for 20,000 pistols. Not until the late 1820's did the War Department fully accept the principle of interchangeable parts. The early arms makers, Whitney, North, and a third Connecticut Yankee, Samuel Colt, who built an automated revolver-manufacturing factory, created important business firms. But due to the nature of the product, none achieved the size or the success attained by the other pioneer large-scale, industrial businesses —textiles and farm machinery.

TECHNOLOGY IN TEXTILES
AND FARM EQUIPMENT

What happened in textile technology is far better known although not necessarily more important than what happened in interchangeable parts armament manufacture. The story begins with Samuel Slater, who brought textile technology to this country. Slater had served an apprenticeship under a business associate of Richard Arkwright, the textile entrepreneur. Convinced that there was little future in England, he sailed for the United States in 1789 with the construction of the Arkwright mill firmly committed to memory. He immediately went to work for the New York Manufacturing Society. Just as quickly, he became convinced that New York could not successfully manufacture textiles because it lacked the necessary water power. Having heard that the Brown family was experimenting with a cotton mill, he wrote Moses Brown and in early 1790, he formed a partnership with Almy and Brown to manufacture cotton yarn.

Initially, textile machinery was built by the mill itself either in a machine shop set up on the mill property or by outside workingmen building the equipment. When the Boston Associates started their project at Waltham, a machine shop was erected to provide the machinery for the mill. When their own mill equipment was completed, the desire to keep the machine shop employed motivated the partners to start turning out textile machinery for other mills. In addition, other mills were licensed to build Waltham-type machinery. Indeed, in some years between 1817 and 1823, income from patent fees and the sale of rights exceeded the profit on the sale of machinery and parts. Although important qualitatively, the total value of textile machinery produced was not great, amounting to only $5 million in 1860.

Technological progress in cotton manufacturing did not stop with the basic power loom. Of special importance were the ring spindle, invented in 1830 by one of Slater's pupils, and various automatic devices that increased the output of both man and machine beyond that of any other factory system in the world. By 1835 the average spinning mule contained more than 300 spindles and by 1860 that number had been doubled. By then the American weaver operated four looms as against two for his counterpart in Great Britain.

Three years after Slater began to operate his mill at Pawtucket, two brothers, John and Arthur Scholfield, emigrated to Massachusetts from

England, and with the financial backing of a group from Newburyport erected a small woolen factory at Byfield, installing what was perhaps the first improved woolen-textile machinery driven by water in the United States. The Scholfields were inevitably followed by others and, despite the uncertainties of the business, by 1810 there were about two dozen woolen mills in operation. By 1816 it was estimated that $12 million was invested in woolen mills producing some $19 million worth of cloth. Connecticut alone had 25 mills, which employed about 1,200 operators and produced about 500,000 yards of woolen goods, and other woolen mills extended from New England as far south as Virginia and as far west as Cincinnati.

Improvements in wool technology lagged behind those in cotton but by 1830, they had also made great strides. The adoption of the spinning jenny was followed by improvements in the weaving process and in finishing machinery. In 1840 the Middlesex Mills started using the Crompton loom, which made possible for the first time the weaving of fancy-patterned woolens on power looms. By 1860, woolen mills extended from New England to Texas, Oregon, and California. The number of mills had grown to about 1,700 employing about 60,000 operators who ran 16,000 looms and 640,000 spindles.

Agriculture, being the largest industry by far in early America, was also the chief beneficiary of technological progress. By 1850 all of the basic farm implements were well on their way to their final form, and the farm equipment business had already produced one of the country's few large industrial enterprises—the McCormick reaper firm.

Early nineteenth-century progress in farm machinery encompassed three main lines of development: the improvement of the plow, the development of a workable reaper to harvest grain, and the invention of a cotton gin. These were the three that contributed the most to the immense increase in farm production that did so much for the American level of living. The cast iron plow enabled the farmer to plow the same number of acres with one-third the manpower that had been required by the crude wooden plow. The 1850 reaper permitted nine men to do the work that formerly had required fourteen scythe wielders. The cotton gin, as has already been explained, enabled the South to produce great masses of cotton.

The task of obtaining machines was great enough in its own right, but it by no means constituted the businessman's entire technological problem. Having obtained the machines, there remained the more challenging task of putting them into operation. That this was accomplished is apparent in the statistics of manufacturing growth.

In 1810, when the largest manufacturing plant in the country was worth less than $250,000, the gross value of manufactured product was estimated at $200 million, almost all produced in households. By 1849, it had climbed to a little over $1 billion and by 1860 to $2 billion. By 1860, the foundations of an industrial society had been firmly established. At the same time New England, the birthplace of American manufacturing, had given way to the Middle Atlantic states as the leading industrial area and was soon to be surpassed by the growing West.

The major manufacturing industries during the first part of the nineteenth century were mostly involved with native raw materials and the production of goods for direct consumption. This was to be expected in a country at the start of industrialization, for such goods were in relatively heavy demand; they were necessities and absorbed only a small percentage of the consumer's income. First in rank in 1860 was cotton cloth manufacturing. It had increased its capacity from 8,000 spindles in 1802, to 800,000 in 1825, to 4.0 million in 1850, to 5.2 million in 1860. The approximately 915 establishments in 1860 employed an average of 130 workers each and represented an average investment of $109,000. Although textile manufacture had dispersed to some extent, almost 75 percent of the industry was still located in the New England states.

Lumbering occupied second place in 1860. About 20,000 establishments had an average investment of $4,000 and an average employment of four. About 38 percent of value added was contributed by the West, 24 percent by the Middle Atlantic, and 22 percent by the South. The manufacture of boots and shoes, in third rank, was also an extremely small-scale business. Its almost 12,000 establishments employed fewer than 11 persons each and represented an average investment of $2,027.

The small scale of many of our early industries is also well illustrated by flour milling, the fourth largest industry. Average investment was only $6,000 and the average labor force numbered only two for the approximately 14,000 establishments. Fifth in rank was the men's clothing industry, with about 4,000 establishments capitalized at less than $7,000 each and employing an average of 28 workers. Of all manufacturing industries, large, medium, and small, two were of especial importance in the business world —textiles and agricultural machinery. Both need more detailed treatment.

THE BEGINNINGS OF THE
TEXTILE INDUSTRY

"Pioneering," Andrew Carnegie is supposed to have said, "don't pay," Hundreds of pages of economic history support his judgement, for in every industry pioneers were unsuccessful. The textile industry was no exception. Before 1800, more than 20 textile mills had been formed in the Northeast; most of them quickly failed. The earliest mills, established before 1790, soon closed. Of these, two in New England had the best chance of success because of the area's superior water power, its available labor force, and the drive of its entrepreneurs. In 1786, the Massachusetts legislature subsidized a textile works in East Bridgewater. In the following year, a group of Boston and Beverly capitalists formed the Beverly Cotton Manufacturing Company. The state again helped by exempting the firm from taxation. Both companies failed because they were not able to build efficient machinery, giving evidence that England's prohibition against the export of technological knowledge was at least to some extent successful.

A more ambitious project—the Society for Establishing Useful Manufactures—appeared in Paterson, New Jersey in the early 1790's. It had a paid-in capital of $625,000 and an extensive land grant, but it failed in 1796. Its management was inefficient and its imported English workers were incapable.

The obstacles lying in the American industrial road were so formidable that the *American Museum* in the late 1780's wrote with much justification:

> to think of manufacturing to any degree of perfection is an absurd attempt, too premature to be carried into effect; that we must not think of this for many years to come; that our want of resources, the high price of labour, and a number of other things render us utterly incapable of such undertakings.

This dismal prognosis did not come true. To be sure, the most successful cotton textile firm, the Boston Manufacturing Co., did not appear until 1813, but the real innovator in the business, the firm of Almy and Brown, had begun its entry into the business much earlier. This Providence firm was certainly the founder of the cotton industry, for it was responsible, directly or indirectly, for creating most of the 27 mills that were operating in middle New England in 1809.

Just as the Brown family had previously studied and planned its entry into candle manufacturing and iron making, so Moses Brown, in 1787, set about learning as much as possible about cotton manufacturing. Early in 1789, he formed a partnership with his son-in-law, William Almy,[7] and bought a spinning jenny and a carding machine. But the business floundered, for the machines were very inefficient. Then, as has been noted, Brown invited Samuel Slater to join in a partnership. Slater built the machinery; Almy and Brown provided the capital and the raw materials and handled the marketing. The profits were divided equally. Eventually, Slater branched out for himself. By 1827, he had been involved in eight partnerships with seventeen different people. He had an interest in mills in four New England states, but he maintained his relation with Almy and Brown through days of agreement and disagreement.

---

[7]Moses Brown soon retired, and the firm of Brown and Almy was reorganized under the name Almy and Brown with Smith Brown, Moses' cousin, as partner.

Although Slater and Almy and Brown were the innovators in mill construction and in yarn spinning, they were not the first to create a fully integrated factory. In the beginning, the firm specialized in one process of one function. It manufactured cotton yarn; it did no weaving, and it did no marketing. The weaving was done by hand loom under the "putting-out" system where much of the labor was performed by rural families in their homes.

The first fully integrated factory was again the result of borrowing freely from the British. While on a trip to England, the merchant Francis Cabot Lowell visited several cotton factories and memorized the construction of the power loom. After returning to Boston in 1813, he, with much difficulty, persuaded a group of merchants, including Nathan Appleton and Patrick Tracy Jackson, to subscribe $100,000 to form the Boston Manufacturing Co.[8] He also enlisted the technical assistance of a remarkable mechanic, Paul Moody.

The Boston Manufacturing Co. was the first factory in the true sense of the word, for it processed the entire textile manufacture from the raw cotton to the finished cloth. Its owners, the Boston Associates, soon dominated the New England economy as well as the textile business. By 1850, they controlled 20 percent of all cotton spindles, 30 percent of Massachusetts railroads, 40 percent of Massachusetts insurance, and 40 percent of Boston banking. They owned million-dollar enterprises at Waltham, Chicopee, Holyoke, and Lawrence, Massachusetts; Dover, Manchester, and Nashua, New Hampshire; and Biddeford and Saco in Maine. A majority interest was also maintained in smaller mills in Peterborough, Somersworth, and Salmon Falls, New Hampshire; and in Taunton and Amesbury, Massachusetts.

In the first seven years of its existence, the Boston Manufacturing Co. was hugely successful, paying aggregate dividends equal to more than the original $100,000 of capital stock. The Boston Associates' success reflected "a virile, purposeful, and imaginative business management." Their guiding spirit, Patrick Tracy Jackson, was an excellent leader. "His actions and letters show foresight, a grasp of both principles and details, a strong sense of self and company interest, and a profound (and sometimes uncritical) enthusiasm for promotion."[9]

The success of the Slater and the Lowell mills, and the fact that it was easy to start a mill with only a few thousand dollars, caused a great surge in opening textile mills. The Great Falls Manufacturing Company was or-

---

[8]Lowell was related to the Cabots through his mother, to the Higginsons through his father, and to the Tracys and Jacksons through his wife. His wife's sister married Henry Lee, and his three Jackson brothers-in-law married three Cabots.

[9]George S. Gibb, *The Saco-Lowell Shops* (Cambridge, Mass.: Harvard University Press, 1950), pp. 59–60.

ganized in 1823, the Amoskeag Manufacturing Company in 1831, the Laconia Mills in 1845, the Pepperell Manufacturing Company in 1850, and the Pacific Mills in 1854. Hundreds of others dotted the New England landscape and shaded its rivers.

The business policies of the early textile manufacturers, their strengths and weaknesses, and their characteristic behavior were an outgrowth of their experience as merchants. As merchants they had depended on others, and as manufacturers they also depended on others. Although well versed in trade and commerce, they realized that they lacked technical knowledge. Consequently, where it was possible, they hired experts as consultants and technicians. The Browns relied on Slater. Lowell depended upon Paul Moody, and the Boston Manufacturing Company at various times employed as consultants Daniel Webster; Nathaniel Bowditch, a mathematician; Jacob Perkins, a mechanical engineer; and Loammi Baldwin, a construction engineer.

THE McCORMICK REAPER

American manufacturing in the first half of the nineteenth century was clearly oriented toward agriculture. Textiles, especially cotton, dominated the consumer goods economy in the early years. But at the middle of the century, it was being challenged by a producers' good farm machinery.

Among the many farm implements that had appeared—plows, harrows, harvesters, threshers, gins, etc.—the harvester overshadowed all others. In similar fashion, the McCormick harvester firm was clearly the most important farm implement manufacturer.

Before McCormick, the farm implement business had always been a small business. In any given farm community, the village blacksmith probably made as many plows as the local factory did. Cyrus Hall McCormick changed all that.[10] He started off slowly, for like his father, his occupation was farming and his avocation was inventing and tinkering with machinery. He claimed to have invented the reaper in 1831, but there had been many reapers before him. His contribution to technology was that he was the first to combine in one machine the seven strategic parts of a reaper.[11] Moving gradually and cautiously, McCormick did not obtain a patent until 1834 and he did not sell a reaper until 1839. As late as 1847, shortly after he moved from Virginia to Illinois, he had sold only 1,278 machines. But the, production and sales rose very rapidly. In the next ten years, almost 15,000

---

[10]McCormick has been exhaustively treated in William T. Hutchinson, *Cyrus Hall McCormick*, two volumes (New York: Appleton-Century-Crofts, 1930 and 1935).

[11]The seven essential parts were side draft, vibrating horizontal knife, divider, fingers, reel, platform, and main wheel.

reapers were sold. By 1860, production amounted to 5,000 a year. McCormick's total output probably equalled one-third of that of all his competitors combined.

The success of the McCormick firm owed much to the external environment and the general economic circumstances of the time. The demand for farm machinery naturally increased as the population increased. But in addition, the westward movement added to the demand, for it brought into cultivation a vast acreage of lush land ideally suited to the mechanized production of staple grains. The continuous scarcity of labor, even while population multiplied at a fantastic rate, added still another incentive to the creation of an intense demand for farm machinery. But the increased production that was made possible through the use of capital goods would have availed the farmer little if he had had no way of getting his goods to market. This problem was solved when the canal, the steamboat, and the railroad enabled the farmer to reach the urban consumer and thus eliminated the last objection to the utilization of farm machinery, especially the reaper.

All the broad economic developments that encouraged the use of farm implements helped the farm equipment business, but they did not explain why McCormick in particular was such an unusual success. Other manufacturers shared in the progress of the general economy, but none of the others succeeded as McCormick did. The difference lay in the nature of the entrepreneurship. McCormick had a large supply of ambition, tenacity of purpose, and the drive to succeed.

Before he began to manufacture reapers, McCormick had tried his hand at the iron business and failed. But the experience was not without value. It sharpened his wits and educated him in marketing, labor relations, the law, and court procedure. "All this," said McCormick in later life, "I have ever since felt to be one of the best lessons of my business experience. If I had succeeded in the iron enterprise I would perhaps never have had sufficient determination and perseverance in the pursuit of my reaper enterprise to have brought it to the present state of success."[12]

It was McCormick who "invented" and improved the reaper; it was he who took the reaper west to Illinois; it was he who clearly dominated the farm implement business. But this is not to say that it was he alone who was responsible for the firm's success. Like all eminently successful businesses, the McCormick reaper enterprise was more like a symphony orchestra than a one-man band. The firm's management operated under a workable, but hardly amicable, division of labor.

Cyrus took his brothers out to Illinois along with the reaper. William ran the office and Leander supervised production. When William died in 1865, Charles Spring succeeded him. Leander hung on until the bitter end,

---

[12]Hutchinson, *Cyrus Hall McCormick*, p. 149.

and bitter it was, for his relations with Cyrus, never very amiable, worsened as the years passed. Cyrus' function in the division of labor was to handle the legal, public relations, advertising, and marketing side of the business. He spent most of his time defending or prosecuting patent and other law suits and in demonstrating the reaper. He traveled to state fairs and to international expositions and was not too proud to visit the farms of large grain growers. In these endeavors, he was eminently successful. The McCormick reaper, for example, won a gold medal at the famous Crystal Palace Exposition in London in 1851 at which three other American manufacturers also won gold medals. But in addition to taking care of his end of the business, McCormick as chief executive officer insisted upon interfering with the other departments. His greatest weakness as an entrepreneur was that he was incapable of creating a managerial organization to carry on the business after he was gone. He brooked no rival as the dominating figure. He did not respect his associates, nor did he treat them as equals. Instead he exploited them. As a consequence, when he was no longer able to run the business, it was left without a leader and spent some years in a state of chaos.

McCormick was far from a likable man, but no realist would expect a phenomenally successful owner entrepreneur to be likable. The qualities that were required for business success in a virgin market were certainly not the qualities that could produce a scintillating social personality. By the same token, the qualities that made for social popularity were the least likely qualities for business success. McCormick thought that success in business was the foundation of everything, and he had a one-track mind in his determination to prove his hypothesis.

In its early years, the McCormick firm for the most part followed the customary production processes of the time. But from the time that manufacture began in Chicago in 1847, the reaper was standardized and the parts were interchangeable. In addition to his own reaper business, McCormick entered into other partnerships or sub-manufacturing agreements most of which ended in dispute. These arrangements were more like licensing agreements than partnerships. Usually, McCormick was paid a patent fee on each machine plus a fee of $2 a day for time spent in the field. Profits were split, fifty-fifty.

It took years before the manufacturing process was fully integrated even within the firm itself. In the beginning, the sickles were made at Fitchburg, Massachusetts at about $1.25 each. Guard fingers were made at Elizabethport, New Jersey. Iron castings were obtained from a firm in Chicago for about $50 a ton. Necessary raw materials such as wood, coal, and iron were bought from a variety of producers all over the Middle West and East. Little time was spent in attempting to make the final product a thing of beauty. The McCormick family was interested in utility, not aesthetics.

Each reaper was given a coat of paint by independent Chicago painters at 14 cents a machine. By 1850, the total cost of building a reaper was a little less than $65, including materials, rent, interest, depreciation, selling commissions, and allowance for bad debts. The selling price at that time was $115 cash or $120 on the installment plan. In practice the cash received at the time of sale varied from 10 to 25 percent of the purchase price, and the balance was collected whenever possible over the next year and a half.

McCormick as the first really big businessman in American manufacturing was an ideal example of an innovator. The reaper company was no one-man business, but a division of managerial labor. Cyrus was, however, unquestionably the decision maker and, therefore, the leader. As a big business in the midst of many small ones, the McCormick reaper firm was far ahead of its time. Consequently, the problems that were relatively minor for most enterprises were of the utmost urgency for McCormick. He apparently thought that marketing was the firm's most important problem, for it was there that he concentrated his attention, and it was in marketing that he made his most important innovations. Raising capital funds did not seem to present any difficult riddles, for the McCormick enterprises enjoyed a liberal line of credit with banks in New York as well as with those in Chicago. In contrast to McCormick, most other firms paid little attention to marketing but found raising capital funds an almost unsurmountable problem. But the problems of the average firm is the topic of the next chapter.

5

BUSINESS PROBLEMS
IN THE EARLY
NINETEENTH CENTURY

It is well to reemphasize the point made in an earlier chapter that although the businessman's problems have differed in degree and in comparative importance, they have always been essentially the same in kind. The businessman's first problem has always been the making of a profit, but at different times capital problems and the problems of competition, marketing, management, and labor relations have vied with one another in the degree of relative importance.

In the early nineteenth century, profit making, capital and credit problems, and the hiring of labor were more important than marketing and management. This should not be taken to mean that the latter two were unimportant. Firms have had to be managed and goods have had to be sold ever since business first began in ancient Sumeria and Babylonia. But a complicated managerial structure was hardly necessary in the relatively simple economy of the nineteenth century. Firms were small,[1] and they performed a single function, so that there was no need for full-time managers and administrators. The "boss" performed many functions in addition to making the decisions that guided the business. In addition to being an entrepreneur, he often performed some tasks in the mill or on the production line. The entrepreneur who spent all of his time in an office was still a half century in the future, and the business leader who was not at home in the factory was still a generation away. Samuel Slater, certainly an important early nineteenth-century businessman, built the machinery in his mill and

[1] In 1811 a Congressman thought it extraordinary that a Philadelphia tobacco manufacturer employed 100 workers and had expenses of $160 a day.

took care of the decisions that had to be made. In addition, "there being no one else to do it," he spent two or three hours on every cold winter morning breaking the ice around the water wheel that provided the power to run the machinery.

Marketing was also not as time consuming and as intricate a puzzle as it was to become later. Manufacturers confined themselves to producing goods. With rare exceptions, they farmed out the marketing function to independent selling agents, wholesalers, and other specialists. At the retail level, the general store and the itinerant peddler continued to serve most consumers.

GOVERNMENT ASSISTANCE TO BUSINESS

Governments—state, local, and federal—were as eager to help business solve its problems as they had been in colonial days, and just as then, they passed laws and adopted policies that were designed to encourage and assist manufacturing and commerce.

Clearly, business must be greatly assisted by such routine activities of government as weather information, census statistics, consular reports, inspection services, licensing, setting standards of weights and measures, and providing coin and currency. But beyond this, there are incorporation laws; subsidies for transportation, communications, and other things that are usually incorporated under the word "infrastructure" or under the term "social capital"; tariffs, bounties, and quotas; and finally, government regulation and control of industry and industrial behavior. Of these four, the first three were tried extensively in the early nineteenth century, but the last did not come into prominence until much later. States, cities, and towns helped new industries, especially textile manufacturing and even more especially cotton textiles, with monopoly grants, bounties, subsidies, loans, lotteries, and tax exemption. In time, they also liberalized their incorporation laws. New York led the way by making it possible to form a corporation without special act of legislation. To be sure, this first general incorporation law of 1811 applied only to manufacturing companies with a capitalization of less than $100,000, but other states soon followed. Connecticut, in 1817, granted limited liability to its corporations. Twenty years later, it passed the country's first comprehensive general incorporation law. By 1860, most of the states had passed similar legislation.

The liberalization of corporate law did not take place without opposition. As early as 1822, Massachusetts had second thoughts about limited liability and partially nullified its previous legislation. Maine changed its mind five times between 1821 and 1856. In the Pennsylvania constitutional convention of 1837 it was proposed that no charter be granted for a project that could be accomplished by a sole proprietor or a partnership. Ohio, in 1851, considered the possibility of substituting partnerships for corporations. In the revulsion against banks that followed the depression of 1837–1841, seven states, two territories, and the District of Columbia prohibited banks by law or in their constitutions.

Corporations, however, had advantages for some business firms and as the law became hesitatingly more liberal, incorporation increased. Apparently, the corporation's greatest advantage was not limited liability, or perpetual life, or, in this early day, the prospect of raising huge amounts of capital. What seemed to have attracted entrepreneurs to incorporate was the prospect of gaining some special privilege in the corporate charter such as the right to issue paper money, or the acquisition of a virtual monopoly in a particular territory.

Regardless of the reasons, the legal form of ownership slowly began to change from the proprietorship and partnership, so typical of a mercantile society, to the corporation. During the years 1807–1818, Massachusetts granted incorporation privileges through special legislative acts to about 90 companies for making cotton and woolen goods. Between 1800 and 1823, eight states incorporated 557 manufacturing companies, capitalized at $72 million ($20 million in New York and $28 million in Massachusetts).

Yet in 1860, most American manufacturing firms were still not incorporated. Data for several states, admittedly incomplete, show that manufacturing firms were slow to take advantage of the liberalized incorporation laws. In Maryland, industrial (manufacturing and mining) incorporations did not exceed five a year until 1825 and then not again until 1835. It was not until the decade 1820–1829 that industrial incorporations accounted for as much as 25 percent of total incorporations. The same pattern prevailed in New Jersey and Ohio. New York had the earliest concentration. Its incorporations exceeded five a year as early as 1809 and amounted to more than 25 percent of the total as early as the 1810–1819 decade.

The federal government's aid to industry was less direct than that of the states and the cities. Just as governmental bodies have always done, it subsidized things rather than people, but whereas local governments gave outright cash subsidies, the federal government made its influence felt through tariffs, patents, navigation acts, and land grants. It used outright cash loans and subsidies only to a small extent and confined these for the most part to transportation enterprises. Between 1816 and 1830, it completed the Cumberland Road and bought stock in four canal companies. But its aggregate financial aid was far less than that of the local governments.

It is impossible to put an exact dollar figure on how much government financial assistance contributed to business progress. State and city financial assistance seems to have been a waste of money, for there is no evidence that any successful firm was helped to its success by direct subsidies and bounties. On the contrary, most of the firms that received such help failed, and those that did succeed did so without government financial help. A side effect of the depressingly bad experience with bounties and subsidies was its effect on future government aid. It converted many to laissez faire and helped to end, at least temporarily, the dominance of the mercantile-paternalistic philosophy, which had been so much in vogue in the previous period. As the Newark *Gazette* said: "There is a time in every country when manufacturers will spring out of necessity and favorable circumstances. In general, government aid is not necessary to produce or support such establishments."[2]

TARIFFS AND EMBARGOES

Economists can argue that except for infant industries, tariffs had little effect on the economy or on business. But businessmen felt much differently. To be sure, not all businessmen looked upon protective tariffs as an unmixed blessing. Those in manufacturing welcomed tariffs and at times sought them passionately. Those in commerce and trade hardly shared this enthusiasm.

Protectionists were probably in the majority, but if they were not, they were certainly more articulate than the free traders. Tariff associations appeared before the country was thirty years old. The American Society (New York, 1816) and the Connecticut Society of 1817 were apparently the earliest, but the Philadelphia Society for the Promotion of Useful Industry by Protective Laws, and its successor, the National Institution for the Promotion of Industry (1820), were the most influential. The latter distributed a paper, the *Patron of Industry*, and it numbered among its members Mathew Carey, the publisher-economist, and E. I. duPont, the founder of the illustrious chemical company.

Long before the formation of these societies, however, Congress had embarked upon a course of protection. Tariff rates were raised approximately every four years, reaching a temporary height in the so-called "Tariff of Abominations" of 1828. Thereafter, and until the Civil War, rates were reduced somewhat.

Certain specific tariffs did encourage economic progress by enabling some infant industries to survive the onslaughts of competition from other more industrialized areas. Tariffs helped the textile industries boom during the War of 1812 and the iron industry in the 1840's. Time after time, as new tariffs were imposed, commission merchants and wholesalers shifted

[2]Quoted in Joseph Stancliffe Davis, *Essays in the Earlier History of American Corporations* (Cambridge, Mass.: Harvard University Press, 1917), p. 498.

from their foreign sources of supply and gave business to local manufacturers.

There is also a widely-held belief that the War of 1812 and the Embargo and Non-Intercourse Acts that preceded it greatly encouraged American manufacturing, especially textiles. The argument is that the prohibition of trade cut off the importation of cotton goods from England. This left the market open to American manufacturers who rushed in to fill the vacuum. Plausible as this argument is, it does not fit all the facts. The embargo's initial effect was to discourage rather than to encourage the textile business. For one thing, English and American goods did not compete as closely as is often assumed. The English made cloth; most American textile manufacturers spun yarn. But what was more important, the embargo produced an economic crisis and severe depression for the New England seaports, and this destroyed much of the demand for cotton yarn. Before the embargo, Almy and Brown, the innovators in the business, sold half of their yarn to Boston and the northern New England towns. The embargo cut this to 17 percent.

The immediate effect of the Embargo and its successor was to dampen the textile business, but its indirect and long-run effect was to encourage it. This experience with the Embargo illustrates an important point in the relations between government and business. Governments wield their greatest influence over the economy and over life in general less by their statutes, their laws, and their specific acts than by "breaking the cake of custom." They shake up the economy, disrupt the usual way of doing things, and bring an end to business as usual. In peace or war, government action pushes producers into different channels of activity and behavior. The years around the War of 1812 were no exception. Capitalists who, because of the embargo, found little investment opportunity in shipping and trade, turned to textiles. With entrepreneurs building spinning mills, cotton yarn was soon being overproduced. The cotton textile business, in which a few firms had been strongly established before the embargo, now became an industry of many producers, most of whom rested on shaky foundations.

Another doubtful thesis concerns the patent system and its assumed encouragement of invention and technological progress. Actually, the government's contribution to technological progress through the patent system was less substantial than the contribution it made by encouraging education and by assisting in the building of transport facilities. The patent argument is based on the heroic interpretation of history. It assumes that inventions are the work of one individual toiling away in the vacuum of a garret. But each invention rests on existing knowledge, and virtually all important inventions have been made almost simultaneously by different individuals, indicating that the basic elements of each had already been discovered and that the time for synthesis had arrived. Thus, the patent system in itself did little to encourage invention. It was rather the American value system, the expansion of population, the accumulation of capital, the construction of transportation facilities, and the institutional framework of the American economy that predetermined a technological civilization and a very rapid industrial growth.

THE CAPITALIZATION OF INDUSTRY

Early American enterprise did not require large amounts of capital funds, for there was little capital-intensive, heavy industry. Once again, however, everything is relative. In absolute terms the demand for funds was not very high, but it was high in proportion to the supply. A disproportion also existed between the demand for fixed capital and the demand for working capital. In the years around 1800, when the productive process seemed interminable, manufacturers needed unusually large supplies of working capital considering the size of their total production. In the cotton mills around 1820, annual production equalled only 60 percent of capital. Then as machinery and transportation improved, goods moved faster through their various stages of production and annual product rose to 97 percent of capital in 1840 and 115 percent in 1860. Thereafter, as frequently happens in economic history, the trend reversed itself.

But whether capital was needed for producers' goods or for financing inventory, it grew at a prodigious rate, doubling every decade from 1820, so that by 1860 the total amount exceeded $1 billion. The average investment per plant, however, was not typically large. In 1832, hundreds of small manufacturers reported total capital investment of less than $1,000 each. Of the Rhode Island factories, 84 percent reported to the Treasury that paid-in capital was less than $50,000. For 119 cotton mills, the average investment was about $43,000, and for 22 woolen mills it was about $15,000. It was possible to start a woolen mill with just over $1,000, but this was the minimum. The manufacture of iron usually required a somewhat larger investment than textiles, but just prior to the Civil War the average rolling mill at Pittsburgh represented an investment of only $150,000.

Although most factories were small operations requiring relatively little in the way of capital funds, there were some at the other extreme. Of 1,094 cotton manufacturers examined in 1850, 41 were capitalized at $250,000 or more or had 25,000 or more spindles. These 41 largest companies had an average capitalization of $830,000 as against an average of $38,000 each for the other 1,053. The total capital of the 41 ($34,000,000) was almost half the total ($74,000,000) of the entire industry. Of the 194 cotton manufacturing companies incorporated from 1825 to 1845, 13 had authorized capital exceeding $500,000, while 41 were capitalized at less than $100,000.

Some of the available figures evidently include accrued earnings such as the $123,000 capital of the Simsbury mill in 1832, and the $215,000 of the Thompsonville Manufactory in 1833, both carpet manufacturers. The Boston Manufacturing Co. had started out with $100,000. The Waltham Company started with capital of $300,000, which was soon increased to $600,000. The Merrimack Company started with $600,000 as did the Hamilton Company, which by 1844 had increased its stock to $1,200,000. Amoskeag started with $965,000 and the Appleton Company in 1828 had the distinction of being the first to start out with resources of $1,000,000. Other million-dollar companies followed: Lyman with $1,470,000; Lawrence with $1,200,000; and Massachusetts with $1,200,000.

THE SOURCES OF CAPITAL

Just as store proprietorship had provided capital for the merchants, merchants were the most important suppliers of capital to manufacturing and industry. Almy and Brown, the backers of Slater, were merchants as were the Lowells, Appletons, and Jacksons of the Boston Associates. Retired merchant John P. Cushing's investments in manufacturing grew from less than $150,000 in 1835 to $427,000 in 1851. As mentioned earlier, merchants from Hartford and Springfield were active in financing factories in the Connecticut River Valley. The Hazard family of Rhode Island and the Derbys of Massachusetts turned their interests from commerce to wool manufacture. A New York merchant firm financed the Simsbury mill and the Thompsonville Manufactory. Frederick Cabot, who had started out in the Far Eastern trade, had among his partners in the Lowell Company Thomas and James Perkins, the Thorndikes, Thomas Lee Jr., Patrick Tracy Jackson, and Patrick's brothers Charles and James, all with merchant backgrounds. Other companies in the carpet manufacturing business with merchant money were A. and E. S. Higgins and John Sanford and Co.

The reinvestment of earnings was an important source of growth capital, so that industrial capital was to an important extent its own progenitor. Once a factory had been firmly established, it could become sufficiently profitable to supply its own capital needs, and many firms grew to a fairly large size by this method. On the other hand, failures were evidently equally abundant, so that this opportunity was not shared by all.

Funds for industry were also obtained from existing industrialists. The merchant-industrialists to some degree carried the principle of diversification into their manufacturing operations. Patrick Tracy Jackson owned shares in at least seven companies as did Nathan Appleton and Israel Thorndyke. All of the original shareholders of the Waltham and Lowell companies also owned shares in other mills. Diversification went further than manufacturing. It was the fortunes of the textile entrepreneurs that financed much of the water and rail transport in New England and later in the Middle West. The Boston Associates financed the Western Railroad to Albany. The Thames Company invested its earnings in packets, and the Spragues of Rhode Island controlled the New York to Providence steamship line and most of the railroads in and about Providence.

As time went on, the original large shareholdings tended to be reduced and the numbers of company shareholders increased. The six largest shareholders in the Waltham Company owned 67 percent of the outstanding shares in 1820, but by 1860 they held only 13 percent. The eleven merchants who contributed 95 percent of the capital of the Waltham Company also reduced their shareholdings after a few years. They owned 571 shares in 1820; by 1828 one of the eleven had dropped out, and the remaining ten owned only 175 shares. By 1836, this had been further reduced to five original stockholders, owning 64 shares, and by 1846, only two of the original eleven were left in the company and owned only 47 shares.

One reason for the decline in the shareholdings of individual merchants was that their stock was being distributed among members of the original families rather than remaining with the individuals themselves. The 1846 records of the Waltham Company show thirty-four Appletons, Lees, Lowells, Abbots, and Jacksons, instead of the five members of these families originally involved.

Employees were also helping to distribute ownership more widely. With the growth of companies, middle managers began to appear. These individuals, more than a few in number and above average in income, together with a few mill workers, were investing part of their savings in company stock. How much this amounted to in absolute terms or as a percent of ownership is impossible to say. According to those commentators who are inclined to overenthusiasm about business' contribution to social welfare, some operatives saved thousands of dollars. According to others, wage earners saved a mere pittance. But one concrete piece of evidence is that in 1845, the operatives of the Merrimac Company owned $60,000 of its stock.

The wealthy merchants supplied the bulk of capital funds for the larger mills, but the smaller ones were dependent on small subscriptions from local sources. The savings of the manufacturer himself, and those of his friends, relatives, and neighbors, were tapped. In many cases farmers exchanged water rights for shares of stock, and local tradesmen risked their surplus funds. Firearms manufacturers, such as Whitney and North, were able to operate on advances from the War Department to build and equip their plants.

THE EARLY FINANCIAL INTERMEDIARIES

Capital funds were also provided by financial intermediaries, that is, the financial institutions that acted as middlemen between savers and investors. Among the stockholder records of eleven large textile companies appeared the names of 35 commercial banks, 7 savings banks, 5 general insurance companies, 5 brokerage firms, 2 private banks, 1 life insurance company, and 1 trust company.[3]

Of the nineteenth century intermediaries—commercial banks, private investment banks, savings banks, trust companies, building and loan associations, and general and life insurance companies—only general insurance companies existed in the Colonial Period. All the others were products of the years between 1781 and 1830, and of the nine intermediaries mentioned above, only the commercial banks, the trust companies, and the private banks were of significant importance to manufacturing. Savings banks in their early years provided significant capital for manufacturing, but later, the savings that were deposited with them flowed out in mortgages, in government securities, or in transportation enterprises.

There were half a dozen reasons why financial intermediaries appeared relatively late. The economy before 1800 was still largely undeveloped, and farming took up the time of nine-tenths of the working population. Whether they were right or wrong, farmers thought they had no need for financial intermediaries. They did need capital, but most of this was raised through their own saving, or, to put it more precisely, through their own labor. Progressive farmers constructed their own barns, fenced their acres, and watched their herds multiply. It was only later as commercial farming spread and self-sufficiency declined that the farmer began to feel a need for financial institutions. A second reason for the late appearance of banks and such was that the needs of the businesses that did exist were not that pressing. Direct financing was possible, and it was even more convenient in the small areas such as existed in the early 1800's. People borrowed from each other rather than from institutions. So it was that local merchants very often acted as bankers in all but name. In every undeveloped frontier area, banking is unspecialized. Country store proprietors advance credit, write insurance, and sell real estate.

There were, moreover, lotteries that could be used to gather up capital funds. Lotteries were originally conducted by volunteers, mostly for colleges, hospitals, churches, and government units. But some manufacturers also used them. By 1820, however, they had been reorganized on a business basis, and their direction had been taken over by professional underwriting

[3] Lance E. Davis, "Stock Ownership in the Early New England Textile Industry," *The Business History Review*, Vol. XXXII, No. 2 (Summer 1958), p. 211.

syndicates. Then their business soared. There were at most ten lottery dealers in New York City in 1824, but at least 150 in 1833. Gradually, public
opinion turned against the lottery. The revulsion was most marked in the
depression years of the 1840's. By then, most states had passed laws prohibiting lotteries, but they had fulfilled a function, and many lottery dealers
were sufficiently agile and sufficiently farseeing to adjust to the changing
times by converting their businesses into banking or brokerage. The House
of S. & M. Allen, the second largest lottery dealer,[4] was the direct ancestor
of the private banking firm of E. W. Clark & Co., which in turn was the
indirect ancestor of Jay Cooke & Co. and the present house of Smith, Bar-
ney & Co. John Thompson, a substantial dealer, accomplished the remarkable feat of founding both the Chase Bank and the First National Bank of
New York.

Two other factors were much more important than any of those mentioned above in explaining the late appearance of intermediaries: the anti-
bank attitude of most of the people and the importance of Europe, especially England, in the American capital and money markets. Both of these
are important enough to deserve a little more attention.

The majority of the population regarded all financial institutions with
suspicion and banks with outright hostility. To the Puritan mind and to
the agrarian sense of values, banking smacked of getting something for nothing. Suspicion rested chiefly on the bank's ability to create money. This
appeared to most people to be nothing more or less than monetary trickery,
and bankers who created money—paper money in those days—were thought
to be no better than gamesmen at the village carnival. Thomas Jefferson
thought that banks were a swindle, and his political opponent John Adams
denounced "every bank of discount" as "downright corruption."

If majority opinion made it psychologically difficult for banks, the
dominance of the English money market made it even more difficult com-
petitively. Before 1815, the colonies were a frontier outpost of the British
Empire. Foreign trade was of immense importance, and the merchants who
imported goods relied on Britain with its well-established financial network
and liberal credit terms. Every merchant of importance had to depend on
his English agent, usually a merchant banking house. The smaller merchants, who had no contact with England, depended on a larger firm to act
as go-between. As has already been said, the most persistent problem in the
early merchant's life was to keep up with his accounts in England, and the
most persistent problem of most other Americans was to maintain satisfactory economic relations with the merchant.

After the rise of industrialism, Americans were still accustomed to
look to England on matters of finance and economics, although this orien-

---

[4]For those who are interested in "firsts," Yates McIntyre was probably the biggest.

tation was diminishing toward the middle of the century. European houses resisted investment in American manufacturing. The Dutch did have a piece of the New Jersey Manufacturing Company and possibly some other holdings, but the English merchant bankers had no manufacturing interest. Nor did they invest in railroads until long after the trains began to run. But they did have a substantial interest in government bonds, banks, and insurance companies, thereby releasing other capital funds for manufacturing enterprise.

COMMERCIAL BANKING AS AN AID
TO INDUSTRY

Despite the general antipathy to banks, banking did thrive. If it had not, its failure to do so would have violated the whole American value system with its business orientation and its emphasis on raising the level of living.

Banking offered a seemingly simple way by which a poor economy could add to its supply of capital funds, and Americans were anxious to take advantage of it. Indeed, one of the basic differences between European and American banking was that in Europe banking appeared because of an apparent excess of funds; in America banking grew because of a dearth of capital.

In every large city, the promoters and original entrepreneurs of the earliest commercial banks were merchants who hoped to provide credit for their main business of shipping and foreign trade. The list is long. It includes among others Morris, Willing, and Bingham in Philadelphia; Wadsworth, Beekman, Livingston in New York; Phillips, Lowell, Appleton in Boston; and the Browns in Providence. They cooperated with one another to the extent that businessmen can cooperate. Each one tried zealously to guard his own territory and to maintain a monopoly in commercial banking, but in their other dealings they maintained a loyalty to their class and to the tradition of the "old school tie." Bankers in the different cities were very cordial to their counterparts in other cities so long as there was no question of direct competition. Branch banking appeared very early, and bankers were constantly alert lest they be swallowed by a larger institution. But correspondent relations between banks came into being as soon as the second commercial bank appeared. By the early 1800's a whole network of such relations had been created. Bankers in the same city also cooperated with each other. They joined together to form the early insurance companies, savings banks, and trust companies. In their lending policies, they were tolerant and generous to their friends while maintaining a conservative attitude toward the public in general.

The merchants rationalized their desire for monopoly by insisting that several banks in a community would "eat each other up" by exhausting each other's specie reserves. Those who were outside the pale—the manufacturers, artisans, and small fry—refused to accept this view. They determined to break the monopoly, and their determination was reinforced by their reluctance to borrow from individuals and their willingness, perhaps eagerness, to borrow from institutions. Before the second decade of the century was over, the nonmerchant businessmen had succeeded in their efforts to invade the field. Indeed, they had flooded the field.

The newer bankers were more aggressive and much less tradition-minded than the merchants, most of whom had been raised under the influence of the English value system. With the shift in control, lending policies did become a trifle less conservative. In fact, conservative critics regarded them as regrettably radical and as "accommodating mere speculators." But these charges were exaggerated. The antagonism between the older and the younger generation was more a matter of words, attitudes, and philosophy than of banking behavior. Neither generation was impetuous in rushing into loans and investments. Long after the newer banks had taken over, it was still a common complaint that the banks were not offering as much credit as business needed. Promoters of enterprises that needed substantial capital tried to solve the problem by forming "improvement banks," that is, institutions formed as subsidiaries of specific large-scale projects, such as canals and railroads.

The charges and counter-charges exchanged between the older and newer bankers were not as contradictory as they seemed. The truth of the matter was that the flow of credit fluctuated widely, and reflected the ups and downs of the business cycle, which in turn reflected the ups and downs of foreign trade and the flow of specie. The banks watched their specie reserves and expanded or contracted their loans as specie flowed in or out. They offered credit liberally in recovery and boom when their specie reserves seemed high and contracted when specie reserves ran down.

The first banks started off with the ambitious intention of making no long-term loans, but of confining their lending to short-term, nonrenewable discounts. Bankers quickly learned, however, that even in the big cities short-term credit was impractical. Economic processes did not move that quickly in that age. Most borrowers could, therefore, make little use of short-term funds. It was not long before even big city banks were granting loans for four months and, in unusual cases, for two years. At the same time, borrowers found it easier to obtain renewals.

What banks were doing was shifting to so-called "accommodation loans," that is, paper that produced business in contrast to trade paper that was produced by business. Or to define the term in another way, accommodation paper was used to finance fixed capital expenditures, while trade paper financed working capital. In a young and developing economy where there were not enough other financial intermediaries to provide the required fixed capital, the commercial banks filled much of the need. Professor Lance E. Davis has estimated that commercial banks provided half the capital for the early textile industry.

As the economy advanced, accommodation loans diminished, but they still retained more than passing importance. Albert Gallatin, in 1831, wrote that " a large portion of bank loans consist of what the merchants consider as permanent accommodation." It is estimated that security loans averaged about 10 percent of bank assets around the middle of the century.

THE COMMERCIAL PAPER MARKET

In pre-1870 America, commercial paper, the bulk of which represented accounts receivable, was even more important than accommodation paper. Critics lumped it together with accommodation paper and considered it the worst of that breed. Yet, commercial paper and the commercial paper market,[5] which is the only financial institution indigenous to the United States, performed an immensely valuable service in carrying on business transactions, for it was the principal means of providing credit for farmers, retailers, and wholesalers who lacked capital.

The country store proprietor commonly acted as a banker for the farmers who were his chief customers. He traded upon an elaborate system of accounts receivable and payable, which needed little cash. A country store frequently went through a week's business without seeing so much as $5 in real money. Since the retailer had no general credit, he established relations with one or two wholesalers. The goods that he bought were mostly staples, accumulated by the wholesaler in anticipation of his busy season. The goods were billed, the bill approved by the buyer and settled immediately either by a promissory note or by draft for acceptance at, for example, eight months' sight. The transaction so far as the sale was concerned was closed; the seller knew exactly the amount and terms of the credit extended, and the buyer often pledged himself to seek no further credit until the note was paid. To obtain money with which to pay the manufacturer or importer for his stock in trade, the wholesaler discounted the notes of the country merchant, endorsing them and thereby making them double-name paper.

Ideally, the three-way transaction was supposed to unravel itself at the harvest season. Sometimes it did and sometimes it didn't. The farmer settled by turning over his crop to the retailer, who in turn shipped the goods to a market where they were sold, and the note to the wholesaler was paid with the proceeds.

[5]By far the best book on commercial paper and the commercial paper market is Albert O. Greef, *The Commercial Paper House in the United States* (Cambridge, Mass.: Harvard University Press, 1938).

The farmer was so dependent upon credit that the seller practically charged whatever price he pleased for his merchandise. Profits were several times what they would have been under a cash system, and people who never did a business of over $300,000 to $400,000 a year retired with fortunes.

The commercial paper business, always of outstanding importance in American trade, underwent a series of significant changes in the decades surrounding the Civil War. These could be grouped under two headings: those that were associated with the general growth of the economy; and those that were induced by the transformation of the prevalent methods of distributing goods.

Early in the century, a middleman had already appeared to create a market in commercial paper. He came with the first banks and the first note brokers. Then as the country's trade and territory expanded and the scale of operations broadened, middlemen became specialized and began to buy and sell commercial paper outright instead of acting as brokers. Private bankers, and to a more limited extent, commercial banks bought and sold paper far from home.

Two other changes of equal importance came in the 1850's when major advancements in transportation, the use of the credit agency, and the spread of country banking encouraged longer sighted wholesalers and jobbers to send salesmen out to the retailer rather than to wait for the retailer to come to them as had been the previous custom. Among other things, this made it possible to buy in smaller lots. The whole evolution brought two important innovations in commercial paper. The terms of credit were shortened because faster transportation speeded the whole process of distribution. At the same time, because of the credit agency, trade bills declined, giving place to single-name promissory notes rather than the two-name acceptance that had previously been the principal document in short-term credit.

The Civil War gave additional impetus to the trend toward shortening credit terms and replacing two-name paper with single-name. Two of the by-products of the War—political uncertainty and rapid currency depreciation—made long-term credit a hazardous adventure. In order to avoid it, wholesalers offered their customers attractive discounts for rapid payment. To take advantage of these discounts, retailers borrowed on their own name in the open market and were encouraged to do so by their bankers.

COMMERCIAL BANK OPERATIONS

Early nineteenth-century bankers considered themselves very busy, but judged by recent standards, the business was extremely small. The Philadelphia Bank employed only nine people in 1803. Around the same time, the Bank of North America, the country's first bank, had only 600 accounts. By the middle of the century the banks had grown, but the biggest one in the country had no more than $2.5 million in deposits and note circulation. The Philadelphia Bank's staff had grown three-fold, while its total assets had grown four and a half times.

The management of these institutions rested in the hands of the cashier, the board of directors, and the president. The decision making power shifted from one to another during the half century considered in this chapter. In the early years, the bank presidents were more or less figureheads. The cashier was the first professional banker. He administered the bank's procedures and took care of day-to-day management. The board of directors made the decisions on loan, discount, and deposit policies. They usually met once a week to pass on loan applications. Their decisions were heavily influenced by friendship, the desire to hold business, and the condition of the money market.

In the early years, the board held the most power, but this could be, and often was, usurped by an able or adroit cashier. By the 1820's, however, the existing arrangement was subject to some penetrating criticism, and things changed once again. Power began to shift toward the bank presidents. Nicholas Biddle, the head of the Bank of the United States, set a dazzling example. He relegated the cashier to a manager and the board to a passive consenting body. At the same time, he created a comprehensive committee system to assist him in running the bank.

Commercial banks were very profitable in the early years of the century, paying 9–12 percent dividends. But competition and the more aggressive behavior of the newer banks lowered the return and at the same time increased the failure rate. By the 1830's, dividends were in the 5–8 percent range. There were no bank failures, as far as we know, until 1809, but by 1815, 208 had occurred. But this resulted partly from a more liberal policy in making loans and was, therefore, not without its advantages. Banking statistics, inadequate though they are, hint that bank loans and investments rose at a rate of better than 5 percent a year, a higher figure than the increase in real national product and somewhat higher than the historical trend in national product in current dollars. To a business system that was starved for capital funds, this was manna indeed.

SAVINGS BANKS AND TRUST COMPANIES

None of the other financial intermediaries—savings banks, trust companies, investment banks, and insurance companies—competed with commercial banks in size or in importance to the total economy.

Savings banks were originally founded in 1816–1819 by merchants "to ameliorate the condition of the poorest classes." As long as the merchants directed them, they conducted themselves in harmony with this original objective. In a few years, however, professional executives took over the management, and the goals and policies of the savings banks changed. Growth now became the main objective, and in order to grow, savings bankers changed both their clientele and their investments. They began to cater to all income groups. They moved out of government obligations and more and more into loans based on "personal security." This change in asset composition could be seen in what happened in specific banks. The Philadelphia Savings Fund began in the 1820's to make three-month loans on a restricted list of securities. The Baltimore Savings Bank had almost three-quarters of its assets in such loans in 1825. In Massachusetts, loans on personal security took about one-quarter of assets in 1835. In the middle 1850's, 40 percent of New York savings bank assets were in stocks, and the largest savings bank in New York City owned more than $4.5 million of stock compared to $2.9 million in bonds and mortgages.

Under the impetus of the more aggressive policy permitted by the changed objective, savings bank deposits grew from about $1 million in 1820 to over $10 million in 1835. But growth had its disadvantages. Savings banks were badly burned in the depression of 1836 and again in 1854–1857. Thereafter they followed a more conservative policy, avoiding business loans and concentrating on mortgages and government bonds.

The largest financial institution of the early nineteenth century and also the most unusual was the Massachusetts Hospital Life Insurance Company chartered in 1818 but commencing business in 1823.[6] The company was similar to a modern trust company, but the funds deposited with it were commingled rather than kept as separate trusts, and it was, therefore, more like a modern investment trust. The diversified merchants and capitalists who founded many of the other early New England intermediaries were also responsible for creating the Hospital Life. Ebenezer Francis, the moving spirit in the Company's founding, was a director of the Boston Bank and later the first director of the Suffolk Bank. William Phillips, the first president, was also president of the Massachusetts Bank and the Provident Institution for Savings. In its first 100 years, one-third of its officers and directors came from 18 proper Bostonian families.

It was, in the words of its first actuary, "a species of savings bank for the rich and middle class." On the liability side, it did not take deposits of less than $500 or for less than five years. On the asset side, it was the most important single source of intermediate-term credit for New England manufacturers. In the years between 1823 and 1860, it loaned $40 million to 42

[6]Gerald T. White, *A History of the Massachusetts Hospital Life Insurance Company* (Cambridge, Mass.: Harvard University Press, 1955).

firms. As a result of its lending policy, it held in 1854 almost $400,000 in stocks. In 1825, 65 percent of its assets were invested in real estate and 32 percent on personal security; by 1835, only 50 percent was in real estate and almost 40 percent was loaned on the personal security of businessmen.

INVESTMENT BANKING

Early American private and investment banks were an outgrowth of shipping, foreign exchange, and merchandizing and later of money brokerage and lottery dealing. Although there were a number of large and respected firms, the business, like all banking in the early nineteenth century, rested on a very weak foundation and most of the early firms failed. The most famous and most respected house was Prime, Ward, & King, but the most important was The Bank of the United States, under the leadership of Nicholas Biddle. There were also J. L. & S. Joseph (agents of the Rothschilds); North American Trust Banking Co.; and Morris Canal & Banking Co. All of these bankers except Prime, Ward, & King failed in the panic and depression of 1837–1843, and Prime, Ward, & King dissolved in the 1840's. Out of the rubble emerged a new group of private bankers, including Drexel & Co.; August Belmont; George Peabody & Co. (later J. S. Morgan & Co.); Speyer & Co.; and E. W. Clark & Co. They remained at the top of the ladder until the 1850's, and some of them—Drexel, Belmont, Speyer and Morgan-Peabody—survived to participate in the intricate banking maneuvers of the late nineteenth and early twentieth century.

The private bankers who began in commerce resembled the British and European merchant banking houses. Indeed, most of them had their origins in Europe. They financed mercantile transactions, followed conservative policies, and became wherever possible family institutions. Alexander Brown was typical. He came to this country in 1801 to start a dry-goods business. Since he had connections in England, he was soon acting as a middleman in foreign exchange, and before long the foreign exchange business displaced the dry-goods business. By 1818, Alexander Brown and his sons were operating branches in Baltimore, Philadelphia, New York, and Liverpool. Although they were great innovators in merchant banking, they avoided investment banking and looked upon the stock exchange with distrust.

The private banking houses that started in money brokerage, that is, in buying paper money at a discount, were altogether different. They were more like investment bankers than merchant bankers, but their activities were quite diversified. Prime, Ward & King, which was founded in 1796 as Nathaniel Prime, Stock and Commission Broker, participated in every security offering in the first quarter century. Most of its business was in gov-

ernment issues, but it also did considerable factoring, insuring, lottery dealing, and merchant banking.

After 1850, the railroads opened a new vehicle for investment banking, and their ascent to titanic heights began at that time. To be sure, all
bankers did not rush immediately to offer the railroads financial help. The
promoters of early New England roads sometimes descended to the level of
soliciting small stock subscriptions from house to house. Winslow, Lanier &
Co., a relatively obscure house, was the real innovator in railroad finance.
In the late 1850's, it was doing a business of $1 million a day. James Lanier
described his firm's activities better than anyone else could:

> At that time there were in operation in the West (Ohio, Indiana,
> Michigan and Illinois) only about six hundred miles of line. These
> roads were chiefly the remains of the old State systems which had been
> sold out to private companies, and were almost without exception
> badly located and imperfectly built. . . . They had, consequently, in-
> volved in heavy loss all who had been engaged in their construction. I
> felt, however, their want of success to be no argument against lines
> properly constructed upon good routes. I undertook to demonstrate
> this in every way in my power, particularly in newspaper articles and
> pamphlets, of which I published great numbers in connection with the
> negotiation of the securities of various companies which we undertook.
> The results of our efforts soon far exceeded our expectations. Although
> we began in a very small way, every step we took gave us increased
> business and strength, and we soon had all the business we could at-
> tend to. . . . We not infrequently negotiated a million of bonds daily.
> The aggregate for the year was enormous. We were without competi-
> tors for a business we had created, and consequently made money very
> rapidly. The commissions for the negotiations of bonds averaged at first
> five percent. . . . Our business soon become so great that it was a ques-
> tion with us, not so much what we would undertake, as what we would
> reject. We not infrequently took, on our own account, an entire issue
> of bonds of important lines.
>
> The negotiation of the securities of companies were followed by ar-
> rangements that made our house the agent for the payment of interest
> accruing on them, as well as transfer agents. Such arrangements nat-
> urally led the way to the banking business to which we afterward
> chiefly confined ourselves.[7]

Meanwhile, too, investment bankers continued to deal in government
securities. The day of important industrial financing was still in the future.

THE BEGINNINGS OF THE STOCK EXCHANGE

Stock exchanges, the milieu of the broker and the investment banker,
first appeared to provide a market for dealing in the public debt, but they

[7]*Sketch Life of J. F. D. Lanier* (New York, 1870) pp. 20–21.

were not active in the early nineteenth century. Federal, state, and local government debt, although growing, was not large; manufacturing companies were for the most part small and closely held; and the general unfamiliarity with securities did not promise a heavy demand for stocks.

In March 1792, a group of New York merchants opened "a stock exchange office" in Wall Street. Eight years later, Philadelphia organized a regular stock exchange, but it never did as much business as the Boston Exchange founded in 1804 or the New York Stock Exchange organized in 1817.

In these early years, there was no such thing as a specialized stock broker. The merchants who dealt in securities did so as part of their diversified financial services. They were also insurers, factors, money lenders, and lottery dealers. The volume of trading in stocks was absurdly low by any standard. Daily turnover averaged 100 shares in 1827 and 1,000 shares in 1830. Yet the dullest day in stock market history occurred on March 16, 1830 when 31 shares changed hands. During the speculative prosperity in 1835, average volume climbed to 6,000 shares. But then after the national debt had been entirely paid off, expert commentators thought that the stock exchange had lost its only excuse for existence. The railroad changed all that. In the boom of the 1850's, transactions over one four-week period totalled almost 1 million shares. By then, $1.5 billion of securities were listed on the exchanges. The New York Central Railroad had 2,500 stockholders and the Massachusetts Western, over 2,300. But there were still no manufacturing stocks traded on the New York Exchange, although there were a handful listed in Boston. In other words, stock exchanges offered no easy answer for manufacturing firms to the problems of raising capital.

6

DISTRIBUTION AND OTHER EARLY NINETEENTH CENTURY PROBLEMS

It is apparent that the problem of raising capital funds—not to mention the problem of acquiring capital goods—loomed large in nineteenth century business. It seemed to most businessmen a more critical problem than the problem of marketing. Yet, at any time, marketing or distribution is a crucial matter.

The problem of marketing encompasses two essential processes: selling goods either directly by the manufacturer or indirectly through wholesalers and retailers, and delivering the goods. Let us consider these activities in reverse order.

Transportation is the real bottleneck in marketing, for there would be little real sense in selling goods if they could not be delivered. One of the preeminent developments in economic and business history during the first half of the nineteenth century was the construction of a comprehensive transportation network. By 1850, the railroad had replaced the rural road, and the steamboat had replaced the flatboat. By then, the transportation channels of domestic commerce were handling over $3 billion in traffic: $1.7 billion in the Atlantic Coast trade; $600 million by canal; $500 million over the railroads; and $300 million on the Great Lakes and the rivers.

There is little point in belaboring what the progress of transportation did for business. If the primary problem of business is to find a customer, the successive stages that were completed in the years before 1850 in the arts of shipping freight went far toward solving half the problem.

SHIPPING GOODS BY NATURAL WATERWAY
AND TURNPIKE

Transporting goods from the place of production to the point of sale had been a persistently thorny problem for the colonial merchant, and it continued to plague the early nineteenth-century businessman. Where possible, goods were carried into the interior areas by water, for natural waterways were inexpensive and more convenient than the primitive means of land transportation. Manufacturers and merchants in Boston, New York, and Philadelphia sent goods north and south along the Atlantic coast. Baltimore merchants had their outlet through the Chesapeake Bay. From the large coastal markets, goods traveled up the Hudson, Delaware, Susquehanna, James, Savannah, and other rivers of all sizes. But the geographic area that rivers could serve was limited. In turn, transport by land had so many disadvantages that it seemed almost impossible. Rutted rural roads were in plentiful supply, but they were for the most part impassable by wagon although they could be traversed by pack horse. Land transportation was, moreover, expensive. It cost as much to ship goods 35 miles inland as it did to ship them to Europe. To ship by pack horse the 300 miles from Philadelphia to Erie cost $250 a ton, almost thirty times as much as the $9 it cost to ship the same goods across the Atlantic.

In a land crying for better means of transportation, the first road of any consequence was the Lancaster Pike, which reached out some 60 miles from Philadelphia to the rich farmlands of the Lancaster area. Its immediate financial success worked up an enthusiasm for building and improving roads, culminating in a turnpike boom, which lasted with undiminished intensity through the middle 1820's and did not die until the mid-1830's. Pennsylvania chartered 86 companies that built more than 2,000 miles of roads at a cost of some $37 million. New York had 135 companies that built 1,500 miles of roads. As early as the 1820's, all the major cities in the United States had been connected by toll roads. Wagon trains were actively carrying freightloads of goods from the coastal cities to places in the interior and bringing interior surpluses back to the coastal cities for export or domestic sale. The teeming traffic was well illustrated by the trade between Philadelphia and Pittsburgh. Despite the difficulties of this hazardous trans-mountain trip, the value of goods shipped by wagon was almost $20 million in 1820. This must have been more than matched by the trade of other better-located eastern cities.

The turnpike companies usually used the corporate form of organization with state legislatures granting charters freely to all applicants. Most of the companies were capitalized at less than $100,000, but several hundred thousands were invested in some of the larger ones. Shares were sold to farmers, professional men, storekeepers, manufacturers, and especially the wealthy merchants, who organized and promoted the companies. State and local governments participated in the financing, some to the extent of complete ownership, and others by the purchase of stock in private companies. About one-third of the financing of Pennsylvania roads was by the state, and Ohio had similar state participation. The total amount of funds invested was considerable for a new nation that had little savings—about $6.5 million in New England by 1840; about $6.0 million in Pennsylvania by 1822; about $5.0 million in Virginia; and comparable amounts in other states.

The turnpikes did cut the time of shipping goods by some 50 to 75 percent, but they were still too time consuming: slow teams averaged only 20 miles a day or 2 miles an hour. On the average it took 26 days to ship goods from Boston to Baltimore and a week from Philadelphia to Pittsburgh. Turnpikes also cut the cost of shipping goods, but it was still expensive. At 15 cents a mile, it did not pay to ship grain or flour more than 150 miles.

River traffic, previously the province of the barge and keelboat, came into its own when Robert Fulton in 1807 demonstrated that the steamboat was commercially feasible. By 1830 it dominated American river transportation and, indeed, all internal transportation. Turnpikes and, later, canals were feeders of river traffic rather than competitors. It was not until the 1850's that railroads proved to be an effective substitute.

Steamboats further reduced the cost and time involved in transporting goods. The first trip up the Mississippi from New Orleans took 35 days as against 90 days on the old flatboat. By 1824 the time was reduced to 10 days, and by 1850 it took only 5 days. At the middle of the century, total tonnage on the Mississippi and on the Great Lakes was twice as much as all the shipping in New York, and the tonnage on the western waterways almost equalled the total tonnage of the entire British Empire. Flatboats and keelboats continued to serve the more isolated areas, but when small steamboats were developed, the more rudimentary craft all but disappeared.

The steamboating business could be entered with a relatively small amount of capital. The cost of a steamboat ran from about $20,000 to $60,-000 for a medium-sized vessel, so that it was not beyond the capacity of a single wealthy individual or a small group. Proprietorships, partnerships, and corporations were all used as legal forms of business with corporations gradually becoming more numerous, especially in the packet-line operations. The initial capital was provided largely by merchants, but with the passage of time, additional investment funds came from reinvestment of earnings, and from businessmen associated with the steamship industry as builders, repairers, and providers of services.

SHIPPING GOODS BY CANAL

With the failure of turnpikes to meet the need for cheap transportation, the country turned to canal building in an effort to solve the problem. The great era of canal building occurred in three waves between 1815 and 1860. Spurred on by the success of the Erie and aided by land grants and stock subscriptions by both federal and state governments, more than 4,200 miles of canals costing almost $200 million were constructed, mostly in New York, Pennsylvania, and Ohio. The canals were effective in reducing the cost of shipping goods. Toll charges ranged from a half a cent to three cents per ton-mile compared with the 15 cents charged by the turnpike. Prior to the completion of the Erie Canal in 1825, it cost a shipper $100 a ton from New York to Buffalo. The Erie immediately reduced this to $15 and eventually to $9.

It was more expensive to construct a canal than to build a turnpike, the average cost per mile being $26,782 in the 1815–1834 period and $64,-206 in the 1844–1860 period. There were only two canals less than one mile in length, and the longest one, the Wabash and Erie in Indiana, was 379 miles long. Clearly, canals required substantial capital investment, so substantial in fact that conservative commentators regarded them as an expensive dream that should be immediately forgotten. *The Albany Gazette and Daily Advertiser* warned Americans against trying to follow the English in building canals. There, it pointed out, "the plentitude of private capital enabled individuals to succeed." Here "individuals generally fail for want of funds."

Certainly domestic private saving did not seem equal to the task of financing the canals. Few individuals invested, and their investment was small. But governments helped solve the problem by making grants and loans and by buying stock in private companies. It is estimated that total public investment amounted to $136.5 million or 73.4 percent of total canal investment of $188.2 million. It is further estimated that about 80 percent of total canal financing (90 percent of the government share) was done by borrowing, so that in the last analysis, most canal investment was financed by private, rather than public sources. At least three-fourths of the $150 million of the borrowed funds came from financial institutions including some $62 million from foreign banking houses, mostly British. Since a great deal of the domestically-purchased bonds were later resold abroad, foreign capital accounted for more than the figures would initially indicate.

Although the canals did succeed in providing a less expensive method of transportation and opened up vast areas of the interior to the coastal markets, only the Erie and a few of the smaller canals were financially successful. The high initial cost of construction, maintenance and repair costs, droughts and floods, under-utilization, and in many cases inefficiency and mismanagement, contributed to their financial woes, which were compounded when the railroads started to provide a faster and more reliable method of transporting goods and people, sometimes with the added indignity of lower rates.

THE RAILROAD

Turnpikes, canals, and steamships had made a considerable contribution to a national marketing system, but the situation was still far from ideal. Goods traveled slowly; bulky goods could not be shipped easily; and there were still too many gaps in the market area. The railroad provided the answer to these problems. It was fast; it had a large carrying capacity; it carried all types of goods; it traveled in all sorts of weather; and man, not nature, could determine its route. The main difficulties in establishing a railroad network were the high cost of construction—in most cases, a minimum of $30,000 a mile—coupled with the scarcity of capital funds and the reluctance of those who had surplus funds to risk them in a new and untried endeavor.

Yet funds were raised, and railroad construction proceeded at a pace so brisk that by 1840 railroad mileage was greater than that of canals. By 1860, the United States could boast of 30,626 miles of railroad. Enough money was raised to meet the $15 million cost of the Baltimore and Ohio, the $30 million of the New York Central, and the $25 million of the Erie. As in the construction of canals, investment came from both public and private sources. Private domestic savings provided most of the initial capital, much of it coming from accumulated profits from foreign trade. Foreign capital, seldom important in initiating a venture, came in later.

Railroad promoters relied mostly on the sale of stock to the more speculative-minded to finance the roads. Sales were made for cash and on the installment plan. Stock was also used to pay for land, labor, and materials. The promoters ignored no prospective investor from the wealthy merchants to the small savers. A popular gambit was to raise funds in a town by a promise to build the road through it.

Governments also assisted in financing early railroads. The federal government contributed by making surveys at government expense and reducing the tariff on iron used in railroad construction. At the beginning of the era some states appropriated funds for railroad construction and some roads were actually completed. Eventually all of these lines passed into private hands. More important was the financial aid given by state and local governments. By 1843, state debts amounting to $43 million were attributed to railroad aid. It is estimated that in the next twenty years, states borrowed another $90 million to finance railroad development. Local and municipal help was even more substantial. By 1870 their contributions equalled at least 20 percent of all railroad costs.

By 1860, railroads had demonstrated their superiority over the other existing methods of transportation. Turnpikes had virtually gone out of existence, and canal building was coming to a halt. Financially, the railroads were a mixed lot. Where efficiently built and conservatively capitalized and constructed to meet an existing economic need, they did well and paid their backers a fair rate of return. Others proved to be disappointing investments. But as the steamships and canals had been responsible for the development of new marketing areas and the growth of new cities, so the railroads furthered this development.

The railroads' indirect effects on business were in the long run perhaps more important than the economies they contributed to the shipping of freight. The real importance of the railroads was that they were innovators in handling large numbers of men and large quantities of money and materials. As such they set an example for manufacturing industry to follow when it reached the stage of big business.

Railroaders, as Alfred D. Chandler has pointed out, "were innovators not because they were necessarily more perceptive, energetic, or imaginative than other businessmen,"[1] but because they were the directors of the country's first big business. The Western Railroad, with only 160 miles of track, cost $7 million in 1842 and the investment in the New York Central, a much longer road, amounted to more than $30 million in 1860. The Erie Canal, which with its 360 miles was in its day the longest canal in the country, cost only $7 million. Other businesses also faded into insignificance when contrasted to the railroad. The cost of one mile of railroad was equal to the cost of one fully equipped river steamboat. In the textile business, the era's leading manufacture, few mills cost as much as $500,000, the equivalent of about ten miles of railroad.

The scale of operations of nonrailroad business was also limited. The largest textile firms employed at most 800 workers; the Erie in the 1850's employed 4,000. The largest manufacturing firms had only one or two plants and could, therefore, be easily administered. The administration of a canal, which might run for a hundred or two hundred miles, was nevertheless equally simple, for the boats that went through the canals were all independently owned. By contrast, railroads ran for hundreds of miles, and their managers had to supervise the operation as well as the maintenance of the equipment that the railroad owned.

Complicated administrative problems, huge construction costs, and heavy investment in equipment produced high operating expenses. It cost the Western Railroad $600,000 to operate in 1850; the Erie's running ex-

---

[1]Alfred D. Chandler, Jr., "The Railroads: Pioneers in Modern Corporate Management," *Business History Review*, Vol. 29, No. 1, Spring 1965.

penses were almost $3 million in 1855, and the Pennsylvania's, a little over $2 million. By contrast, it cost less than $300,000 a year to operate a big textile mill and even less to run a canal.

By its mere size, the railroad presented business and society with new problems and new questions that brought new solutions and new answers. The railroad caused governments to alter their whole attitude toward business. It ended the groping for laissez faire and ushered in a new era of regulation. Labor relations also changed because of the railroad. As Chandler has pointed out, the large national craft union appeared first in railroads.

But it was in business operation that the rails had their greatest impact.[2] They were the initiators of many of the "firsts" in corporation finance, accounting, and management and administration. As we previously pointed out, the railroads were responsible for the first sharp uptrend in stock market activity. At a time when the national government was reducing its debt and few manufacturing firms had "gone public," activity in railroad stocks nourished investment banking and brokerage. Railroads, too, were the first to issue convertible bonds and preferred stocks, and they were the first to use the holding company device.

Heavy capital investment and the complicated financial structure and diverse ownership that this brought about made a fruitful climate for the accounting profession. Bondholders and stockholders were intensely interested in what financial statements could tell them. Freight agents wanted some figures on which they could base their rates. Those in the treasury department wanted to be protected against dishonesty. Those in the controller's office wished to know what should be allocated to fixed capital and what to working capital. Accounting had the answers to all these questions.

It was in the management field, however, that the railroad business wrought its revolution. It was there that the first professional managers appeared in business. These were for the most part engineers who were more or less anonymous in contrast to the promoters and financiers who received the publicity and reknown that were strewn so lavishly throughout the railroad business. As full-time career executives, they were interested only in the mundane task of running a railroad. Even before the 1840's, officials from different roads were visiting each other and discussing how things were done and how they should be done. As Professor Leland Jenks has put it: "They were talking the language of formal organization, distinguishing officers, departments, and divisions from the persons assigned to do the work."[3] They recognized the problem of allocating authority and responsibility.

[2]Alfred D. Chandler, Jr., ed., *The Railroads: The Nation's First Big Business* (New York: Harcourt, Brace & World, Inc., 1965).
[3]Leland H. Jenks, "Early History of a Railway Organization," *Business History Review*, Vol. XXXV, No. 2, Summer 1961.

These engineer-managers understood how substantially the problems of the large road differed from those of the short lines. Daniel C. McCallum, the Erie Railroad's general superintendent, described the difference succinctly. "A superintendent of a road fifty miles in length," he said, "can give its business his personal attention. . . . In the government of a road five hundred miles in length a very different state exists. Any system that might be applicable to the business and extent of a short road would be found entirely inadequate to the wants of a long one."[4]

The engineers visualized an organizational structure quite different from that of Europe. Ideally, this structure would incorporate the advantages of managerial specialization and division of labor. The road would be split into divisions, the functions and the lines of authority of each manager would be carefully defined, and channels of communication would work smoothly to gather and disseminate the information necessary to make the railroad run efficiently. Executive authority would be concentrated in the president of the road, who would operate through departments. He and his directors and top officials would make top-level decisions on such matters as whether and when to expand, how to compete and cooperate with other lines, and how to raise capital. The everyday management—the running of the railroad—would be the job of the road's superintendent and the mass of the road's employees.

None of these innovations in railroad operations appeared suddenly. They were the outcome of years of evolution rather than of a couple of weeks of inspiration. Three managers—Benjamin H. Latrobe, chief engineer of the Baltimore & Ohio, McCallum, and J. Edgar Thomson, president of the Pennsylvania—were responsible in the decade of the 1850's for the initial moves. Latrobe was the first to systematize his railroad's operations. This happened in 1847 when the B. & O. began to extend its line from Harper's Ferry to Wheeling. Before that the road had been only 80 miles long, and it operated reasonably well under a structure that vaguely outlined rather than concisely spelled out the responsibilities and duties of the principal officers. Latrobe's chief innovations were first, to create two departments to oversee the railroad's operations (one to supervise the running of the road and the other to handle the collection and disbursement of revenue) and second, to define clearly the objectives, responsibilities, and duties of the various management officials.

In 1853, the directors of the Erie Railroad, then the longest road in the country, were alarmed by its high cost of operations. They split the road into five divisions, each under the direction of a division superintendent. Then they turned the whole thing over to McCallum to work out an administrative system. In doing so, McCallum followed six general princi-

[4]Quoted in Chandler, *The Railroads*, p. 101.

ples: a proper division of responsibilities; sufficient power to carry out responsibility; the means of knowing whether the responsibilities were being faithfully executed; great promptness in reporting derelictions of duty; daily reports and checks; and a system by which the general superintendent could immediately detect and fix responsibility for errors. Guided by these principles, McCallum worked out lines of authority and responsibility for running the road and channels of communication through which there flowed a stream of information to help the executives in the complicated process of administration and decision-making. To illustrate the new system, McCallum drew a detailed organization chart, one of the first in American business.

What the Erie did was developed to a more sophisticated stage by J. Edgar Thomson of the Pennsylvania. Following the Erie's example, he divided the Pennsylvania into several geographic divisions, each under a superintendent. Then he went further and established a more concise relationship between the operating divisions and the central office. He imposed on McCallum's organization chart a line and staff organization under which the chief executives handled people and the staff executives handled things. His top executives were decision makers, and the divisional, or middle managers handled day-to-day operations.

What the railroads had done was, of course, to create a corporate bureaucracy. Whether this was fortunate or unfortunate was beside the point. It was inevitable because a big business or a big organization could be administered only through a bureaucracy. It was no simple coincidence that the railroads were the first to retain corporation lawyers and the first to employ whole armies of office workers. A business as big and as complicated as a railroad could not proceed except with large numbers of people gathering information, classifying data, keeping records, and managing legal problems. Such routine administration was the very essence of bureaucracy, but any other arrangement would have produced chaos.

SELLING GOODS BEFORE 1850

Distribution requires not only transportation facilities, but also organizations of businessmen to provide the mechanisms through which goods may be exchanged. In addition to roads, railroads, and waterways, distribution or marketing requires a variety of wholesale and retail outlets and ancillary services, such as advertising, to expedite the transfer of goods from the producer to the consumer.

Trade has always been an immense business. Even in the early 1800's, wholesaling and retailing must have accounted for 5 percent of the national income and 4 percent of the labor force compared to its present figures of

15 percent of income and 20 percent of the labor force. In the early nineteenth century, however, the distributive organization was very amateurish. But it did fulfill its function of serving an economy characterized by a small but rapidly growing population, a confused money system, slow transportation facilities, and an agrarian way of life.

In disposing of their goods, manufacturers rarely took care of their own marketing. To be sure, some did experiment with the idea. Early textile mill owners took their goods to Boston, Providence, and other cities, selling or consigning wherever they could to country storekeepers along the way and trading the remainder for raw materials or other goods. Connecticut clockmakers peddled them through the country. Iron manufacturers in western Pennsylvania peddled their wares from flatboats on the Ohio and Mississippi Rivers. Many of the carpet manufacturers marketed their goods directly. In the first few years of the reaper, the McCormick family was the sole agent. They delivered the machines, put them in working order, and instructed the farmers in their use. In these years, McCormick's marketing problem was largely one of teaching the farmer to use machinery, which gives us a clue to why the whole mechanism of direct marketing was temporarily abandoned.

Once an industry could produce large quantities for distribution over a large territory, direct marketing proved cumbersome, and several other types of procedure came into practice. To some extent auction markets were still used for the disposal of surplus stocks that had grown too large for sale through normal channels, and to introduce new styles in order to test their acceptance and obtain some idea of the price at which they could be sold. But a much better and more typical way of distributing goods was through wholesalers, commission merchants, and selling agents. The methods used by Almy and Brown illustrate what happened. In their first years of operation, they sold most of their yarn to weavers in Rhode Island, Connecticut, and Massachusetts. As they expanded production, they began to sell all through New England to retail shopkeepers who took the goods on consignment for a commission. When the West became the main outlet for their product, they found it impossible to find local shopkeepers of reputation to whom they could ship consignments. They resorted, therefore, to commission houses in Philadelphia and Baltimore, the two primary distributing centers for western trade.

COMMISSION MERCHANTS AND SELLING AGENTS

Commission merchants operated on the consignment system, that is, ownership of the goods remained with the manufacturer until the sale was made and the goods delivered to the purchaser. In the major distribution centers, a different arrangement prevailed. There, wholesalers purchased directly from the mill or the commission merchant and supplied both the city retailers and the jobbers who resold to the country trade. The third middleman, the selling agent, was originally much the same as the commission merchant. He was still an agent rather than a principal, and still handled goods on consignment. The important difference at first was that he had an exclusive agency. Later, he took on a more important role in the firm's affairs. The practice seems to have originated with Nathan Appleton, who had financial interests in the Boston Manufacturing Company and in B. C. Ward & Co., a commission house. The Boston Company arranged for B. C. Ward to sell the output of the mill. Before 1819 Ward sold the goods at auction, but in that year a contract was made establishing Ward as exclusive agent for a commission of 1 percent. The Pepperell Manufacturing Co. also followed this procedure, using Francis Skinner & Co. of Boston and New York. Skinner, like most agents, handled the output of several mills. The maximum commission allowed him was 1¾ percent. Subagents in Boston and Philadelphia received an additional 2 percent.

The use of an exclusive selling agent created a much more intimate relationship. The agent assumed full responsibility for marketing and used whatever selling methods he thought necessary. But he also took on several other functions that were helpful to the manufacturer. At a time when business obligations were paid mainly by promissory notes due six or eight months from date and when many banks either refused to discount such paper or would do so only at high rates of interest, the selling house became the manufacturer's banker. Relying on the sales of goods to reimburse them, the selling houses extended funds in sums of $5,000 to $10,000 and were often the manufacturer's creditor to the extent of $100,000. There were years when the interest on funds thus advanced provided the selling house with nearly 20 percent of its total income.

Selling agents also assumed all debts arising out of a sale, thus freeing the manufacturer from the risks of nonpayment. For this "factoring" function, a charge of 2–4 percent was made. A court ruling in 1839 decreed that payment to agents advancing funds on goods could be made only from the proceeds of the sale of the goods. This increased the agent's risk on advances, for declining prices could result in a considerable financial loss for the agent who advanced too large an amount. Because of this, agents started to take a more active role in manufacturing policy. It was a common practice for them to buy shares in manufacturing companies, and it was not at all unusual for them to be represented on the board of directors of the mill.

During the first half of the century, the use of exclusive selling agents was the prevalent mode of marketing, but toward the middle of the century, another variation developed. This was the dealership, a forerunner of the present method of selling automobiles. The first wide use of dealers began in 1845 when Cyrus McCormick hired his first agent. Like the selling agent, he sold on commission, and the machine was delivered to the buyer when he met the initial down payment. The agents worked under a contract that provided that they should maintain a sample machine, canvass the wheat districts in their territory, deliver reapers, instruct purchasers in machine operation, stock spare parts, repair machines, collect bills, and distribute advertising. They often operated through sub-agents who were the first farm implement retailers. They were supplied with sales arguments, but when competition was strong, they were expected to rely on their own ingenuity.

McCormick was an innovator in other areas of marketing as well. He was a heavy advertiser, a regular attender of agricultural fairs, and an early user of installment credit. As his grandson later expressed it, McCormick invented the reaper, and he also invented the means to make it attainably useful to farmers.

WHOLESALING AND RETAILING

In the underdeveloped economy of early nineteenth-century America, it was not uncommon for one firm to handle wholesaling and retailing and all the ancillary institutions connected with distribution. As in colonial days, a merchant, especially on the frontier, was a wholesaler, retailer, banker, insurance agent, and real-estate operator.

Gradually, specialized houses stepped in and replaced the jack-of-all-trades merchant, taking over each of the subordinate steps. The process began in wholesaling, and before the nineteenth century was very old, its organization had already become complicated. Sedentary merchants in the large seaport cities imported goods and sold them for their own account. In domestic trade, commission merchants sold for their own account and for others; jobbers vended dry goods to country retailers; factors financed producers and acted as their agents in the sale of goods, especially cotton textiles; selling agents were already active in disposing of goods made by domestic producers; and dealers handled farm equipment.

The usual trade channel for foreign goods was from the importer to the jobber to the retailer to the consumer. But the auction system flourished from the end of the War of 1812 to about 1830. Under the auction system, goods were sold through agents to retailers who came to the market cities about twice a year. The system was especially economical for British producers, who had a large volume of goods to sell, for eliminating the importer and the jobber could save as much as 25 percent of the costs of distribution.

So long as imported goods were so important, and so long as retailers continued to come to the Atlantic seaboard cities in large numbers, the auction system worked very well. But when domestic production began to catch up to foreign production, and when competition forced producers to adopt more aggressive selling methods, the auction system began to fail. Cincinnati and St. Louis developed as wholesale centers in the late 1840's, and as wholesaling became established in the West, western retailers no longer found it necessary to take the long journey East to buy goods. Moreover, by buying at private sale rather than at auction, buyers could obtain better credit terms.

Although wholesale trade was already specialized as early as 1800, it took much longer for most retail trade to become similarly specialized. Because of poor transportation facilities, most of it continued as in colonial times to be conducted in limited areas. The country trade was still at mid-century carried on by "country pay," that is, by barter on an open book account. Peddlers were still in business, although their trade was declining rapidly. Traveling along remote trails, and by raft or flat boat on the waterways, they called on farmers in outlying regions, trading thimbles, needles, and other things for farm products, rags, and other articles. Occasionally, these petty capitalists were large-scale operators, employing as many as 200 horses and 100 men and supplying trading posts and country stores in the outlying areas with goods from the market centers on the Atlantic Coast. Both the peddler and the community market have survived to the present day, but by the early nineteenth century, they were already far behind the small-town general store and the city specialty shop. As early as 1840, there was one store for every 300 people, which meant a severe curtailment of the peddler's opportunities.

As in colonial days, the general store was the principal intermediary between the wholesaler and the consumer. As its name implied, it sold a wide variety of goods, for the demand for any one class of commodities was not large enough to permit specialization. Except in the large cities, retail stores carried a miscellaneous stock of imported manufactures, tropical goods, such as sugar and spices, and the staples of the surrounding country. Thomas Ashe's description of a Western Pennsylvania store in 1806 would apply equally well to any frontier retail store at a later date:

> These storekeepers are obliged to keep every article which it is possible that the farmer or manufacturer may want. Each of their shops exhibits a complete medley; a magazine where are to be had both a needle and an anchor, a tin pot and a large copper boiler, a child's whistle and a pianoforte, a ring dial and a clock, a skein of thread and trimmings of lace, a check frock and a muslin gown, a frieze coat and a superfine cloth, a glass of whiskey and a barrel of brandy, a gill of vinegar and a hogshead of Madeira wine.[5]

5Quoted in Fred Mitchell Jones, *Middlemen in the Domestic Trade of the United States, 1800–1860* (Urbana, Ill.: University of Illinois, 1937), p. 44.

Although the general stores carried a wide variety of articles, their total stock was small. Many stores occupied only a few square feet, and a box or chest held the entire stock. The stock of luxuries or finery was especially small because the demand for them was limited, it was difficult and expensive to transport them, and the store owner did not think the turnover large enough to warrant putting much money into them.

Usually, the general-store proprietor went in person to the large market cities—Philadelphia, Baltimore, and New York, in the early nineteenth century, and also to Cincinnati and St. Louis around the middle of the century. He bought goods at auction or from wholesalers on very liberal credit terms. The cost in time and money for this annual or bi-annual visit was high. It cost, for example, $300 and took anywhere from $1\frac{1}{2}$ to 3 months for a merchant to make the trip from Cincinnati to Philadelphia around 1820. The average country store did about $15,000 to $20,000 business a year, but sales ran as low as $1.25 a day and as high as $60,000 a year. Because the operation was small and the storekeeper usually held a local monopoly, markups were high: 25 percent over and above all expenses barely kept the proprietor in business; 50 percent was fair; but prosperity required 75 percent.

Most country stores' trade was conducted on a barter basis, but there were certain "cash articles" that could not be bought except with money. These included tea, coffee, leather, iron, powder, and lead. But linen, cloth, feathers, beeswax, deerskins, and furs were regarded as money when offered by the would-be purchaser. Because of the prevalence of barter, storekeepers had little cash, but wholesalers and manufacturers accepted as pay the goods that the storekeepers had acquired in trade, and the storekeeper disposed of any surplus by shipping it down river to a commission merchant. In time, of course, this practice became outmoded, but it was quite common in the late 1830's and had not completely disappeared by the 1850's.

Transactions in frontier stores were more often than not a matter of bargaining between the store owner and the shopper. In the sale of specialized products like dry goods, haggling was universal. On basic commodities, many stores followed a one-price policy; but where a proprietor had a monopoly position over a relatively wide area, it was customary to bargain. In such extreme cases, something as basic as coffee sold anywhere from 25 cents to $1.25 a pound, depending on the financial status of the buyer.

There was little competition among storekeepers. There was no price competition, because the general stores usually had a monopoly. Nonprice competition seemed pointless because of the shortage of goods. If the supply was limited, there was no reason to make any special effort to drum up demand by the usual strategies of product differentiation, such as special packaging, service, advertising, and emphasis on brand names.

The general store in every small town, especially on the frontier, was an economic and social institution—as important as the church and probably more important than the school. The country-store proprietor was an unusually influential citizen. No specialist himself, he enabled others to specialize. He was often banker as well as merchant. By buying goods on long-term credit and selling them to customers on open-book account, he brought capital to the outlying regions from the better-developed areas. To be sure, the system was expensive. Prices were about twice as high as back East, but this was the price that had to be paid for small-scale operations, the large volume of credit business, and the high cost of shipping goods.

In the big cities these disadvantages did not exist or they were much less important, permitting specialized retailing to appear fairly early. By 1800, specialty stores handled groceries, hardware, and dry goods. There were drug stores and book stores; but it was not until 1831 that a haberdashery appeared in New York City, and there were no retail jewelry, furniture, or shoe stores before 1850.

THE PROBLEM OF A LABOR SUPPLY

Entrepreneurs needed money, materials, and markets, but they also needed men—or, in this early day, children—to run the machinery, to wait on the customers, and to keep the books and records. Despite the rapid increase in the population, the lure of the land remained strong enough to create a relative labor scarcity. However, the continued growth of the native population and the later influx of immigrants provided a gradual solution to the problem.

The lack of adequate transportation facilities imposed another obstacle in the way of recruiting a labor force. A small manufacturer, hiring only a few hands, might depend on those in the immediate area, but when large mills were constructed requiring a commensurately large labor force, both skilled and unskilled, a different solution had to be found. Either the factory had to be constructed where a labor force already existed or the labor force had, in some way, to be brought to the factory.

The early New England factory entrepreneurs developed two ways of hiring labor to provide the necessary hands to work the machines: the family system and the boardinghouse system. The Slater mills were the outstanding example of the family system. When the first mill opened, all nine operatives were children. To augment his labor supply, Slater persuaded whole families to move to Pawtucket. Naturally, the system recruited many more children than men and women. By 1801, Slater employed more than 100 children between the ages of four and ten.

The mills that used the system were usually equipped with the spinning mule and used the men for this heavier and more arduous work, with the women and children performing the lighter and easier work. Usually, the families occupied company houses. Although it would seem that employers would have to build housing that was appealing enough to attract families from other areas, this was not the case. Company housing was just as grim as workers' houses were in the textile centers of Europe, and they added an austere note to what might otherwise have been an attractive village.

The boardinghouse or Waltham plan was quite different from the family system of hiring, and nothing in modern employment remotely resembles it. The Boston Associates invented the plan in order to provide a labor supply for their rural mills where no local labor supply was available. The basic idea was to recruit young women from New England farms and to provide housing for them in dormitory-type residences near the factories. The system not only economized on food and shelter, it also provided respectable surroundings and supervision of the girls' conduct while away from home. They were required to be in their rooms by 10 P.M., to attend church services, and to be modest and industrious.

Conditions at the boardinghouse mills seem to have been better than those at the family-type, with wages ranging from about $2.50 to $3.50 a week from which was deducted about $1.25 a week for board. Despite the low rate of pay, some of the ex-farm girls managed to save a bit each week, and their dormitory-type living conditions were certainly no worse than those of factory workers elsewhere including Great Britain. At about 1835, domestic service offered only about 75 cents a week plus board, a school mistress could earn about $2.00 plus board but her employment was for only four and a half months, and seamstresses earned about $1.00 a week in Philadelphia and Baltimore, and 75 cents in New York.

The hiring of women and children was a permanent policy during the first half of the nineteenth century. In 1820, children constituted about 45 percent of all Massachusetts cotton-mill workers and 55 percent of those in Rhode Island. This high rate decreased by 1832, but it still covered 21 percent of labor in Massachusetts and 41 percent in Rhode Island. Women supplied much of the rest of cotton-textile labor. In 1832 there were three women for every two men, and in the Pepperell Mills in the 1850's, 66 percent of the workers in Mill 1 and 80 percent of those in Mill 2 were women.[6]

In the woolen mills, children were not so prevalent even in 1820. In the Massachusetts mills the ratio was 48 percent men, 28 percent women, and 24 percent children; and for the country as a whole, 50, 17, and 33 percent. After 1820, the use of children decreased and that of women increased, just as it did in the cotton mills. By 1832, the number of children employed in the factories of the leading woolen producers had declined to 8 percent

[6]Evelyn H. Knowlton, *Pepperell's Progress* (Cambridge, Mass.: Harvard University Press, 1948), pp. 30–47.

of the labor force. The percentage of women workers had meanwhile increased to 49 percent. The use of women was of particular benefit to the mill owners, for they were paid about half the wages paid to men.

The supply of labor for the growing industries was also augmented by the flow of immigrants. Of only minor importance in the first quarter of the century, their ranks swelled in the years 1833–1837, and again in the 1840's and 1850's. In 1826, only 38 foreigners were employed at Fall River out of a total of 612 operatives; twenty years later they were a majority of the factory workers in that district. Lowell relied much longer on native labor. In 1842, only 50 out of 1,500 workers in the Merrimac mills were foreigners.

Clark writes that "from the time our first factories were started . . . , a continuous immigration of spinners and weavers ensued from northern England and Ireland." But actually spinners and weavers (only a small part of total immigration) averaged only 289 a year from 1820 to 1860 and far less during the latter two decades of that period. Only in the 1830's did they arrive in large numbers, averaging 660 a year. Nevertheless, immigrants did make a conspicuous contribution to the labor force, especially in the years after 1840. Of great importance was the fact that from 1820–1860 more than 60 percent of the immigrants were males and 81 percent of them were of working age (15 and over). 74 percent of female immigrants were also of working age. Over the period, only 0.2 percent of the immigrants professed to be weavers and spinners. But it is more than likely that although a large percentage of immigrant labor performed unskilled work on roads, canals, and railroads, many of the so-called unskilled found their way into the mills and factories.

Foreigners found ready work in the carpet mills as both supervisory personnel and workmen, with a predominance of English, Scotch, and Germans. Scotch weavers at the Thompsonville mill were so numerous that Orrin Thompson was said to have "colonized his village." When improved machinery permitted the substitution of women for men as carpet weavers, the mill-owners were pleased to lessen their dependence on the foreign-born artisans, for by the late 1840's and early 1850's, it was thought that immigrants were a disturbing influence in the labor force.[7]

WAGES AND WORKING CONDITIONS

No one could rightly accuse the early manufacturing entrepreneurs of being profligate in the wages they paid or of being over-fastidious in the working conditions they provided. Undoubtedly, wages and working condi-

[7]Arthur H. Cole and Harold F. Williamson, *The American Carpet Manufacture* (Cambridge, Mass.: Harvard University Press, 1941), pp. 37–38, 57–58.

tions varied from place to place and mill to mill, but in most places the lot of the factory worker like that of the Gilbert and Sullivan policeman was not a happy one.

Industry's prevailing wage theory was more attuned to the commodity theory than to paternalism. Employers paid what they had to in order to attract suitable labor to the mills. As expressed by the agent of a Fall River industrialist:

> As for myself, I regard my work-people just as I regard my machinery. So long as they can do my work for what I choose to pay them, I keep them, getting out of them all I can. What they do or how they fare outside my walls I don't know, nor do I consider it my business to know. They must look out for themselves as I do for myself. When my machines get old and useless, I reject them and get new, and these people are part of my machinery.[8]

It can be said that on the average, workers were paid about $1 a day in the years 1800 to 1860, but there was some variation over time and considerable variation among different occupations. Over the first thirty years of the century, average wages were more like 80 cents a day, and in the 1840's and 1850's, they were more like $1.25 than $1.00.

TABLE 3 Median and Average Daily Wages, 1800–30 and 1830–60

Occupation	1800–30		1830–60
Workers at Boston Mfg. Co.			
1817 median	.60		––
1817 average	.85	(1851–60)	1.03
Metal fabricators			
Mass. median (1829)	.80	(1859)	1.22
Machinists (1817)	1.43	(1832)	1.20
Carpet workers, average (1829)	1.00	(1849)	1.00
Woolen workers (1829)	.85		––
Agricultural machinery			
Smiths	––	(1856)	1.25
Foremen, bricklayers, carpenters	––		2.50

Skilled workers—machinists, mule spinners, foremen, and such—made approximately twice as much as the average. Supervisory employees and executives, of which there were a constantly growing number, made much more. Factory overseers, *circa* 1830, earned as much as $18 a week and clerks as much as $9. An 1825 bank paid its president $2,000 a year. Toward the

[8]Norman Ware, *The Industrial Worker, 1840–1860* (Boston: Houghton Mifflin Company, 1924), p. 77.

middle of the century, a railroad president cost $3–5,000 a year. The agent of the Pepperell Mills earned $3,500, and the treasurer of the Lowell Mills, $3,000. By the 1860's, the general superintendent of the McCormick Plant was being paid $7,000.

There were, of course, many more who worked in business at the other end of the pay scale. Women earned approximately half what men earned. Children received the lowest wage of all, approximately half of what women earned. The businessman, in short, had a simple rule of thumb, not an elaborate economic theory, by which to guide his wage policy. The average pay for a skilled male worker was $1 a day, the maximum for a female was 50 cents, and the most for a child was 25 cents. Apprentices, who were a special case, were ordinarily paid $25-$30 the first year, $40 to $50 the second, and $60-$75, the third.

Some industries were notoriously low payers. The needle trades were outstanding in this respect. In 1845, seamstresses were working for as little as 10 cents a day. Although most received more, average weekly earnings were about $1.50-$2.00. Things were no better in the 1850's when journeymen dressmakers in New York worked 14 to 16 hours a day for $1.25 to $2.50 a week. The Phoenix Manufacturing Company of Paterson, New Jersey paid unusually low wages. In 1828 men received $3.90 a week while women received $2.75. It paid its child workers a miniscule 23 cents a day. The Troy Company did even worse, paying as little as 33 cents a week.

Forging and smelting, although better than the clothing industry, were nevertheless below the average. In the Baltimore Iron Works in 1843, laborers did arduous and heavy work for 66 cents a day, while the furnacemen received the princely sum of $1.00. Rates in Pittsburgh iron foundries were about the same. Lead smelters at Galena made as much as $6.25 a week, but laborers, only $4.00.

The cost of living was, to be sure, much lower then than it is now. Budget makers thought that a family of five could get along on $600 a year, but this was just getting along on a mere subsistence basis, and most workers could not afford even that. Fortunately for them, they were not the only wage earners in the family. But even so, any unforeseen emergency pushed the average working family over the precipice of poverty.

The most common of these unforeseen emergencies was business recession or depression. In the first 60 years of the 1800's, there was probably one year of recession for every one and a half of prosperity. Workers were especially hurt in the depressions of 1819, 1837, and 1857. During the depression of 1819, estimates of unemployment in Philadelphia ranged from 5,000 to 20,000, and in Pittsburgh the total employed decreased by more than 60 percent. During the depressed 1830's, wage reductions were a constant source of friction between workers and mill-owners. The workers at one mill in Philadelphia had their wages cut from $1 per cut making tickings to 60 cents. At other Philadelphia mills, wages were reduced by 20 to 25 percent. Similar reductions were also made by the New England mills, and they continued into the 1840's. In 1840, a Congressman wrote that "labor commands but little more than half the wages it did a year ago." In the early 1840's, the Mayor of New York bitterly remarked:

> Our streets are filled with wandering crowds. . . . Petitions signed by hundreds asking for work are presented in vain . . . thousands must therefore wander to and fro on the face of the earth, filling every part of our once happy land, with squalid poverty, and with profligacy.[9]

Labor suffered equally in the late 1850's when cotton textile employment in Rhode Island fell by 68 percent, jewelry by 78 percent, and ironworks employment by 43 percent. Congress was informed that not 20 percent of the nation was steadily employed, and skilled artisans offered their services in Philadelphia at 60 cents a day.

There were other working and living conditions that made life difficult for the industrial worker. Hours of work were from sunup to sundown, six days a week, which meant a 72- to 75-hour week, or roughly twice as many hours as today.

Workers were bound by contracts that specified the terms under which they were to work—the length of the contract, the wage, method of payment, the work they were to perform, and the rent of the tenement if they were to live in one. Families were required to live up to the letter of the contract under penalty of discharge, eviction, and at times the blacklist. Enforcement was at the option of the employer. The Cocheco Company required the employees to "conform in all respects, to the regulations which are now, or may hereafter be adopted, for the good government of the institution; to work for such wages as the company may see fit to pay." Typical was the following:[10]

1. The hours of work shall be from sunrise to sunset, from the 21st of March to the 20th of September inclusively; and from sunrise until eight o'clock, P.M., during the remainder of the year. One hour shall be allowed for dinner, and half an hour for breakfast, during the first mentioned six months; and one hour for dinner during the other half year; on Saturdays, the mill shall be stopped one hour before sunset, for the purpose of cleaning the machinery.
2. Every hand coming to work a quarter of an hour after the mill has been started, shall be docked a quarter of a day; and every hand

[9]Stanley Lebergott, "The Pattern of Employment Since 1800," in Seymour E. Harris (ed.) *American Economic History* (New York: McGraw-Hill Book Company, 1961), p. 295.
[10]William A. Sullivan, "The Industrial Revolution and The Factory Operative in Pennsylvania," *The Pennsylvania Magazine of History and Biography*, Vol. LXXVIII (1954), pp. 478–479.

absenting him or herself, without absolute necessity, shall be docked in a sum double in amount of the wages such hand shall have earned during the time of such absence. No more than one hand is allowed to leave any one of the rooms at the same time,—a quarter of a day shall be deducted for every breach of this rule.

3. No smoking or spirituous liquors shall be allowed in the factory, under any pretense whatsoever. It is also forbidden to carry into the factory, nuts, fruits, etc.: books or papers, during the hours of work. . . .

• • •

7. Every hand (excepting those who rent a tenement belonging to this concern), shall give at least two weeks' notice of his or her intention to depart from or cease working in this factory, and the said hand shall continue to work in it, if required so to do, during and until the expiration of the said two weeks. In case of failure herein, the said hand shall forfeit all the wages which may be due to him or her at the time of leaving the mill.

If employees left without giving two weeks' notice, they were to forfeit two weeks' pay. They were not to organize or strike under penalty of a fine. The employers' power over the workers was just about complete, and they maintained and circulated a blacklist that excluded further employment in all boarding-house mills and many which were not. The Lowell Mills issued "discharge papers" to employees who left for good cause (management's evaluation), and no other mill was supposed to hire a person who did not have these papers.

The mill continued to pursue the worker even after his daily work was presumably finished. Wages in the family mills were seldom paid in cash, but in all or in part by due-bills drawn on the company store. Cash payments while reckoned on a daily basis were paid quarterly, monthly, and sometimes semi-monthly but seldom more frequently than that, and even then there were delays in payment because of intermittent shortages of cash. Mills sorely in need of workers would advertise cash and bi-weekly payment as added inducements. In the Lowell shops wages were computed daily and paid twice a month. At Brittania wages were computed monthly and settled quarterly.[11]

The company store was an important part of the business to many a manufacturer. It usually carried dry goods and food, which were sold to the employees at "the usual profit of country trading stores." As a condition of employment, workers at the Slater mill in Webster signed an agreement that, "I further promise and agree that I will not trade, or make purchases, at any store whatsoever, during the above period" except at the stores "belonging to Mr. Slater." In the boot and shoe industry in the 1850's workers

[11]George S. Gibb, *The Whitesmiths of Taunton* (Cambridge, Mass.: Harvard University Press, 1943), pp. 39, 143; George S. Gibb, *The Saco-Lowell Shops* (Cambridge, Mass.: Harvard University Press, 1950), p. 54.

received their $1.00 to $1.33 a day "mostly in cash" but also in cheese, flour, butter, and leather stock. Even where no formal agreement was made, announcements such as the following served the same purpose and usually the same result:

> Notice. Those employed at these mills and works will take notice that a store is kept for their accomodation, where they can purchase the best goods at fair prices, and it is expected that all will draw their goods from said store. Those who do not are informed that there are plenty of others who would be glad to take their places at less wages. Crompton Mills, Feb. 1843.

Attempts by labor to better its lot occurred mostly in the skilled trades but even there it met with little success. The boardinghouse girls walked out several times, but without organization, leadership, and a strike fund, they gained nothing. The organized unions suffered from the same handicaps as well as opposition from the press and the courts. But unions were organized and strikes did take place. Between 1834 and 1837, Commons notes the organization of 152 unions. During the same period about 170 strikes were declared.

COMPANY PROFITS AND PERSONAL FORTUNES

A true picture of the profitability of the early manufacturers is difficult to develop. For one thing, accounting records are not good enough to lead to an accurate conclusion. Undoubtedly, they were an improvement over those kept earlier, but they were far below later standards. The usual records kept in the mills included daybooks, cash books, bill books, lists of invoices, payroll accounts, production records, mill expenses, and records of cotton waste disposal. The Boston Manufacturing Company kept close control over its operations to the point of using a crude but workable cost-accounting system, with cost-allocation of administrative expenses, but this was considerably beyond what most other firms did.

Even the meager records available leave much to be desired. It would seem, however, from the available data, reports, and statements, that profits were a function of size of plant, prices, competition, and the vagaries of the business cycle. There was a high mortality rate among the smaller firms, and most firms were small. Someone once asked the prominent merchant, Nat Griswold, how many businessmen had succeeded over the previous fifty years. "The average," he replied, "was seven in the hundred. All the rest, ninety-three in the hundred of untold thousands, have been bankrupts." But the great merchants and the large mechanized mills with sufficient capital and the economies of mass production were able to weather the periodic storms and return substantial profits. At least, this is what we may conclude from the accounts of the fortunes accumulated by individuals from their business activities. *Hunt's Merchants' Magazine* said, in 1846, that Boston had 456 people with fortunes of from $100,000 to $6,000,000.

At about the same time, almost 1,000 fortunes of $100,000 or more were counted in New York. Of these, 96 were estimated at $500,000 or more. Apparently, the best way to riches was through success as a merchant; 40 of the 96 made their fortunes by this means; 22 inherited money; 9 made it in land; but only 6 in manufacturing and 4 in banking and brokerage.

In 1831, Samuel Slater reported that most manufacturers earned slight profits. That is to say, they earned very little above their wages and the ordinary interest on their investment.[12] This should be taken with more than the usual grain of salt, for profit in those days was often defined as the amount of income above the legal interest rate. Slater's judgment applied particularly to the small factories that were typical of American manufacturing during the years prior to 1830. These mills did not necessarily close, for unprofitable mills could contribute to the profits of the mill-owner's store where workers were paid in goods. But they could not withstand the storms and stresses of depression. In 1828, woolen manufacturers testified that they had been losing money, and in 1832 it was estimated that up to that time all the money invested in American woolen mills had been lost to the original owners. The eastern Pennsylvania iron manufacturers, similarly small businessmen, suffered severely during the depression of the 1830's and early 1840's with almost one-third of them passing through the hands of the sheriff.

On the other hand there were industries and firms reporting large, though not necessarily consistent, profits during the period. An account of dividends paid by 24 New England textile companies from 1839 to 1849 indicated an average return of 10 percent on aggregate capital exceeding $20,000,000. The highest average was 14 percent by the Merrimac Company, the largest of the reporting companies. From 1846 to 1850 a select list of cotton mills owned by Boston industrialists also averaged a 14 percent return on capital. Iron ore furnaces, a very cyclical business, were reported in 1832 to have paid average dividends of 18 percent, and according to one authoritative report, earnings of foundries and machine shops ranged from 10 to 25 percent in the mid-1840's, after the earlier depression had exhausted its blows.

Evidence suggests that profits for the larger cotton mills were high during booms and low during depressions with a general decline over the entire period. According to Caroline Ware, the entire industry showed an average return of a little above 3 percent on all invested capital. The rela-

---

[12]Caroline F. Ware, *The Early New England Cotton Manufacture* (Boston, Mass.: Houghton Mifflin Company, 1931).

tively high profits of the more successful mills were averaged out by lower returns and failures of the others.

Contrary to what classical economic theory may have taught, profit of individual firms strayed far from the norm. From 1816 to 1826, the Boston Manufacturing Company earned 18.75 percent. The Masonville Company in Connecticut earned 50 percent a year from 1827–1831. Pepperell was consistently profitable; in some years profits exceeded 50 percent of capital stock. The Lowell Manufacturing Company earned 12 percent from 1831–1836, 8 percent from 1837–1842, and 7 percent from 1843–1852. The Hartford Carpet Company averaged 12 percent a year from 1854–1859, during which period Lowell earned 8.6 percent. At the Boston Manufacturing Company machine shop profits averaged about 50 percent of sales from 1817 to 1823.

Dividend payments by the large textile mills show a definite cyclical trend. The dividends of the manufacturing corporations listed on the Boston Stock Exchange averaged 11.4 percent through 1836, 9.7 percent from 1837 through 1846, and dropped further to 5.86 percent from 1847 through 1859. The Appleton Company, which had paid out 15.6 percent in the period 1831–1835, was paying only about 7 percent in the 1840's and 1850's. Chicopee went from 10.0 percent (1831–1835) to 1.2 percent in the 1850's, and similar declines in dividend payouts were true for Dwight, Hamilton, and others.

TABLE 4   Average Dividend Payments of Textile Mills, 1830–60 (percent of par value)

Mill	1831–1835	1836–1840	1841–1850	1851-1860
Appleton	15.6	3.4	6.7	7.5
Bartlett			7.4	6.3
Chicopee	10.0	5.0	4.2	1.2
Dwight			11.0	3.8
Great Falls		2.0	10.5	6.7
Hamilton	15.6	5.4	7.4	7.7
Lawrence		6.4	8.6	6.2

Source: Gras and Larson, *Casebook in American Business History,* pp. 672, 703.

The chief culprit in keeping profits down was the business cycle, but it had a close rival in competition. Like the business cycle, there was little that businessmen seemed able to do to control it, except in the short run. Producers constantly resorted to gentlemen's agreements to fix prices. Temporarily, these were successful, but as has long since been proved, there were few gentlemen involved in a gentlemen's agreement.

7

THE APPEARANCE
OF BIG BUSINESS,
1850–1900

During the last half of the nineteenth century the United States completed the transition from an agricultural to an industrial economy. Production and business activity soared as never before. Although many of the leading industries of the pre-1850 period continued to grow with the country, it was the appearance of new industries and new types of entrepreneurship that provided the romance and excitement of the late nineteenth century. There emerged a group of business leaders patterned after Schumpeter's "heroic entrepreneur," although they were described by others in somewhat less flattering phrases. Be that as it may, by the end of the century the United States had emerged as the industrial leader of the world, and her business leaders had become household names to the millions of Americans who were eager to emulate their success.

THE ECONOMIC BACKGROUND

The Civil War dealt a shattering blow to population growth. To be sure, population did continue to increase, but at a lower rate than in the pre-Civil War period. By 1900 the United States contained 76.1 million people, about two-and-one-half times the 1860 number. The increase from 1820 to 1860 had been about three times. As the population multiplied we also became much more urban. City population surpassed farm population by 1890. By the end of the century, only 35 percent of the labor force was in farming, and 40 percent of the people resided in urban areas, double the percentage in 1860. At the same time, however, the population was spreading out. The Census Bureau announced the end of the frontier line in 1890, and by 1900 more than one-third of the continental population lived in the Middle West.

The United States was also becoming a more productive and richer country. It is estimated that the gross national product in real terms increased from an average of $12.8 billion (1947 dollars) in the 1869–1873 period to $52.3 billion in 1897–1901.[1] Although the data are admittedly even rougher than most estimates of this important economic statistic, they unmistakingly indicate the trend.

There are still other ways of noting the growth and changes in the postwar economy that had more than passing significance for business. In 1860 mass production was still rare. By 1894, when she produced twice as much as Great Britain did, the United States had definitely taken world leadership in manufacturing. As a natural consequence of this growth, the structure of American industry changed radically. Manufacturing was no longer so closely confined to processing agricultural products, but had moved into producers' goods as well. Of the ten leading industries at the end of the century, four were in producers' goods. By 1900, there were twenty-six industries with a net product of more than $50 million a year, compared with only two in 1860. Only five of the ten 1860 leaders were among the first ten in 1900. Cotton textiles, first in 1860, had dropped to seventh place in 1900, and the leading industry of 1900 (foundry and machine-shop products) had not been in the top ten in 1860.

The economic progress that was demonstrated by the rapid rise in the national income, thriving industrialism, and the transformation of the industrial structure did not take place in a straight line. It was not a case of onward and upward in a steady climb to successive peaks of prosperity. On the contrary, the last fifty years of the 1800's witnessed a series of economic disasters—the panics and depressions of 1857, 1873, and 1893—that were among the longest and most severe in the country's economic history.

Technology was the precipitating factor in whatever transformation had occurred in American society. Consider this roll call of later nineteenth-century technological achievements: the accelerated use of agricultural machinery, the extensive construction of railroads, the Bessemer and open-hearth processes that turned the age of iron into the age of steel, and the introduction of electricity and the internal combustion engine in the 1890's. In addition, equally important if less publicized developments took place in the office and its environs—the typewriter, the telephone, the linotype, the rotary press, and, wonder of wonders, carbon paper.

[1] In per capita terms the increase was from $360 to $795, or 120 percent.

THE HEROIC ENTREPRENEUR

The changed composition and structure of American business in the late nineteenth century, with its increased emphasis on machine production, its new sources of energy, its changed product mix, and its need for larger units of capital investment brought with it a need for a new kind of entrepreneurship.

The new entrepreneur, known variously as the "industrial capitalist," "heroic entrepreneur," "empire builder," and "robber baron," achieved prominence in the 1870's. Philosophically, he was an individualist with an enormous ego. Although he would not have recognized the term, he was a Social Darwinist, believing that the principle of the survival of the fittest applied in economic life just as much as in biological life. In addition to the profit motive, he had an immense drive for accomplishment and an exaggerated power complex. The game was important to him, and profits were like the chips in the game; they were the badge of accomplishment, rather than the ultimate objective.

Those who conformed most closely to the industrial capitalist prototype had magnificent strengths and magnificent weaknesses. They possessed the unique abilities that were required to exploit the surging market that appeared in this era of vast expansion. Their abilities in production enabled them to fill an untapped market in an incredibly short span of years, contributing in an important way to economic growth and a rising scale of living. Being concerned more with production than with demand, they often took demand for granted. But their problem and function was to create an organization to run a large-scale plant. This required specialization, and the industrial capitalist soon adjusted himself to the role of a specialist. As Andrew Carnegie put it, it was best to put all one's eggs in one basket and then watch the basket. In the process of watching the basket, the entrepreneur was becoming a specialized decision maker rather than a jack-of-all-trades business administrator. He differed from his predecessors in manufacturing in that he no longer spent all his time in the factory. He was, in the words of Thorstein Veblen, changing from a captain of industry to a captain of business.

Although production was his chief forte, the industrialist also had some ability and interest in marketing. He understood instinctively that price competition moved goods in a virgin market. To put this in another way, he understood the importance and the application of what the economist calls price elasticity. Further than that, however, his sophistication did not go. Given the nature of his market, there was little point in making a valiant effort to create demand. He therefore took little interest in the more complicated forms of marketing that were to come into vogue when replacement demand and income elasticity became more important than original demand and price elasticity.

He was even less interested in the niceties of management than he was in marketing, and he was almost completely uninterested in intricate corporation mechanisms. These weaknesses in corporation finance and management often brought him close to disaster. He grossly underestimated the value of carefully planned managerial practices. At a time when the mode of production lent itself to a centralized administrative structure, he did his best to run his business as a "one man show." He was an optimistic, nonintellectual hunch player who scoffed at management theory and regarded all office work except accounting with disdain. He had even greater contempt for the trappings of finance. His business was with minor exceptions organized as a partnership or a closed corporation. Therefore, he had neither need nor use for such things as earnings per share, capital budgeting, and depreciation allowances. He distrusted the financial world and looked upon Wall Street as a hotbed of financial manipulation and chicanery.

Despite their innovations and their disregard for some of society's current mores, businessmen, like most people then as now, were not overly enthusiastic about change. They were reluctant to replace costly equipment or install untried methods if the existing product was satisfactory. The leading businessmen and firms were rarely the pioneers in technology. McCormick, for example, was very late in manufacturing a good mower, and Carnegie spoke for most industrialists when he stated that pioneering didn't pay. What he probably meant was that pioneering an unproved process didn't pay, but once a policy or process had demonstrated its worth, it was necessary to push it with all vigor and resources. "In no other country," read a report of the Industrial Commission,

> has skill in the organization and administration of productive enterprises been so highly developed as in the United States. Our "captains of industry" are quick but sure in their judgements, self-reliant, and of boundless energy. They are less conservative than their competitors abroad, more ready to seize upon improved methods, and to incur risks where there is a fair chance of conspicuous success.[2]

THE BEGINNINGS OF BIG BUSINESS

Among the many spectacular developments in the economic history of the late nineteenth century, the beginnings of big business in manufacturing stood out above all others. As we saw in Chapter 6, the railroads were

[2]*Report of the Industrial Commission*, 1902, p. 519.

already a big business in the 1850's. But as late as the 1870's, most industrial firms were still oriented toward the processing of farm products, and the conduct of their business was not much different from what it had been in the early days of the Boston Associates. Things began to change rapidly after the severe depression of 1873, and by the beginning of the twentieth century, indeed by the 1890's, heavy industry was an accomplished fact. In this evolution from light to heavy industry, the conduct of business had become altogether different from what it had been less than a generation before.

Mass-production methods had brought a new set of problems. To be used economically and efficiently, they required mass-consumption markets. Goods pouring out of plants in a steady and seemingly inexhaustible stream required a steady and inexhaustible stream of buyers. In the fight for a place at the top, no quarter was given and none asked. In order to keep the factories running at full blast, business became a rougher and less gentlemanly affair than it had been in the earlier period of history.

Contemporary descriptions of how business conducted itself in the nineteenth century are as scarce as descriptions of how Americans lived. Natives, especially, took their world for granted and what little description we have has been contributed by foreign travelers and emigrants who found the new world absorbing and fascinating. Such a commentator was Peter A. Demens, an unknown Russian immigrant who became a successful lumber operator. Demens left us a description of some aspects of business conduct in the middle years of the last half of the nineteenth century. Like many manufacturers, he resented the so-called middleman who took care of distributing the goods. This was an ancient source of irritation, however. For example, there is a note in *Hunt's Merchants' Magazine* in August 1852 that complains about "the ruinous and increasing prices of marketing. . . . Something is not right. The consumer pays enormous prices and the producer gets but a modest return." Demens' resentment against the middleman interfered with his objectivity, but it also left us a colorful and informative summary of some of the marketing practices of the time.

According to Demens, nine-tenths of all American commerce was in the hands of various commission men and brokers.

> It is almost impossible to buy anything directly from the producer; every factory sells off its entire production to some sort of broker, who then resells it to retail merchants throughout the entire Union. Furthermore, as soon as the broker has some degree of monopoly over a given branch of production, he designates local wholesalers for a given territory—sometimes a state, sometimes several counties, sometimes one large city. . . . The commission men even control the commerce in such merchandise as cotton and woolen fabrics, although these are made in factories dispersed throughout the country.
>
> Such an abnormal position is easily explained. In America a mass of

free capital constantly seeks investment, and therefore competition is great in all manufactured articles. Overproduction appears now in one, now in another branch of industry, and then goods cannot find a market. . . . The chief anxiety of every factory owner is, then, how and where to sell his product. . . . If there is not a rapid turnover, the entrepreneur must have two or three times the normal capital to be in a position to conduct his business. . . .

From their own point of view, the agents naturally try in every way to expand their business. They usually have extensive resources and use all sorts of cunning devices, the more quickly and the more profitably to sell the goods. Huge sums are spent in advertising of every kind. Nowhere in the world is there such a mass of newspapers; in the majority of cases these hold almost nothing but advertisements. There are also many other methods. All the fences, the sides of buildings, and often the roofs are inscribed with signs. Many commercial houses have specially organized publicity departments which spend tens of thousands of dollars annually; the mails are choked with the circulars, throw-aways, and brochures of these enterprising men of letters. . . .

But the most expensive, the most widespread, and the most unpleasant means of advertising is the dispatch of special people, called "drummers." These are clever, brash, nimble-tongued young gentlemen, usually foppishly dressed, uninhibited in manners, and supplied with an inexhaustable fund of shrewdness and impudence. The drummer is provided with great trunks of samples of the goods he sells. Sometimes he works for a commission, but more often for a fixed salary, and his boss pays all expenses. . . . Such a migratory young man costs a commercial house no less than $3,000 a year; the smart ones may even cost $5,000, and especially good ones get up to $15,000. . . .

Closely related to the questions of trade in America is that of credit. Both in wholesale and in retail business agreements in terms of cash are exceedingly rare; everything is sold over a period—thirty days, sixty days, three, four, six, and even twelve months.[3]

The economy that Demens described was one of small business with many unintegrated firms dependent upon many marketing middlemen. His picture was exaggerated, but it was true in kind if not in degree.

By 1900, contemporary observers were describing a quite different world, a world of vertically integrated big business. A few large firms whose interests spread out over the whole country dominated every major industry. The McCormick and Carnegie companies clearly overshadowed all their competitors in farm implements and steel. In consumer goods, too, there was apparent oligopoly with the big five (Swift, Armour, Morris, Cudahy, and the predecessor of Wilson & Co.) in meat packing; the three beer barons (Schlitz, Pabst, and Anheuser Busch) in brewing; James Buchanan Duke in tobacco; Washburn-Crosby in flour milling.

[3]Oscar Handlin, *This Was America*, (Cambridge, Mass.: Harvard University Press, 1949), pp. 350–355. Quoted by permission.

REASONS FOR THE BEGINNINGS
OF BIG BUSINESS

The elimination of the middleman constituted the most important innovation in the process of growth and concentration. Several causes blended together to produce this innovation and the striking transformation of business that it reflected. In the earlier years, the market for goods had been so scattered that it had been impractical for manufacturers to distribute their products directly. Attempts on the part of resourceful entrepreneurs like Almy and Brown to do so proved abortive and were soon abandoned. Distribution continued to be handled by commission merchants, selling agents, and jobbers. The wholesalers were probably well satisfied with the traditional ways of doing things, but the ambitious industrialists who were in the process of building big business found the existing methods of marketing intolerable. The middleman was an annoying barrier in the way of their ambitions to use their accumulating resources for business expansion.

Convinced that the wholesalers were not doing everything possible to push their product, aggressive entrepreneurs set about constructing their own nationwide marketing organizations. These attempts at vertical integration, for such they were, were assisted by various factors outside as well as inside the business world. Continuous population growth and continuous urban concentration created a national market, and the spreading railroad network provided a fitting means of penetrating it. Thus all the ingredients necessary for innovation were present. We can see how the process worked by taking four diverse examples, two from producer goods in the 1850's and two from consumer goods in the 1870's and 1880's.

Among the most important innovators in building vertically integrated firms were Cyrus McCormick in farm equipment, Edward Clark in sewing machines, Gustavus Swift in meat packing, and Frederick Pabst in beer brewing. There were, of course, other innovative entrepreneurs, so it should not be inferred that these four made up the entire roster of those who shook up the business world in the late nineteenth century.

Cyrus McCormick began before 1850 to sell his products through commission agents. Gradually, this built up to a franchise agent system of a type that later became common in the automobile business. In the sewing machine industry, Edward Clark, the brains of the Singer Company,[4] recognized, as McCormick had, that his company would have to demonstrate the machine and give instructions and service to the customer. Under his supervision the sewing machine became the first consumer appliance to be sold through a complete franchise system. Later, when more control was sought over retail outlets, he established branch stores to replace the franchise ar-

---

[4]Clark directed marketing and finance, 1852–1863. The partnership between Clark and Singer ended in 1863 when the company became incorporated. Clark was president 1876–1882.

rangement. The first of these branches appeared in Boston in 1852; by 1859, there were 14 of them. Singer also sold through commission agents who bought the machines at discounts ranging from 20 to 40 percent. Commission agents were supposed to provide demonstration and repair service, but they did not perform these services well. To give better service and to cut costs, the company gradually took over the agencies. This move toward vertical integration—for that was what it was—received encouragement from the peculiarities of Civil War taxation. The federal government levied a tax on each sale. A final product that passed through the hands of a series of different producers carried as many taxes as there were producers. On the other hand, products made by an integrated producer were taxed only once. Integration, therefore, offered obvious tax advantages, and Clark took advantage of this. By 1867, when it began to make its own cabinets, Singer was integrated from raw material to final customer.[5]

Clark also innovated by selling on the installment plan. As early as 1856, he began to sell sewing machines on liberal consumer credit terms— $5 down and $3 a month for a $125 machine. These policies involved certain risks because they required increased working capital to carry credit customers, to operate the branches, and to train and keep the trained personnel to demonstrate the machines to potential buyers. But apparently the risks were worth it.

The McCormick and Singer companies went into marketing deliberately, but to some extent the meat packers, the brewers, and other consumer goods manufacturers were forced to assume the marketing function. In the late seventies, Swift conceived the novel idea of shipping refrigerated meat from Chicago to the densely populated cities of the East. His notion horrified some and dismayed others, and he ran into a wall of opposition. Local butchers tried to persuade the public that shipped meat was poisonous, and local retailers were reluctant to handle so dangerous a product. Swift met the problem by setting up a chain of branch offices that sold to and sometimes controlled retail outlets. By the 1890's, Swift's marketing organization, centrally directed from the head office in Chicago, covered the whole country. Thus, he was a pioneer innovator in both marketing and management.

The Milwaukee and western beer barons faced a different, but equally knotty, problem. In the early 1870's, beer brewing was essentially a local business. The five largest producers were located in five of the largest cities.[6] But things were already changing. The Milwaukee firm of Best & Co. was selling beer in Chicago as early as the 1850's. Then in the late sixties and seventies, beer production in Milwaukee far outran local demand. The

---

[5]Andrew B. Jack, "The Channels of Distribution for an Innovation: The Sewing Machine Industry in America, 1860–1865," *Explorations in Entrepreneurial History*, first series, Vol. IX, 1957.

[6]Best & Co. (Pabst) in Milwaukee; Seip & Lehmann, Chicago; George Ehret, New York; Bergner and Engel, Philadelphia; Christian Moerlein, Cincinnati.

brewers had to find a market in other cities. But this was not easy, for the cost of transportation precluded Milwaukee beers from engaging in price competition with local beers. Aggressive, marketing-minded Western entrepreneurs met the challenge by using the techniques of monopolistic competition. They differentiated their product by advertising and publicizing it. In order to be assured of retail outlets, they financed saloon keepers by buying stores and renting them or by making capital available. The western premium beers sold in the eastern cities at twice the price charged for the local product, but the saloon keepers were well satisfied, for their profit margins were higher than on the local product. By the 1890's, Pabst, Anheuser-Busch, and Schlitz accounted for a major share of American beer production. Many of the former leaders—Seipp, Ruppert, Moerlein, Bergner—had sunk way down in the competition.[7]

MARKETING CHANGES IN TEXTILES

The shift in marketing strategy that occurred as part of the process of vertical integration is more than important enough to deserve a few added examples.

In the marketing of cotton textiles, the second half of the nineteenth century began where the first half left off, but as the century grew older, changes took place here as well. To some extent the older system of mill-agent relationship remained, but to this textile leaders added several new methods.

Generally speaking, there evolved four methods of distributing cotton textiles. The selling agent still continued to exert an important influence, especially where other services such as advancing funds and fashion advice were important aspects of the relationship. Brokers also remained in the field but only to a small extent. The two important changes were the growth of direct sales to clothing manufacturers and sales to converters. Converters appeared on the scene in the 1880's, and were in effect middlemen and merchants. They usually operated without a manufacturing or finishing plant, but purchased the cloth from the mill and had it converted into finished goods.

Gradually the middlemen became less important in the industry as the textile entrepreneurs turned to direct selling for both economy and control. By 1872, the textile directories indicated that "nearly all of the Fall River print cloth mills were selling direct, without a selling agent." In 1890, the New York Chamber of Commerce bemoaned the fact that "the desire to

[7]Thomas C. Cochran, *The Pabst Brewing Company* (New York: New York University Press, 1948).

economize had led a number of mills to dispense with agents and commission houses."

Admittedly, the above statements were somewhat exaggerated. Not all mills, not even all the large mills preferred direct selling to the agency system. When the Pepperell Manufacturing Company, in 1870, was faced with the failure of its selling agent, Francis Skinner & Co., "there was no consideration of a change from the customary method of distribution through a commission selling house." Pepperell selected a new agent, J. S. & E. Wright & Co., who agreed by contract "to endorse the notes of the corporation or sign as surety for the payment of such notes as the need of the corporation for money on occasion may require without additional charge."[8]

Some evidence of the decline of the selling agent may be inferred from the experience of the Wright Company. The number of manufacturer accounts handled reached a peak in 1873 and probably remained fairly stable until the early 1880's. By 1899 the number had declined from 16 to 11, and by 1912 it had gone down to 9. It is possible, however, that the lost accounts had been shifted to other selling houses, for the selling house did more than sell the cotton cloth, especially patterned cloth. Aside from supplying advances on sales, which for some mills was a necessity, the sales merchants through their knowledge of market demand and styles performed valuable services in advising on fabrics.

In the sale of woolens, the expansion of the market at first resulted in the use of additional wholesalers and jobbers located in the new areas. The mills ordinarily sold their output through commission merchants who in turn sold to the wholesalers and jobbers who distributed the goods to clothing manufacturers (mostly men's) and retail outlets.

The first change from this round-about system came before the Civil War when direct sales were made to clothing manufacturers, but a more concerted effort to break away from the dependence on the hierarchy of middlemen came later. Both the mills and commission merchants used traveling representatives who sold by sample, thus bringing the manufacturers to both jobber and consumer as they bypassed the wholesalers. In addition, sales were made, on a much larger scale than in the past, directly to large purchasers—primarily department stores and wholesale clothing manufacturers.

Direct sales to clothing manufacturers were not strictly speaking a new method of marketing cloth, but the increase both in volume and diversity of this trade after 1870 produced almost a difference in kind instead of merely in degree. The extent of this area of the business can be seen in the change that took place in the clothing business itself. Between 1869 and

[8]Evelyn Knowlton, *Pepperell's Progress* (Cambridge, Mass.: Harvard University Press, 1945), pp. 73, 183-6.

1899, value added in men's clothing increased from \$62 million to \$132 million. The increase in women's clothing was even more striking—from \$6 million to \$75 million, or more than tenfold.

So, by the end of the century, the shift to direct selling by both manufacturers and sales agents had permeated the industry, and wholesalers had largely left the field. The jobber supplied the small buyer, and selling agents and commission merchants still provided selling services for many mills that were too small to undertake direct selling or that preferred the older customary methods. But most major producers sold directly through their own sales divisions.

The difference between emphasizing growth and enjoying stability rested in the last analysis on the difference in the entrepreneurs, and, more specifically, on the different ways in which different entrepreneurs looked at marketing. McCormick, Clark, Swift, Pabst, and others whose firms achieved glamorous success in the late nineteenth century replaced the commission agents with branch offices and exclusive agencies. They were growth oriented. They recognized that marketing was an important function of the firm to be placed on an equal level with production and to be pursued with energy and ingenuity. They advertised their product. Where possible they differentiated it and where possible they serviced it. McCormick, for example, traveled all over the world displaying his reapers. Pabst, in consumer goods, constantly contested for blue ribbons at county fairs as well as at world fairs and at the annual encampment of the Grand Army of the Republic. Other less aggressive, more stability-minded businessmen ignored or avoided becoming involved in marketing, and their business reflected their aloofness. A historian of a well known textile machinery firm tells us that its executives "believed that sales promotion was unessential and almost unethical and that the best way to sell a product was to improve it. . . . For the first half of its existence, the company maintained no sales force." At first, the company used a few commission agents, but after 1860, one selling agent had an exclusive contract. The company issued no catalogues. Instead of illustrating its wares, the firm urged customers to visit the factory to see the equipment's manufacture and operation.[9]

OTHER FACTORS IN THE BEGINNINGS
OF BIG BUSINESS

We have just seen how vertical integration contributed to the growth of big business by grafting marketing functions on firms that had previously been engaged only in manufacturing. At the same time, bigness and concentration were being propelled on their way by the appearance of heavy in-

[9]Thomas R. Navin, *The Whitin Machine Works Since 1831* (Cambridge, Mass.: Harvard University Press, 1950), pp. 95–97.

dustry, by the railroad's tendency to encourage greater competition, and by the effects of the long and severe depression of 1873–78. Each of these deserves additional explanation.

The economy's transformation from light to heavy industry was epitomized by the oft repeated statement that the first half of the nineteenth century was the Age of Iron; the second half was the Age of Steel. Iron could be forged by firms with small capital, but a steel works required a huge investment. By 1900, for example, it required $50 million to build a steel plant, an amount far beyond the capacity of anything but a big business.

The railroads, which were the country's first big business, encouraged other big business in at least two ways in addition to providing the model. As we have already said, they were a cardinal factor in creating a national market, and in doing so, they put a sharper edge on intramural competition. They broke down monopolistic market positions by making it possible for firms to invade each other's territory. To protect themselves from the wounds and bruises of competition, businessmen integrated horizontally as well as vertically, thus giving another boost to big business.

Depressions added another dimension to the underlying economic trends that were driving business inexorably to what later became known as "giantism." The severe economic downturn of 1873–78, the longest in American history, played an especially important role, for, either by coincidence or as part of cause and effect, the movement toward bigness in business picked up speed in the seventies. The evidence favors the cause and effect relationship, for so many entrepreneurs catapulted to success in the 1870's and early 1880's that it would be stretching credibility too far to assume that it was nothing but a coincidence. Charles Pillsbury organized C. A. Pillsbury & Co. in 1872. In the same year, General DuPont formed the Gunpowder Association. Andrew Carnegie and his associates erected their first steel plant in 1873. Philip Armour became head of his firm in 1875. John Wanamaker opened his Grand Depot in 1876. Gustavus and Edwin Swift formed their partnership in 1878. The "Standard Oil Crowd" had all taken their places by 1879. James Buchanan Duke began making cigarettes by machine in 1881.

By further aggravating the businessman's dissatisfaction with existing methods of marketing, the depression of the seventies encouraged vertical integration. It also encouraged his flirtation with horizontal integration as a way of avoiding the worst effects of competition.

BUILDING AN ADMINISTRATIVE STRUCTURE

Vertical integration required much more sophisticated business methods than had sufficed for the merchant and the small businessman of the early nineteenth century. The innovators in industrial expansion needed far more capital and much more complicated forms of business organization. In addition, they had to build an administrative structure, something that had not been needed in the previous generation. It was necessary to develop a nervous system in the form of a middle management office force to complement the physical growth of the factory. To express this in another way, the expanding firm had to create a bureaucracy, for the big business firm could only operate under a system of routine administration, and routine administration is a synonym for bureaucracy. Strange things were happening in business life—things that must have made individualistic industrialists very uneasy indeed. The administrative end of business was growing, and it was apparent that nothing could be done to stop it. For example, Cyrus McCormick, certainly no champion of office work, watched his office staff grow from two to three clerks who had barely enough to do in 1854 to sixteen men who were hard pressed to answer the correspondence in 1879.

Like every other business action and intellectual process, what was occurring in administration was not brand new. The building of a bureaucracy had its antecedents in the army, the church, and, as we explained in the previous chapter, especially in the large railroad. Only later did it appear in the integrated industrial firm. Some business administrators certainly knew this. H. M. Barksdale, who contributed so much to the DuPont organization, was well aware of the railroad experience, for he had been trained in the Baltimore and Ohio. According to James Stillman of the National City Bank, the Standard Oil company "borrowed" its idea of "strong centralized government (with certain other doctrines) from the Roman Catholic Church." A member of the management staff of the vast Pennsylvania Railroad system, William P. Shinn, became the Carnegie Company's first office manager. But in most cases, those who put together an administrative structure were unaware of the existing precedents. Their organizations were slapped together or just grew as expedience and necessity dictated. Nevertheless, by the 1890's, business leaders like Clark, Swift, and Duke had set up departments to run their widespread activities. They had also created strong central offices to oversee and coordinate the various departments. These organizations worked, although not in the most orderly fashion. There were no clear lines of authority or responsibility and no separation of long-term planning from day-to-day operation. Some holding companies were also operating companies, and the functions of one committee or department often overlapped those of others. This was often the fault of the entrepreneur, who, individualist that he was, tried to interfere in everybody's business including his own. In time this too would be corrected, but we will return to this theme a little later.

ANCILLARY INSTITUTIONS

In developing an administrative structure, businessmen relied more on ancillary institutions than had been their habit in the early 1800's. They saw no pressing need for public relations advisers, management consultants, or the more sophisticated assistants of the present day, and, as long as they could, they tried to avoid investment bankers. But the handful of business enterprises that were growing to gigantic size in the 1880's found it advisable to employ specialized corporation lawyers to solve the legal riddles associated with growth. They also depended heavily on the very large commercial banks to meet part of their immense needs for capital funds. There were, however, very few of these gigantic banks. Even at the outbreak of World War I, there were only about a dozen that were large enough to lend $1 million to one customer.

The increasing complexity of the manufacturing process affected accounting more than any other ancillary. Routine administration, the pressures of competition, the need to depreciate a huge capital investment, and the more intricate processes of roundabout production necessitated more careful record keeping and made somewhat more advanced accounting an indispensible adjunct of efficient business. The shrewdest businessmen understood this; it was one of the insights that made them shrewd. McCormick, who would have failed an elementary business school course in management; Rockefeller, who it was once said had the soul of a bookkeeper; and Carnegie, who had an inherent contempt for office work, recognized the value of careful accounting. To be sure, their systems were much less sophisticated than the systems of today, but they did have the rudiments of cost accounting, and they used them well. McCormick, for example, was able by 1879 to know not only the cost of building one of his machines, but also the portions of this sum that were chargeable to labor, materials, and "running expenses," including light, heat, insurance, and so on. Because the timekeeper recorded in his book on each of his hourly rounds the class of work each man was doing, and the rate of pay prescribed for that service, it was possible for the office to determine both the labor cost of an entire implement and of any one of its parts.[10]

But once again, it was the railroads that led the way. Albert Fink, an immigrant from Lauterbach, Hessen-Darmstadt, Germany, was an especcially important innovator in accounting. He had started as a bridge designer and construction engineer and eventually became president of the

---

[10]William T. Hutchinson, *Cyrus Hall McCormick* (New York: Appleton-Century-Crofts, 1930), Vol. 1, p. 609.

Louisville and Nashville Railroad. Fink broke the railroad's accounts into four classes, each of which represented a distinctive type of cost. The expenses entailed in *maintenance* of the road were fixed. *Movement expenses*, on the other hand, were variable, and *station expenses* were a mixture of fixed and variable costs. The *cost of capital* was, of course, in a class by itself. Fink's essay into sophisticated accounting was not simply academic. It had a practical purpose in rate-making. "We," he asserted, "can not make the average cost per ton-mile the basis for a tariff, if it is to be based upon cost; we must classify the freight according to the conditions affecting cost of transportation, and ascertain the cost of each class separately."[11]

The ultimate importance of Fink's contribution far transcended its importance in introducing cost accounting. The railroads were the first businesses to depart from making prices on the basis of an analysis of impersonal supply and demand. They were the first to make scientific cost determination the main basis for price. As industrial firms grew larger, they would follow the same path, that is, the path of monopolistic competition. But in these early years, it was the rare businessman who followed the example of the railroads and of Carnegie and Rockefeller. Public accounting, academic training in accounting, and the first book on cost accounting appeared in the 1880's. But again the advance was confined pretty much to big businesses and not to all of these. The first controller of an industrial enterprise was not appointed until 1892. Even as late as 1918, at least one relatively large and long-established manufacturing firm was still using single-entry booking.

THE DECLINE OF THE "ONE-MAN" COMPANY

The late 1800's witnessed the decline but not the total fall of the "one-man" company. The growing size and increasing intricacy of the integrated firm, the variety of functions that had to be carried on, and the need for expert advice and information required an administrative structure that transcended the individualistic one-man organization. The notion that a single individual "ran the whole show" in the large firms of the late nineteenth century is as much a legend as is the rags-to-riches road to success popularized in the Alger stories. The great empire-building entrepreneurs were undoubtedly the central driving figures in their companies, but they received invaluable assistance from their associates and this in increasing quantities as time went on. Indeed, the history of management's progress can be described as a continuous movement that transformed the executive from a one-man band to the leader of a symphony orchestra.

[11]Quoted in Alfred D. Chandler, Jr., *The Railroads: The Nation's First Big Business* (New York: Harcourt, Brace & World, Inc., 1965), p. 115.

In Standard Oil, few men made decisions or recommendations solely on their own. It was a community of interest led by John D. Rockefeller. The DuPont company owed as much to H. M. Barksdale and J. Armory Haskell as it did to General Henry DuPont. Carnegie had the help of his brother Thomas and his friend Henry Phipps, the production genius of Captain Billy Jones, and the executive ability of Henry Clay Frick.

A group of men managed each large firm. In the process, they built up a highly centralized organization. They set up a number of departments, each of which took care of one or more of the various functions performed by a large, integrated business. All activity was supervised by the central office. In some cases, the executives created committees, and although many of them hated to do so, they conscripted an office force to provide data and information for the officers, the committees, and their aides. But we can get the best inkling of how this change from a one-man firm to a collective enterprise occurred by returning once again to our reliable model—the railroad. In the pioneer period of railroad management, the chief executive was the superintendent. He was a monarch on the order of Louis XIV. He consulted no one; he issued orders to everyone—to the operating personnel as well as to middle management. But this mode of operation could not continue. No executive had the necessary strength, energy, and stamina to run a one-man road. In a short time, some decentralization of power inevitably occurred. By 1870, in most of the major roads departmental autonomy was well entrenched. The executive transmitted his directives through department heads, and all reports were made through them. In time, too, this would occur in industry, but it would not occur until the late nineteenth and would not become common until the twentieth century.

CORPORATE ORGANIZATION COMES INTO ITS OWN

One of the ways in which businessmen adjusted to the changing conditions of the late nineteenth century was by changing the legal form of organization. The use of a corporate charter increasingly replaced the partnership agreement as the business firm grew in size. The importance of this in the everyday life of the average citizen can hardly be exaggerated. Indeed, a strong case can be made for the proposition that the increased use of the corporation was the most important institutional innovation of the century.

From a business point of view, the partnership had several disadvantages for firms that needed large amounts of capital and more pliable forms of business organization. Each partner was individually liable for all partnership debts, creditors had to sue all the partners, and dissolution of the partnership could come about by death of a partner or for several other reasons including a transfer of a partnership interest. The corporation gave the individual owner limited liability, and owners could sell or transfer their shares without disturbing the operation of the business, thus giving the firm a sense of permanence that it had previously lacked. It also allowed firms to tap the funds of those who had neither the desire nor the ability to manage.

By the middle of the century, many states had passed legislation permitting incorporation under general incorporation laws rather than by special act of the legislature. By then, too, all nonbank charters limited the liability of shareholders to the subscription price of their stock. By 1875, 24 of the 37 states, including all the important industrial states except Delaware, had passed free incorporation laws, so that after that date, the special charter had become a thing of the past for most fields of enterprise.

Limited liability, although important, was not the cardinal consideration for incorporation, for about the same number of corporations were formed in some of the states that did not grant limited liability as in those states that were more lenient. What made the corporation more desirable was that it fitted the needs of a thriving business world better than did the proprietorship and the partnership. Through the sale of stocks and bonds, entrepreneurs could raise larger amounts of capital funds. This had been important to the large banking and transportation ventures of the antebellum period and was equally important to industrial firms when they were organized on a large scale.

Businessmen were enchanted with the advantages of incorporation, which on the one hand permitted them to raise large amounts of capital and at the same time permitted the stockholders the relative safety of limited liability along with the right to sell their shares at any time they wished. From the entrepreneur's point of view, the corporation had one disadvantage: dissident stockholders could annoy and even interfere with management.

The increased use of the corporate form is indicated by the increase in the number of incorporations, especially in the industrial states. New Jersey, which had issued 561 charters in the decade of the 1850's, was issuing twice that number in the seventies, and twenty times as many by the nineties. Maine, during the 1850's, had issued 364 charters, which grew to 4,918 by the nineties. Other states showed a similar growth in business incorporations.

Most of the firms, although organized as corporations, were in reality incorporated partnerships whose shares were not bought or sold in the open market. This was to come later. In the late 1880's, the Pullman Company was the only large manufacturing company listed on the New York Stock Exchange. The stock of some textile companies—Amoskeag, Wamsutta, and so forth—traded on the Boston Exchange, but these were not giant firms. The shares of most of the largest organizations, including Armour, McCormick, Singer, Swift, were held by a small group and not available to the general public. The Carnegie enterprises were typical. They were not even incorporated until 1892. At that time there were only twenty-five stockhold-

TABLE 5   Number of Incorporations, 1840–1899

State	1840–49	1850–59	1860–69	1870–79	1880–89	1890–99
Connecticut	142	548	583	62[3]	902	1483
Maine	226	364	384	671	2886	4918
Massachusetts		176[1]	758	773	1539	2335
New Jersey	159	561	924	1101	3861	11355
Ohio		623[2]	1762	3048	5945	8059

[1] 1851–1859
[2] 1850–51, 1855–59
[3] 1870 only
Source: George Heberton Evans, Jr., *Business Incorporations in the United States, 1800–1943* (New York: National Bureau of Economic Research, 1948), pp. 12, 15, 18, 19, 111–113, 119–120.

ers whose ownership interest ranged from less than 1 percent to 58½ percent. Under the terms of an "ironclad agreement," stockholders could sell their shares only to the company. Moreover, any holder's stock could be bought at book value if 75 percent of the stock so voted. This type of arrangement assured control to the insiders, but it also prevented the corporation from taking full advantage of its capital-raising powers. In almost all companies, management had to rely on a small group of stockholders, retained earnings, and bank borrowing to raise the sizable capital it needed. Retained earnings, for example, swelled the size of the Carnegie enterprises from $700,000 in 1873 to over $400 million in 1900. Standard Oil paid out only a little over half of its prodigious earnings in the decade of the 1880's.

8

GOVERNMENT, LABOR, AND PROFITS

The term "heroic entrepreneur" may be too melodramatic to describe the "industrial capitalist." J. P. Morgan may have been a modern Henry II, but Rockefeller did not look like a Norse god, nor did Carnegie resemble Ulysses. Important though the individual entrepreneur was in the growth of business, he was a man of his times. The era and the economic environment in which he lived had much to do with his outstanding success. In the nineteenth century, the culture of the day made business a highly respected, if not the most highly respected, occupation, and the whole community was well aware of this.

GOVERNMENT AND BUSINESS IN THE NINETEENTH CENTURY

In the last half of the century, as in the first half, government, especially the federal government, continued to encourage and assist the entrepreneur. Laissez faire might have been extolled as an abstract principle, but it did not guide government policy. Throughout the nineteenth century, business and government rode tandem in a harmonious relationship that was believed to be beneficial to all concerned.[1] State governments be-

[1] A belief that was by no means peculiar to the United States. In every country that experienced an impressive economic growth, the government encouraged the entrepreneur. The examples are legion: mercantilism in England and Bismark's German paternalism in the late nineteenth century. Surely the best example is Japan, of which it has been said, there was scarcely any important Japanese industry of the Western type . . . which did not owe its establishment to state initiative.

haved much as Massachusetts behaved. It "conceived of the beneficent hand of the state as reaching out to touch every part of the economy . . . the organization of education, the public works undertaken, codes of law administered, and the type of taxes imposed, as well as more direct guidance, all would shape the enterprise of the region."[2] On the federal level, Congress and the Executive exerted themselves all through the last half of the century to assist business by subsidies to transportation, tariffs, contract labor laws, and other devices.

Most business leaders showed no interest in playing an active role in politics.[3] They regarded it as a parasitic occupation and looked upon its practitioners with tolerant contempt. The few who refused to become emotionally involved were "independent voters," distributing their financial manna between the major parties as Henry O. Havemeyer, the sugar tycoon, freely stated in a Senate investigation. These were, however, a small minority. Most business leaders supported the party of their choice, and the party of their choice was in the majority of cases the Republican party. For every Southern Democrat like Cyrus Hall McCormick and Thomas Fortune Ryan, there was a score of Mark Hannas in the GOP.

Today, it is fashionable to think that direct business involvement in the political arena is a recent development. This is not so. Although few businessmen at any time became actively involved, today's business leaders are no more active than yesterday's. From the so-called Essex Junto in early Federalist America to Charles Percy and George Romney, businessmen have been occupying political office by election or appointment. Ten of the 66 members, or 15 percent of the 1860 Senate, and 16 or 18 percent of the 1900 Senate were businessmen. In fact, the number in the Senate before the 1910 Constitutional amendment provided for direct election was so large that it came to be called the "Millionaire's Club."

For many years in the early part of the century, Nathan Appleton, the New England textile magnate, was an important member of the House. In the latter part of the 1800's, Abram S. Hewitt, the iron manufacturer, was chairman of the House Ways and Means Committee. Nelson Aldrich, Rhode Island businessman and father-in-law of John D. Rockefeller, Jr., was one of the "big five" in the Senate during the Progressive Era. Marcus Alonzo Hanna has been given credit for nominating and electing William McKinley President. John Wanamaker was Postmaster-General, and Levi P. Morton, the investment banker, was Vice President.

[2]Oscar and Mary F. Handlin, *Commonwealth: A Study of the Role of Government in the American Economy, Massachusetts, 1774–1861* (New York: New York University Press, 1946), pp. 54–55.

[3]"Politics, as a profession belong not to the merchant" (*Hunt's Merchants' Magazine*, Vol. 2, January 1840, p. 23) seems to have represented majority business opinion.

TARIFFS AND SUBSIDIES

Government intervention in business continued to follow the traditional lines that had first been laid down in mercantilist England and colonial America. Government encouraged business with tariffs and subsidies. In addition, in the late nineteenth century, the federal government took up where state governments had left off in the regulation of industry and industrial behavior.

After the Civil War, protectionism reached new heights. It was, however, based upon a new rationale, for the infant-industry argument had become by then a trifle shopworn. In the 1880's, a political candidate in a moment of innocence labeled the tariff a local issue. The remark deserved more respect than it received, for it was closer to the truth than most people understood. In Congress, free traders and protectionists argued back and forth, but each was well aware of its own special interests, so that the century culminated in the protectionist McKinley Tariff of 1890, the rates of which were ultimately surpassed by the Dingley Tariff of 1897.

In all the give-and-take over rates and duties, victory belonged to the side that spoke the loudest and had the better organization. By the 1880's, this was well recognized, for by then the organized businessman had assumed the upper hand in tariff negotiations. By then, largely through the energetic efforts of John L. Hayes, the lobbyist for the woolen industry, Congress had conceded industry's right to send its spokesmen into every committee hearing and to stand at every Congressman's door. The size of a duty came to vary according to the size of the organization. The quinine makers, of whom there were only four, were unable to get their product off the free list, but the pottery fabricators of whom there were many, obtained a 13 percent increase. Joseph Wharton as the sole nickel producer had to submit to a 50 percent reduction, but as an ironmonger, standing with many others, he suffered a reduction of only 4 percent on pig iron.[4]

Businessmen were divided on the tariff issue, but no similar disagreement existed about the merits of government contributions to social capital. Like the nonbusiness public, they were correctly or incorrectly under the impression that government intervention was absolutely necessary if turnpikes, canals, and railroads were to be built.

When private capital did not flow freely, which was more often than not, railroad promoters were not averse to seeking financial assistance from governments. Indeed, many of them went to considerable lengths to get the government involved, using the argument that public aid to the railroads would benefit society more than it would benefit the railroad owners.

---

[4]Ida Tarbell, *The Tariff in Our Times* (New York: The Macmillan Company, 1911), p. 131.

It is not possible to state exactly how much governments contributed, because their assistance took many forms that could not be measured in cash. They made outright gifts, subscribed to stock, much of which was lost, and made loans, which were not all paid back. They guaranteed credit, an activity that was often a prerequisite for obtaining capital funds but on which no money value could be set. They remitted taxes, provided and paid for surveys, offered drawbacks (reduced rates) on tariffs, gave roads the privilege of issuing paper money, and made them gifts of land. The Federal Coordinator of Transportation in 1940 conservatively estimated government aid to transport for the whole of American history, excluding the purchase of securities, at $1.4 billion, a very large amount in absolute terms, but small in proportion to the total cost.

Before 1850, the federal government provided much engineering assistance, but its other aid to railroads was negligible. State and municipal governments, on the other hand, provided some $300 million, probably about one-third the cost of the pre-Civil War network. The nature and magnitude of this help varied from section to section. In New England, Massachusetts was the only state that contributed, although towns and cities were active. Government aid was much more important in the Middle Atlantic states. Most of the capital for the construction of the Erie Railroad, for example, came from government loans. In the Middle West, governments began with very generous support, but this diminished abruptly because of heavy losses during the depressions of 1837 and 1857. Nevertheless, government aid made a substantial contribution in Ohio, Indiana, Illinois, and Michigan; Missouri contributed almost as much to internal improvements as did New York.

Governmental assistance was far more important in the South than in any other section. Over half the cost of southern railroads was paid by states, cities, and towns. South Carolina subscribed for as much stock as did private investors. Maryland, Virginia, Georgia, and North Carolina paid for much more than half. The ways in which this aid was given varied widely. But no matter what form it took, government help was profoundly important. In 1840, the South, where government played the major role, had more railroad mileage than any other section, a phenomenon which was, to be sure, short-lived.

The Jacksonian philosophy that prevailed in the early years of the railroads effectively prevented the federal government from playing an important role in the construction of the eastern roads. But in the 20 years after 1850, federal aid became much more important. To be sure, the only financial help given by Washington was to the Union Pacific and Central Pacific railroads in the form of $65 million of first-mortgage loans all of which were eventually paid off. These federal loans were greatly overshadowed by $95 million in state aid and $175 million in local help. However, the federal government also made huge land grants, about 180 million acres in all. These grants, which were designed to encourage the construction of railroad lines through the vast, sparsely populated West, were for 100 feet of right of way and six square miles on alternate sides of the track before the Civil War, and for 10 miles in the states and 20 miles in the territories after the war. One road, the Northern Pacific, got a grant of 20 miles in the states and 40 miles in the territories. Seventy railroads shared in the government's largesse. Four (Northern Pacific, Santa Fe, Southern Pacific, and Union Pacific) received 73 percent of the total. Immense as the grants were, however, they contributed to less than 20,000 miles, or only 8 percent of the country's total railroad mileage.

Land grants gave an immense psychological impetus to the business of railroad building. They nourished the promoters' usual optimistic belief that any road would pay. It came to be assumed that free land meant the difference between a tidy and a vast fortune. But in most cases, the faith in land grants was a delusion, for the roads were not able to sell land quickly enough to meet construction costs. Thus, the grants failed to fulfill the principal goal that the government had in mind. But the misinterpretation of what the land grants would do also accelerated the building of a western railroad system. Attracted by the prospect of profits from land grants, many entrepreneurs rushed in to build railroads long before railroads would ordinarily have been constructed. Moreover, in their anxiety to turn their lands into cash, railroad companies engaged in aggressive and elaborate sales campaigns here and abroad. They publicized and advertised. They sold on credit at prices ranging from $1.25 to $20 an acre. Although the money did not roll in, settlers did, and the West was populated much more quickly than it would have been without the land grants.

Although the western railroads were built much sooner than would have happened in an economy directed solely by market forces, construction was usually sloppy and inefficient. Emphasis was on speedy growth, not stability, and many of the western roads had to be rebuilt shortly after their original construction. To those who believed that the market should be the sole determinant of economic development, and that economic progress should be slow, steady, and "unwasteful," the land grants were, on balance, economically harmful. Those who emphasized the short run and believed that speed was of the essence thought the land grants made a significant contribution to economic development.

Actually, it was not really economics that brought a halt to government aid to railroads. Heavy financial losses and revelations of bribery and graft on all levels chilled the initial ardor for government help, and public aid stopped. Most state governments dropped out in the depression of the 1850's, the federal government quit in the 1870's, and most local governments were no longer giving assistance by the 1890's. Of course, in the twentieth century, they would all be back with highway, airline, and new kinds of railroad subsidies.

FEDERAL REGULATION OF INDUSTRY

Although the federal government from its beginning regulated commerce through such measures as the Navigation Acts, historians share the belief that the Interstate Commerce Act of 1887 was its first important legislation in the regulation of business behavior. Certainly the ICC was the model for the federal legislation that later mushroomed.

For many years, it was assumed that the ICC was the creation of farmers and liberals—the "people against big business," so to speak. But this view is both oversimplified and inaccurate. That amorphous group known as "The People" rarely express well-defined feelings about economic issues. Their dissatisfaction, moreover, seldom translates itself into constructive legislation. The ICC and the federal intervention that it set in motion arose out of the peculiar economic circumstances of the railroads, and it was businessmen as much as farmers and the people who sought federal regulation.

From the day they started, the railroads were in trouble both among themselves and with the rest of the public. They had disrupted the existing channels of trade, and thereby antagonized merchants along the rivers, lakes, and canals. By offering cheap and convenient means of transportation, they brought widely separated merchants into competition with each other and thus aggravated existing irritation. But these were petty irritations compared to the aggravations caused by competition among the railroads themselves. As networks stretched across the country, individual roads found it increasingly difficult to achieve satisfactory earnings.

Objective observers who sympathized with the railroads' plight offered constructive criticisms. One of the most common was to urge the roads to compete by improving service rather than by cutting rates. But roads that took this path of product differentiation were flirting with disaster. Railroads that confined their activities to improving service rather than working for new traffic were almost certain to become bankrupt. A better way to success or survival was to build or purchase feeder lines in order (1) to achieve a safe or monopoly position, (2) to undercut competitors' rates on routes where competition existed, and (3) to raise rates where competition did not exist, and to enter into pools with competitors. All of these tactics had their disadvantages, and none of them was designed to win friends. Cutting rates antagonized other roads. Discriminating between long and short hauls was especially infuriating to shippers both in manufacturing and in farming. Pools were notoriously weak, because any road felt free to violate its rate agreements if opportunity presented itself.

By 1886, when the states had proved themselves incapable of dealing with the railroad problem, a majority of businessmen were resigned to accepting federal regulation. By then, the business community could be divided into five groups. A large number were enthusiastic in their belief that federal regulation would put a halt to discriminatory rates. A second group chiefly among railroaders were similarly convinced that regulation would put an end to rate cutting and establish a sound floor for railroad earnings and thereby solve the railroad problem. A third bloc wanted some type of legislation, but they were not very sure what form this should take. The fourth group, consisting of the leaders of the largest railroads, emphatically opposed government intervention. A last small fraction of the business population included manufacturers and merchants who opposed anything, including government intervention, that might benefit the railroads.

In all of this mixture of opinion, philosophical principles, such as laissez faire, were of slight importance. Self-interest was the incentive behind the support of the ICC. As a perceptive student has pointed out:

> Businessmen were more interested in solving particular problems than they were in adhering to any "business philosophy. . . ." The great majority of them rejected laissez faire economics and cared little for the theory of the survival of the fittest. . . . The desire for economic protection was the one and only unifying force among those who supported regulation.[5]

THE LABOR SUPPLY FOR BIG BUSINESS

Burgeoning industry required a growing labor force, which continued to be supplied by an expanding native-born population and by immigration, but the mix was somewhat different from what it had been earlier in the century. The increase in native population, although still high in absolute terms, had slackened somewhat. Immigration, on the other hand, was much higher than in the years before 1850. After slowing down drastically during the Civil War, it increased after the War was over, especially during periods of recovery and prosperity. Peaks of immigration occurred in 1873, 1882, and 1892, years that also marked peaks in the business cycle.

Equally important for industry was the mix of immigrants. Immigrants provided most of the unskilled labor who did the rough, heavy work. The skilled miners, weavers, silk workers, and iron puddlers and rollers

[5]Edward A. Purcell, Jr., "Ideas and Interests: Businessmen and the Interstate Commerce Act," *The Journal of American History*, December 1967.

among the immigrants reduced the training time involved in developing a supply of specialized workers. By 1870, foreign born constituted 53.3 percent of the labor in mining; 37.6 percent in certain of the textile industries; and 43.4 percent in some areas of the iron and steel industry. By 1890, the percentages in mining and steel had fallen a little, to 49.1 and 37.9 percent, but in textiles it had risen to 42.8 percent.

Governments, both federal and state, helped business by encouraging immigration. Congress, in 1864, passed a law exempting immigrants from the draft and allowing prospective employers to enter into contracts with immigrant workers to advance the passage money against a lien on future wages. Thus, the colonial practice of indentured servitude was to some extent revived. Individual states set up boards of immigration, distributed pamphlets, and by other means tried to encourage immigration. Although these efforts no doubt met with some success, they were not as effective as the work of labor agents. The Central Pacific Railroad hired several thousand Chinese for railroad construction through an agent who prepaid their passage; and the American Immigrant Company, with the backing of Secretary of the Navy Welles, Senator Sumner, Chief Justice Chase, and the Reverend Henry Ward Beecher, was active on the east coast in recruiting immigrants from Europe.

Most of the immigrants were males, but in the native-born labor force, women expanded their share of the job market. In 1870, women accounted for 14.6 percent of the labor force; by 1900 this figure rose to 18.3 percent of a much larger labor force. The total number of females in the labor force increased (1870–1900) from 1.8 million to 5.3 million, predominantly in domestic service and the teaching profession, although 16 percent of all manufacturing workers were women. In textiles and clothing, women made up almost 70 percent of the labor force, in cigars and tobacco, almost 35 percent, and in paper and printing, almost 25 percent.

Children also continued to contribute to the labor supply. In 1900, a little less than 20 percent of those between 10 and 15 were in the labor force.

WAGES AND HOURS

The attitude of the post-Civil War industrialist toward labor differed little from that of the industrialist of pre-War days. He opposed unions and supported long hours and low pay. Only a small minority recognized that hours, wages, and productivity were interrelated. Labor was regarded by most businessmen and by most of the public as a commodity, and in the interest of economizing on resources, it behooved the businessman to buy it at as low a price as possible and in as small amounts as possible.

Aside from the long-established practice of periodic wage payments—quarterly, monthly, weekly, and, occasionally, daily—three unusual systems deserve some mention. Of these, the best known was the inside-contracting system under which a contractor brought in the labor force and the company provided the factory or mine, and the raw materials and sold the finished product. The advantage of nonsupervision and training of labor was, however, outweighed by the necessity of closer inspection of the product and the danger of misuse of the machinery. A small number of firms used profit-sharing plans, but since the efficient and inefficient alike benefited, and some minimum wage had to be paid, the arrangement had little appeal. The third system, piecework payment, which became the customary method for paying incentive wages always dissatisfied the slower and less efficient workers and antagonized all workers when the piecework rates were periodically reduced.

In terms of wages and hours, workers made respectable strides in the late nineteenth century. The average daily real wage in manufacturing increased about 50 percent between 1860 and 1890, while the hours per day decreased from eleven to ten.[6]

Of course, wages and salaries differed from firm to firm and from occupation to occupation. Based on 1860 prices, real weekly earnings in the cotton textile industry jumped from about $4.50 in 1860 to about $7.00 in 1900, about the same as the increase in manufacturing as a whole. Skilled workers in steel and other industries earned about $12 a week in 1860 and $18 in 1900, again about the same as the manufacturing average. Unskilled workers did not do quite as well, the average increasing from about $6.25 a week to $8.80 a week.

Real wages in the United States were higher than in Great Britain, and probably in the rest of the world, although the differential with Great Britain was smaller toward the end of the century than in 1860. In 1860, the American textile worker's real wage was $4.48 a week; the Englishman's, $2.82. By 1906, the American earned $6.85 and the Englishman $5.81. Most of the difference was clearly attributable to productivity, which even as late as 1909 was estimated to be twice as high in America as in Great Britain.

Factory wages also differed from those in other occupations. Farm workers whose pay averaged about $165 a year with keep in 1860 had progressed to $180 in 1900. Loggers doubled their wage between 1860 and 1900; so did clerks who received $600 a year "tops" in 1860. Executives did even better. Middle managers made $3-5,000 a year in 1860 and a top executive earned $10,000. By 1900, the latter's income was as much as $25-30,000.

The bare data on wages and hours do not, however, tell the whole

[6]Estimates of the increase in real wages made by four distinguished economists range from 48 percent to 74 percent.

story. Prosperity alternated with depression, and during the depressed period wage reductions and unemployment hurt labor severely. The conditions under which industrial labor worked and lived fitted poorly the American dream and provided a strong impetus for the development of unions. Truck payment, long hours, periodic wage reductions, company towns and stores, sweatshops, unsanitary and dangerous working conditions, and the lack of protective legislation pushed labor toward organization for its own protection and progress.

Employers resisted the union movement with a single-minded tenacity of purpose that contrasted harshly with their lack of a general labor policy. There was no doubt in their minds that unions could raise wages. In the McCormick Reaper plant, for example, unions clearly influenced the wage level. Before 1887 when unions were strong in the McCormick works, McCormick wages were much higher than those paid by nonunion competitors. After Cyrus McCormick II broke the union, McCormick wages were the lowest in the industry.[7]

But the opposition to the unions was certainly not based solely on economic considerations. It was more a question of power than of maximizing profits. The unions threatened the entrepreneur's way of life, and he reacted hostilely even at the expense of productivity and profit.

Again the McCormick Company provides a case in point. The company did what it could to prevent unionization even at the expense of profit. It resorted to strike breakers, machines, bonuses, wage increases, discriminatory discharges and promotions to fight the union. In 1886, the company installed $500,000 of machines to replace the skilled molders who had, through their union, won a strike in 1885. In that year, foundry costs had been $3,000 a week. In 1886, with machines and unskilled labor, they were $8,000 a week. "Time and again," writes Ozanne, "Cyrus McCormick II was to make concessions while withholding . . . the workers' right to participate in union activity without discrimination."

There is no reason to believe that what happened in the McCormick Company was unique. Companies resisted the unions individually and collectively. Employer associations were organized in practically every industry to destroy the union movement, to oppose the demands of disgruntled workers, and to help enforce their own attempts at wage reduction. The early organizations were usually informal and temporary. With the growth of the market area, they became more formal and more lasting.

The associations used a variety of tactics, including injunctions, summary discharges, blacklists, lockouts, and labor spies, in its struggles with the unions. But it received its greatest help from economic recession and

[7]See the illuminating studies by Robert Ozanne, *A Century of Labor-Management Relations at McCormick and International Harvester* and *Wages in Practice and Theory* (Madison, Wisc.: University of Wisconsin Press, 1967 and 1968).

depression. In good times, the union had the advantage. In hard times, the employer did not have to worry so much about strikes, for when business was bad, the plant might just as well be shut down. Later, in the 1920's, an entirely different set of circumstances would apply. But this is a matter for a later chapter.

PROFITS AND MORTALITY

Unfortunately, the data on profits in general for the late nineteenth century are scattered and meager. At best, the generalizations and conclusions are indicative rather than conclusive. Such information as does exist indicates that on the whole profits were not typically exorbitant relative to either capital investment or assets; they seem to have exhibited a downward trend during the period; and the eagerness of entrepreneurs to expand during prosperity resulted in unused capacity and falling profit margins as their markets became more and more saturated.

Because of Dun and Bradstreet, we have better data on failures and mortality than on profits. Their statistics go back to 1857. The lowest rate of failure in the late nineteenth century—58 per 10,000 firms—occurred during the Civil War. The highest rate—242—was one of the distinguishing features of the panic year 1857. As one might expect, the failure rate varied directly with the business cycle. During the prosperous early seventies, mortality was less than 100 per 10,000 firms. During the severe depression, 1873–1878, thousands of weakly capitalized or poorly managed firms were thrown into bankruptcy. The failure rate climbed to 158 in 1878. Again in the short depression of the mid-1880's, failures reached 121 per 10,000. In the five depressed years surrounding 1895, the rate at one time reached 133 per 10,000. Yet, in both depression and prosperity, the average liability per failure did not vary much, although there was some tendency toward decline over the whole fifty-year period. In the 1860's and 1870's, for example, the average liability per failure hovered around $28,000. In the 1890's, it had sunk to $14,000.

In several industries over-capacity seemed to be the rule rather than the exception. In 1884 the American Iron and Steel Association bemoaned the fact that it was almost the exception for the industry to produce at more than 50 percent of capacity. The whiskey industry also generally operated at less than 50 percent of capacity. In the manufacture of bread, the National Millers Association members were informed that the industry was characterized by keen competition and small profits. The president of the National Association of Stove Manufacturers complained in 1888 that it was "a chronic case of too many stoves, and not enough people to buy them."

In the textile industry, the available data suggest that for the most part returns to capital were cyclical and declining. A sample group of eleven New England companies showed definite cyclical returns during the period. Returns to net worth averaged 10.8 percent a year from 1866 to 1873, 3.4 percent a year during the depression of the seventies, 12.1 percent a year from 1880 to 1882, and fell to 2.5 percent a year over the following four years. For the entire 21 year period the net return averaged slightly below 7.5 percent. Returns to sales showed a similar trend. For the entire industry it was estimated that by 1890 profits were 7.6 percent before depreciation and 5.8 percent after a 3 percent depreciation charge.[8]

At the Pepperell Mill the cyclical trend was also evident. Returns to stated capital (not adjusted for changes in retained earnings) dropped. They ran between 16 and 26 percent in the prosperous years and between $11\frac{1}{2}$ and $14\frac{1}{2}$ percent during depressions. The 15.7 percent average return on sales during the period 1871–74 was not again equalled during the remainder of the century. The profit margin dropped to an average of about 8.5 percent until 1893 when it fell further to about 7.5 percent. In 1899 it declined again, to 5.4 percent.[9] The companies studied by McGouldrick showed a similar pattern.

In other areas profitability did not differ greatly from that of textiles. Individual companies did well or poorly, but on the whole the records are not impressive. In the new electrical industry, Thomson-Houston Electric was organized with $1,000,000 of authorized capital. In its nine years prior to the merger into General Electric it amassed retained earnings of more than $8.5 million. The newly merged General Electric Company with assets of $50 million earned the equivalent of only a $4\frac{1}{2}$ percent return on its assets during the first eight months of operation after which it earned 2 percent in 1893 and 0.5 percent from 1894 to 1898. The United States Lighting Company incurred losses of $1.5 million from 1882–1889.[10]

Returns to sales similarly deteriorated in other companies and other industries. The Lowell Machine Shop held up well until the mid-eighties, averaging 14.3 percent a year from 1869 through 1884, but the average for the next 13 years was only 6.4 percent. Smith and Griggs, a small brass fabricator, showed returns to sales of about 16 percent from 1865 through 1879, but only 8.4 percent for the remainder of the century. Armour and Co., the meat packer, reported a steadily diminishing ratio of profit to net

[8]Paul F. McGouldrick, *New England Textiles in the Nineteenth Century* (Cambridge, Mass.: Harvard University Press, 1968), pp. 81, 99; Broadus Mitchell, *The Rise of Cotton Mills in the South* (Baltimore: The Johns Hopkins Press, 1921), p. 262.

[9]Evelyn H. Knowlton, *Pepperell's Progress* (Cambridge, Mass.: Harvard University Press, 1948), pp. 454, 468.

[10]Harold C. Passer, *The Electrical Manufacturers 1875–1900* (Cambridge, Mass.: Harvard University Press, 1953), pp. 30, 148, 327–28.

worth. Starting from an average of 42.6 percent annually in 1869–73, the ratio declined consistently reaching 11.2 percent from 1889–96.[11] On the other hand, there are several examples of firms that did well throughout the period. The Carnegie companies and Standard Oil, which we shall discuss in more detail, did very well. But some small businesses did the same. The Dennison Company, for example, averaged 18 percent on assets from 1878 through 1900 with a decline setting in only after 1895.

Dividends in the McGouldrick sample behaved similarly to profitability. They averaged 12.5 percent of paid-in capital for 1866–73, 6.5 percent during the depressed seventies, 8.7 percent in 1880–82, and 5.4 percent in 1883–86. Gras and Larson arrived at similar results. Their nine textile companies paid an average of 15.3 percent a year from 1866 to 1873 after which dividends declined, reaching 4.6 percent a year during the depression of the nineties. Dividend payments at Pepperell were atypical compared with the other textile companies. They ranged from 10 to 12 percent on capital stock from 1871 through 1880 and from 12 to 14 percent during the following 20 years. In three years (1887, 1892, and 1899) extra dividend payments increased the yields to 52, 64, and 44 percent respectively.

Dividend payments of mining corporations dropped from 3.4 percent in 1871 to 2.8 percent in 1890 and returns to gaslight company shareholders fell from 13.1 to 4.7 percent during the same period.[12] Investors in the Lowell Machine Shop enjoyed a return averaging 24 percent from 1869 to 1884. But then they suffered at an average of 8 percent from 1885 to 1897. In the railroad industry conditions became increasingly poor. In 1882, 52 percent of railroad stock was not paying dividends, and by 1897 the figure had reached 71 percent. The average dividend rate on all railroads fell from a low 2.93 percent in 1882 to an even lower 1.49 percent in 1897.

Except for railroad shares, American industry was poorly represented on the New York Stock Exchange. Textile shares were inactively traded on the Boston Exchange, and a few coal companies were traded in New York. Not until the end of the century did the term "industrials" come into general use.

The stocks that were traded did not do well. According to the Cowles Commission, industrial issues between 1871 and 1896 gained 11 percent, railroad issues lost 12.5 percent, and utilities gained 18.4 percent.

Individual issues in general followed the speculative cycle. From their 1876 highs to their 1877 lows, 3 coal issues dropped from an average of $118

[11]George S. Gibb, *The Saco-Lowell Shops* (Cambridge, Mass.: Harvard University Press, 1950); Theodore F. Marburg, *Small Business in Brass Fabricating* (New York: New York University Press, 1956), p. 100; Gras and Larson, *Casebook in American Business History* (New York: Appleton-Century-Crofts, Inc., 1939), p. 631.

[12]National Bureau of Economic Research, *Trends in the American Economy in the Nineteenth Century* (Princeton, New Jersey: Princeton University Press, 1960), pp. 431–32.

a share to $21 a share. Average railroad prices fell from a high of $70 in 1873 to a low of $21 in 1877, peaked again at $102 in 1881, and declined to the end of the century.[13]

In textile stocks the indications are that prices depended less on speculative activity than on the record of the mill. In the 1880's, the shares of South Carolina mills were reported to be worth an average of $125 a share with the highest selling at $173 and none below $100. Shares in the Pepperell Mill rose from $550 in 1871 to a peak of $1,500 in 1896 and never sold below $550. In 1899 when Pepperell merged with Laconia, the shares were selling at an average price of $1,400.

[13]Sereno S. Pratt, *The Work of Wall Street* (New York: D. Appleton and Co., 1921), p. 254; Francis Eames, *The New York Stock Exchange* (New York: Thomas G. Hall, 1894), pp. 58, 61, 64, 66–68.

9

BUSINESS COMPETITION AND THE MERGER MOVEMENT

As industrial firms took advantage of widening markets and better transportation, industrial production galloped ahead. In the early 1880's, it was twice as high as in the early 1870's. Since production tended to increase faster than demand, businessmen were harassed by problems of excess capacity and ruthless price competition. This was especially apparent when the economy turned down. During such depression periods, thousands of weak, poorly managed, poorly capitalized firms were thrown into bankruptcy. The rate of failure doubled between 1871 and 1875. Similar trends occurred in the recession of the mid-eighties and the depression of the mid-nineties. Things were equally poor in railroading. Between 1882 and 1890, only 41 percent of the capital stock of all roads paid a dividend, and by 1894, receivers and trustees were operating almost 25 percent of total mileage.

MEETING THE PROBLEM OF COMPETITION

Businessmen continuously sought a solution to the problems presented by the inexorable law of supply and demand. Traditional methods of controlling price competition centered on the trade association. Because written contracts aiming to fix prices or to curtail output were forbidden by common law, competitors resorted to so-called "gentlemen's agreements" and pools. In both of these devices, all or most of the producers in an industry or a particular market agreed to maintain fixed prices or to share the market according to some quota arrangement. The pool was, however, a more formal affair than the gentlemen's agreement.

Both of these attempts to control competition were almost as old as economic history. They began in colonial times and persisted thereafter. The Browns of Providence formed a gentlemen's agreement in candle manufacturing before Independence. In every subsequent manufacturing venture, they endeavored to convince their fellow producers that agreement was a better method of securing maximum profits than competition. When other mill owners dropped their prices, Almy and Brown urged them to reconsider, arguing that when the tide of economic activity turned, "it would not be an easy matter to again raise" the prices that had been so thoughtlessly lowered.

There were other pools. In 1817 the salt producers of the Kanawha Valley organized the Kanawha Salt Company, which set production quotas, determined prices, and sold the product for the group. Pools were also used by the early transportation companies in a desperate but frustrated effort to regulate rates. Ohio salt manufacturers formed a joint-stock company in 1851 to regulate the quantity of salt manufactured and its price. In 1853, the American Brass Association was formed to alleviate the hazards of competition. In 1854, the Hampton County Cotton Spinners Association was organized, and in 1855 the American Iron Association appeared. But pools seemed to become a common way of business life in the 1870's with the beginnings of big business.

RAILROAD POOLS

The railroads with their immense fixed capital investments were especially vulnerable to the fluctuations of the business cycle. In the depression of the 1870's, competition and rate wars lowered the rates to a point where returns to railroad investment were constantly threatened.

The situation had become so serious by the 1870's that cooperation seemed the only way for railroads to protect their interests and maintain the profitability of their organizations. The first pooling attempt of any importance was the agreement entered into in 1870 by the Northwestern, the Rock Island, and the Chicago, Burlington, & Quincy Railroads to divide the traffic between Council Bluffs (Omaha) and Chicago. Each of the roads retained 45 percent of its passenger revenue and 50 percent of its freight revenue with the remainder divided equally among the three members. The pool, with some changes, remained in operation until 1885.

Albert Fink of the Louisville & Nashville carried the pool idea much further and soon led the movement. He outlined his plan in a letter to the convention of the Southern Railway and Steamship Association in September 1875. On the basis of Fink's proposal, the Association, which included most of the important southern lines, organized a pool with Fink as commissioner. The pool set rates and apportioned freight according to formula. The portion allotted each road was based on its previous experience. Rates were set by committees for each junction point at which the roads involved were represented. Each year the traffic allotment was changed and reallocated on the basis of the amount of business each road had obtained on a nonrate cutting basis. No secret rebates or price cutting of any sort was to be used to gain an individual advantage over other members of the pool. The pool was passably successful in reducing the number and severity of price wars and maintaining rates at a profitable level and remained in effect until the Interstate Commerce Act was passed in 1887 with its provision forbidding pooling.

The roads competing for the traffic between Chicago and the East had also indulged in price wars and rate cutting. When the Baltimore and Ohio was completing its road into Chicago, the presidents of the four trunk lines met in Saratoga, New York in order to forestall another rate war. Although an agreement was reached, it was not observed, and the price cutting that followed resulted in huge losses for all the roads. Finally, an agreement was reached with Albert Fink's help, leading to the organization of the Eastern Trunk Line Association, an organization similar in most aspects to the Southern Railway and Steamship Association. Under the pooling arrangement the New York Central and the Erie Railroad each received 33 percent of all westbound freight from New York; the Pennsylvania received 25 percent; and the Baltimore and Ohio, the remaining 9 percent.

Although pooling was entered into with great gusto by railroad entrepreneurs (in 1880, 115 companies had joined combinations), by June of 1881 rate wars began again, and Fink was voicing his disappointment in railroad managers. The rate wars lasted until the summer of 1885, when J. P. Morgan established a temporary peace through consolidation of several of the competing roads. In 1887 the Interstate Commerce Act, much to the delight of many railroaders, put an end to pooling but not to the businessman's efforts to evade or circumvent the "evils" of competition.

Even before the ICC appeared, and indeed even before J. P. Morgan's intervention, railroad executives turned to combination and consolidation and self-sufficiency as a means of survival. Eastern roads consolidated operations through purchases, leases, and mergers. In the West, roads that did not run to strategic big cities tried to reduce their dependency by constructing additional mileage to the gates of large market areas. The Atchison, Topeka & Santa Fe was in the late nineteenth century the outstanding example of this strategy. In 1884, it began to build to the Pacific Coast. Then it bought a connection to the Gulf at Galveston. In 1887 it entered Chicago. By 1893, it was the longest road in the country, but it was also bankrupt.

INDUSTRIAL POOLS

Industrial pools closely followed the example set by the railroads. One of the most accomplished was the Michigan Salt Association, organized in 1876. The association was set up as a closed corporation with each producer holding one share of stock for each barrel of daily capacity of output. Each member could turn over its entire output to the association. Or it could lease its plant to the association, which in turn would manufacture and sell the salt at a fixed price. The pool handled about 85 percent of the salt produced in the area for the fifteen years of its existence, and it was just about as successful as a pool could be.

Steel rail producers also organized an important industrial pool in August, 1887. Unlike the salt pool, the steel rail pool regulated output, but did not, at least contractually, regulate prices. The pool members accounted for as much as 90 percent of total output, and by agreement each company was given a quota. Though it was disbanded after six years of operation, the pool succeeded in bringing some stability to the industry. In 1894 the pool was reorganized, but the quotas were continually violated and the final termination took place in February, 1897. Then the price of steel rails dropped from $28 to $16.50 a ton, but this may have been more because of the depression of 1893–97 than because of the pool's demise.

Other pools had mixed success. The pool in wire nails, set up in 1895, succeeded in raising the price from $1.20 to $2.55 per keg within a year, but lasted only until the end of 1896. Pools in the cordage industry had existed since 1860 but rarely lasted more than three years. The American Wall Paper Manufacturing Association included almost every company in the industry. It fixed prices and production and even attempted to exclude the middlemen, but it also failed as secret price cutting reduced its effectiveness. It was followed by the Continental Wall Paper Company in 1898, with practically the same membership and volume of output. The Continental arrangement was similar to that of the Michigan Salt Association. The Continental acted as sole selling agent for the pool members with profits distributed according to plant capacity. It thus controlled both the output of the individual companies and the prices. Jobbers could buy only from the members, and they were under pressure to maintain resale prices. In addition the two manufacturers of wall paper machinery sold only to members of the group. A contemporary charged that this pool was probably the most complete monopoly of a commonly used article ever accomplished.

Meat packing pools that determined the quantity that each packer was to ship existed from 1885 on. In 1893 the meat packers entered into a more comprehensive agreement. Weekly meetings were held, and each company reported its shipments into the various geographic areas during the week and the prices received. Fines of 40 cents per 100 pounds were imposed for exceeding quotas, and new quotas were set for the following week. In order to avoid legal difficulties, the members were designated by alphabetical letters. In 1897 the effectiveness of the pool was hampered by the competition of Schwarzschild and Sulzberger, a nonmember. The following year a new pool was organized, which included the troublesome competitor, and lasted until 1902, when as a result of public indignation and agitation, the pool was dissolved and all its records destroyed.

One of the most audacious agreements was entered into in 1894 by the Addyston Pipe and Steel Company and five of its competitors. The companies all manufactured cast iron pipe and sold principally on a bid basis to public utility companies, municipal corporations, and other large buyers. The agreement divided the market into three parts: reserved cities, pay territory, and free territory. Reserved cities were to be the exclusive domain of certain specified companies, while the free territory was open to all without restriction. The major part of the country (36 states), however, was pay territory, and it was here that the companies were to carry on business only according to the rules promulgated by the pool. All inquiries for pipe received from buyers in pay territory were to be referred to a board that determined the price at which the pipe was to be sold. All companies could bid on the order, but the one that agreed to pay the pool the highest bonus was to receive the order at a price predetermined by the board. The remaining bidders entered fictitious bids higher than the winning one to ensure that they would not be successful bidders. The bonuses received by the board were divided annually among the members according to their sales in pay territory. The pool was finally overthrown in 1899 in one of the Supreme Court's most famous decisions.

Pools rarely lasted very long because they offered no positive solution to the problem of competition in a climate of excess capacity. They neither cut costs nor increased demand. They could work only if each member refrained from producing as much as he could. Time soon showed that not all the gentlemen in a gentlemen's agreement were gentlemen and that not all the participants in a pool could be trusted to behave themselves. Market forces may not have worked as perfectly in the real world as in the theorist's model, but they worked well enough to break almost all voluntary combinations. Supply eventually exerted itself in a rough way. Members found it easy to evade the self-imposed restrictions. Sooner or later, especially in depressions when total sales were falling, one party sold below the agreed upon price, and the whole delicately contrived scheme collapsed. Outraged members could not resort to the courts, for pools were not legally enforceable. American enterprise then sought a new and stronger device for restraining competition and found it, first in the trust and later in the holding company.

The cardinal motive behind such devices as the trust and the holding company may have been to acquire and maintain power. Certainly, it was a most important consideration in the behavior of business entrepreneurs. But meeting competition and overcoming its problems was an equally, if not more, important motive.

THE TRUST DEVICE

Corporation lawyers and business entrepreneurs soon created a new form of organization that gave much more flexibility to the corporate form by expanding its capital-raising powers and at the same time confining control to a small group of insiders. This new refinement, called the trust, first appeared in the Standard Oil Trust of 1879 and in the more famous Standard Trust of 1882. The innovation was essentially the brainchild of Standard's brilliant legal adviser, Samuel C. T. Dodd, but many others contributed their ideas. Under the 1882 agreement, 41 stockholders in 40 different companies, controlling 90 percent of the country's refining capacity, turned their stock over to nine trustees in exchange for $70 million in "trust certificates," representing all the stock in 14 of the companies and most or a large block in the 26 others. The company stock was held by the trustees in joint rather than individual account so that each stockholder lost his individual interest in his own company and received, instead, a proportionate share in the total property and income of the entire trust. Stockholders continued to receive dividends. In the mysterious world of legal magic, they owned the companies but they had no vote in the trust. In the trust, in other words, ownership was effectively separated from control.

The powers of the trustees were similar to those of directors of a single, unconsolidated company. They collected all the income and distributed it *pro rata* among the certificate holders as they thought best. They could use trust funds to buy securities of other oil companies for the benefit of the trust members. The trustees had the power to discontinue operations at poorly located plants and build others at better locations. Provision was also made for the inclusion of new members. The agreement was to last for 21 years after the death of the last surviving trustee, or it could be dissolved by approval of nine-tenths of the value of the certificates within one year of its organization or by two-thirds within ten years. At the time of its supposed dissolution in 1892, the Trust had outstanding $97,250,000 of certificates representing shares of 84 companies.

The success of the Standard Oil Trust caused many imitators to pick up the idea. The Cotton Oil Trust, formed in 1884, involved about seventy plants in the business of manufacturing and refining cottonseed oil. In May 1887, the Distillers and Cattle Feeders' Trust encompassed about 80 companies in whiskey distilling—controlling 85–90 percent of total output. The

Sugar Trust arose as a result of technological improvements in refining that increased the optimum plant size and resulted in overcapacity. Between 1867 and 1887 about 36 refineries had closed leaving only 26 in business. To stabilize the industry, Henry O. Havemeyer, in August 1887, set up the Sugar Refineries Company, a trust controlling 20 refineries that produced about 78 percent of the nation's sugar output. The eleven trustees distributed $50 million of trust certificates to the shareholders in return for their stock certificates. The trustees ran the separate companies, thus providing effective consolidation. Of the twenty plants acquired, they dismantled twelve and consolidated the remaining eight into four.

Many other trusts were organized during this period: linseed oil (1885), lead (1887), cordage (1887), starch (1890), wall paper (1892), and leather (1893). "In an incredible number of the necessaries and luxuries of life, from meat to tombstones," commented Henry Demarest Lloyd,

> some of the inner circle of the "fittest" has sought, and very often obtained, the sweet power which . . . the sugar trust had: It can close every refinery at will, close some and open others, . . artificially limit the production of refined sugar, enhance the price to enrich themselves and their associates at the public expense, and depress the price when necessary to crush out and impoverish a foolhardy rival.[1]

It is easy to see why the device was so popular. It enabled a group of entrepreneurs to control many different companies in many different states —a practice that was not permitted under existing corporation law. It also enabled them to raise capital and convert some of their holdings into cash without relinquishing any of their control, for trust certificates could be bought and sold in the open market. Indeed, a few of them quickly became important playthings for stock exchange investors and speculators.

But to those who were not in the "in group," "trusts" soon became synonymous with "monopoly," and states, resentful over attempts to evade their control, began actions to dissolve them by antitrust proceedings. Louisiana attacked the cottonseed oil trust in 1887. New York revoked the charter of the North River Sugar Refining Company, one of the members of the sugar trust. Nebraska, in 1890, ordered a distiller to withdraw from the whiskey trust. But it was Ohio, in 1892, which applied the *coup de grace* when it broke up the Standard Oil Trust by ordering Standard Oil of Ohio to withdraw from the organization.

By then, however, ingenious lawyers and promoters had developed another form of organization, the holding company, which promised an equally expedient method of exercising control. Actually, holding companies of a sort had appeared earlier in the century in railroads and public

---

[1]Henry Demarest Lloyd, *Wealth Against Commonwealth*, New York, 1894, pp. 4–5.

utilities, but they were rare and were chartered by special acts of legislation. The holding company first became an important legal organizational structure when New Jersey in 1889 passed an amendment to its incorporation law permitting corporations to own stock in other corporations. This act, copied as it was by other states, permitted a group of entrepreneurs acting through a parent company to gain control over a large number of subsidiaries scattered over a wide area at the price of a relatively small investment.

GOVERNMENT REACTION TO
POOLS AND TRUSTS

The trust was a far more binding arrangement than the pool. The pool's success depended on the cooperation of the members, but the trust was controlled by a handful of trustees. The pool could and often did become a cacophony of discordant voices; the trust spoke with one voice.

But like the pools, the trusts fell afoul of the law. It did not matter what the trust was doing, or whether the trustees argued that combination was in the best interests of society, or whether the trust was economically efficient, the state courts held that trusts were hostile to competition and therefore hostile to the public good. When Standard of Ohio was ordered to withdraw from the trust, the Ohio court, anticipating a later debate, said:

> Much has been said in favor of the objects of the Standard Oil Trust and what it has accomplished. It may be true that it has improved the quality and cheapened the costs of petroleum and its products to the consumer. But such is not one of the usual or general results of a monopoly; and it is the policy of the law to regard, not what may, but what usually happens. Experience shows that it is not wise to trust human cupidity where it has the opportunity to aggrandize itself at the expense of others.[2]

All governments have always abhorred uncontrolled or unregulated monopoly. Yet most businessmen who had a possibility of achieving a monopolistic position strenuously exerted themselves to do so. Some governments, such as England, met the problem by putting some monopolies in the hands of a chosen few and attacking all others through the common law. Other nations, notably Germany, deliberately encouraged industrial firms to collaborate with each other in cartels under stringent government regulation. In the United States, by contrast, monopoly was considered an inherent evil that restricted production and inflated prices, thereby exploit-

---

[2]The most thorough historical study of antitrust is Hans B. Thorelli, *The Federal Antitrust Policy* (Baltimore: The Johns Hopkins Press, 1955).

ing the consumer and giving undeserved windfall profits to an antisocial few. Monopoly, or a market structure close to monopoly, was to be tolerated only when no alternative was possible. In the debates on what course of action should be followed in regulating business, it was taken for granted that free competition was the norm, the advantages of which were "too self-evident to be debated, too obvious to be asserted." Consequently, the economic rationale that underlay what came to be known as antitrust policy freely assumed that the elimination of monopoly would produce competition. Behavior and policy, therefore, concentrated more on opposing monopoly than on shoring up competition.

Although ostensibly concerned solely with economic issues, antitrust policy was just as much the offspring of social and ethical values. Indeed, at times economic considerations played an out-of-tune second fiddle to social and ethical considerations in the enforcement of the antitrust laws and the regulation of business. Sociologists and anthropologists have pointed out that Americans have always admired control over things, but have resented control over people. Laymen have always been impressed with the American's sympathy for the underdog. Thus, in government regulation of business, the objective of protecting the weak in the economic market place has been as important as the elimination of monopoly and certainly more important than supporting competition. In antitrust activity, this has meant attacking big business and protecting small business even at the possible expense of economic growth. As Judge Learned Hand put it:

> Throughout the history of these (antitrust) statutes it has been constantly assumed that one of their purposes was to perpetuate and preserve, for its own sake and in spite of possible cost, an organization of industry in small units.

Business leaders found this hard to understand. Their bewilderment was well expressed by James J. Hill when he heard that the Supreme Court had ruled against the Northern Securities Company, a merger of three important railroads. "It really seems hard," said Hill, "when we know that we have led all Western companies in opening the country and carrying at the lowest rates, that we should be compelled to fight for our lives against the political adventurers who have never done anything but pose and draw a salary."

THE SHERMAN ACT

Government regulation of business in America began in the Colonial Period. At that time, when goods were scarce relative to the economic ambitions of the citizens, and when medieval and mercantilist thought prevailed, governments used medieval precepts in trying to protect consumers. The concept of a "just price" was deeply ingrained in the legislation of the times, and the colonies enacted laws designed to prevent anyone from gaining a monopoly or cornering the market.

As production increased and laissez-faire economics, with its emphasis on market forces, attained respectability, direct government regulation of business diminished. Under the assumption that the normal forces of competition would constrain the businessman's propensity to monopolize, the federal government did not try to regulate the internal operation of business, and on the state and local level, regulation was on a small scale. But a deep distrust of big business and the corporation always prevailed.

State government regulation became more active in the late nineteenth century. Acting under the common law, various states moved against the trusts, which had become a popular form of business organization. Their actions seemed to have been signally successful, for the trust device was abruptly abandoned. But perhaps this was more because business entrepreneurs had discovered in the holding company a more effective method of consolidation than because of state activity. In any event, the use of the holding company immunized large scale enterprises from effective local regulation. As in other instances, the elimination of the state as a policeman, instead of shaking confidence in government regulation, led to a popular demand for federal participation.

The national government first entered the business of formal regulation with the Interstate Commerce Commission in 1887, and then on a broader basis with the Sherman Act of 1890. Labeled "An Act to protect trade and commerce against unlawful restraints and monopolies," it made illegal "every contract, combination in the form of trust or otherwise, or conspiracy, in restraint of trade or commerce among the several States, or with foreign nations." Every person who monopolized, attempted to monopolize, or conspired to monopolize any part of interstate trade or commerce was guilty of a misdemeanor subject to a fine of up to $5,000 and imprisonment for up to one year.

The Sherman Act got off to a slow start. The officials who were supposed to enforce the legislation had neither the funds nor the inclination to do so. In fact, one of the early attorneys general characterized antitrust policy as "a little narrow pinchbeck policy." Given this disinclination, it was not surprising that the act was invoked only 18 times in its first ten years, and four of these cases involved labor unions.

The first case to reach the Supreme Court was *U.S. v. E. C. Knight Co.* in 1895. The American Sugar Refining Co., which refined 65 percent of American sugar, purchased E. C. Knight and three other producers to bring its capacity up to 98 percent of total production. The government tried to enjoin the purchase, arguing that it would produce a monopolistic combination in restraint of trade. The court decided against the government on the ground that "manufacture and commerce are two distinct and very different things. The latter does not include the former."

The sugar case is usually considered a milestone in antitrust history, but its importance has been exaggerated. It is charged that the court's ruling dealt a critical, almost fatal, blow to antitrust policy, because, if manufacturing was not interstate commerce, most of the so-called trusts could not be touched. But this charge makes little sense in light of the fact that only half a dozen cases had been raised under the Sherman Act. Moreover, the court's extremely parochial definition of commerce could not continue very long. It began to break down when the court in *Addyston Pipe and Steel Company v. U.S.* (1899) held that manufacturers had violated the Sherman Act by setting up a system of collusive bidding. It was completely shattered by the Northern Securities case (1904) and *U.S. v. Swift and Co. et al.* (1905), which held that "whatever combination has the direct and necessary effect of restricting competition is in restraint of trade." In subsequent decisions, the courts have continuously broadened the definition of interstate commerce until today it may include almost any economic behavior, including the operation of a small country store in a small country town.

MERGERS AND GIANT ENTERPRISE

The attempts by businessmen to control markets and to solve their competitive headaches were not altogether frustrated by adverse legislation and adverse decisions in the courts. For by that time businessmen and their legal aides had discovered several new methods to accomplish old purposes and yet stay within the letter of the law and its interpretation. Mergers, consolidations, and holding companies not only offered a way of overcoming the obstacles that governments had imposed to thwart the trusts, but they were also immensely important as a primary force in building big business.

In the history of American business, there have been three or four waves of mergers and consolidations. The first took place in the years around 1900. It was the most important of all, for it produced all the giant corporations that dominated American business in the early years of the 1900's. It was *the* innovation, for it paved the way for the other merger waves later in the century. The second wave occurred in the 1920's; and the third in the late 1950's and again in the late 1960's. Although it is often assumed that mergers took place in periods of business stagnation, this was not the case. To the contrary, each merger epidemic occurred in a booming economy; and a prerequisite was an active, spiralling stock market.

Actually the term "merger" is used for any of three types of business combination all of which result in the same end. In a merger the firm being merged becomes a part of the remaining corporation. In a consolidation a new corporation is formed to incorporate the two or more firms being merged. In a holding company voting control of the merged firm is acquired by the parent company while the merged firm still remains a corporate entity. The holding company is, therefore, a simple modification of the "trust," with the shares of the holding company being substituted for trust certificates. In all three methods, payment for the absorbed companies may be made in cash, or in securities of the remaining corporation. In the literature each of these combinations was frequently referred to as a "trust." But then like all institutions, the "trust" had lost its specific meaning. It became a generic term used to identify a near-monopoly or a giant combination.

REASONS FOR MERGERS

In general, mergers were the result of the same basic causes that had produced vertical integration and trust agreements in the previous generation. One objective was to attain market control and eliminate or minimize competition. When, for example, the American Ice Company was formed, its stated intention was to bring under single control all the leading ice companies in the country. The United Shoe Machinery Company, formed in 1899, was not so explicit, but a letter to a competitor's stockholders left little to the imagination. It explained that the United Shoe Machinery Company had already contracted for more than a majority of the capital stock of Goodyear Shoe Machinery Company, Consolidated and McKay Lasting Machine Company, McKay Shoe Machinery Company, Goodyear Shoe Machinery Company of Canada, International Goodyear Shoe Machinery Company, Eppler Welt Machine Company, International Welt Machine Company, Davey Pegging Machine Company, besides stocks in other shoe-machinery companies, letters patent, and other property. It went on to say that the company would also from time to time acquire other shoe-machinery properties, either by direct ownership or by purchase of shares of their stock.[3]

The American Tin Plate Company, according to its president, was formed to do away with "foolishness" in making prices. In the negotiations that preceded the formation of International Harvester, the legal adviser to the McCormicks, although not adverse to a complete monopoly, argued that a few competing firms would serve to deter new entrants into the field,

---

[3]The United Shoe Machinery Company is discussed extensively in Eliot Jones, *The Trust Problem in the United States* (New York: The Macmillan Company, 1922). Although fifty years old, this is still a valuable source.

and "it is more than likely that, without adopting any 'crushing' policy the business of such competing firms can be restrained by the combination within reasonable limits."[4]

Businessmen also resorted to mergers in order to relieve the strains of declining profit margins. It was generally accepted that large-scale enterprises created by integration and consolidation could gain substantial economies of scale that were not available to small- and medium-sized firms. To some extent this turned out to be true but not to the extent envisioned, which seemed to border on the edge of infinity. Economies could be and were achieved to some extent in production and administration. The large firm could gain some economies in purchasing and in distribution. It could make use of ancillaries, such as lawyers, banks, and accountants, which were not available to small firms on the same scale. An important additional impetus and result of horizontal mergers was the increased ability to integrate vertically. One of the factors in the harvester combination, for example, was the difficulty of either Deering or McCormick to undertake further expansion on its own.

Other reasons also played their part in the consolidation movement taking place as it did and when it did. Individual and institutional savings were growing, and the business prosperity of the late 1890's brought a heightened interest in industrial securities. The relatively poor showing of railroad securities compared with the few listed industrial combinations in the depression of 1893 changed investor attitudes. At the same time, the industrialists (or their heirs) had much to gain by being part of a listed corporation, for it was much more difficult to sell a closely held business than to sell one's shares on the Stock Exchange. Even if a sale could be successfully consummated, the price received would be lower than the owner could get by going public. It was a common rule of thumb that a closed company went on the block for about three times earnings while a publicly owned and listed company could command about ten times earnings. To the industrialist who wished to retire or to his heirs who would rather spend their patrimony than continue the family business, a merger offer was indeed a golden opportunity.

Not to be overlooked was the activity on the New York Stock Exchange which, by providing a market place, allowed the public to share the gains from the new giants of industry. The public rushed to take advantage of its opportunities. Sales rose from 55 million shares in 1896 to 139 million in 1900 and then, after a few years of lesser activity, to 282 million in 1906. The Dow Jones industrial average was pushed up relentlessly from a low of 38.49 in 1897 to a high of 77.08 in 1901 when the frenzy subsided. The

---

[4]Quoted by Helen Kramer, "Harvesters and High Finance," *Business History Review*, Vol. XXXVIII, Autumn, 1964, p. 290.

eagerness of the public for stocks provided an easy market for the shares of the new merger promotions, and promoters were certainly not loath to provide the shares whether or not the consolidation was economically warranted. The process was to be repeated (with similar results) in the later merger periods.

It was clear that economic considerations were not the only reasons for the outbreak of mergers. Businessmen, argument to the contrary notwithstanding, are human beings, and human beings are not motivated solely by the objective of maximizing profits. Ambition and a drive for power also exist, and they were important factors in the merger movement. Promoters and businessmen often looked upon mergers as an ideal means of building empires, even though some empires did not pay.

THE INITIATORS OF THE
MERGER MOVEMENT

Nothing in the economic world has ever occurred by itself, and consolidations were no exception. Someone had to provide the plan, secure the approval and the cooperation of those involved, and where necessary, raise the capital funds. In short, someone had to act as the promoter of every merger.

Actually, there were three types of promoters. In many cases the manufacturers themselves performed the promotion function. In others, investment bankers took the lead. But in most cases (about two out of three) professional promoters put the combination together.

Manufacturers were responsible for putting together such giants as the American Tobacco Company, United States Leather, National Cordage, National Salt, and American Sugar Refining. In many cases manufacturers began the promotion, but couldn't agree to terms and then called in an investment banker to arbitrate. This happened in the Harvester combination with J. P. Morgan and Company ending up with a 13.4 percent ownership in the new firm. The House of Morgan also created the largest combination of the era, the United States Steel Company. But professional promoters put together most of the new giants. Judge William H. Moore and his brother were responsible for the National Biscuit Company, Diamond Match, and American Tin Plate. Charles R. Flint, the "father of trusts," brought into being United States Rubber and United Starch among others. Elbert H. Gary helped John W. Gates consolidate the barbed wire industry and create the Federal Steel Company. There were others as well, including John Dos Passos, astute corporation lawyer; John W. Young, who promoted the ill-fated United States Shipbuilding Company; and Joseph B. Greenhut, who breathed life into the Glucose Sugar Refining Company.

FINANCING THE MERGERS

The promoters of a consolidation had financial problems that differed substantially from those faced by the organizers of a trust. The trust had involved a simple exchange of trust certificates for ownership shares, but the merger promoter needed a backlog of cash to get the consolidation started. First, there was the need for option money for the merged properties (which might be lost if the merger didn't go through). In addition, since the merged companies usually retained their cash balances, cash was required to start the operation of the new company. Also, in many cases some miscellaneous debts of the merged companies had to be paid.

In a typical payment procedure, the owners of the merged companies received some cash and the remainder in securities. The securities that were paid consisted ordinarily of preferred stock equal to the book value plus a bonus of common stock with a par value equal to the preferred. When cash was required, it was raised by the sale of securities on the open market. In order to make the new securities more attractive, buyers were offered the same bonus that the insiders had already received. That is, they were also given an equal amount of common stock when they bought the preferred. Infrequently, bonds were sold to raise part of the necessary funds.

This arrangement of issuing securities in excess of book value commonly called "watering the stock" or "over capitalization" was a common financial practice that many critics were quick to deplore. But this is a naive interpretation of value. The promoters were merely capitalizing the new corporations at a multiple of expected earnings. Unfortunately, at times the earnings were more expected than real. But evaluating a going concern on its book value was never a valid method of evaluation, and there is little evidence to support a conclusion that the recipients of the common stock ever considered it to be more than a risk security. As Judge Moore put it in his testimony before the Industrial Commission in 1899, "Everybody knows what they are getting when they get common stock; they know they are not getting anything that represents assets."

THE EXTENT OF MERGER ACTIVITY

Mergers took place prior to 1898, but they were few in number compared with the activity in the five following years. In all, there were only 138 recorded mergers in manufacturing and mining in the three year period 1895 to 1898, while there were 2,653 in the 1898–1902 period. Many industries previously characterized by small- and medium-sized firms were now dominated by one or a few leaders, setting the stage for the oligopolistic business structure, which has characterized much of American industry in the twentieth century.

Most of the firms that became big businesses did so via the merger route rather than by internal growth. As one would expect, the consolidation movement was accompanied by a general increase in plant size and capacity and by the disappearance of a number of individual companies. Of the more than 3,200 mergers that took place in manufacturing and mining between 1898 and 1906, more than 350, or over 10 percent, involved major firms; and 22 firms, including United States Steel, American Tobacco, American Smelting and Refining, and American Can, grew to massive size as a result of mergers.

By 1900, the Bureau of the Census reported that there were 185 combinations controlling 2,216 plants with a total capitalization of $3,619,039,-200. The 185 combinations represented 8.4 percent of all establishments, paid 9.6 percent of wages, and accounted for 14.1 percent of production.

Consolidations resulted, of course, in the absorption of many firms. Between 1898 and 1902, 2,653 companies disappeared, over 1,200 in 1899 alone. In the three depressed years 1895–'97, consolidations absorbed less than 140 firms.

MERGER SUCCESS IN ACHIEVING MARKET CONTROL

Since one of the prime reasons for the merger movement was to achieve market control, it was to be expected that some of the new industrial giants would account for a substantial share of production. In his

TABLE 6   Some Large Companies Formed by Consolidations as of 1900

Firm	Total Stock Issued (Millions of Dollars)	Firm	Total Stock Issued (Millions of Dollars)
Federal Steel	99.7	Pittsburgh Coal	64.0
Continental Tobacco	97.7	American Bridge Co.	61.1
Standard Oil of N.J.	97.2	National Steel	59.0
American Steel & Wire	90.0	American Car &	
National Tube	80.0	Foundry	58.2
Amalgamated Copper	75.0	American Smelting	
Pullman Co.	74.0	& Refining	54.8
American Sugar Refining	73.9	National Biscuit	53.0
American Tobacco	68.5		

Source: *Report of the Industrial Commission*

study of 313 industrial mergers, Nelson found that 86 achieved control of at least 42.5 percent of the market. But the 86 constituted only 27.5 percent of the mergers, so that the remaining 72.5 percent either merged for other reasons or failed in their objective.

Some other studies of the period concluded that a much higher percentage of horizontal mergers acquired overwhelming market control. John Moody found that in 92 large mergers, 78 controlled 50 percent or more of the output in their industries; 57 controlled 60 percent or more; and 26 controlled 80 percent or more.

Even in Dewing's study of 14 mergers that failed, 11 were found to control from 40 to 85 percent of their market. Evidently, market control did not guarantee success.[5]

Whether the consolidation movement as a whole did or did not succeed in achieving monopolistic control over the market remains a debatable question. What conclusion one reaches rests very largely on the size of the sample and the criteria one uses to measure market control. But certainly, many individual firms did achieve market control. Some retained such control for an extensive period of time, but for others control was fleeting and ephemeral.

Of all the consolidations that took place around the turn of the century, the United States Steel Corporation, created in New Jersey in 1901, was by far the largest and most ambitious. Upon its organization, it controlled about three-fifths of the nation's steel business. It was fully integrated with hundreds of millions of tons of iron ore, more than 50,000 acres of coal lands, more than 1,000 miles of railroad, more than 100 lake vessels, and large holdings of limestone and natural gas properties. Although it was not a complete monopoly, its proportion of several products was quite impressive. It produced 65 percent or more of seamless tubes, tin plate, steel ingots and casting, and wire nails, and 55 percent or more of structural shapes, plates and sheets, rails, and pipe and tubes.

In its first few years, the corporation added extensively to its facilities. It constructed the largest steel plant in the world at Gary, Indiana at an eventual cost of more than $62 million. It also added a steel plant at Duluth, Minnesota and a large cement plant at Buffington, Illinois. It acquired valuable iron ore and coal properties by buying Union Steel, Clairton Steel, and Tennessee Coal and Iron and by leasing Chemung Iron, Canistee Mining, and part of the Great Northern Railroad ore lands.

Yet, despite its numerous acquisitions, United States Steel's share of the market declined steadily in many areas of production. By 1910, it pro-

[5]Ralph L. Nelson, *Merger Movements in American Industry, 1895–1956* (Princeton, N.J.: Princeton University Press, 1959), pp. 100–103; John Moody, *The Truth About the Trusts* (New York: Moody's, 1904), p. 487; Arthur S. Dewing, *Corporate Promotions and Reorganizations* (Cambridge, Mass.: Harvard University Press, 1914), p. 526.

duced less than 60 percent of eleven different products, and in five of the eleven its share was less than 50 percent.

The American Sugar Refining Company was another example of a consolidation that had temporary control of the market. The company grew out of a trust that had been declared illegal by the New York courts in 1890. Acquiring all the refineries except one, American Sugar had, by 1892, about 98 percent of the country's sugar refining capacity.

With almost total control of the business, the company raised sugar prices so sharply that new refineries constantly entered the field, and much of the company's time, energy, and ingenuity were spent in absorbing independents or working out agreements with them. And all to little avail, for the company's market control steadily declined from 98 percent in 1892 to 70 or 43 percent in 1909.[6]

The International Harvester Company held on to a position of market control much longer than Steel or Sugar. The two prime movers in the combination effort were the McCormicks and the Deerings, with the latter proposing that the combination include all the firms in the industry. The McCormicks, fearing government and farmer hostility, held out for combining only the five largest firms. When the combine was finally organized, the McCormicks received 42.6 percent of the stock, the Deerings 34.4 percent, and the remaining 23 percent divided among three other companies, one of which was by that time owned by J. P. Morgan and Company. The new corporation controlled about 90 percent of total production of grain binders and 80 percent of mowers.

During the following few years, the Harvester company acquired several competing firms—D. M. Osborne and Company, the Minnie Harvester Company, the Aultmann Company, and the Keystone Company. Until 1905 the acquisitions were not made public and the companies passed as independent firms. Control of other noncompeting areas of the farm equipment industry was also sought with the acquisition of the Weber Wagon Company and a manure-spreader factory, the development of new lines of equipment at its existing plants, and the purchase and construction of foreign plants.

In 1902, International Harvester produced an estimated 90 percent of grain binders, 83 percent of mowers, and 67 percent of rakes. In 1911, they still produced 87 percent of binders and 75 percent of the mowers, and their rake production had increased to 72 percent of the total.

In terms of controlling the market, the "tobacco trust" was much more successful than most. Market control began in 1890 with the organization of the American Tobacco Company, a consolidation of the five leading cigarette manufacturers—W. Duke, Sons & Company; Allen & Ginter; Kinney Tobacco Company; W. S. Kimball Company; and Goodwin & Com-

---

[6]The 70 percent was the Government's estimate; 43 percent was the Company's.

pany. The five produced about 90 percent of all cigarettes, but less than 8 percent of smoking tobacco. Subsequent acquisitions enabled the company to gain entry into other tobacco products. By 1900, it had a major share of cigarettes, snuff, chewing and smoking tobacco. It was weak only in cigar making, which was still a handicraft industry. But until its dissolution in 1911, it was not only able to maintain, through various acquisitions and reorganizations, its position in the domestic industry, but extended it worldwide. It had a working agreement with the Imperial Tobacco combination in Great Britain, and through its two-thirds interest in British-American Tobacco, had a dominant interest in other foreign tobacco markets not under government control.

The United Shoe Machinery Company offered another example of successful market control. At the outset, United produced from 70 to 80 percent of the important bottoming-room machinery. Within ten years, it had absorbed another fifty firms, and market control became almost complete. By 1911, the combine produced 95 percent of all bottoming machines, except outsole-stitching machines, of which it produced 78 percent.

MERGERS AND PRICES

Entrepreneurs tried to gain market control primarily to achieve "price stability," which, they hoped, would result in a satisfactory rate of profit. To what extent combinations and consolidations, or in other words, big business, succeeded in achieving this objective is a question that cannot be answered with an assured generalization.

Undoubtedly, the arrival of big business changed the process of price making. In the industries dominated by giant enterprise, prices were no longer solely the result of the interaction of impersonal forces of demand and supply. As had happened in railroading a generation before, some industrial firms had grown big enough to have an influence over prices through their control of supply. Instead of accepting supply and demand as uncontrollable forces, entrepreneurs paid more attention to their own costs in arriving at the prices they charged. Costs of production, in other words, became a primary force in the price mechanism.

Large firms could also practice price discrimination on a broad scale. But this is not to be taken to mean that large-scale enterprises could set prices wherever they wished. There was always the danger that if prices were too high, competitors would enter the field, or potential customers would resort to substitutes. Then too, if the demand for the product was elastic, buyers might simply drop out of the market. In short, discretionary pricing was not as easy as it appeared to be in mechanistic models.

We have already seen what happened to American Sugar Refining when it tried to "stabilize prices." But Standard Oil afforded a better example of price making in a giant enterprise. Standard Oil rejected charging what the traffic would bear, even though it had a near monopoly in oil refining. Instead, it set prices at a point not too high to attract competition, but high enough to make a profit. Where competition did not exist, it practiced price discrimination. Thus, net prices in 1904 ranged from 8.5 cents a gallon in Ohio to 13.9 cents in Arkansas and from 7.2 cents in southern California to 12.4 cents in northern California. The tactic was very similar to what led to the strange disparity between long and short haul rates in railroading. Where roads competed with each other, rates were pared to the bone. Where competition did not exist, roads tried to make up what they had lost in competitive territory. Thus it cost 30 cents to ship a tub of butter 900 miles from Elgin, Illinois to New York City, but 65 cents to ship a similar tub 165 miles from upper New York State to New York City.

PROFITABILITY OF MERGERS

The profitability of mergers is open to the same qualifications as their effect on prices. Depending on what is considered an adequate return on investment, the data can lead to different conclusions. Combinations in the period 1900–13 earned between 2.5 and 7.4 percent annually. During the entire period, they earned 10 percent or more only about 10 percent of the time, 7.5 percent in about one-quarter of the years covered, and 5 percent only about half the time.

About half of the consolidations of the period resulted in complete failure or reorganizations in which creditors as well as shareholders suffered. Atlas Tack, organized in 1891, went into receivership in 1896, was reorganized a year later, went into receivership again in 1899, was reorganized and again went into receivership in 1901, and was finally dissolved. National Cordage suffered a similar experience, undergoing four receiverships and reorganizations until it was dissolved in 1912. The American Bicycle Company also went through several receiverships and final dissolution in 1913. Although these are extreme examples, they demonstrate that business combination was no profit panacea. Good management and realistic capitalization were far more important. This could be seen in the experience of the Standard Oil Company, which, from 1882 to 1906, never earned less than 10.9 percent on its capital stock and in some years earned more than 80 percent. For the entire period, earnings averaged more than 35 percent of capital stock, and dividends to shareholders averaged 24 percent a year. The American Sugar Refining Company, reflecting its early strength, paid an average dividend on its common stock of 12.3 percent a year from 1891 to 1899, going as high as 22 percent in 1893. In 1900 the dividend dropped to 6½ percent, then rose the following year and was maintained at 7 percent.

The tobacco combination was also very profitable. Between 1890 and 1908 the average annual return on its assets amounted to 16 percent, and in only one year did the return fall below 10 percent. From 1890 to 1903, dividends on common stock, never lower than 6 percent and as high as 29 percent, averaged 11 percent a year.

United States Steel and International Harvester showed only moderate success in their early years. In its first decade Steel twice omitted a dividend and in the remaining years it paid from 1.5 to 5.5 percent. Harvester, in its first decade, earned an average of 7.34 percent. It paid a dividend of 3 percent in 1903, 4 percent in 1904–06, and none in 1907–09.

Another way of measuring the profitability of business organization is by the market price of its common stock. A stockholder who bought one share of stock in each of 42 large corporations would have lost in 17 and gained in 25. The gains were, however, much larger than the losses, so that an investment of $2,009 in 1903 or earlier would have grown to $3,889 by 1913 for a gain of $1,879 or 93 percent. The shares would have been held for various periods of time—one for only five years and six for twenty years or more, with an average time holding of 13.7 years. Computed on a basis of 13 years the gain works out to a compounded rate of only 5.2 percent a year. Furthermore, if two companies, American Radiator and Eastman Kodak, had been excluded, the gain would have declined to $889 on an initial cost of $1,863, which would have reduced the total gain to 48 percent, and the annual compounded rate to about 3.1 percent. From the stockholder's point of view, unless he was fortunate enough to have bought the large gainers, the profits were far from glamorous.

Undoubtedly, the horizontal merger movement of the turn of the century was an innovation in business structure. Undoubtedly, it set the structural patterns of business in the United States in the twentieth century. Undoubtedly, the initial growth of the firm provided, in many cases, certain desired benefits from the economies of scale. Intraplant economies, such as mechanization, mass production, and the use of scientific management techniques, could more easily be utilized by the large firm rather than the small one. But the economies were limited. They were, moreover, often phantom economies that served as a rationale to cover other complex motives. Where the consolidation was not based on sound economic necessity, the results were likely to be disastrous whether initiated by promoters, bankers, or the manufacturers themselves.[7] Some businessmen who took part in extravagant consolidations were empire builders who were interested in growth for

[7]Six of fourteen consolidation failures studied by Dewing were formed by the manufacturers themselves, two acting also as promoters. The great J. P. Morgan also promoted some magnificent failures.

TABLE 7   Market Value per Share of Stock in 42 Large Corporations, from Origin to 1913

Company	Start	1913	Net Change
Allis Chalmers	$ 20.13	$ 1.02[a]	$ − 19.11
American Agricultural Chemical	27.75	47.84	20.09
American Car and Foundry	17.23	46.83	29.60
American Chicle	66.72	200.96	134.24
American Hide and Leather	10.95	4.21	− 6.74
American Linseed	11.71	9.68	− 2.03
American Locomotive	27.47	33.52	6.05
American Radiator	42.50	519.33	476.83
American Shipbuilding	25.46	43.81	18.35
American Smelting & Refining	40.61	66.02	25.41
American Steel Foundries	11.44	7.64	− 3.80
American Sugar Refining	81.76	110.66	28.90
American Tobacco	119.02	237.49	118.47
American Type Founders	32.70	43.90	11.20
American Window Glass	28.15	16.33[b]	− 11.82
American Woolen	16.91	17.97	1.06
American Writing Paper	3.21	1.48	− 1.73
Chicago Pneumatic Tool	37.33	50.79	13.46
Colorado Fuel & Iron	41.65	31.13	− 10.52
Crucible Steel	24.93	15.08	− 9.85
Diamond Match	139.20	100.49	− 38.71
Eastman Kodak	103.45	617.18	513.73
General Chemical	64.21	197.98	133.77
General Electric	112.03	181.21	69.18
Harbison-Walker Refractories	4.83	46.83	41.99
International Paper	56.55	9.42	− 47.13
International Silver	18.09	110.00	91.91
International Steel Pump	28.88	8.69	− 20.19
National Biscuit	37.48	118.66	81.18
National Carbon	21.06	120.66	99.60
National Enameling & Stamping	26.08	13.07	− 13.01
National Fireproofing	35.69	8.32	− 27.37
National Lead	38.71	47.39	8.68
Pittsburgh Plate Glass	111.00	97.52	− 13.48
Pullman	186.91	253.74	66.83
Railway Steel Spring	32.89	27.08	− 5.81
Union Bag & Paper	29.64	5.30	− 24.34
United Fruit	138.58	163.64	25.06
United Shoe Machinery	36.09	111.03	74.94
U.S. Cast Iron Pipe & Foundry	13.12	12.36	− .76
U.S. Rubber	43.19	73.04	29.85
U.S. Steel	44.04	59.52	15.48
Totals	$2,009.35	$3,888.81	$1,879.46

[a] 1912
[b] 1907

growth's sake. Others were more interested in financial control and speculative profits. Although some mergers turned out to be eminently successful, the merger movement itself did not fulfill its economic justifications. When economic logic was subordinated to speculative objectives or to a drive for power regardless of cost, the mergers usually failed.

10

TWO CASES IN LATE NINETEENTH-CENTURY MANUFACTURING

Individual firms and individual entrepreneurs had different approaches and essayed different solutions to the common business problems of the late nineteenth century. The generalizations we have been making about business history in that era may lead to a misapprehension of this simple truth. To correct any inferred misunderstanding, we offer a brief summary of the history of two of the outstanding business successes of the late nineteenth century—the Carnegie Steel company and Standard Oil.

The use of cases also serves another equally important objective. Cases give more pertinence to the abstractions of business history by relating them to specific personalities and specific business firms. Not that the Carnegie companies and Standard Oil were in any sense typical or average business firms. In contrast to business organizations in general, these two firms were hugely successful. But average or not, their histories show how two firms expanded and met the business problems of their day.

THE CARNEGIE STEEL COMPANY—AN EXAMPLE OF SUCCESSFUL INDUSTRIAL CAPITALISM

It is easy to succumb to the "great man" explanation of history when the subject is Andrew Carnegie and the Carnegie steel companies. Carnegie had that peculiar mixture of admirable and unadmirable qualities that make a fascinating personality. He had more than a fair share of ambition, self-confidence, and self-reliance. Many of his contemporaries and associates, with good reason, considered him vain, boastful, cocksure, and reckless. Yet, he was also an effervescent individual of vast personal charm. In business, he was a quick decision maker and suffered fools impatiently. He could forget friendship and loyalty, but never stupidity, or what he considered stupidity. One of his associates, Thomas Miller, astutely described him, "To Andy, Napoleon that he was in business, blunder was worse than a crime. He could forgive the one; he could never excuse the other."[1]

Carnegie was a tenacious, opportunistic, and crafty competitor. "Whatever I engage in," he once said, "I must push inordinately." To fail in any enterprise was for him an unendurable experience. Even in cards and golf where no stakes were involved, he was a hard loser, brooding over every defeat. A salesman rather than technician or engineer, he manipulated people rather than things. Although he wrote and said much about his philosophy and beliefs, much of it was fantasy. Nor was consistency one of his strongest traits. He was a talented coin phraser, but many of his phrases hardly matched his behavior. Two of his most noted aphorisms were: "Pioneering don't pay" and "Put all your eggs in one basket, then watch the basket." But his early behavior in business, that is, in the years before he was forty, violated both precepts and violated them radically. He did pioneer and his eggs were in many different baskets. But then Carnegie's memory was very convenient; he remembered circumstances and events more as he wanted to than as they actually happened. All in all, Carnegie was probably more a sinner than a saint, but saint or sinner, he was a winner!

Carnegie held the controlling ownership interest in the Carnegie enterprises throughout most of their history, but it would be a mistake to conclude that he was the company and that he was solely responsible for its success. The Carnegie companies were, as most successful enterprises, the result of the efforts of many talented people of whom Carnegie was by no means the least.

No matter how talented and how innovative Carnegie and his colleagues may have been, however, their efforts would not have been successful had it not been for the favorable environment of the late nineteenth century. Before this, American iron production, although voluminous in the aggregate, was a small-scale, unintegrated, decentralized business. Steel production was so small as to be practically nonexistent. In the second half of the century, however, both the demand and the supply sides of the industry were radically affected by numerous developments of which the most significant were the Bessemer and the open-hearth processes on the supply side, and railroad construction and the structural steel building on the demand side. The Bessemer process (1856), which was ideally suited for rails,

---

[1]Quoted in Joseph Frazier Wall, *Andrew Carnegie* (New York: Oxford University Press, 1970), p. 255. This is by far the best biography of Carnegie.

eventually made it possible to produce five tons of steel in half an hour in contrast to the previous method, which took fifteen days to make fifty pounds.

By 1880, rails were absorbing 740,000 of the 900,000 tons of steel then produced. In time, as rail production declined and other steel uses increased, the Bessemer method lost much of its value, but then the open-hearth process, better suited to the newer needs but not much more economical, came to the fore. By 1900, four-fifths of pig iron production was being converted into steel. It was in this ideal environment that Carnegie achieved his enormous success.

Andrew Carnegie was born in Scotland in 1835. Like many of the stars in this age of heroic entrepreneurs, he was the son of a dominant mother and a colorless or ne'er-do-well father. With his parents, he immigrated to the United States when he was 13 and went to work as a bobbin boy in a textile factory for $1.20 a week. In 1850, he became a telegraph boy at $2.50 and before the year was out, he had become an operator at $4 a week. Throughout his life, Carnegie and good fortune were intimate friends. As an operator and as a person, Carnegie had impressed Tom Scott, who in 1853 became superintendent of the western division of the Pennsylvania Railroad and hired Carnegie as operator-secretary at $35 a month. Scott became very fond of Carnegie and financed him in ventures that soon made him independently wealthy. An extraordinary example occurred in 1858. At that time, Carnegie acquired a one-eighth interest in a sleeping-car company formed by Thomas Woodruff, who had invented one of the many such cars. Carnegie borrowed the first payment ($217.60) from the bank and paid the remainder from dividends.[2] Finding this strategy of borrowing to cover his investments eminently successful, Carnegie resorted to it over and over again. His first investment had been in Adams Express; he borrowed the money from Scott and later paid it off by mortgaging his mother's home. When he entered the steel business, he borrowed heavily from commercial and investment banks. One of his chief sources of capital at that time was J. S. Morgan & Co.

The Woodruff purchase turned out very well, paying him $5,000 a year by 1860. When he began in later life to preach the ingredients of success, Carnegie warned his young audience to avoid speculation and to concentrate on specialization. This was more than ironic, for the Woodruff stock purchase was a speculation, and it violated the rule of specialization. A foolish consistency, however, was to Carnegie as it was to Emerson "a hobgoblin of small minds."

---

[2]According to Carnegie, he was mainly responsible for bringing Woodruff into contact with Scott. This was a typical piece of Carnegie's fancy. Actually, Scott made an agreement with Woodruff and as was his habit, he insisted that "his boy Andy" be counted in for a piece of the action.

THE FORMATION OF THE
CARNEGIE COMPANIES

In 1859, Carnegie succeeded Scott as superintendent of the Pennsylvania's western division. By then, steel was on the threshold of its extravagant expansion. But Carnegie did not enter the business until 1863. The firm with which he then became closely involved had been started by the Kloman Brothers in 1858. By 1863, Andrew's brother Thomas and two of Andrew's friends, Thomas Miller and Henry Phipps, had become partners in the business. Andrew had advanced the money for his brother, but he was not able to get a share in the business for himself. Soon after the partnership formation, Andrew Kloman[3] elicited Phipps' help in an attempt to oust Miller. Andrew Carnegie was called in to arbitrate the matter. He persuaded Miller to reduce his share drastically. Along with Miller, he then started the Cyclops Iron Works. This company was not successful because it lacked technical talent. In 1865, in the last year of the Civil War, which had made the iron business extraordinarily prosperous, Carnegie resigned from the Pennsylvania. In the same year, at the suggestion of Thomas Carnegie, Kloman and Phipps consolidated with Cyclops to form the Union Iron Mills, a specialized firm that manufactured structural shapes from wrought iron but manufactured no pig iron. At about the same time, Carnegie, with no cash investment of his own, had become part owner of the Keystone Bridge Company. Far from being specialized, Carnegie's interests were at this time remarkably diversified. He was associated with Miller in oil, telegraphy, and banking and with William Coleman, Thomas Carnegie's father-in-law, in oil.

Events moved rapidly in the next few years. Miller continued to find it impossible to work with his old friend Phipps, and he sold his share of the company to Carnegie for $71,362, considerably less than the $142 million that it would eventually be worth. In 1867, Carnegie, who was now managing the company's finances and sales along with his other diversified interests, moved his headquarters from Pittsburgh to New York—a move of more than ordinary significance in managerial history. In New York, Carnegie spent most of his time selling his companies' products through his wide contacts in the railroad and other businesses. In 1870, the company erected the first of a series of blast furnaces to make its own pig iron, and at the same time took the daring and altogether unusual step of hiring a chemist.[4]

By 1870, Carnegie's income was well over $50,000 a year, and he toyed with the idea of giving up business. Instead, he followed his later oft-quoted

---

[3]The other Kloman brother, Anthony, had already been bought out by Miller.
[4]This was apparently the brainchild of Henry Phipps, who had an obsession with cost reduction that matched Carnegie's.

advice. Putting all his eggs in one basket and watching the basket, he became a specialist in steel. He had flirted with steel as far back as 1866, but up to 1872 his public pronouncements had extolled the advantages of iron and downgraded those of steel. But then for one reason or another he became convinced that steel was to be king. It has been said that the initiative for the first of Carnegie's steel companies came not from Andrew, but from Thomas Carnegie and William Coleman, both of whom were superb production men. But Carnegie's most recent biographer scoffs at this as well as at the idea that Carnegie held back from innovation. He claims, on the contrary, that Thomas, Kloman, and Phipps were the cautious ones, holding Carnegie back from the risks to which his recklessness would naturally have taken him.

Regardless of who was primarily responsible, Carnegie, McCandless & Company built the Edgar Thomson steel works at Braddock, Pennsylvania in 1873.[5] Note that this was just at the peak of the business cycle and that the entry into the business and the construction of the plant took place during the longest and one of the severest depressions in economic history. Carnegie was to repeat this strategy later. Depressions were looked upon as a time for ambitious and thorough overhauling, retooling, and capital formation. During the depression of 1893, for example, the Carnegie companies completed a process of vertical integration. They were then in a position to produce everything in steel except some end-products such as tubing. At the same time, the company rationalized the production process by putting in the open-hearth method.[6] Of course, all this expansion required substantial capital outlays. Carnegie raised the funds for his initial ventures by selling some of his other holdings and by borrowing from the banks. Later expansion was financed for the most part by retained earnings.

CORPORATION FINANCE AND MANAGEMENT
IN THE EARLY STEEL BUSINESS

Carnegie, McCandless & Co. represented an investment of $700,000. Andrew Carnegie's interest was $250,000. William Coleman put in $100,-000, and seven others, including Thomas Carnegie, Kloman, and Henry Phipps invested $50,000 each. In their subsequent history, the Carnegie enterprises adjusted their capitalization sporadically rather than year by year as earnings were plowed back into the business. In October 1874, Carnegie, McCandless & Co. was dissolved and succeeded by the Edgar Thomson Steel Co., Ltd. to take advantage of Pennsylvania's new law giving limited liability to all the partners in a Pennsylvania Association.

[5]Alexander L. Holley was actually responsible for building the works.
[6]Carnegie insisted on putting two Siemens open hearths in the first plant.

During the depression, four of the partners, needing money, sold their interest to Carnegie. By 1878 when the company was once again reorganized, Carnegie owned $741,000 of $1,250,000. Another consolidation occurred in 1881, and when Carnegie Brothers & Company emerged, Andrew owned $2.7 million of the $5 million capital. Thomas Carnegie and Henry Phipps owned $878,000 each. Another reorganization took place in 1886 when Carnegie Phipps & Company was formed to operate the Lucy Furnaces and the Homestead Mills, which had been purchased in 1883.

In the early 1880's Carnegie Brothers began to integrate backward to the raw materials. The process brought Henry Clay Frick and the Frick coke business into the company in 1882. When Thomas Carnegie died, Phipps became temporary chairman, but Frick took over the job in 1889. It was during the reorganization of 1886 that the company created the famous iron-clad agreement, under which any stockholder's stock could be purchased at book value by a vote of 75 percent of the stock. The stock of any stockholder who left the company for any reason had to be sold back to the company at book value.

During all this time, the company's management operated under a loose division of labor. Carnegie had no office, but he was unquestionably the executive of last resort. Frick, whose relations with Carnegie deteriorated steadily, was chairman of the board. Phipps was the accountant and in charge of raising capital funds chiefly through bank loans. Thomas Carnegie, Captain Bill Jones, and later, Charles M. Schwab, were the production men.

In 1892, the enterprises were again reorganized. Carnegie Brothers and Carnegie Phipps were sold to Carnegie Steel Company, Ltd., a new firm with a capital of $25 million. Andrew owned 58.5 percent; Phipps, 11 percent; Frick, 6 percent[7]; George Lauder, 4 percent; Schwab and 20 others, 1 percent. Meanwhile, relations between Carnegie and Frick were deteriorating to the point of no return. Carnegie persistently interfered in matters that were not his business. Moreover, he treated the brilliant Frick—and brilliant he was[8]—as an office boy, embarrassing him by vetoing some of his decisions and making sneering remarks behind his back. The last in a series of crises bordered on the absurd. Frick and Carnegie had made an informal agreement whereby Carnegie Steel was assured of as much coke as it needed for the next three years at a price below the existing market price. Frick on second thought abrogated the agreement on the ground that he had no

[7]Frick had originally 11 percent, but he owed Carnegie for much of this. When he paid off his note to Carnegie, his share fell to 6 percent.

[8]From a reading of the evidence, it is evident that Frick's business ability has been grossly undervalued. He was as able as Carnegie and perhaps abler, but unfortunately his personality lacked Carnegie's charisma. See George Harvey, *Henry Clay Frick, The Man* (New York: Charles Scribner's Sons, 1928).

authority to negotiate a selling agreement. Legally, Frick was correct; he had acted in excess of his authority. At first glance, the matter seems to have been a piece of trivia, since the same individuals owned both companies even though they were still legally independent enterprises. But this is misleading, for Frick and the H. C. Frick Company owned much more of the Coke Company than of the steel company, and Carnegie owned a larger share of Steel than of Coke. In any event, Carnegie came to regard the matter as one of principle, and since Frick would not give in, Carnegie forced him to resign and then attempted to use the iron-clad agreement to force Frick to sell his stock at its book value. Frick, of course, objected.[9] He insisted that the $25 million value placed on the company by the iron-clad agreement was absurd. Since the company earned $21 million in 1899, his argument was valid, no matter how little it suited Carnegie. On the basis of earnings, the company was worth at least $210 million, and its prospects for future growth were, to say the least, encouraging.

What added to Frick's case was that he had already offered to buy the company for $320 million. Carnegie had accepted the price and had given a $2 million option to buy. Frick negotiated with the Moore Brothers, well known corporation promoters, and they agreed to pay $1 million for an option. All it then took to satisfy Carnegie's share was another $170,000, which Frick and Phipps deposited. But the plan never materialized because the promoters could not raise the necessary cash. The options were forfeited to Carnegie, which did nothing to improve relations.

The difference of opinion about the iron-clad agreement did come to court, but the pressure on Carnegie and his shaky legal case resulted in a settlement in 1900. The company was reorganized as the Carnegie Company, Inc. with a capital of $320 million, half in common stock and half in bonds. Frick emerged with $30 million, but he was forever forbidden to hold office in the company.[10]

THE UNITED STATES STEEL CORPORATION

Meanwhile, other steel companies were allying and uniting in this era of trustification. In the late 1890's, the House of Morgan put together the National Tube Company and an integrated steel company, the Federal Steel Company; the Moore Brothers floated the National Steel Company

[9]If the reports of those who knew were true, this is a major understatement. It was reported that when Carnegie told Frick what he was about to do, Frick erupted, "For years I have been convinced that there is not an honest bone in your body. Now I know that you are a god damned thief." He thereupon advanced upon Carnegie with fists clenched. But Carnegie got to the door first.

[10]In the later formation of U.S. Steel, Frick received $15.8 million in bonds, $23.8 million in preferred stock, and $21.8 million in common.

and a handful of specialized companies. In retaliation, Carnegie threatened to build a tube plant, a railroad from Pittsburgh to Tidewater, and anything else that was necessary to compete all along the line.

Before these plans could be consummated, however, Morgan stepped in, bought the Carnegie companies for $480 million, and consolidated about 60 percent of the steel business in the giant United States Steel Corporation, the world's first billion dollar industrial corporation. Morgan was, of course, accused of having flagrantly watered the stock of the new company by having issued stock in excess of the company's stated value. Actually, the value set by the Morgan interests was much more realistic than the value set by the Carnegie company. After a few shaky years, United States Steel settled down and became part of the bedrock of the Stock Exchange. If the company had been so overcapitalized, the so-called "water" in the stock would not have dried up nearly so fast.

PRICING POLICY IN THE CARNEGIE COMPANIES

Carnegie, McCandless was a late starter in the steel business even though the industry was small at that time. For some years, the ironmasters who were now in steel had tried to divide up the business in a pool arrangement under the auspices of the Bessemer Steel Association. It was not a dog-eat-dog industry but one that followed the maxim; "fight and shake hands." Carnegie was not sympathetic, and throughout his career he was the maverick in every pool arrangement.

The first meeting of the Steel Association that Carnegie attended allotted the Carnegie Company a 9 percent share. The largest quota, 19 percent, was assigned to Cambria. Carnegie insisted that he would have as large a share as any other firm. When this was greeted with laughter, he told the assembled delegates exactly how much salary and expenses each was receiving. He then informed them that he would undersell them because his company could make a profit at a price of $65 whereas they needed $70 to break even.

Carnegie, more than anyone else, made steel a prince and pauper business, cutting the price sharply in recession and setting it high when demand was increasing. According to J. P. Morgan, with whom Carnegie had little in common, Carnegie demoralized the industry. This could very well be, but in a new industry producing an undifferentiated product, price competition was the only competition possible. In a free enterprise system, some producer or other was sure to recognize this homely truth and put it to use.

One of the reasons why Carnegie's pricing policy was superior to that of his competitors was his interest in and respect for accounting. When the Edgar Thomson works opened, Carnegie enticed W. P. Shinn, a career executive in the Allegheny Valley Railroad, part of the Pennsylvania system, to become general manager in the new plant. Shinn installed an accounting system similar to the one employed by the railroad. The firm kept careful track of costs and prices by means of daily cost sheets. It accepted no order until cost had been carefully calculated. It used its accounts in making decisions about technological modernization, output, and prices. As one of the company's executives somewhat ruefully explained, "The minutest detail of cost of materials appeared . . . in the accounts and . . . every man in the place was made to realize it. The men felt and often remarked that the eyes of the company were always on them through the books." This concentration on costs reflected a Carnegie obsession. As one of his partners said, "Carnegie never wanted to know the profits. He always wanted to know the cost."[11] And he wanted to know it meticulously in the objective language of numbers. As he himself put it, "Figures, my friend, figures!"

LABOR RELATIONS IN THE
CARNEGIE PLANTS

Labor relations in the Carnegie companies were not handled in any clearcut fashion. There was no concise answer to the question of who was responsible for what. This was especially true after Frick became chairman. Before him, Andrew Carnegie made policy presumably on the supposition that labor relations fell in the area of major decisions for which he was responsible.

On the whole, what Carnegie thought and did about labor was not much different from what other businessmen thought and did. He had his difficulties with the Amalgamated Association of Iron and Steel Workers and presumably with the workers too. The Amalgamated represented skilled workers and, therefore, more or less ignored the unskilled who made up most of steel's labor force. Originally, there were some Amalgamated members in the Homestead works, but management certainly did not encourage them. Indeed, it was labor trouble that persuaded the Homestead owners to sell out to Carnegie Brothers in 1883. As soon as Homestead was acquired, Carnegie announced that the company would no longer negotiate with the Union on the ground that the Union represented only a minority of the workers.

Carnegie's principle was that in case of a strike, management would "confer freely" with the workers and "wait patiently until they decided to

11Wall, *Andrew Carnegie*, p. 337.

return to work." He insisted that no strike breakers would be used. In 1887, the Carnegie labor policy met its first severe test. The company announced a 10 percent cut. It was refused, and the Edgar Thomson works were shut down. Carnegie then announced that future wages would vary with the price of steel. There would, however, be a minimum below which wages would not be allowed to fall. At that time, the Thomson plant was on an eight-hour day, one of only two mills so operating. The Knights of Labor had promised to apply pressure for an eight-hour day on competing companies, but it had not done so. Carnegie then restored the twelve-hour day,[12] and in the ensuing strike, the works were shut down for six months before the workers capitulated.

In 1889, the first Homestead strike took place as a protest against the sliding scale. Carnegie was in Europe, and the works manager brought in strikebreakers. Riots broke out before a compromise was agreed upon. The strikers accepted the sliding scale with a three-year agreement at a rate higher than first proposed.

When the agreement ran out in 1892, the second Homestead strike, one of the most notorious in American labor history, occurred. Although the economy was at the height of prosperity, Frick, who was now chairman, proposed to lower the floor to which the sliding scale could drop. Only 325 out of 3,800 workers would be affected, but they might be subject to a cut of 15 percent. The company also wanted to eliminate the union completely and it stipulated further that contracts should expire in January not June.[13] Negotiations between Carnegie and the spokesmen for the workers resulted in some concessions on both sides, but not enough for agreement. Carnegie then left for his annual stay in Europe, leaving Frick to negotiate. Frick, however, had no notion of negotiating any further. He was preparing to bring in strikebreakers from the Pinkerton agency, a fact of which Carnegie must have been aware. When the strikebreakers arrived, an all-day battle broke out in which a number were wounded and some were killed. The strikers won the skirmish, but Frick appealed to the Governor, who dispatched the national guard to protect the plant. Gradually, the workers returned. The Carnegie Company had won, the union had been destroyed, and Carnegie's reputation had descended to its lowest point. The *St. Louis Post-Dispatch* said of him:

[12]From an economic point of view this move seems to have been irrational. According to Captain Jones, the 8-hour day was an important reason for the Carnegie Company's ability to produce many more tons of steel than any of its British competitors. What seems to have been lost in an 8-hour compared to a 12-hour day was more than made up by increased productivity.

[13]At the time, Homestead workers made a maximum of $7.60 a day, but only 4 workers earned this; 113 averaged between $4 and $7.60; 1,177 made $1.68 to $2.50; and 1,625 made $1.40 or less.

Count no man happy until he is dead. Three months ago Andrew Carnegie was a man to be envied. Today he is an object of mingled pity and contempt. In the estimation of nine-tenths of the thinking people . . . he had not only given the lie to his antecedents, but confessed himself a moral coward . . . say what you will of Frick, he is a brave man. Say what you will of Carnegie, he is a coward.[14]

THE REASONS FOR CARNEGIE'S SUCCESS

Undoubtedly, the Carnegie enterprise was vastly successful. Indeed it was so successful that it swayed public opinion into the mistaken belief that all business firms wallowed in wealth. To the contrary, the Carnegie experience was most unusual. It was a growth firm in a growth business. In 1883, the company's profits passed $1 million. By 1887, they were $3 million; in 1896, $6 million, and in 1900, $40 million. But at the same time, steel prices declined secularly from $65 a ton in 1875 to $17 a ton in 1898. Production increased inversely. In 1872, the United States produced less than 100,000 tons; by 1900, the Carnegie works alone were turning out 4 million tons, roughly half of American production, which in turn was roughly half the world's total.

It is not too difficult to explain the Carnegie Company's success. It was a case of a group of talented men taking advantage of the right time and the right environment. It is not so easy, however, to explain what made Andrew Carnegie so extraordinarily successful. It was certainly not because he worked hard in the sense of being chained to his desk for eight or nine hours and to his briefcase for another four. To the contrary, he spent half of every year in Scotland, although undoubtedly he kept in touch with the business wherever he was. Nor was it because of his analytical talents or his innovative genius. He was not really an inventor or a pioneer. Alexander Holley and John Fritz were the American innovators of the Bessemer process.

What then did he have? What did he contribute? Aside from being an outstanding salesman, which was no mean accomplishment, he was the first in the steel business to realize the importance of mass production. He encouraged any method that would increase output and cut costs. He pioneered in scientific analysis and in cost accounting. But above all, he recognized and understood the function of a chief executive in a big business. He worked only on major decisions, on the big things, not on details. He would not have been able to do this had he not possessed an enviable talent for picking able men to help him. He found the men and he drove them

14Quoted in Wall, *Andrew Carnegie*, p. 572.

hard. He was much like Henry Ford in a later period. The Carnegie enterprise was never one big happy family. Men were expendable, executives as well as laborers. Miller went, Kloman went, Scott went, Shinn went, and even Frick went, but the Carnegie mills kept on going. Perhaps, eventually, Carnegie, like Napoleon and Ford, would run out of manpower, but by then, Carnegie too was out of the business.

All in all, Carnegie personified in the steel business what Veblen described as the transition from the captain of industry to the captain of business. Before Carnegie, the great men in steel had been self-taught engineers who were at home in the factory but out of place anywhere else. After Carnegie, steel executives were much more at home in an office than in a factory. Carnegie bridged the gap. He had no place in the factory and not much more place in an office. He knew that steel could be sold at a dinner table or in a club as well as in an office. Indeed, no office was big enough to confine him. As Fritz Redlich has said, "It is doubtful whether the development of the American iron industry would have been otherwise if Carnegie had never lived, but it is also doubtful if the development would have been as rapid."

STANDARD OIL AND JOHN D. ROCKEFELLER

The Standard Oil Company and John D. Rockefeller[15] met and handled their business problems much differently than the Carnegie companies did. One important reason for this was that Carnegie and Rockefeller differed markedly from one another in their philosophy, beliefs, and approaches to business and its management. Neither Carnegie nor Rockefeller ran a one-man company; both were magnificently assisted by men of unusual talent. But Carnegie, despite his magnetism, found it difficult to get along with many of his associates and left no doubt about who dominated the firm. Rockefeller, on the other hand, was much more a company man than Carnegie. Although his personality was not nearly as striking as the little Scotsman's, and although it was said that "he was 100 years old when he was born," he got along much better with his colleagues. Then too, unlike Carnegie and other contemporary business leaders, Rockefeller was more a generalist than a specialist. He knew the oil business. In the early years, he was not adverse to taking part in the physical labor associated with the business. He was always interested in raising capital, watching the books, the manufacturing process, and personnel problems. But as time moved on, he delegated more and more of the details of ad-

---

[15]The early years of the Standard Oil Company and John D. Rockefeller's business career are treated exhaustively in Ralph W. and Muriel E. Hidy, *Pioneering in Big Business* (New York: Harper and Row, 1955) and Allan Nevins, *John D. Rockefeller*, two volumes (New York: Charles Scribner's Sons, 1941).

ministration. He was that most adept entrepreneur, a brilliant leader of a brilliant orchestra. In his generalized knowledge and his increasing concentration on broad policy decisions, he anticipated the professional executive of the next generation.

Rockefeller was born in 1839, the magic late 1830's that produced so many business leaders—Carnegie, J. P. Morgan, Mark Hanna, and James J. Hill among others. Rockefeller's family was not average American, judged either by its mode of life or by its income. Like so many other extraordinarily successful businessmen, he had a strong-willed mother who was more respected than loved. She taught him the bourgeois virtues of thrift, thoroughness, responsibility, and religious faith that would be of enormous help to him in his later business success. His father was, to say the least, peculiar. A man of many parts in business, his chief occupation was peddling. He was a successful, itinerant medicine man, who sold oil in large and small bottles to those who could be lulled into believing that it was a panacea for man's aches and pains. His movements were mysterious, and since he was rarely at home his family saw little of him. He was not, however, entirely bereft of paternal virtues. One of his objectives was to teach his sons to be "sharp." In this he was extravagantly successful, although his strategy was somewhat unorthodox. It was said that one of his tactics was to cheat his sons out of the few cents they earned. Be that as it may, his prosperity enabled him later to help John D. financially.

In high school, Rockefeller showed a talent in practical subjects that would later come in handy in his business and economic life. He was a master of mathematics but of little else. He started early on his career of money-making by beginning at age seven to sell turkeys off the family farm, just as the nine-year-old Gustavus Swift sold chickens and ten-year-old Leland Stanford sold chestnuts.

After four years as a bookkeeping clerk, John D. at twenty formed a commission merchant partnership with a man named Maurice B. Clark. By this time, he had already formed his philosophy and determined his objectives, and he was soon to demonstrate his life-long business methods. "I'm bound to be rich," he announced. But money was not the only goal. Business to him was more than a road to wealth. It was a great, an exciting, a serious game. Accomplishment, he taught years later, was the thing. "Some say that because a man is successful and accumulates wealth, all he is after is to get wealth . . . . How blind!"

Although throughout his life he constantly thought about and analyzed his business affairs, he did not work hard in the usual sense of spending long hours at the office or of "remaining in the saddle" until he was old and tottering. He began to retire from Standard Oil in 1890 when he was hardly 50, and he retired from the company completely before he was 60.

In private life he was very conservative, practicing rigid economy and faultless order. In his business relations, he was a radical. To be sure, he avoided hunches. He looked at every problem coldly, unemotionally and as nearly as possible in the clear light of logic. He insisted upon complete mastery of detail, but his business campaigns and tactics were those of a bold innovator. He was growth-minded, expanding the business as rapidly as possible and depending as much as possible on what he could borrow. He had the precision of a bookkeeper, the temperament of an unemotional surgeon, and the imagination and thrust of a military genius.

In both his private and his business life, he was secretive and close-mouthed and had few, if any, close friends. He boasted that he could tell a man's income a few minutes after meeting him. "Don't be a good fellow," was the only advice he ever gave the well-attended Sunday school class that he taught for years.

ENTRY INTO THE OIL BUSINESS

In the same year that Clark & Rockefeller started in business, Col. Edwin L. Drake had drilled an oil well in western Pennsylvania. Nine years earlier, in 1850, James Young had patented in Scotland a process for extracting a liquid hydrocarbon from coal and shale and distilling it to produce naphtha, kerosene (coal oil), and paraffine.

With Young's technology, Drake's discovery set in motion what was to become the gigantic petroleum industry. But in the early 1860's, it still had all the characteristics of a new industry. It was a young man's industry, boisterous and rowdy. In the very beginning, there were many small firms, each specializing in one aspect of the business. Some were producers, some were refiners, and some were in marketing. Some made barrels and others provided castings. These early oil men borrowed heavily from existing industries, but a few added something of their own. As early as 1865, a man named Van Syckel built the first successful pipe line as a means of eliminating the teamster with his horse and wagon. But most lived simply for the short run. Price cutting was an unpopular but widely practiced sport. All prices fluctuated sharply, but the squeeze was on the refiner. In the years 1869–71, for example, crude prices fell 19 percent, but kerosene dropped by 25 percent, or almost half again as much as crude. Naturally, failures were common both among producers and refiners.

In order to instill a semblance of order to the industry, some entrepreneurs began to integrate both horizontally and vertically. For example, Jacob Vandergrift was active in production as well as in marketing. But these were few and the business was still a hurly-burly one when Clark and Rockefeller came in. They had been doing very well in produce what with the Civil War and Rockefeller's ambition. Then in 1863 they joined with Samuel Andrews and Maurice's two brothers, Richard and James, to form the Excelsior Oil Works to refine crude oil. Andrews, helped by Richard Clark, handled production, James Clark bought the raw material, and Rockefeller and Maurice Clark handled the finances and management. There was, however, really nothing for Clark to do because Rockefeller took charge. Moreover, James and Richard did not like Rockefeller, and the feeling seems to have been reciprocated. In addition, John D.'s business tactics seemed too reckless for the Clarks' temperaments. He was too impatient to expand the business. It was his intention to gain a monopoly in refining, which he recognized as the bottleneck of the business. He had long since concluded that unbridled price competition would keep everybody poor. Whether he was right or wrong from society's point of view, he thought that competition hampered research, injured the competent, and redounded against the consumer. He had every intention of preventing expansion from getting out of hand, for he realized that careful accounting was the foundation of a stable business, but he also knew that large credit facilities were essential to steady expansion. And he was certainly not adverse to borrowing. In fact, in his own words, he "wore out the knees of his pants" obtaining credit from the banks. It must be remembered that the capital needs of the early refining business were not as great as they might seem and certainly far less than they were to become later. As late as 1875, one of Standard's strongest competitors built a refinery for only $65,000. But this is all a relative matter. Rockefeller could use all the capital he could get. Then as later, the company relied on plowed-back earnings, bringing in new owners, and bank loans.

By 1865, it was clear that the business was too small for Rockefeller and too big for the Clarks. In an auction, the former bought the latter out for $72,500 plus his share of the commission business. Rockefeller and Andrews were then the largest oil refiners in Cleveland. Although Andrews stayed on, he too would eventually sell, for his temperament was also not equal to Rockefeller's radical business strategy.

TOWARD VERTICAL INTEGRATION

Rockefeller and Andrews emphasized vertical integration even before the Clarks left. In 1864, at John D.'s urging, they began to make their own barrels and shortly purchased tracts of land to provide timber. In 1866, Rockefeller, recognizing his own limitations, but desiring to become more involved with the marketing end of the oil business, brought his brother William in to set up a marketing export office in New York. In 1867, Rockefeller persuaded Henry Flagler and Flagler's uncle, Stephen

Harkness, to join the company, the latter as a silent partner. With their entrance, Rockefeller, Andrews, & Flagler became the largest refinery in the world.

Flagler brought with him not only capital, but brains and experience. He took charge of the transportation end of the business. As the traffic manager, his job was to get the best rates he could from the freight agents, and he did very well. Indeed, it has been said that Standard Oil's success rested on the solid foundation of the rebates Flagler was able to obtain. This is a highly oversimplified explanation. For reasons that we are about to explain, the railroads had been giving rebates with a free hand ever since the oil business began. Standard Oil was a success less because of rebates than because it excelled in efficiency. It put its by-products to use better than its competitors did. It practiced vertical integration earlier and more thoroughly. It had better facilities. Andrews was an efficient production man, and Rockefeller used cost accounting before any one else in the petroleum industry.

It could be assumed that the refiners in the oil fields would have an advantage over those in outlying areas, such as Pittsburgh, Cleveland, Philadelphia, and New York. This advantage of being on top of the well was, however, neutralized by the fact that producers in the field had to bring in from distant points what they needed for production. But what really hurt them and also Pittsburgh was the relative sparcity of transport facilities. The Pennsylvania Railroad and pipe lines were the only ways out of western Pennsylvania, and the railroad was not about to forget this fact. It therefore charged what it thought the traffic would bear. The consequence was that the oil fields were in a disadvantageous position vis-a-vis Cleveland, which had a plethora of means of transport: the Pennsylvania; the Atlantic and Great Western Railroad, atttached to the Erie; the Lake Shore & Michigan Southern, a creature of the New York Central; the Great Lakes; and the Erie Canal.

Since there was not enough traffic to satisfy all the roads, each of them competed for the existing business by granting rebates. These were, of course, secret, and every freight agent tried to concede as little as possible.

Flagler undoubtedly did well, but Standard Oil of Ohio, which was incorporated in 1870 at Flagler's suggestion, was not satisfied. The goal was to consolidate the oil business, or at least most of it, in order to do away with dog-eat-dog competition. Pools would not work nor would gentlemen's agreements. Horizontal integration through merger was in Rockefeller's opinion the only answer. But this did not come to fruition at that moment. Instead, the plans for a wholesale consolidation were detoured by the South Improvement Company, a scheme concocted by the railroads and some refiners. The objective was to divide as much of the refining business as possible among the three major railroads. The South Improvement Company, which was theoretically open to any refiner who cared to join, proposed to ship 45 percent of its oil over the Pennsylvania and the rest equally between the Erie and New York Central. The tariff was to be raised, but the members of the SIC would get a 40-50 percent kickback on their crude and 25 to 50 percent on refined. Nonmembers in Cleveland who shipped to New York would pay an overall cost of $2.80 a barrel on crude and refined compared to the old cost of $2.40, but Standard would pay only $1.90. The members of the cartel would, moreover, receive a drawback on every barrel shipped by a nonmember. Whether Flagler and Rockefeller were the instigators of this device is a moot question, but they certainly supported it with enthusiasm. Clearly, this arrangement would drive all nonmember competitors out of business. But the Machiavellian scheme failed. The Pennsylvania legislature, under the onslaughts of an army of producers and independent refiners, many of whom would later become executives of Standard Oil, repealed the South Improvement Company's charter. It was a complete defeat for Standard and Rockefeller, one of the few out-and-out mistakes in his business career.

BUILDING THE MONOPOLY

From a business standpoint, Standard Oil put together a superlative organization. But intellectually and philosophically, it represented a mass of inconsistencies. Most of the oil business executives, like most business leaders, practiced so-called "cut-throat" competition and tried to achieve monopoly while extolling the virtues of competition. Rockefeller and Flagler did not share this inconsistency. They understood their objectives clearly. It was John D., Jr., not Sr., who defended consolidation by saying that the best way of obtaining the best rose was to cut off all the buds except one. He may have said it, but the philosophy was his father's.

As has been mentioned, the oil business suffered from chronic overproduction at the refinery and even more so at the well. It was dog-eat-dog in interminable warfare. Railroads fought canals and each other. Teamsters and railroads fought the pipelines and each other. Producers hated refiners and vice versa. Everyone fought and hated everyone else. Pools were proposed time and time again to deal with the problem. The South Improvement Company was really a pool. So was the "Pittsburgh Plan," a grandiose scheme whereby the refiners would fix the prices of both crude and finished product with each member being assigned a quota. Neither of these and none of the many subsequent pooling arrangements worked. Rockefeller and Flagler were hardly disappointed, for they had never really believed that pools were workable. They, therefore, returned with enthusiasm to their original plan of putting an end to overproduction by consolidating the whole business. They proposed to begin with refining, the strategic bottleneck in the chain from the well to the consumer. Soon they would get around to marketing and finally to extraction.

"What we did," Rockefeller later reminisced, "was to take the large concerns first." Standard had three great advantages in its early consolidation campaign. It was by far the most efficient producer. Second, it had strategic relations with the railroads. It controlled the terminal facilities in Cleveland. The railroads were making no bones about threatening the producers through the proposed South Improvement Company. And since Standard shipped more oil than anyone else, it got the best freight rates and in addition it often obtained rebates. Finally, as a result of the depressed business conditions of the early 1870's, all the other oil companies were losing money. Many of them found it difficult if not impossible to continue in business.

Even before the depression set in, Standard, in 1871, bought its largest Cleveland competitor, Clark, Payne & Co.,[16] which had been losing money. In the same year, it purchased Jabez Bostwick & Co., a New York refiner and exporter. By 1872, it had bought all the Cleveland refineries. In the next few years, it bought William Warden's Atlantic Refining in Philadelphia, Charles Lockhart in Pittsburgh, Pratt & Rogers in New York, John D. Archbold in the oil region, and Camden & Co. in West Virginia. Through Warden, refineries were purchased in the Baltimore area. Warden negotiated for those in the Philadelphia area, Archbold handled negotiations in the oil regions, and Pratt and Rogers did the same in New York.

Many of the sellers insisted that they had sold only because Standard and the railroads had threatened to ruin them. They also insisted that Standard had paid them much less than their plants were worth. Standard, on the other hand, insisted that it paid a fair price, and the evidence supports its claim. It always urged sellers to take stock rather than cash. Where this was done, the seller eventually made far more than if he had sold for cash and far more than if he had remained in the business. But Standard Oil was never a charitable institution. Rockefeller was deeply religious, taught Sunday school, and gave generously to charity. Some of his partners were equally religious. But in business, they were ruthless in meeting competition. Price cutting, rebates, and more violent tactics would be used without compunction to make a recalcitrant competitor "sweat" or "feel sick." Tactics were especially ruthless after Standard entered local distribution in 1879.

By the mid-seventies when Standard was about to embark aggressively into new functions, it produced more oil than all the New York refineries

[16]This was the second time Rockefeller bought out Maurice Clark.

put together. Its production exceeded the combined output of Philadelphia, Pittsburgh, and Baltimore. Yet despite its moves toward integration, Standard was still very much a manufacturing company. It owned no wells. It had no retail outlets. It had no control over the middlemen. In 1873, the company entered distribution by buying a half interest in Chess, Carley & Co., the leading southern jobber. In 1875, it bought into Waters-Pierce of St. Louis. In the same year, Neyhart & Grandin, marketeers in the oil region, were brought into the fold. In 1877, it absorbed Alexander McDonald & Co. of Cincinnati, and during all this time it was developing its own distribution network. Meanwhile, too, Standard was gaining a foothold in other means of transporting oil. In the early 1870's, it obtained some pipelines. In 1877 it formed United Pipe Lines. This set off a competitive struggle with the Pennsylvania Railroad. Fearing that Standard would take much of its regional business, the Pennsylvania, through its affiliate the Empire Transportation Co., decided to enter refining. In the battle that followed, Standard, aided by a disastrous strike against the railroad, soundly defeated the Pennsylvania and then bought the Empire's entire oil interests. Rockefeller raised the cash for this by going from bank to bank saying, "I must have all you've got." In time, further pipelines were purchased, the main one being the Tidewater Pipe Co. in 1881. Integration also continued in raw materials. But as late as 1881, Standard owned only three or four wells. By the end of the decade, however, Standard, with its usual energy and aggressiveness, emerged as a major factor in the field as well as at the refinery.

MANAGEMENT AND OTHER PROBLEMS

By 1877, the absorption of so many different companies so widely spread from the Middle West to the Atlantic seaboard had resulted in near chaos legally and administratively. To be sure, consolidation and amalgamation had produced enormous rewards. The organization was extremely prosperous. It had almost 100 percent control over refining and a large chunk of the rest of the business. Amalgamation had also brought with it most of the executives who were running the company. Oliver H. Payne was one of the members of the executive committee,[17] Ambrose McGregor succeeded Andrews. Jacob Vandergrift was in charge of pipe lines. Rogers was active in marketing. But all these individuals and all their companies were held together in a loose confederacy. It was difficult for the home office to keep a tight rein over the subsidiaries that were not

---

[17]The directors in 1873 appointed an executive committee consisting of John D., Flagler, and Payne. William Rockefeller and Jabez Bostwick were an advisory committee. The two committees were combined in 1878.

under its immediate control. This was especially apparent in the distribution end of the business. F. D. Carley of Chess, Carley and Henry Clay Pierce of Waters-Pierce often refused to follow the policies and instructions sent down from above. They made their own pricing decisions, paying no attention to home office directives. They were rough competitors, especially adept at cutting prices, but they were not averse to entering into partnerships with competitors who were then allowed to enter their territory. The one thing that made their conduct bearable was that each made a substantial profit. But eventually, when opportunity presented itself, both firms were eliminated.

One of the principal difficulties in the way of a unified business was a legal one. Under state law as it then existed, no firm could buy stock in an out-of-state firm without special act of the legislature. Standard, therefore, resorted to various subterfuges. Jabez Bostwick managed Bostwick & Co. after its acquisition. All the earnings, however, were turned over to Standard. When the Long Island Oil Co. was purchased, its stockholders turned their stock over to Henry Flagler as trustee in exchange for cash and Standard Oil stock. Similar arrangements were made with other owners. All of these acquisitions were kept secret, a talent that Standard Oil possessed in profusion. But the arrangements were far from satisfactory. The loose arrangement was an obstacle to smooth operation, and what, for example, would happen if the trustee died?

The legal problem was solved by the creation of a trust in 1879, and its improvement in 1882. The trust was not the masterwork of any one man, but certainly, Samuel C. T. Dodd, the corporation's brilliant attorney, was primarily responsible. Under the agreement, 41 stockholders turned over to nine trustees all the stock in 14 companies and part of the stock in 26 more for trust certificates amounting to $70 million.[18] The advantages of the new arrangement were immense. It increased management control although, as we shall see in a moment, not to the extent desired. It ensured secrecy and freedom from nonmanagerial interference, and it gave ownership more flexibility.

The trust took care of the firm's legal organization until 1892 when it was ordered dissolved by the Ohio court. But it did not do much to iron out the administrative problems of what was by now the world's largest manufacturing company. Since the beginning of its existence, Standard had been seeking the perfect administrative structure. As the organization grew, the problem naturally became increasingly complex. A variety of functions had to be integrated. The company had always taken a long-

---

[18]The original trustees were the two Rockefellers, Flagler, Payne, Bostwick, Pratt, Brewster, Warden, and Archbold. Payne, Bostwick, Brewster, and Warden retired in the 1880's. They were succeeded by Rogers, Horace A. Hutchins, and Wesley H. Tilford. There were only eight in the 1890's.

range view, but with increasing size, planning became more intricate. More information, more consulting, and more experimenting were necessary, for decision-making was in Standard a "synthesis of opinion."

Early in its career, Standard started to develop a committee system. The Executive Committee went back to 1873, and it existed informally even before that, for Rockefeller, Flagler, and Andrews (especially the first two) spent much of their time consulting with each other.

The formation of the trust gave a fillip to administrative progress. According to James Stillman, the head of the National City Bank and a close friend of William Rockefeller, Standard used the Roman Catholic Church as a model in building its structure. By 1886, the committee system had been completed. At the top of the pyramid was the executive committee consisting of the top managers who were present on any given day at 26 Broadway. Then came: case and can, cooperage, domestic trade, export trade, lubricating oil, manufacturing, and transportation.

The executive committee handled both general policy and routine management, which was clearly a mistake, for its activities became bogged down in detail, which delayed decision making.[19] It also found it difficult to force subordinates to go along with its decisions. In short, friction was an ever-present ingredient in the relations between executives and managers.

A word must be said about labor policy and price making in Standard in the late nineteenth century. The company paid its executives well, and its wages were as high as any in the industry. Indeed, they appear to have been higher than anyone else's. This, however, is not saying much, for by later standards wages were extremely low. In 1889, Standard's median wages varied from 80 cents a day for boys to $8.33 for superintendents. The median for all manufacturing workers was $1.86. Laborers, the largest group, averaged $1.50 a day.

Standard's executives seemed to think that supply and demand determined labor's wages, but in practice the company's management followed a recipe that combined a large measure of the wages fund theory and a generous helping of paternalism. Paternalism in labor relations was still the order of the day, and Standard was no exception. General working conditions were abominable but no worse than in other places. There was much of what later became known as welfare capitalism, but there were also frequent complaints of favoritism on the part of foremen and superintendents.

Standard's executives also seemed to think that supply and demand determined prices. In a sense this was true. For example, if supply in-

[19] For example, the executive committee insisted on ratifying any appropriation of over $5,000, any new construction for over $2,500, and any salary increase of over $600 a year.

creased, prices *tended* to go down, and if at the same time demand fell, prices *tended* to go down even faster. But this had to be qualified, for price making seemed to have moved far away from the ancient truths. A new variable—the power of large-scale enterprise—had inserted itself in the picture. Supply and demand was now tinged with the tactics of monopolistic competition; oil refining was a case of oligopoly in which much attention was paid to what the competition was doing. Yet, here too, the monopolistic model was too neat and too simplistic to explain how prices were made in the Standard Oil colossus. Certainly, no one in the executive committee had any notion of where marginal cost equalled marginal revenue. In actual practice price making was a vague tactic greatly influenced by judgments and philosophy. Rockefeller, it was said, argued for prices that were not high enough to attract competition, but high enough to make a profit. Some of his colleagues wanted to charge as much as the traffic would bear. As in most cases, the Rockefeller view prevailed.

THE REASONS FOR SUCCESS

As one wit once put it, Standard Oil refined everything but the Pennsylvania legislature, but most of all it refined millionaires. It was estimated that at one time Rockefeller, by far the wealthiest in the Standard Oil crowd, was worth $850 million and in addition he had given away $750 million. Over a period of thirty years Standard Oil earned breathtaking profits. In 1883, it made $11.2 million and paid $4.3 million in dividends. In 1890, it made almost $20 million. Between 1882 and 1906, dividends amounted to $500 million, and all this was divided among forty stockholders. John D. was the largest with almost 9,000 shares. Flagler was next with 3,000, and Harkness held a little less.

Explaining success is at best a complicated business. In the case of Standard Oil, it is even more complicated. Yet, some things stand out. First of all, it was in no sense a one-man company subject to one man's foibles and peccadilloes. "The secret of success of Standard Oil," Rockefeller recalled, "was that there had come together a body of men who from beginning to end worked in single-minded cooperation . . . who reached all their decisions after fair consideration. . . . They considered all possibilities before deciding."

Rockefeller's chief talent, and he had many, was that he had brought this dazzling array of business brains together. "These men," said William H. Vanderbilt, "are smarter than I am—a great deal. They are very enterprising. I never came into contact with any class of men so smart and able as they are in their business."

Standard Oil was far ahead of its contemporaries in overall business strategy. It made a fetish of integration. It utilized its by-products, employed a chemist, practiced meticulous accounting, and developed an administrative organization. Others did some of these things too, but not as thoroughly as Standard did.

There were other reasons for its success. It was a ruthless competitor. It made secret agreements with railroads. It charged different prices in different sections and for different customers. It dumped its products abroad, practiced espionage, and as a business organization it cared little for public opinion and did not know the meaning of "social responsibility." Yet, bankers and railroad men trusted Standard Oil when they would not trust each other.

11

DOMESTIC TRADE
AND FINANCE

Thus far in dealing with the last half of the nineteenth century, we have talked only about the railroads and manufacturing as though that was all that business consisted of in the late 1800's. This was clearly not true. Trade (both wholesale and retail) and finance (commercial banking, investment banking, and other financial intermediaries) continued to be immensely important.

The growth of the nation in size, population, production, and wealth brought with it a growth in trade, which made necessary an expansion of distribution facilities.

The vast improvement of transportation and communication produced by the railroad, the telegraph, the cable, and the telephone in turn permitted larger distribution units and greater specialization in distribution functions. From mid-century on, the focus of marketing shifted from the commission merchant, who sold on consignment and commission, to the jobber, who bought the goods outright that he hoped to sell later.

WHOLESALE AND RETAIL TRADE
IN THE BUSINESS COMMUNITY

Between 1870 and 1900 employment in retail and wholesale trade increased from 785,000 to 2,460,000 or by more than 200 percent. To put it another way, employment in retail and wholesale trade rose from 6.1 percent of the labor force in 1870 to 8.6 percent in 1900. These figures become more impressive when compared with the decline in production employment from 70.0 percent to 62.7 percent of the labor force during the same period.[1]

Although trade employment grew at a better than average pace, its share of the product did not show a similar advance. Value added by wholesalers and retailers increased from 32.7 percent of retail value in 1869 to 35.4 percent in 1899, representing respectively 15.7 percent and 16.8 percent of national income.

The growth and spread of urban markets coupled with improvements in transportation and communication created many changes in marketing techniques. A variety of middlemen were still active in moving goods from factory to consumer, but gradually their position deteriorated. As mass production and mass consumption gained momentum, both manufacturers and retailers developed more sophisticated and more aggressive selling policies to meet the pressures of increased competition. Direct buying and selling by manufacturers became more common. By 1880, many manufacturers were advertising their products, offering goods on trial, hiring their own local salesmen and agents, and in some cases bypassing the retailer as well as the wholesaler.

Producers who declined to assume the marketing function by opening branch warehouses or organizing sales and marketing departments had perforce to depend upon additional wholesale outlets. At the start of the period, wholesaling did expand, but the peak seems to have occurred about 1879. The expansion came somewhat later in the West than in the East as the trends in distribution followed population movements.

To replace or augment the wholesalers' efforts, the traveling salesman or "drummer" appeared. By 1860, there were at least 1,000 traveling representatives taking orders and promoting sales. Despite punitive license fees and high taxes imposed to protect local merchants, their ranks multiplied rapidly. A committee of the Society of Commercial Travelers estimated their number at 50,000 in 1869. The *New York Herald* thought there were 100,000 in 1877, but the Census counted 7,300 in 1870, 59,000 in 1890, and 93,000 in 1900.

THE DEPARTMENT STORE

By the late nineteenth century, the general store of early America was to be found only on the frontier, and even there it was fast disappearing as frontier villages grew. Its place was being gradually taken by the

---

[1] The estimates are from Harold Barger, *Distribution's Place in the American Economy Since 1869* (Princeton, New Jersey: Princeton University Press, 1955), pp. 4–6. *Historical Statistics* gives somewhat different statistics.

department store, which is really a giant general store or a collection of specialty shops.

Technically, a department store is one in which both merchandising and management are organized along departmental lines. This definition would make Lord and Taylor in New York the first department store, but the definition itself leaves much to be desired. An informed student insists that a department store encompasses a dozen characteristics.[2]

1. a central location
2. many departments
3. free services
4. one price
5. low mark up
6. aggressive advertising and promotion
7. selling for cash only
8. large volume of business
9. centralization of non-selling functions
10. buying for cash
11. disposal of old stock at bargain prices
12. open-door policy

Many pioneers in retailing undoubtedly followed some of the above practices. The policy of selling for cash only, for example, was at least as old as 1806 when Wheaton and Dixon of Dedham, Massachusetts advertised for cash only. But a pioneer in business is one who blazes a trail that no one follows. The innovator is the one who sets the example that many others follow. In department store retailing, the innovators were A. T. Stewart in the 1830's and 1840's, R. H. Macy in the 1850's, and John Wanamaker in the latter 1800's. Of these, Stewart did more than any one else to shake up the retail business.

By any standards, A. T. Stewart's dry-goods firm was a big business. In the 1860's, he was responsible for 10 percent of the imports at the New York Port. His total sales in 1865 were $50 million of which $8 million were retail. Macy's would not reach $1 million until 1870; Field, Leiter in Chicago did $3.4 million in 1874; and Wanamaker reached $10 million in 1896. Stewart was the innovator in at least 10 of the dozen characteristics enumerated above. In addition, he was the first American department store owner to open a foreign office.

Stewart compensated for his superlative merchandising skills by an apparent lack of managerial talent. Like his fellow department store owners, he was either unwilling or unable to train anyone to succeed him. When he died, his successor quickly ran the business into the ground, and it was eventually purchased by John Wanamaker, who was solidly em-

---

[2]Harry E. Resseguie, "Alexander Turney Stewart and the Development of the Department Store, 1823–1876," *Business History Review*, Vol. XXXIX, Autumn, 1965.

bedded in Philadelphia retailing. Wanamaker, too, failed to develop a managerial succession, and so did Marshall Field and R. H. Macy. But Captain Macy did solve the problem obliquely. In the early 1870's he leased several departments in his store, and one of the tenants, the Straus family, in time bought control of the store and established a generation-by-generation managerial succession.

Wanamaker innovated in many of the department store's operational details, especially in labor relations and in advertising. The department store industry had a well-deserved reputation for notoriously bad labor conditions. At the middle of the century, stores paid sales clerks $500 a year for a 12-14-hour day, 6-day week. This meant that work began at 6:30 A.M. and continued until 7:00 P.M. and on Saturdays until 10:00 P.M. In addition, many stores were open on Sundays. Shortly after Wanamaker opened his first store in 1861, he reduced the business day drastically, and by 1900, his stores closed at 5:00 in the summer and 5:30 in winter.

Wanamaker was famous for advertising more than for anything else. It was said that of the first day's sales of $20.67, $20 was spent for advertising. But he pursued still other audacious stratagems. He was the first to have branch stores, opening them temporarily in Pittsburgh and Richmond to dispose of Philadelphia's swollen inventory. He at one time manufactured some of his own goods, but abandoned the practice when it proved impractical. He was also one of the first to move "uptown" or "out in the country," but his failure to follow through on this policy was one of his worst mistakes. Department stores, it seems, must be mobile, continuously moving from what were once the business centers. Arnold Constable offers a typical history. In 1825, Aaron Arnold opened a dry goods store on Pine Street in lower New York. The next year, he moved to Front Street and in the following year to Canal. In 1869, the firm moved uptown to 19th Street and in 1914 way uptown to 39th Street. In 1937, a branch was opened in the Westchester County suburbs. Three years later, another branch opened on Long Island, and finally after World War II, still another branch in northern New Jersey.

THE MAIL-ORDER HOUSE

In the cities, the department store replaced the general store. In the rural areas at the same time, the position of the general store was severely damaged by the appearance of another retailing innovation—the mail-order house.

Specialized mail-order business dates back to early history, but it did not become firmly entrenched and institutionalized until the 1870's. Even then, it is unlikely that a comprehensive mail-order business would have appeared had it not been for two extraneous circumstances—the opening of rural postal delivery and the extreme agricultural discontent that accompanied the secular price decline of the post Civil War economy.

The first diversified mail-order house appeared in 1872 when Aaron Montgomery Ward, a former Marshall Field employee, and his brother-in-law George P. Thorne invested $2,400 in what they called "The Original Grange Supply House." Clearly, Montgomery Ward intended to cater to the farmer, and it did so with great success. In its first year, it issued a single 8 x 12 sheet to publicize its wares. By the early 1890's, it was distributing an 8 x 11, 540 page catalogue that carried more than 24,000 items. Its business was then over $1 million a year.

Sears, Roebuck & Co. was a late starter, founded in 1893. It did not achieve any impressive growth until the late 1890's. In 1895, it was doing a volume of $750,000. Then Julius Rosenwald entered the business. He proved to be the balance wheel that the mercurial Richard Sears needed. Sears devoted himself to advertising, the catalogue, and selling, and Rosenwald handled the more mundane, but overwhelmingly important business decisions. By 1906, when the present corporation was formed with a capital of $40 million through the offices of Goldman, Sachs & Co., the company's annual business amounted to $38 million.

THE CHAIN STORE

Chain stores have wrought a greater change in American life than either the department store or the mail order house. They are older, there are more of them, and they have attracted more customers.

Like most economic institutions, the chain store appeared long before the latter part of the nineteenth century. But most students of the subject rather arbitrarily take 1859 as the date at which it first became important. It was in that year that George Hartford and a leather dealer named George F. Gilman founded the Great Atlantic and Pacific Tea Company, an institution which, according to a rival chain store executive, "made a greater contribution to raising the standard of living in America than anyone else including Henry Ford."

Hartford was an aggressive and energetic salesman with a talent and personality for retail innovation. He imported tea directly and by eliminating the middleman cut the price from $1 a pound to 30¢. He sold door-to-door as well as from the store at low markups. He gave trading stamps, crockery, dishpans, and baby pictures, and business was so prosperous that by 1870, there were eleven stores. Eighty-nine more outlets were opened in the next decade, but phenomenal expansion did not begin until the 1880's, when Hartford's two sons, George L. and John A. entered the business. By then, Gilman had retired, and the firm was completely family owned.

The young Hartfords soon demonstrated an aggressiveness and an innovating spirit, and far surpassed their father's tactics, which had appeared so unique. George L. pressed for vertical integration and soon put a chemist to work mixing baking powder in the back of the original store in downtown New York. John had ideas that were more difficult to sell. He was convinced that the business would be more successful if cash-and-carry replaced credit and home delivery. It was difficult to persuade the senior Hartford, but in 1912 John finally had an opportunity to try the idea out. The firm anonymously opened a cash-and-carry outlet around the corner from its most profitable store. Within six months, the cheap store had driven the service store out of business. Thereafter, expansion took place at a breathtaking rate. At one time, the pace was fifty new stores a week for a full year. With its enormous number of outlets, the chain began to use its power to gain an advantage over competitors in much the same way that Standard Oil had done. A. & P. with its extraordinary volume was able to buy at much better prices than could its competitors. Sellers who refused to give the chain favorable terms soon regretted it, for A. & P. did not hesitate to move into the production end of the grocery business if that seemed more advantageous.

Meanwhile, other chains had started. Frank Woolworth opened his first successful store in Lancaster, Pennsylvania in 1879; the Jones Brothers (now Grand Union) in 1872; the Kroger chain in 1882; Kress and Kresge in 1892 and 1896; and J. C. Penney in 1902.

By 1900, the business of retailing was much different from what it had been in 1850. The country store, a solid base at mid-century, was fading fast by the 1870's. Physics tells us that nothing ever disappears completely. There are still some general stores in the South and the Far West, and there are general store characteristics in the department stores of downtown and the suburban shopping center. But as an institution, the general store was fast being replaced by specialty shops and eventually by collections of specialty shops known as department stores. The general store's doom was marked by rural free delivery, the automobile, and the boll weevil. The first produced the mail order house; the second bypassed the small-town market center; and the third undermined the cotton crop on which the southern country store's credit system was based.

ADVERTISING IN THE
LATE NINETEENTH CENTURY

Advertising,[3] almost as old as business itself, grew at a creeping pace until the 1870's. Before then, advertisements were more like news items,

[3]There is no very good history of the advertising business in general. Ralph Hower, *The History of an Advertising Agency: N. W. Ayer & Son at Work, 1869–1949* (Cambridge, Mass.: Harvard University Press, 1949) contains more information than more general histories.

serving primarily to notify the public. The business was small even for the standards of the day. According to tax returns, publishers' income in 1870 was about $10 million. The American economy was, after all, a producer's economy. Discretionary income was limited. Product differentiation and other such tactics of imperfect competition seemed hardly necessary. There were, moreover, no media with a regional or national circulation, and newspapers opposed display advertising, not simply because of inertia, but also because of costs and technological difficulties.

Nevertheless, some pioneering had already been accomplished. Volney B. Palmer, in 1841, founded the first agency. It represented publishers, not the advertiser. Palmer was eventually absorbed by N. W. Ayer, founded in Philadelphia in 1869. Ayer would be the leading innovator among advertising agencies in the late nineteenth century.

By 1860, there were 30 advertising agencies selling space in periodicals to advertisers. By then too, newspapers had grown and the printing had progressed to the point where new methods of advertising were not only feasible but attractive. The first machine-made newspaper appeared in 1827. The *New York Sun* in 1833 was the first penny newspaper and the first one sold by newsboys. A 9 x 12 paper, it claimed that its 20,000 circulation was the largest in the world. In 1846, a major invention, the Hoe press, made printing much cheaper and much quicker. By 1856, the *New York Ledger*, a weekly, had a circulation of 400,000. Robert Bonner, its proprietor, was a major innovator in his own right. When he was refused space for display advertising, he took a full page in the *New York Herald* on October 4, 1856 for repetitive small advertisements for his own publication. He thereby became the first to use a full-page advertisement and the first, except for patent-medicine advertisers, to spend $150,000 a year for newspaper advertising. His pioneering effort liberalized the newspapers' current customary rules, paving the way for a change in advertising usage for other businessmen. Yet it would take another ten years before department stores and financial houses forced newspapers to accept display advertising.

The sudden blossoming of advertising induced a rash of competition among the agencies. George P. Rowell, a young Bostonian, saw a way out of the competitive war. He became a space wholesaler, buying volumes of space in country newspapers and selling it to advertisers. Ayer carried this further when, in 1876, he devised the open contract. Under the plan, the agency acted for the advertiser. It placed all the ads for a customer, charging a commission on the net cost of the space.

Meanwhile, under pressure from aggressive agencies, magazines opened up to advertisers. *The Atlantic, Harpers* and *Scribner's accepted advertising* in the 1860's, but it was not until the J. Walter Thompson Agency appeared in the late 1870's that advertising spread to almost all magazines.

Other media also came in. Outdoor advertising was being attacked as early as the 1860's as a "mania" and "nuisance." In 1891, a huge electric sign, the first of many, was put into operation on New York City's Broadway. Two years before that, William J. Carleton and George Kissam started to sell street-car advertising on a national basis. By 1895, it was a $2 million business.

Agencies introduced new tactics as well as new media. In 1877, Henry Nelson McKinney, partner in N. W. Ayer, undertook a market survey, the first of its kind. After 1880, agencies further expanded their service to include the preparation of advertising copy. Previously it was thought that the advertiser himself was best qualified to write his own advertising copy. Many of the larger advertisers, however, hired their own copywriters or used free-lance experts to prepare copy. In 1893 the use of color in advertising was introduced by Mellin's Food in the World's Fair edition of the *Youth Companion*, adding an additional eye-catching technique.

Agency market surveys were instrumental in forging changes in design and packaging. By the 1860's, a few articles were already wrapped and brand names such as Burnett's Vanilla (1845), Babbitt's Lye (1855), Robert Burns Cigars (1857), and Eagle Brand Milk (1857) were easily recognized. But these marketing appurtenances did not become common until much later. By then too, slogans had come into wide use. They differed from other advertising copy in that they gave no reason to buy except a catch phrase. But in a few years most Americans became familiar with "Absolutely Pure" (Royal Baking Powder), "You press the button; we do the rest." (Eastman Kodak), "It floats" (Ivory Soap), and "Yours for Health" (Lydia Pinkham).

Just before the close of the century, McKinney inaugurated the first fully integrated national advertising campaign, using several marketing devices in order to publicize "Uneeda Biscuit" for the National Biscuit Company. It involved the creation of a new package, a trade mark, a trade name, and all the media then in use. It had become evident that advertising was a potent weapon in the selling arsenal. One enthusiastic adherent went so far as to say that, "Advertising is the medium of communication between the world's greatest forces—demand and supply. It is a more powerful element in human progress than steam or electricity."[4]

Expenditures by businessmen for advertising increased rapidly. From about $50 million in 1867, they multiplied more than ten times to about $542 million by 1900. In the mid-1890's, the advertising budget for Baker's Cocoa was estimated to be about $200,000 a year, $500,000 a year for Royal Baking Powder, $400,000 a year for Sapolio Soap, $250,000 a year for Pearline Soap, and $100,000 a year for Quaker Oats. By the late 1890's,

[4]Frank Presbrey, *The History and Development of Advertising* (New York: Doubleday, Doran, 1929), p. 341.

Eastman Kodak was spending $750,000 a year. (R. H. Macy was spending more money on advertising and had a larger percentage of sales as well.) By 1902 the ratio of advertising expense to sales was about twice what it had been in 1888. The media did well with all this expenditure. *Harper's*, with a circulation of 125,000, charged $250 a page. *The Ladies Home Journal*, going into 850,000 homes, charged $4,000 for the back cover.

Of all the entrepreneurs who had a talent for marketing, or what in this case would better be called selling, few equalled John H. Patterson of the National Cash Register Company. Peer of American Tobacco Company's George Washington Hill and teacher of IBM's Thomas Watson and hundreds of others, Patterson achieved enormous success more through his innovations in selling than because of anything else. He did not seem to be at all interested in management. He despised knowledge for knowledge's sake, and even though he was a graduate of a noted liberal arts institution, he was strongly prejudiced against college. Unlike many of his successful contemporaries, he had no use for accounting. But like most of his successful contemporaries, he had little interest in finance. He did not differentiate between fixed and working capital, and he was chronically short of cash. He concentrated on the demand rather than the supply side of business. Thus he did not try to cut costs when business turned down. Instead he devoted even more attention to increasing sales and income. He was an ideal marketing man; it was selling and all its ramifications that intrigued him. It was said that no American sales organization with more than 25 members was without a man who at one time had been in the Patterson training program.

Patterson was not the inventor of the cash register. It cannot even be said that he saw its possibilities when others didn't. In a way, his connection with business machines was accidental. He had bought a controlling interest in a cash register company in 1884 and regretting it, he tried without success to get his money back. The only alternative was to sell cash registers, and this he proceeded to do enthusiastically and convincingly. He changed the name of the company to National Cash Register, built up a selling organization that was second to none, and made the cash register company his whole life. His first step was to establish exclusive territorial sales agencies manned by former cash register salesmen. His agents worked solely on commission as did many salesmen for many other firms. But here the similarity ended. Most firms gave little assistance to commission salesmen; Patterson worked along with them. He viewed advertising as an ideal means to increase sales.[5] From each of his first ten agents, he secured a list of five hundred prospects. For each of the five

[5]His biographer, Samuel Crowther, *John H. Patterson* (Garden City, N.Y.: Doubleday, Page, Inc., 1923), claimed that Patterson was the father of modern advertising. This is an exaggeration, but Patterson was an immense contributor to the art.

thousand prospects he then prepared eighteen different pieces of advertising, each piece giving a reason why the purchase of a cash register would benefit the buyer. Like the McCormick newspaper ad, the Patterson material contained testimonials from satisfied users. Each day the prospect received one of the letters, and the ground was well prepared for the salesman's inevitable visit. Eventually, the Patterson organization surveyed the whole national market and divided it into districts of 400 people each. Every salesman was assigned a quota, and the sales force's goal was to sell one cash register per year for every 400 people.

Patterson exerted himself to the limit of his ability to help his salesmen achieve their goal. He insisted that they memorize a meticulously prepared sales talk and follow it to the letter when talking to a potential customer. The company in 1894 inaugurated the first training school for salesmen. It was also one of the first, if not the first, to hold an annual convention and to publish a regularly issued house organ.

Patterson's business and personal life was filled with childish idiosyncracies that made him a fascinating character. Although he employed many men of great talent, none of them could be sure of the next day's employment. In this and many other things, Patterson resembled Henry Ford. "When we get to the point where everything depends on one man, let's fire him" epitomized his relations with his executives. He fired people for using butter and pepper and because he listened to a face reader. He expected superhuman effort on projects that bordered on the irrational. At three o'clock one afternoon he rode past a hall that was used as a restaurant and told the manager, "Have this place ready for use as a riding academy by 6:00 A.M." He played dangerously with his own life as well as the lives of his associates. Somewhat of a hypochondriac, he followed health fads as intensely as he created means of selling cash registers. He took four or five baths a day, drank a cup of hot water every half hour and was fair game for any quack or charlatan. But regardless of his peculiarities, he was a genius in business.

FINANCIAL INTERMEDIARIES—
THE ERA OF FINANCE CAPITALISM

Although most nineteenth-century entrepreneurs were not interested in finance, they did require capital funds, and these they raised by tapping every available source. The railroads with their enormous demand for funds relied heavily on state, local, and federal government, foreign investors, and domestic buyers of bonds and stocks. Manufacturing and trade were not so fortunate. They had to rely on domestic savings and on the financial intermediaries that grew gigantically in the last of the nineteenth century.

The growth in the material prosperity of the middle class provided a volume of savings, and the easiest way of channeling this saving into industry was through the pipeline of financial intermediation. The assets of three main intermediaries soared from approximately $1.0 billion in 1860 to almost $15 billion in 1900. In the same time span, national wealth, a most difficult thing to estimate, rose from $15 billion to $85 billion. Assets of financial intermediaries thus climbed from 6 percent to 17 percent of national wealth.

Commercial banks remained the largest intermediary. Their number grew from 932 to 12,427, and their assets from approximately $850 million to $10.0 billion. Their total loans of over $5 billion in 1900 were the source of most of the capital funds for American business. Yet, at the end of the century, there were only a dozen banks in the whole country whose capital and surplus was large enough to allow them to lend $1 million or more to any one customer. Savings banks made equally impressive progress. Their number remained about the same at around 625 all through the late 1800's, but assets rose from less than $200 million to $2.4 billion.

THE GROWTH OF THE
LIFE INSURANCE BUSINESS

Although they did not grow any faster than the savings banks or the commercial banks, life insurance companies had a much more spectacular set of years than any of the other intermediaries. Certainly, more innovations were introduced in life insurance at this time than in any of the other intermediaries.

In 1841, only 1,211 policies were written and only $4 million were in force. Total premiums were only a little over $250,000. At that time,

Table 8   Assets of Financial Intermediaries, 1860–1900 (in millions of dollars)

Year	Commercial Banks	Savings Banks	Building & Loan	Life Insurance	General Insurance	Total Assets
1860	851	149	n.a.	24	81	1,105
1870	1,781	550	n.a.	270	182	2,783
1880	2,518	882	n.a.	418	239	4,056
1890	4,601	1,743	300	771	352	7,767
1900	10,011	2,430	490	1,742	484	15,157

Source: Data derived from *U.S. Census Bureau, Historical Statistics of the United States; All Banks Statistics; Annual Report of the Superintendent of Insurance, State of New York, 1961; Institute of Life Insurance;* Year end reports made to insurance commissioners of various states; Raymond Goldsmith, *Financial Intermediaries in the American Economy Since 1900.*

there were 14 companies in operation, and their assets were negligible. Then came two developments that propelled the industry forward. The first was the inauguration of mutual companies that catered to all members of society, and the other was the creation of the agency system and the beginning of aggressive selling. Life insurance took on the distinction of being the financial industry that was most anxious to sell its service, and the results were spectacular. The number of companies almost doubled, and by 1900 the 84 companies in the field had assets of $1.7 billion compared with the $24 million in assets held by 43 companies in 1860.

Willard Phillips of the Boston merchant family formed the first modern mutual company—the New England Mutual in 1835. It was modeled after the Massachusetts Hospital Life Insurance Company, and it was because of a fear that it might have to emulate the Hospital Life's contribution to charity that it did not begin operations until 1842. By then, as with all innovations, the idea was being picked up by other ambitious and energetic men: Morris Robinson of the Mutual of New York, Benjamin Balch of the State Mutual of Worcester and the National Life of Vermont, and Robert L. Patterson of the Mutual Benefit. Of all these, Balch probably had the most fertile imagination and the largest stroke of genius, but his personality was not built for business success. He drove people hard and got them to do things, but he was not popular and he was a restless rather than a happy person. Robinson made a more permanent contribution to the business. He was the first to separate life insurance from the trust business. He advertised and he started personal solicitation. He was, in other words, the trail blazer in marketing life insurance, and for this he was paid the princely salary of $1,500 in 1843 when he launched the Mutual Life of New York.

Carrying Robinson's ideas a step further, the Connecticut Mutual had an agency system as early as 1846. It was not, however, until 1853 that the first sales manager or general agent, Henry H. Hyde of the Mutual Life, appeared. Hyde was very successful, but it was his son, Henry Baldwin Hyde, who really launched aggressive selling. As the representative of the Mutual and later of the Equitable, Baldwin Hyde was the stereotype life insurance man, who gave rise to the limerick: "No one has as much endurance as the man who sells insurance."

By 1850, there were 48 life insurance companies with assets of about $10 million. In any new business that is growing spectacularly, there will paradoxically be a great deal of shaking out of competitors; the number of firms will narrow, but the total business will soar. So with the life insurance business in the 1850's. During the decade, 21 companies were formed, and 26 went out of business, so that in 1860 there were only 43 companies, but their assets were almost $25 million. The companies that were doing most of the business were the recently founded mutuals. Of

the $205 million life insurance in force, $125 million had been written by
five mutual companies: The Mutual of New York ($40 million), Connecticut Mutual ($26 million), Mutual Benefit ($25 million), and the New
York and the New England ($16 million each).

As the business grew, new policies and new ideas were introduced
voluntarily or by request of government agencies. The nonrenewable term
policy, which had been the principal contract written when trust companies did most of the insurance business, faded into insignificance. Its
place was taken by the whole life policy, which appeared in the 1840's,
and the endowment, a product of the fifties.

Once having established a base, the life insurance business embarked
on an extraordinary rise. There were four main reasons for this. The
first and most important was the revival of a hardy perennial of the insurance business—the tontine.

The tontine, which originated in seventeenth-century France, originally stipulated that the sums deposited by the participants plus interest
thereon would be paid to the last surviving member of the group. This
extreme form was never popular in the United States, since it was believed
that it encouraged homicide and was against public morals. But at some
time or other various modified forms of tontines aroused much excitement
among Americans. The famous Old Tontine Coffee House, the City Hotel,
and the Park Theatre, in lower Manhattan, were financed by an arrangement whereby the property would revert after a specific number of years
to those investors who were still surviving. A tontine also preceded the
Union Bank of Boston and the Insurance Company of North America.
The financing of the Old Tontine Coffee House was an excellent example
of how a tontine worked. It was erected in 1794 by the contributions of
203 members. The agreement was that the last seven survivors would share
the property, an event that finally occurred in 1876.

The tontine fell out of favor in the early 1800's, but the idea never
died. It was revived in 1876 by Henry Hyde and quickly adopted by his
competitors in the Mutual Life of New York and the New York Life.

Under the Equitable's tontine plan the beneficiaries of policyholders
who died received the face value of the policy; those who let their policies
lapse received nothing; those who kept their policy in force until the end
of a stipulated period (10, 15, or 20 years) were paid the face value of the
policy plus their own accumulated dividends for the whole period, plus
a share of the dividends of those who died, plus a share of the accumulation of those who let their policies lapse. The policyholder could now
view his insurance not just as family protection in the event he died, or
as a way of saving small amounts, but as a speculation in which he was
betting on outliving the majority of participants.

The tontine feature, coupled with aggressive salesmanship, enabled a few companies to take over the business and build up large reserves, which helped them to become important forces in the capital markets. Companies like the Connecticut Mutual that refused to offer the tontine policy sank rapidly. Second largest in 1878, it had dropped to fourteenth by the end of the century.

A second innovation accounting for the growth of the life insurance companies was the introduction of industrial life insurance. The regular life companies sold their policies primarily to the upper and middle income classes. Not only were persons of limited means unable to acquire protection, but the life companies were failing to provide a means of gathering the petty savings of these millions of individuals. It was to remedy these defects that the Prudential Insurance Company of America, under the leadership of its founder, John F. Dryden, in 1877 brought industrial insurance into the United States from England, where it had originated in 1854.

Companies like the Prudential, the Metropolitan, and the John Hancock, which specialized in industrial insurance while also writing regular life coverage, grew rapidly to huge size. The Metropolitan, which had been eighteenth in size among life insurance companies in 1875 with $25 million in force, became the largest company in 1910 with over $2 billion on the books. The Prudential, which in 1876 had but $250,000 in force, expanded to $139 million in 1890.

Still a third reason for the industry's emergence was the liberalization of government restriction in the seventies and eighties. In 1869, New York, like many other states, had passed a law limiting investments to government securities and New York mortgages. In the seventies, investment power was somewhat broadened geographically, and in the eighties, New York companies were permitted to lend on mortgages anywhere in the country. New England had long since made the same concessions to a national market.

The insurance companies were in a position to do something about capital mobility. They had the funds, and rates of return were higher in the West than in the East. All of them kept some of their deposits in banks far from the home office. According to a plan decided upon at the time of its formation, the Connecticut Mutual was the first to make substantial investments in western securities. In 1861, it began to lend on farm mortgages. President Greene said in 1896 that in its fifty years, the company had loaned $146 million to 60,000 westerners. Other companies also advanced money on agricultural loans. The Aetna, in alliance with the Illinois Central Railroad, made many loans to small farmers in Illinois at 10 percent interest. The Northwestern had $30 million in Illinois mortgages, the Union Central was active in Indiana, and the Mutual Benefit all through the Middle West.

In the process of spreading their investments, the life companies drastically changed their investment portfolios. At first, they had been conservative investors. The New England Mutual in 1860 had one-eighth of its assets in railroad, manufacturing, and bank stocks; one-third in real-estate loans; one-tenth in government bonds; and about one-twentieth in loans on personal security. Much of this was due to the influence of government regulatory agencies, which were constantly being expanded. Massachusetts, in 1837, passed a law restricting life insurance investments in stocks to a small list of local companies. In 1849, Wisconsin and New York passed similar laws.

When state legislatures liberalized their rules for life insurance investments, the percentage of assets invested in stocks and bonds rose from 10 percent to over 35 percent, and the portion invested in mortgages and real estate fell from over 60 percent to less than 50 percent.

The motivating powers putting all of these forces together were the ambitious, aggressive entrepreneurs who emerged at the heads of the fastest growing companies: Hyde of Equitable, Frederick S. Winston and Richard McCurdy of the Mutual; William H. Beers and John McCall of the New York Life; Dryden of the Prudential; and Joseph F. Knapp and John R. Hegeman of the Metropolitan. Certainly, these men had much to do with the astonishing growth of the industry. They all shared an insatiable enthusiasm for growth at almost any cost. Profits and rates of return faded into the background, and the motive became not profit maximization, but as one competitor put it, "more, perhaps, for the pride in doing it than otherwise."

As the life insurance business grew to become a great fount of capital, it also took on the barnacles, the decay, and the stultification associated with growth. The structure became honeycombed with bureaucracy, the leading firms became intermeshed with other financial intermediaries in the banking world, the aggressive entrepreneurs tired, and the business became a tool rather than an entity of its own. Home office staffs grew to awesome size. The Prudential's staff rose from 89 to 250; the Metropolitan's to 1,081 in 1897. The president of the latter company was referred to as "a business machine," and its home office proudly proclaimed that it had more typewriters than any other office building in the world.

Boards of directors deteriorated to playing a rubber stamp role. Committee minutes became a mass of cliches. Elaborate home office buildings were erected to house the trappings of bureaucracy. Inevitably, the leaders of yesterday could echo the words of John Hegeman, "the business some time ago outgrew me." As they tired, they gave way to the bright salesmen and the financial wizards. George Perkins took over in the New York Life, Gage Tarbell in the Equitable, and Haley Fiske in the Metropolitan.

Relationships with banks and trust companies reached the point where insurance companies were described as "the financial annexes to Wall Street interests." The Mutual in the 1890's depended upon the finance committee headed by George F. Baker of the First National Bank; the New York Life, on George Perkins, a Morgan partner; the Equitable, on General Louis Fitzgerald of the Mercantile Trust. The Prudential relied on the brokerage house of Robert Winthrop & Co., the Metropolitan, on Vermilye & Co. But insurance companies also had a controlling interest in banks and trust companies even if they did not exercise it; The Equitable, in the Mercantile, the Equitable, the Commercial in Philadelphia, and the Franklin National; the Mutual in the Guaranty, the U.S. Mortgage & Trust, and the Morton Trust Co.; the Metropolitan, in the Hamilton Trust in Brooklyn and the National Shoe and Leather; the New York, in the New York Security & Trust; the Prudential, in the Fidelity Trust.

THE EMERGENCE OF INVESTMENT BANKING

Although not nearly as large as the commercial banks, investment banks were more fascinating and through their dealings in the securities markets, they moved more capital funds into the railroads, heavy industry and government than the commercial banks did.

Investment banking really came into its own in the late nineteenth century, for it was then that the American economy emerged as the largest in the world. An environment characterized by rising income and saving, heavy industry, the beginnings of big business, and a relatively large national debt could only invigorate investment banking.

On all sides, commentators of the day from the English political scientist and traveler, Lord Bryce, to the broker, James K. Medbery, remarked on the ubiquity of security speculation. "Today," wrote Medbery in 1870, "the wires of our telegraph companies are constantly burdened with orders to brokers . . . or stock operators. . . . Many of these persons are large capitalists; the majority are salaried men, small merchants, individuals who deem it an averagely safe business to divert their surplus to chances of the market."[6]

Admittedly, these commentators spoke from a biased sample. Medbery was a broker and Bryce, as one wit expressed it, "looked at America over a champagne glass." But activity in the securities markets did spring from peak to peak in the seventies and eighties. The volume of shares traded averaged 51.2 million a year in the last years of the 1870's, 104.4 million in the early 1880's, and 83.1 million between 1885 and 1889. And it was not just the volume of business that attested to the fact that the

[6]James K. Medbery, *Men and Mysteries of Wall Street* (Boston: Fields, Osgood Co., 1870), p. 11.

securities business was thriving. The Dow Jones average appeared in the 1890's, and in 1890 F. W. Hopkins, a partner in S. V. White & Co., delivered a lecture on industrial securities at Yale University.

In back of these brokers and professional stock-market players stood the conservative, mysterious investment bankers. They could be divided into five groups. The first group was headed by Jay Cooke & Co. and included Vermilye & Co., Henry Clews, and John J. Cisco & Son. Cooke had been the government's agent in the borrowing that had financed most of the cost of the Civil War. After the war, the house of Cooke declined. Other bankers successfully competed with it for the government's various bond refunding operations, and Cooke went into the railroad business with more optimistic enthusiasm than careful consideration. The Northern Pacific Railroad proved his undoing, and his house failed in the 1873 panic. But Cooke's contribution to finance had been immense. He gave the public more education about bonds than anyone else before or since, and through his sales organization he tapped the savings of the little man and brought him and the small local banker into the national capital market. Henry Clews, an English-born broker, also contributed an important financial innovation. His firm was the first commercial paper house in the modern meaning of the word. Clews bought and sold commercial paper. His predecessors had acted as brokers, rather than as principals.

The German-Jewish investment bankers formed the second group, even though they rarely acted as a disciplined entente. Most of these houses had their forebears in Frankfurt or Hamburg, Germany. For example, the house of Philip Speyer & Co., which opened a branch here in 1837, went back to at least the middle of the fourteenth century. James Speyer, who succeeded to the senior partnership in 1899, achieved great prestige, but he was a lone wolf in the true sense of the word. He seemed to have had no interest in the continued existence of the firm. He trained no successor, and the house dissolved upon his retirement. Abraham Kuhn and Solomon Loeb were originally peddlers, and they operated general stores in Indianapolis and Cincinnati before entering the banking business. But this house, which eventually became second in fame and prestige to J. P. Morgan, did not begin to ascend to its pedestal until Jacob Schiff and the Warburgs, both from the old-line German banking houses, entered the business, Schiff in the early 1870's and the Warburgs later. J. & W. Seligman Brothers were also peddlers and clothing dealers before they entered banking. In the 1870's, they became importantly involved in government finance, and they were the most influential house before J. P. Morgan and Kuhn, Loeb came to dominate the business.

A third entente consisted of the Yankees from Connecticut and Vermont. Fisk & Hatch, Vermonters, formed a firm in 1862 that later, 1885, became Harvey Fisk & Sons. Levi P. Morton, also from Vermont, was the senior partner in two houses (Morton, Bliss and Morton, Rose) before he decided he liked politics better. Junius Spencer Morgan from Connecticut joined Peabody & Co., an English firm formed by an ex-Baltimorean. Eventually, Morgan took over the business, and its name was changed to J. S. Morgan & Co., but his fame really rests on being the father of J. P. Morgan.

Still another group consisted of the Boston houses, Kidder, Peabody & Co., and Lee, Higginson & Co. Founded by representatives of Boston-Salem merchant families, they achieved immense reputation and prosperity, but toward the close of the century, they were becoming mere satellites to the House of Morgan. In the twentieth century, Lee, Higginson would again emerge as an innovator, but that is an item for a later chapter.

Finally, there were a number of firms that were not particularly allied with any of the larger ententes. Small though they were, however, some of them contributed importantly to the development of investment banking. August Belmont, for example, had started in the United States in 1837 as agent of the Rothschilds. He soon went his own way, and gained for some reason or other the wide respect of the financial community even though he came to spend more and more of his time at the races and in society. The much smaller and less well-known house of Winslow, Lanier & Co. was a much more significant innovator, especially in railroad finance.

J. P. MORGAN—THE PERSONIFICATION OF FINANCE CAPITALISM

Werner Sombart, the penetrating German economic historian, was originally responsible for the term "finance capitalism." He coined it to describe an economy dominated by bankers of the commercial as well as the investment variety. Whether the term has any real meaning or usefulness is still a moot question, but in any case, during the late nineteenth century investment bankers undoubtedly emerged from behind a cloud of anonymity to take their places among the empire builders of the day.

The most luminous star in the galaxy of investment banking was undoubtedly J. P. Morgan & Co. J. Pierpont Morgan was born in 1837, in those magic years of the late thirties that produced so many other business leaders. His father was a wealthy banker, and Morgan had the opportunity of acquiring what was then considered the best education. He attended Göttingen University, where he did not distinguish himself academically although he was proficient in mathematics. All his life, he had what the Germans call *Rechenhaftigkeit*—the enjoyment of numbers and figures that Sombart called an essential characteristic of the bourgeoisie.

Morgan returned to the states in 1857 and found employment at no salary with Duncan, Sherman & Co. He spent his time studying the cotton market, but most of these early years were spent in apparently unproductive efforts. A change in his career took place in 1861 shortly after he opened his own office. He married Amelia Sturges, who suffered from consumption, which at that time was a fatal disease. He took her to Europe, but she died a few months after the marriage.

In 1863, Charles Dabney became the senior partner in Dabney, Morgan & Co. The firm was at that time a combination of merchant and investment banking. It bought and sold securities, bills of exchange, and acceptances drawn against imports. It also dealt in foreign exchange and gold. Morgan spent much of his time keeping his father well informed about what was going on in the United States.

Following the Civil War, Dabney, Morgan & Co. (Drexel, Morgan & Co. in 1871)[7] made dazzling progress. The firm had many advantages. Vast opportunities for investment continued to open in the United States, and the dollar volume of saving was increasing. But until it became adequate to meet investment demands, the Morgan firm had excellent rapport with European capital markets through J. S. Morgan & Co. In addition, the firm had talent and a division of labor to put the talent to work. Dabney was a first-class accountant, and Morgan was a resourceful, energetic, self-confident entrepreneur with a philosophy more akin to the feudalism of medieval Europe than to nineteenth-century industrialism. He believed in rights and duties, just price, and a cooperative rather than a competitive economy.

Morgan soon had an opportunity to show his force. In a famous contest with Jay Gould and Jim Fisk over the control of the Albany & Susquehanna Railroad in 1869, Morgan won "not only by litigation but by force of arms."

Morgan spent the 1870's in government finance. His firm and others with close European connections, such as Belmont and Seligman, soon dominated the government refunding operations. But all the refunding was accomplished by the late seventies. By then, too, the government was paying off its debt, thus removing part of the raw material used by investment banking.

In 1879, Morgan turned his attention to financing, refinancing, and reorganizing railroads. His first large operation was the sale of 250,000 shares of New York Central from the portfolio of William H. Vanderbilt.[8] The syndicate that Morgan set up moved the stock without causing more than a ripple in the market, a noticeable achievement when daily trading

---

[7]Still later, in 1894, J. P. Morgan & Co.

[8]Vanderbilt had been threatened with heavy taxation, which caused him to sell. The episode also caused him to coin the much publicized phrase, "The public be damned."

on the Exchange was still well below 1,000,000 shares a day. In 1880, Drexel, Morgan & Co. with the aid of Winslow, Lanier, and August Belmont underwrote $40 million of Northern Pacific bonds.

Morgan's antipathy toward competition and overexpansion made him a champion of order and live and let live. The railroad business, with its sporadic price wars, violated his sense of what should be, and he spent most of the remaining years of the century in attempting to restore peace in the industry. At first, he tried to achieve his goals through "community of interests," but this was much like a gentlemen's agreement and it did not work. He believed that government regulation might accomplish what he had in mind, but the ICC disappointed him. After one last attempt in 1889 to establish a workable gentlemen's agreement, Morgan shifted to the policy of "Morganization," that is, of gaining a strong influence in the administration of roads that were in financial trouble. When the Morgan firm reorganized a road, and it reorganized almost every well-known road in the country, it followed a set pattern. It set up a voting trust to control management. It reorganized the management. It did not cut the capitalization, but raised the stock-bond (equity to debt) ratio, thus lowering fixed charges. It restricted production and created reserves. The objective of all of this was the maintenance of a set of rates that would make the road pay. This did not sit well with the industrialists who wanted the cheapest rates possible, and it was one of the many reasons why they disliked Morgan intensely.

In time, the Morgan firm also became involved in the industrial merger movement. Its first venture into this field came with the formation of the General Electric Company in 1892, at the very beginning of the late nineteenth-century merger wave.

The House of Morgan could not have accomplished what it did had it not controlled a vast reservoir of capital funds. Its own capital was never large enough to finance its innumerable financial reorganizations, and it did not possess the facilities to dispose of sizable security issues. But what it did not have, it obtained through a complicated set of interlocking directorates and alliances. The Morgan firm became the strategic unit in an alliance with George F. Baker's First National Bank and James Stillman's National City Bank, an alliance that was eventually (in 1912) labelled "The Money Trust." The Morgan-Baker-Stillman entente held 341 directorships in 112 companies with over $22 billion in assets at a time when the national wealth was estimated at $186 billion. A Morgan partner, Henry P. Davison, organized the Bankers' Trust. The Guaranty Trust was commonly known as a Morgan bank. So was the National Bank of Commerce. Morgan held the controlling interest in the Equitable Life Assurance Society and was chairman of the Mutual Life's Finance Committee. George Perkins occupied the same position in the New York Life.

The existence of a workable agreement with other money powers and a number of distribution outlets for securities was only one of the reasons for the Morgan firm's success. An even more important reason was that the Morgan organization had put together a group of men with immense talents, Charles H. Dabney, Charles H. Coster, Egisto P. Fabbri, J. Hood Wright, F. L. Stetson, and many more. Each had his specific specialty; each had his unique talent. The firm was completely departmentalized, and talent under the circumstances could not go to waste. Most of the partners in the Morgan enterprise found life short and exciting but not too merry. And over the whole loomed the personality of J. Pierpont Morgan, confident, tenacious, energetic, ruthless, and serene in his notion that he had the ultimate answer to rights and duties; a throwback to the lords of medieval feudalism.

12

BIG BUSINESS
BECOMES A REALITY

The previous chapters emphasized that in order to thrive and in some cases even to survive, businessmen had to adjust their tactics (strategy) and organization (structure) to changes in economic and political institutions, to shifts in market forces, and to technological evolution. In the first seven decades or so of the nineteenth century, both the internal structure of business and the external environment it faced were relatively simple and posed few problems. Most businesses were small and, except in the giant railroad, the owner-manager was the typical entrepreneur. Labor unions were weak, and the political system was as friendly as businessmen could realistically expect. The most dynamic features of the economy were the extraordinary growth of a highly mobile population, the continuous rise of the city, and the construction of a railroad network.

THE ECONOMIC BACKGROUND

The economy took a somewhat different course in the twentieth century. The rate of population growth slowed down appreciably, to 20 percent in the first decade, 15 percent per decade in 1910 to 1930, and 7 percent in the 1930's. World War II, unlike other major wars, spurred population growth to 15 percent in the forties. After surging to 18 percent in the 1950's, it slipped back to 13 percent in the sixties.

Per capita income in dollars of the same purchasing power almost quadrupled in the century's first sixty years. But the upward march was certainly not continuous. Measured by what the dollar could buy in 1958, average income was approximately $1,000 in 1900. By 1929, it had climbed to approximately $1,600. But in the deep depression, 1929–1933, it dropped back to $1,100, approximately what it had been thirty years before. By 1940, at $1,740, it was still only about $100 more than it had been in 1929. Following World War II, however, per capita real income achieved a substantial gain, and it did even better in the 1960's. At the beginning of that decade, average output in real terms was estimated at $2,700. By 1970, it had risen to $3,600. Surely, it was a heady atmosphere for business.

The twentieth century has been labelled the era of the "knowledge revolution." Although the expression is more melodramatic than accurate, the 1900's did witness a sharp change in the form of technological progress. In the early nineteenth century, the emphasis had been on the creation of machinery; in the late nineteenth and early twentieth century, the stress shifted toward the development of new sources of power;[1] the middle of the twentieth century was a time of research and managerial evolution. The process of technological progress that had been extensive in the nineteenth century became intensive in the twentieth century.

The new technology had major ramifications on how Americans made their living. At the beginning of the century, most members of the labor force were still involved in primary production, that is, in farming, manufacturing, and construction. By mid-century, a majority were engaged in tertiary occupations, that is, in distribution and service. The so-called "white collar" occupations—clerical, professional, sales, and management—that made up only about 20 percent of all workers in 1900, had grown to approximately 50 percent by the late 1960's.

Technological improvements, especially in transportation and communication, also widened the market area, and by mid-century produced a manufacturing and managerial decentralization that had been impossible in the early part of the century. In 1890 the vast majority of the companies were sectional. Only a handful of giants, such as Singer, McCormick, and Standard Oil, served a national market. To be sure, these giants had already gone beyond their national boundaries, but their international business was more an intrusion than a full-scale invasion. In the 1960's, by contrast, American business was not only national but multi-national. International phone service, airplanes, and computers made it possible by this time to cover a world market in less time than it had taken to cover a local market at the beginning of the century or the national market at the end of World War II. Direct investment in foreign subsidiaries totalled over $70 billion, ten times as much as at the end of World War II. American companies produced abroad over $200 billion a year in goods and services.

---

[1]As late as 1900, coal generated over 70 percent of all consumed energy. Fifty years later, it generated less than half as much. Electricity, gas, and petroleum generated 10 percent in 1900 and 70 percent in 1950.

ADJUSTING TO CHANGE

At all times, the entrepreneur's primary problem has been to use his resources rationally in a world of shifting market forces. By whatever label we may know him, the industrialist, industrial capitalist, owner-entrepreneur, or empire builder of the late nineteenth century dealt with this problem in his own distinctive and individualistic fashion. He was at his best in dealing with a virgin market. Although the term itself was unknown to him, his marketing techniques rested on a firm faith in price elasticity. He believed that it was price that made people buy; the lower the price, the greater the sales. He was at home in the vast untapped markets created by the city and opened up by the railroad. He carried business enterprise somewhat beyond the brink of bigness. His mills, packing-houses, factories, and refineries turned out a flood of goods. But expansion was not easy to accomplish, and capacity production often affected profits adversely. He dealt with the problems of expansion and competition by pursuing horizontal and vertical integration, often with the objective of achieving a monopoly position. In its effect on economic growth, this was laudatory, for nothing encourages growth as much as the pursuit of monopoly, provided the goal is never reached.

But from the point of view of the business enterprise, the strategy and tactics of the industrialist were not altogether satisfactory. By the last quarter of the nineteenth century, it was clear that his kind of business system required much revision and modification. Very often, his financial policies were too weak to withstand the rigors of business recession, and his managerial organization was not geared for smooth operation of mass-production enterprise. He did not disappear altogether, and he returned in full force each time a new product appeared or a new market called for invasion. So, at a later date, Henry Ford, who perhaps most closely resembled the composite industrial capitalist, took full advantage of the infant automobile industry. By the early 1900's, however, most of the spectacular, often flamboyant, owner-entrepreneurs who had starred in the great growth that began in the 1870's had retired from active business life. Clark retired from the Singer presidency in 1882. McCormick died in 1884. Pillsbury sold his flour mill in 1889. Rockefeller and Armour began to withdraw from management in the early 1890's. Carnegie and his associates sold their holdings to United States Steel in 1901. Swift died in 1903.

The old order was giving way to new, both in personalities and in behavior. Either by force of circumstances or by voluntary decision, steps were taken to change the existing structure and to overcome some of the enterprise system's weaknesses. Frequently this change came from outside industry. When a great industrialist's vast enterprise began to totter for want of cash, or when price competition threatened to "demoralize" an industry, it was not uncommon for the investment bankers of New York's Wall Street or Boston's State Street to step in to protect their own interest or those of other creditors or stockholders. To be sure, bankers had been active participants in the railroad and textile business for years, but it was only in the last quarter of the nineteenth century and the early years of the twentieth that their intervention in manufacturing and in retailing became more active.

In their business policies, the investment bankers differed fundamentally from the industrialists. Unlike most industrialists, who specialized in a single branch of production, the bankers spread their influence over many different industries. Consequently, their interests were too diversified to permit them to assume a continuous entrepreneurial role. Within the firm, they picked the managers and delegated to them most of the actual power to make decisions. Thus, they paved the way for professional managers to take over the reins of business later in the century.

As one might expect, investment bankers were more interested in financial policy than in any other aspect of business. They preferred the discipline of corporate finance to that of industrial management. Income statements and balance sheets, earnings per share, security prices, capitalization, and security flotations absorbed their interest much more than did the index of industrial production, the output of pig iron, or the volume of car loadings. Because bankers and industrialists were so different, it is not surprising that bankers disliked industrialists and that production men loathed bankers. Morgan thought that Carnegie was a dangerous man who had "demoralized" the steel industry. For his part, Carnegie abhorred the bankers and the promoters. He boasted, not without reason, that he could operate a steel business much better than a lot of "stock-jobbers" who paid more attention to security manipulation than to steel-making. Rockefeller, too, disliked the bankers. He thought they had an unjustified superiority complex. Speaking of Morgan, he said, "I could see that Mr. Morgan was very much—well like Mr. Morgan; very haughty, very much inclined to look down on other men. . . . For my part, I have never been able to see why any man should have such a high and mighty feeling about himself."[2]

Because they were so much concerned with financial matters, the investment bankers were more at home in reorganizing and consolidating existing businesses than in creating and building new ones. They were not particularly venturesome or bold in expanding production. They were more interested in dividends, stability, and the protection of stockholders' interests than in plowing back earnings and expanding plant. They were opposed to price competition. Instead, they favored a spirit of "live and

[2]Allan Nevins, *John D. Rockefeller* (New York: Charles Scribner's Sons, 1941), Vol. 2, p. 419.

let live," with stable rather than volatile prices. With such a set of beliefs, it was not surprising that the bankers exerted an important influence in bringing to the fore a concept of "fair prices" similar to the "just price" of medieval times. Judge Gary, of the United States Steel Corporation, a managerial representative of the bankers, expressed the idea very well when he said: "I think any of us would rather have the prices of our tailor or our grocer substantially uniform, assuming that they are fair and reasonable, than to have the prices very low in time of panic and depression, and then in other times very high and unreasonable."

Ultimately, this drift away from market-determined prices toward "fair and reasonable prices" invited government regulation and even government control, for, if prices were no longer to be determined by the market, they might just as well be administered by government as by businessmen and bankers. As the Telephone Company's Theodore N. Vail, who opposed government ownership but supported government regulation, said in 1912, "There are few big captains of industry who can run a great corporation, but there is any quantity of men who could review their acts and who . . . could say whether or not the men who were doing things were doing them right."

The problem of adjusting to major changes assumed different overtones in the twentieth century. Like everything else, it became much more complicated. In the institutional environment, there were three important developments that taxed the resiliency of the entrepreneur. The ownership of the large corporation became more fractionalized and more widely dispersed. In the labor field, business unionism with its emphasis on bread-and-butter objectives finally emerged victorious over welfare unionism, which stressed more abstract and metaphysical goals. In the political field, the federal government played a more and more active role in economic life in general.

The ramifications of these developments sank deep into the foundations of business life. First of all, the professional manager replaced the industrialist and the financier as the prototype of the influential entrepreneur. This, in turn, brought forth a set of enigmatic and previously unheard-of problems, which could be subsumed under the general heading "The Corporation Problem," and which included such matters as the separation of ownership from control, the vitiating effects of corporate bureaucracy, and the legitimacy of the corporate hierarchy.

Changes in economic and political institutions also led the businessman to put more emphasis on functions that had previously been largely neglected. Public relations, labor relations, and government relations assumed an importance they had never enjoyed in the past. Business literature devoted more space to the businessman's social responsibility. Critics on the left derided what was happening as blatant hypocrisy.

Critics on the right were alarmed by the seeming departure from profit-mindedness. Still other critics charged that the businessman had become a manipulator of people rather than a manipulator of things, as his predecessor had been.

The behavior of market forces in the twentieth century was also different enough to create new problems of adjustment for the businessman. The growth of population slowed down, and, although new and important means of transportation were devised, they did not open new areas as the railroads had. Because the domestic market did not expand as rapidly as in the past and because in many industries the virgin market of the nineteenth century was being succeeded by the replacement market of the twentieth century, businessmen had to exercise more active initiative in developing markets and in dealing with the problem of so-called "excess capacity." In response to the challenge, they tried to stimulate the domestic market by multiplying the quantity and intensity of their advertising and their use of consumer credit. In addition, entrepreneurs diversified their activities on a broad front. They began to exploit intensively international markets. They created new products through research and development, and they branched out into entirely new businesses. The net of all this was a change in the nature of competition and an equally important change in the internal organization of business. Competition became more a struggle between marketing departments and less a battle of prices. Or, to express this in another way, emphasis on service, product differentiation, and other tools of monopolistic or imperfect competition came to rival and even to surpass price competition as income elasticity superseded price elasticity in the market place.

GIANT ENTERPRISE

Big business in the absolute sense is a modern creation. It is probable that no single plant in the early nineteenth century controlled as much as 10 percent of the output of any manufactured product. But there can be no argument that big business is one of the facts of the modern world. If we are to believe the statistical evidence, the change took place in the two decades surrounding 1900, for it was then that big business in manufacturing first became a reality.

In 1885, manufacturing companies with a net worth of more than $10 million were very large. They were relatively analogous to today's $1 billion firm. Perhaps there were five in the whole country. Companies of $5 to $10 million were also rare. Many of the best known industrial plants fell far below or just made the select few. McCormick Reaper's net worth was only $2.5 million, and the Carnegie Company's net assets were valued at only $5 million. Two wholesalers, H. B. Claflin and Marshall Field, were the largest firms in distribution. Wanamaker and Macy were medium size; A. & P., Woolworth, and Montgomery Ward were first beginning to grow. At the same time, however, each of the ten largest railroads had a net worth of over $100 million, and the Pennsylvania's assets were over $200 million.

The speed of growth accelerated toward the end of the century. In 1897, there were eight companies with over $50 million in assets. The first billion dollar manufacturing company, United States Steel, appeared in 1901. By 1904, there were 40 companies in the $50 million class, over 100 with $10 million, but only three with over $200 million and less than 1,000 with over $5 million. At that time there were 1.2 million business firms, 200,000 of which were in manufacturing. This meant that only one half of one percent of all industrial firms could be considered large-scale businesses by a liberal definition of the word. Some of the best known companies—American Tinplate, American Woolen, International Paper, U. S. Rubber—had assets of less than $50 million.

By 1919, big business in manufacturing was a well recognized fact. There were in that year more than 100 companies with over $50 million in assets. Since then, business firms have grown apace. Today's corporations originate 65 percent of all business income. Among these corporations, only 2/10 of 1 percent own assets of $50 million or more, but they control 60 percent of all corporate assets. General Motors, the largest industrial corporation, employs more people than the entire population of St. Louis. Its annual sales are two and a half times as much as California's total revenue. The number of stockholders in the American Telephone and Telegraph exceeds the entire population of all but three cities.

CONCENTRATION AND CONTROL

Although it is evident that big business has continued to grow, no such clear-cut answer can be given to the question of whether business has become more concentrated, that is, whether small business has been disappearing and whether the economic area not occupied by agriculture and the government has been completely usurped by big business.

There are more businesses in proportion to population today than there were in 1900. Moreover, the proportion of small business to the total business population is a little higher today than it was then. In addition, it is estimated that monopolistic firms constituted 32 percent of the manufacturing population of 1899, 28 percent in 1937, 24 percent in 1947, and about 24 percent today.

But there is also evidence that there has been some slight increase in the relative importance of the very large corporate units in the last half-century. The 100 largest firms controlled about 20 percent of all corporate assets in 1919, 40 percent in 1948, and 50 percent in 1968. Among these 100 firms, the 20 largest held almost 50 percent of assets in 1919, over 54 percent in 1958, and slightly over 50 percent in 1969.

In the normal backing and filling that takes place within the business population, the degree of mobility among the largest firms is relatively large. In the last 50 years, almost 200 companies have at one time or another been included in the 100 largest firms. Of the original 100, 39 are still included, 22 disappeared as a result of mergers, and 4 failed. But, on the other hand, of today's 100 largest companies, only 33 had not been included in the business "who's who" at some time before 1948.[3]

MERGER WAVES IN THE
TWENTIETH CENTURY

As any historian would expect, much of what took place in the twentieth century was a repetition, with different emphasis, of nineteenth-century phenomena. In the 1900's, big business grew, as it had in the late nineteenth century, both by internal expansion and via the merger route. But mergers were a far more popular way of achieving giantism. Of the 100 largest industrial companies in 1969, more than two-thirds had achieved most of their size by absorbing other small or large companies.

Mergers took place in waves. The consolidation movement of the late 1890's was repeated during the speculative 1920's and again when the

TABLE 9   Departures and Arrivals Among the 100 Largest Companies in Manufacturing and Trade, 1909–1969

	1909	1919	1929	1935	1948	1958	1969
Departures	—	40	31	16	20	16	31
Arrivals	100	40	31	16	20	16	31

Source: Collins and Preston "The Size Structure of the Largest Industrial Firms," AER, 1961; The Fortune Directory.

[3]See, for example, G. Warren Nutter, *The Extent of Enterprise Monopoly in the United States, 1899–1939* (Chicago: University of Chicago Press, 1951); M. A. Adelman, "The Measurement of Industrial Concentration," *Review of Economics and Statistics,* Vol. XXXIII (1951); Solomon Fabricant, "Is Monopoly Increasing?" *Journal of Economic History,* Vol. XIII (1953); Norman R. Collins and Lee E. Preston, "The Size Structure of the Largest Industrial Firms," *American Economic Review* (1961); A. D. H. Kaplan, *Big Enterprise in a Competitive System* (Washington, D.C.: The Brookings Institution, 1964).

stock market took off in the 1950's and 1960's. But there were some significant differences between 1890, 1920 and 1950. Fewer giant corporations participated in each successive merger wave. In the 1890's, the very large corporations consummated many of the alliances; in the 1920's, it was the middle-size group; and in the post-World War II era, most of the participants were small. As George Stigler described it, "In the early period, the leading firms seldom merged less than 50 percent of the industry's output; in the later period the percentage has hardly ever risen this high. The new goal of mergers is oligopoly."[4] A second difference was that in the twentieth century, bank mergers were as fashionable as mergers in manufacturing, mining, and transportation. Finally, the later merger movements were more concerned with conglomerate consolidations. In the 1890's, mergers continued the horizontal and vertical integration of the previous 20 years; in the 1920's, mergers of firms in different industries were interspersed with vertical integration; in the post-World War II period, diversification was the prevailing theme.

In absolute numbers, the rate of merger in the 1960's surpassed all others. For the whole decade, the average was 1,300 a year in comparison with 660 in the 1920's, 360 in the first merger wave, and 430 in the 1950's. In the years of the bull market of 1925–1929, mergers averaged over 900 a year, reaching a high of 1,245 in 1929. Again in the bull market of the 1960's the urge to merge took on a frenzied pace, reaching 1,500 in 1967 and 2,655 in 1968.

Qualitatively, the merger movement of the 1920's rivaled its predecessor and far surpassed its successor. As has been said, giants merged in the 1890's, large companies merged in the 1920's, and small companies joined forces in the 1950's and 1960's. Indeed, if merger movements were defined to encompass only major consolidations, the immediate post-World War II era would not qualify as a merger movement. On the other hand, the 1890's would be memorable for having produced big business and the 1920's for having narrowed the gap between the big and the very big.

MORE ON MERGERS

The basic objectives were much the same in all four merger waves. Entrepreneurs sought to gain competitive advantages by (1) acquiring additional capacity, (2) diversifying the product line, and (3) achieving

---

[4]George J. Stigler, "Monopoly and Oligopoly by Merger," *American Economic Review*, Proceedings, Vol. XI (1950), reprinted in Richard R. Heflebower and George W. Stocking, eds., *Readings in Industrial Organization and Public Policy* (Homewood, Ill.: Richard D. Irwin, Inc., 1958).

economies of scale by vertical and horizontal integration. Large-scale enterprise seemed to offer additional nonmarket advantages such as the possible ability to retain more competent legal counsel, the possibility of wielding political influence, the enhancement of public relations, and the probability of being able to borrow more easily and greater amounts.

Noneconomic motives were also involved in merger movements. Businessmen are not and have never been robots automatically responding to the calculus of pleasures and pains. For example, the empire building propensities of the nineteenth-century tycoon were reproduced in his twentieth-century successor, even though empire building did not necessarily lead to maximizing profits. Then too, tax avoidance or tax saving, a consideration that did not exist in the earlier merger waves, became of more than passing importance in the 1950's and 1960's.

It is not easy to assay the success of the twentieth-century mergers. Not enough time has passed to develop the same kind of picture of survival and bankruptcy that we have for the 1890's. And in the complicated world of today, accounting methods of measuring profits have become an exercise in obfuscation. Consider a hypothetical case of a large company with sales of $1 billion a year. By conservative accounting standards, the firm netted $54 million or $8 per share. By more liberal standards, it made $69 million or over $12 per share. Clearly, it is exceptionally difficult to measure profits in the complicated world of conglomerates.

Regardless of what accounting practices are used, it would seem that the advantages achieved by merger would result in an enhanced profit performance. Economies of scale and diversification should pay off. But it is always necessary to qualify what would seem to be in order to make it conform to reality. The gigantic conglomerates that appeared in the 1950's and 1960's enjoyed spectacular success in their youth. Their earnings per share were much higher than the average earnings in Standard and Poor's list of 500 stocks. Their shares sold at much higher multiples of earnings. But toward the end of the sixties, many conglomerates fell on evil days, and it appeared that the experience of the early merger waves, in which failures were about equal to successes, would be repeated.

DIVERSIFICATION AND DECENTRALIZATION

Merger activity collapsed during the depressed 1930's, averaging only 114 a year from 1933 to 1939. But although mergers ceased to be in style, the search for profit increased in intensity, and manifested itself most evidently in diversification moves by big business. Indeed, the diversification of business activities and the decentralization of business organization have been among the most important developments in the last 40 years of business history.

By the 1920's, most large firms were organized in centralized structures. They operated under departments, such as production, sales, law, and so forth. Although they had many functions, with few exceptions they still dealt in a single product. Steel companies produced steel. Tobacco companies made cigars, cigarettes, and pipe tobacco. Oil companies pumped oil, refined it, and sold it. But entrepreneurs were not satisfied with this. In order to utilize their expanding resources and at the same time to assure a further measure of security against the vicissitudes of the business cycle, they inaugurated campaigns of ambitious diversification. They moved exactly opposite to Andrew Carnegie's famous dictum, which admonished industrialists to put all their eggs in one basket. Electric-machinery manufacturers entered the appliance market, meat packers manufactured soap, automobile producers turned out refrigerators, oil companies expanded their international activities, and so on, through a long list of businesses, until only the metal companies and the processors of a few agricultural products were not diversified.

Some pioneering entrepreneurs were quick to recognize that diversification required an entirely different kind of managerial approach. The structure that had worked so well for a single-product firm was not good enough for a multiproduct firm. The top executives were too often busy with administrative rather than entrepreneurial decisions. The heads of departments ran into difficulties in handling a number of diverse products. Sales departments, for example, did not find it easy to sell both automobiles and refrigerators. Procurement of raw material and routing the production of different goods caused continuous headaches.

According to Chandler, DuPont, General Motors, Sears Roebuck, and Standard Oil were the business innovators in solving the problem of adapting the managerial structure to the strategy of diversification. In the 1920's, they were the first to decentralize their organizations, to operate through divisions rather than departments, and to divorce their chief executives from day-to-day administration, leaving them free for long-range planning. During the 1930's, the shift from a centralized to a decentralized structure quickened, and it attained a rapid tempo after World War II.

Decentralization was selective. It came most quickly in companies that had grown mostly by merger, in firms with diversified product lines and heavy investment in research and development, in businesses that were very complex, and in companies that were headed by career executives. It came slowly or not at all in companies headed by the "empire-building" executive and in lines with no diversification and little research and development. Indeed, Chandler, on the basis of a large sample of companies, concludes that the three D's traveled together: diversification and development could not succeed without decentralization. Decentralization appeared unnecessary without the other two.

The experiences of the DuPont Company afford the best illustration of how strategy and structure changed in an immensely successful firm.[5] In the dozen years before World War I, DuPont, principally because of the efforts of H. M. Barksdale, J. Amory Haskell, and Pierre duPont, developed a very successful, departmentalized, centralized managerial structure. The loss of an antitrust suit in 1912 and the stimulus of World War I caused the company to diversify into other lines. Barksdale foresaw, "When the war is over, our difficulty is going to consist of making a creditable showing in earnings because of the huge increase in manufacturing facilities." Peace would pose for DuPont a problem of resource utilization. Further expansion in explosives was not attractive because the demand would decline, and in any event it was not possible because of the antitrust judgment. The company, therefore, poured its resources into a varied series of investments. In addition to investing substantially in General Motors, it began to manufacture and market, through its existing departments, chemicals, paints, celluloid, dyestuffs, and synthetic fibers.

To its surprise, DuPont suffered heavy losses on its diversified lines. By 1921, these losses were in the area of $30 million, and management was taking a very hard look at major changes in its organization. The young men were sure they understood the problem. Diversification had greatly increased the demands on the administrative office, and the departmental structure was not attuned to many different products. Selling paints, it was clear, was not the same as selling explosives; procuring raw materials for explosives was not a problem for a specialist in buying pigments. In 1920, the young group proposed as a solution a reorganization on the basis of product, not function; but after considerable thought, Pierre duPont vetoed the idea. However, when the company lost another $1.3 million in early 1921, Pierre and the veteran executives capitulated. The company adopted a new structure of five autonomous divisions (cellulose, paint, purolin, dyestuffs, and explosives) overseered by a general office with staff specialists and general executives. Each division head was responsible for administrative decisions, and the central office was relieved of all day-to-day operations. Under the new arrangement, the company once again became successful, and the structure remains today essentially what it was forty years ago. Indeed, critics are inclined to think that it may be time for another change.

    [5]For the DuPont Company's business history see: Alfred D. Chandler, Jr., *Strategy and Structure* (Cambridge, Mass.: The M. I. T. Press, 1962); Alfred D. Chandler, Jr. and Stephen Salisbury, *Pierre S. du Pont and the Making of the Modern Corporation* (New York: Harper & Row, 1971); Ernest Dale, "Du Pont: Pioneer in Systematic Management," *Administrative Science Quarterly*, Vol. 2, No. 1 (June 1957); Ernest Dale, *Great Organizers* (New York: McGraw-Hill Book Company, 1960).

THE GOVERNMENT'S ATTITUDE TOWARD
MERGERS AND LARGE-SCALE ENTERPRISE

Government showed no clear understanding of what was going on in the world of business. As big business became a reality, the government behaved like a rudderless ship floundering in turbulent waters. It did not know whether it wanted to accept big business or to reject it.

In the late 1890's, the federal courts began to reinterpret the language of the Sherman Act. In *U.S. v. Trans-Missouri Freight Association et al.* (1897), the majority of the Supreme Court held that the Sherman Act condemned *every* restraint of trade, but Justice White, in a dissenting opinion shared by three other justices, enunciated what later became known as "the rule of reason." "The words restraint of trade," he said, "embrace only contracts which unreasonably restrain trade, and, therefore, reasonable contracts, although they, in some measure, restrain trade, are not within the meaning of the words."

During the Progressive Era, writers such as Herbert Croly and Charles Van Hise openly questioned the traditional view that competition was the norm of economic life even in a free society. They argued that large-scale enterprise was inevitable, and that policy makers should cut their cloth accordingly. Van Hise proposed that any firm controlling more than 50 percent of an industry should be looked upon as in restraint of trade and should be regulated by government. President Roosevelt was much impressed by this view. "Combinations in industry," he said, "are the result of an imperative economic law which cannot be repealed by political legislation. . . . The way out lies not in attempting to prevent such combinations but in completely controlling them in the interest of public welfare." The Supreme Court was also much impressed by the so-called "new competition." The rule of reason, which had been in the minority, now emerged as the prevailing view, at first as an obiter dictum in the Northern Securities case (1904), and then more fully in the Standard Oil and American Tobacco cases of 1911. In the Standard Oil case, Chief Justice White, speaking for what was now a majority, held that the Sherman Law was intended to prohibit unreasonable restraints of trade where there was an intent to monopolize and where unfair competition ruled in the place of free competition. In other words, there were good trusts that should continue and bad combinations that should be dissolved.

The promulgation of the rule of reason was the last of a series of incidents that convinced many original proponents that the Sherman Act had not accomplished its mission. It had not clarified the perennial confusion over the nature of competition nor had it eliminated and outlawed all monopolistic practices. Indeed, some overzealous critics labeled the act "the mother of trusts," for, although it apparently prohibited agreements among independent firms (so-called "loose-knit" combinations), it did not forbid close-knit combinations, that is, mergers or consolidations. Some Congressmen recommended that a firm that controlled over 30 percent of its market must be broken up because it was in restraint of trade.[6] But this was a minority view. Instead, in order to clear the antitrust air, Congress, in 1914, passed the Clayton Act and the Federal Trade Commission Act.

The Clayton Act was designed to prevent monopolies before they happened. It prohibited interlocking directorates, price discrimination, and the acquisition of competitors where the result would be a substantial lessening of competition. The Federal Trade Commission was supposed to prevent unfair competition.

During the 1920's, antitrust policy reverted to the doldrums that had been its outstanding characteristic in the early 1890's. Prosperity and the political climate were primarily responsible for this, but businessmen also lent a helping hand. Judge Elbert H. Gary's tactics, for example, were always colored by a concern for the Sherman Act. His annual reports, news conferences, and pursuit of good public relations showed that he was fully aware that United States Steel was frequently in the antitrust courts.

Although it was a time of good feeling between government and business, at least two cases in this era were of more than passing significance in antitrust history. In 1920, the Supreme Court extended the rule of reason in deciding against the government in the U.S. Steel case. The majority opinion interpreted the government's brief as contending "that strength in any producer or seller is a menace to the public interest and illegal, because there is potency in it for mischief." After dismissing this as a "manifest fallacy," the Court continued, "The corporation is undoubtedly of impressive size. . . . But we must adhere to the law, and the law does not make mere size an offense, or the existence of unexerted power an offense." Much of this thinking was to be abandoned in less than a generation. A similar fate was to meet the Court's logic in *Thatcher Manufacturing Co. v. Federal Trade Commission* (1926). Here the Court held that the Clayton Act strictures against the purchase of a competitor applied only to stock purchase. This meant that there was no violation of the Clayton Act where one competitor bought the assets of another. In 1950, this interpretation was specifically negated by the Celler Amendment to the Clayton Act.

GOVERNMENT'S FLIGHT FROM COMPETITION DURING THE GREAT DEPRESSION

At various times during the Progressive Era and after, Congress chipped away at the faith in competition that underlay the antitrust policy.

[6]The Stanley Committee in 1912. Senator La Follette (Wisconsin), introduced such a bill in 1913.

In 1918, it passed the Webb-Pomerene Act, which permitted cartels in international trade by exempting them from the antitrust acts. In 1920, the Transportation Act encouraged combination in railroading. During the 1920's, too, the so-called new competition further infiltrated business thinking. A new breed of businessmen, the professional managers, looked back with disapproval at the old breed's competitive tactics. The new theory was perhaps best stated by Judge Gary. After paying lip service to "the natural law of supply and demand," Gary continued:

> We never reach out intentionally to get a competitor's business. If the price of a commodity has been sufficiently established to secure publication in the journals, we never cut under that price . . . for two reasons: first, it would not be the fair thing to do; and secondly, it would only be a question of time before . . . we would feel the effects of it, because someone else might cut our prices . . . even worse than we had cut their prices.[7]

Another eminent company, National Biscuit, found that attempts to control prices and production were too expensive. In its Annual Report for 1901 it wrote:[8]

> When this company started, it was thought we must control competition, and that to do this we must either fight competition or buy it. The first meant a ruinous war of prices, and a great loss of profit; the second, a constantly increasing capitalization. Experience soon proved to us that, instead of bringing success, either of these courses, if persevered in, must bring disaster. This led us to reflect whether it was necessary to control competition. . . . We turned our attention to improving the internal management of our business, to getting full benefit from purchasing our raw materials in large quantities, to economizing the expenses of manufacture, to systematizing and rendering more effective our selling department; and above all things . . . to improve the quality of our goods. . . . It became the settled policy of this company to buy out no competition.

In line with the tenets of the new competition, there occurred a proliferation of trade associations, which intentionally or unintentionally were designed to circumvent the Sherman Act by restricting competition. Their activities included "fair trade practices" and "open price" arrangements, which published each member's prices and production for all to see. These cooperative activities had the blessing of the political administration of the 1920's.

Perfect cooperation, however, was, like perfect competition, more a state of mind than a reality. At least, businessmen seemed to find it neces-

---

[7] *Addresses and Statements of Elbert H. Gary* (privately printed, no date).
[8] Quoted by Alfred D. Chandler, Jr., "Beginnings of Big Business in American Industry," *Business History Review*, Vol. XXXIII, Spring, 1959.

sary to create artificial means to control man's "propensity to compete." This became quite evident during the great depression of the 1930's when, under economic stress, cooperation quickly reverted to what was called "cutthroat competition." A number of businessmen and business spokesmen urged that something be done about this unfair competition. They believed that overproduction had caused the depression. Almost as soon as the gloomy era began, they called for changes in the antitrust laws to permit business "to enter into contracts for the purpose of equalizing production and consumption." The United States Chamber of Commerce and other influential organizations argued that economic recovery could be greatly advanced through business cooperation under the aegis of Federal and state legislation. They urged the administration to adopt the Swope plan,[9] or something similar. The Hoover administration rejected the whole idea with a sweeping condemnation, "There is no stabilization of price without price fixing. . . . It is the most gigantic proposal of monopoly ever made in history."

But other administrations were much more amenable. In 1931, California passed a "fair trade" law, permitting producers to establish by contract with dealers minimum retail prices for their goods. Within a short time, 43 other states adopted similar legislation. But the most extreme departure from the traditional American policy of resisting monopoly and economic collusion came with the National Industrial Recovery Act of 1933. Through the NIRA, the government tried to persuade the firms in each major industry to create, through a trade association, a code of fair practices, setting minimum prices, minimum wages, and production quotas. It was hoped that this elaborate blueprint for industry planning would protect the economically weak and enable the economy to pick itself up by the bootstraps, so that depression would give way to recovery.

The NIRA was declared unconstitutional in 1935, and the New Deal immediately reversed its policy and inaugurated the most vigorous antitrust campaign in history. At roughly the same time, the Supreme Court began to press a much harder line, but Congress, ostensibly to protect small business, continued to restrict competition. In 1936, it passed the Robinson-Patman Act. In a sense, this law encouraged competition by prohibiting price discrimination on sales that were otherwise identical. But the act was really designed to protect small business, for it prohibited firms from selling more cheaply in one part of the country than another and selling at "unreasonably low prices for the purpose of destroying competition." A second example of Congress' restrictions on competition came in 1937 with the Miller-Tydings Amendment, which exempted fair-trade contracts from the Sherman Act. Later, when resourceful businessmen invented ways and means of avoiding fair-trade restrictions, Congress passed the McGuire

[9]A plan for the "self-regulation" of business proposed by Gerard Swope, head of General Electric.

Act (1952), which not only continued the exemption of price maintenance, but gave firms the right to enforce fair-trade agreements against nonsigners and to fix prices not only at a minimum, but at any point. Again, however, resourceful businessmen cut the underpinning from this legislation, this time by attacking fair-trade laws in the state courts. Today, there are only 23 states in which nonsigners of price agreements are bound by fair-trade laws.

ANTITRUST AND THE COURTS SINCE 1945

In the forty years between the enactment of the Sherman Act and the outbreak of the depression, certain interpretations of the antitrust laws achieved a status of respectability. Among these were the principle that the Sherman Act applied only to unreasonable restraints of trade and the doctrine that size alone was no proof of monopoly. This line of reasoning evolved during a period when economists defined competition as a condition in which two or more sellers each tried to maximize income without regard to the action of the other. But then in the depression, under the influence of imperfect competition theory, competition took on a quite different meaning. "Pure competition" was defined as a situation in which many sellers, no one of whom could influence the price, dealt in products that were exactly the same. "Monopoly" continued to be defined as a one-seller market. Both pure competition and monopoly were very rare. The most common market structure—indeed, the only market structure in manufacturing and distribution—was a combination of competition and monopoly recognized as monopolistic competition, imperfect competition, or oligopoly.

Some economists looked upon imperfect competition as a fact of life about which nothing could be done. In formulating policy, they examined the behavior of a given market structure, that is, they were more interested in performance than in structure. Their yardsticks for deducing the existence of insidious monopoly were not the number of sellers or the ratio of concentration, but ease of entry, effect on economic growth, price behavior, unused capacity, and technological innovation. Where a given industry scored well on the above tests, the market structure was described as one of "workable competition," the effects of which were analogous to pure competition.

It is, of course, impossible to say how much influence the new concepts had on the courts, but the latter did refer increasingly to imperfect competition theory. Impressed by the alleged evils of oligopoly, the courts jettisoned the rule of reason and the strictures against regarding huge size as evidence of monopoly. Judgment of antitrust violation reverted to questions of structure rather than of predatory performance. In five of the most important antitrust cases decided after 1945, four rested on the criterion of size and only one referred to the doctrine of workable competition.

In the *Cellophane* case, the United States brought a judgment against the DuPont Company, charging an illegal monopoly in cellophane. The district court held in favor of the company on two grounds: first, that DuPont acted like a competitor and not like a monopolist; second, that, although DuPont had substantial control over cellophane, it had only a small share of flexible packaging. The Supreme Court in 1956 affirmed the judgment, emphasizing that the flexible packaging market, not the cellophane market, was the relevant one for determining market control. The Cellophane decision was the only important victory for a large industrial firm. It was also an uneasy victory, because it was a four-to-three decision.

In four other decisions, size and market control ruled as the decisive factors in government victories. In 1945, in the celebrated Alcoa case, Judge Hand effectively obliterated both the rule of reason and the concept that size alone was not evidence of monopoly. In holding the Aluminum Company in violation of the Sherman Act, Judge Hand said, "Congress did not condone 'good trusts' and condemn 'bad' ones; it forbade all." He put the question of monopoly strictly on a yardstick basis: a 90 percent share of the market "is enough to constitute a monopoly; it is doubtful whether 60 or 64 percent would be enough, and certainly 33 percent is not."

In the Bethlehem-Youngstown case (1958), the government argued that the proposed merger would substantially lessen competition. The companies took the then novel position that the number of competitors in a market was much less important than the strength of the individual competitors. They argued that a market of four competitors, one very large and three small, was less competitive than a market in which there were two competitors of like size. The district court held in favor of the government on the ground that the proposed merger violated the Celler Amendment to the Clayton Act because there was a reasonable probability that it would substantially lessen competition.

The decision in *Brown Shoe Company v. U.S. (1962)* carried antitrust to much greater lengths. The government sought to nullify Brown Shoe's purchase of the Kinney Shoe Chain. Brown argued that even though it was the third largest shoe producer it accounted for only 4 percent of total production, and that even though Kinney was the largest retailer it accounted for only 1.2 percent of all sales. Moreover, the companies were in different lines, the one in medium- and the other in low-priced shoes. The court held that the Celler Amendment of 1950 intended "to arrest mergers at a time when the trend to lessening competition in a line of commerce was still in its infancy." It therefore decided in favor of the government.

One other case touched on so many points that it deserves to be quoted in more detail. In 1949, the government brought a Clayton Act suit against the DuPont Company, seeking to force it to divest itself of its 23 percent share in General Motors. The government contended that Du-Pont's stock interest gave it an unfair advantage in selling finishes and fabrics to General Motors. The government pointed to the fact that DuPont supplied two-thirds of General Motors' finishes. The defendant pointed to the equally incontestable fact that this was only 3 1/2 percent of DuPont's production. Which, then, was the relevant market, General Motors or the universe of finish users? The court in 1957 held in favor of the government. In doing so, it said:

> We agree with the trial court that considerations of price, quality and service were not overlooked by either du Pont or General Motors. Pride in its products and its high financial stake in General Motors' success would naturally lead du Pont to try to supply the best. But the wisdom of this business judgment cannot obscure the fact . . . that du Pont purposely employed its stock to pry open the General Motors' market to entrench itself as the primary supplier of General Motors' requirements for automotive finishes and fabrics.

> Similarly, the fact that all concerned in high executive posts in both companies acted honorably and fairly, each in the honest conviction that his actions were in the best interests of his own company and without any design to overreach anyone, including du Pont's competitors, does not defeat the Government's right to relief. It is not requisite to the proof of a violation of Section 7 to show that restraint or monopoly was intended.

> The statutory policy of fostering free competition is obviously furthered when no supplier has an advantage over his competitors from an acquisition of his customer's stock likely to have the effects condemned by the statute.

Antitrust policy has never been guided by a set of specifically defined objectives. Its goals, as near as they can be discerned, have been to resist monopoly, to prevent business concentration, and to protect (for moral, ethical, social, and sentimental reasons) the structure of what is vaguely known as small business. Although at times economic growth was considered to be an indirect goal ancillary to the prevention of monopoly, antitrust policy was never designed to promote or encourage economic growth directly. The Attorney General's National Committee on the Antitrust Laws made this clear in 1955. In its opinion, a company that practiced "undue restraints of competition" could not be excused by proof that its actions represented progressive managerial policy or that it had benefited the public. In other words, competition was desired not so much for its economic efficiency as for its constraint on economic power.

In similar fashion, antitrust policy has been evaluated much more on moral and ethical grounds than on its addition to or subtraction from economic growth. Business critics have concentrated on the fairness of the policy. Probably the most extreme expression of this view was delivered by Henry Lee Higginson, the Boston banker. "The Sherman Law," said he, "is probably the most vicious and unreasonable law that was ever passed by any legislative body."

Antitrust policy has discouraged the natural tendency to resort to the more invidious forms of market control: price fixing, collusive bidding, and the division of the market. It has also been a necessary spur to counteract the temptation to let well enough alone. It has, in other words, kept big business "on its toes." But beyond this, its effects become fuzzy. Supporters of rigid antitrust policy rest their case on three heroic premises. They equate pure competition with economic growth. They imply that big business is inefficient. They assume that political-legal action can produce pure competition. It is at least somewhat questionable whether pure competition has always done a better job than imperfect competition in fostering economic growth. It is also questionable whether big business has been inefficient in comparison with small business. What is most questionable is whether political-legal action can break down business concentration and produce a purely competitive market structure. Here, defenders of antitrust policy tend to exaggerate both its potentials and its accomplishments. It has been argued that stringent interpretation of the laws has had a significantly restraining effect on consolidation whereas loose interpretations have encouraged combination and monopoly. Thus, it is said that the *E.C. Knight* case was a great victory for monopoly. Yet the American Sugar Refining Company, which won the great victory, controlled 98 percent of the business in 1895 but less than 50 percent when Henry O. Havemeyer, its entrepreneur, died in 1907. From the time of its victory, it was beset by new competitors, notably Claus Spreckels and John Arbuckle, each of whom entered the field and stayed to be successful. In 1910, when the company manufactured 42 percent of the country's sugar, it owned 7 of the 21 cane sugar refineries and had an interest in 33 of the 68 beet sugar factories.

It is also claimed that the *Sugar* case inaugurated the merger movement of the 1890's and the *Northern Securities* case ended it. But the merger movement really did not begin until 1898, three years after the *E.C. Knight* decision, and it did not end until 1906, two years after the *Northern Securities* decision. To be sure, the great merger movement of the 1920's took place in an environment of relaxed antitrust enforcement, but the same could not be said of the period since 1950. The growth of big business, whether fed internally or externally, seemed to proceed along a trend line regardless of the lax or rigid attitudes of antitrust enforcers.

13

SOME PROBLEMS OF
PROFESSIONAL MANAGEMENT

In a previous context, we said that the twentieth century confronted the businessman with a new set of problems. The most important of these involved the separation of the control of business from the ownership of business.

THE SEPARATION OF OWNERSHIP
AND CONTROL

The 1957 *DuPont* case, in which the Supreme Court ordered DuPont to divest itself of its stock interest in General Motors, was much more than a trivial incident in the DuPont-General Motors chronicle or in the perennial contest between the government and big business. For forty years, some member of the DuPont managerial hierarchy had taken an active part in General Motors, ostensibly to protect DuPont's substantial investment. The 1957 decision was, therefore, a kind of benchmark in the continuous trend toward the separation of the ownership and control of business enterprise.[1] A few economists, especially the late Joseph Schumpe-

---

[1]Note what William Z. Ripley wrote in *Main Street and Wall Street* (Boston: Little Brown & Co., 1927), pp. 131–2: "General Motors is peculiarly fortunate in that . . . there is a 60 percent concentrated ownership in a small group almost, one may say in the DuPont family. But this ideal situation—under which the DuPonts, with their unusual technical training and ability and their innate sense of trusteeship, stand sponsors for success through having the major property stake in success or failure represents unfortunately only a transitional stage in development. When this generation passes on its way, will that guarantee for continued success be possible of continuance?"

ter, thought that this trend was one of a parcel that posed a much greater threat to economic growth and the continued existence of the free enterprise system than did the evils of imperfect competition. Some businessmen also recognized the dangers in what was taking place. Alfred P. Sloan, Jr., wrote in the October 1927 *World's Work*:

> There is a point beyond which diffusion of stock ownership must enfeeble the corporation by depriving it of virile interest in management upon the part of some one man or group of men to whom its success is a matter of personal and vital interest. And conversely at that same point the public interest becomes involved when the public can no longer locate some tangible personality within the ownership which it may hold responsible for the corporation's conduct.

Theoretically, control of a corporation rested in the board of directors, but this was more theory than fact. Legally, of course, the board was responsible for the conduct of the enterprise, which made the board an anomaly, for in the large corporation, the board was more often than not the creature of the management. This was especially the case where management was strong and efficient. The correspondence between Sloan as chairman of General Motors and the representatives of the DuPont Company, which owned a substantial stake in GM, gives us an insight into the importance of the board and the alleged power of the finance capitalists. In proposing a slate of directors, which to all intents meant selecting the board, Sloan wrote that he would (1) oppose "further representation of bankers," (2) give consideration to "geographical location," (3) exclude those "who represent interests that have relationship with General Motors, especially in the buying and selling area," (4) allow the DuPont Company to pick its representatives on the GM board, (5) avoid making more than one recommendation from the "same line of industry," and (6) ignore holdings of GM stock as an essential qualification.

In explaining the reasons for his guidelines, Sloan went to some lengths to explain that a director "can do very little." He "felt" that "we are all apt to exaggerate what a director can contribute to any large corporation. . . . The smaller the company and the smaller the board, the less of course this applies because they can get closer to the business." Sloan, and probably his other big-business colleagues, resented the oft-heard allegation that professional managers were nothing but office boys for bankers. "Judge ---," he wrote to Walter Carpenter of DuPont, "was heard to say that I . . . could not adopt any policy without it being approved by Mr. Morgan. You can just see how far reaching that type of thing goes." In reacting to this false opinion, Sloan resorted to a strategy for which he had little sympathy. "I do not want you to think," he admonished Carpenter, "I have accepted the philosophy that the public relations is determining the policies of General Motors. As a matter of fact, I am fighting that policy all the time because there is too much of it already."[2] Rather than giving ammunition to those who thought Wall Street pulled the strings in what they conceived to be the puppet show of big business, he opposed further banker representation on the board.

WHY THE SEPARATION TOOK PLACE

The separation of ownership from control was an inescapable result of the growth of big business and the influence of finance capitalism. For, almost by definition, ownership was split off from control as soon as it became distributed through shares that could be bought and sold on stock exchanges. Even if shareholders had the desire and the knowledge to make the many intricate decisions involved in running a mass-production business, they could not do so, for it was physically impossible for all of them to meet together and to formulate policy in a kind of entrepreneurial town meeting.

Similarly, it was beyond the capacity of one man to handle the intricate problems and decisions associated with large-scale enterprise. What was needed was a set of specialists who could take care of such matters as marketing, labor relations, and capital budgeting. Instead of being in the hands of those who owned the business, control in the sense of the power to make important decisions vested more and more in a group of professional executives whose ownership stake in the companies they managed was relatively small. This was but another link in the everlengthening chain of division of labor. The "industrial revolution" and the factory system had separated the worker from the instruments of production. Large-scale enterprise, in turn, did the same thing to the owners.

Although it was inevitable, the process of separating ownership from control was encouraged and sped on its way by the bankers, who by their financing had so much to do with big business. A few examples, admittedly extreme, must suffice to illustrate the nature of what was happening in the 1920's. The most famous example was Dodge Brothers, Inc. Dillon, Read & Co. bought the business for approximately $150 million. They then offered for public sale $160 million of bonds and preferred stock and 1.5 million shares of Class A nonvoting common. The voting common (500,000 shares) was kept for management. In another example, the Industrial Rayon Corporation sold 598,000 of nonvoting common while management held 2,000 of the voting shares.

[2]Quoted in Ernest Dale, *Readings in Management* (New York: McGraw-Hill Book Company, 1965), p. 64.

THE CAREER EXECUTIVE

The ascendancy of the career executive or professional manager did not take place overnight. There was no managerial revolution. The evolution, as we have seen, began in the railroads around the middle of the nineteenth century, and it began there because they were gigantic businesses. It appeared in manufacturing and trade almost simultaneously with the appearance of large-scale enterprise. At first, like all innovations it passed unnoticed, but by the 1920's, it had become commonplace. In 1912, Andrew Carnegie, in what must have been for him a painful moment, told a congressional committee: "Private partnerships are out of fashion. There is not a big concern in America that I know today that is managed except by officers under salaries."

Carnegie was more farsighted than most, and his judgment was a little premature. It is estimated that in 1910, approximately 80 percent of all nonfarm managers were still self-employed, and one-quarter of the capital stock of a large sample of sizable companies was owned by executives. But the movement was well under way, and it proceeded at an accelerated rate. One study has shown that 76 percent of the business executives born in 1771–1800 were owner-operators; 5 percent were career managers. In the next generation, those born in 1831–1860, 56 percent owned businesses they had built; 21 percent were "bureaucrats." Of the 1891–1920 group, 18 percent were owner-operators; 48 percent were career men. Let us look at this increase in professional managers in another way. In 1950, 60 percent of all executives were still self-employed; but by 1960, only 40 percent owned their own business, and 60 percent worked for someone else. Among the largest corporations, the rapidity of change was understandably more impressive, for professional management is a necessary characteristic of gigantic size. In 1929, owners controlled either outright or by a substantial stock holding 34 percent of the 200 largest firms and 46 percent of the largest firms in industry and trade. Management controlled 44 and 40 percent respectively. Forty years later, owners controlled slightly over 10 percent of the 200 largest companies and not quite 20 percent of those in industry; management controlled 85 percent and 80 percent. In only 15.5 percent of today's largest corporations does an individual, a family, or a cohesive group own as much as 10 percent of the stock.[3]

The professional manager was and is a person of diverse talents. According to Crawford H. Greenewalt, president of DuPont, "Specific skill in

[3]Committee on Investigation of United States Steel Corporation, 1912; F. W. Taussig and W. S. Barker, "American Corporations and Their Executives," *Quarterly Journal of Economics*, Vol. 40 (1925); *U.S. Census of Population, U.S. Summary, Detailed Characteristics*, 1960; Reinhard Bendix, *Work and Authority in Industry* (New York: John Wiley and Sons, 1956), p. 229; R. J. Larner, "Ownership and Control in the 200 Largest Non-financial Corporations," *American Economic Review*, September, 1966.

any given field becomes less and less important as the executive advances through successive levels of responsibility. Today, for example, there are thousands of people in the DuPont Company whose expertness in their special field I can only regard with awe and admiration."[4]

The career executive's role was to act as trustee for a collective enterprise in which management, owners, creditors, workers, competitors, consumers, and government had an interest. It was his function to keep all of these sometimes antagonistic groups as happy as their divergent interests would permit. This meant broadening the motives and objectives of business enterprise. The profit motive worked very well when business had only its owners and customers to satisfy. In the new environment, business enterprise had to emphasize new motives and new objectives in order to placate the government, the public, and the different conflicting strata of management. The profit motive still dominated, but it was much more qualified and less uncompromising. According to Thomas C. Cochran, "Good organization men were probably less aggressive risk takers, less relentless in the quest for profits than the owner managers of smaller enterprises."[5] The professional manager thought more in terms of long- than short-run profits, and his profit goals were always tempered by prestige objectives. Growth for growth's sake in terms of the firm's share of the market and the slope of its sales curve were high on his slate, as were the desire for personal security, personal prestige, and the perpetuation of the business.

Ideally, the career executive was the cognitive or sophisticated entrepreneur described by Arthur Cole. He was supposed to be concerned, not with day-to-day activities, but with long-range plans and objectives. He required a broad knowledge of the total business situation as well as a knowledge of his own company. No single entrepreneur possessed this breadth of knowledge or the time and energy necessary to make the thousands of decisions that daily faced the large-scale enterprise. Management, therefore, broke its activities into specialized pieces, just as it had previously split the job on the production line.

Although nothing replaced what is referred to vaguely as "business judgment," management used applied mathematics, advanced accounting, statistics, economics, sociology, psychology, and the magic of the computer to help solve its riddles. Executives came to depend on large internal administrative staffs and ancillary institutions for information and data. Thus, a vast office force came into being. Again, this phenomenon had appeared at a much earlier date in the railroad business. In 1860, for

[4]Herrymon Maurer, *Great Enterprise* (New York: The Macmillan Company, 1955), p. 146.

[5]Thomas C. Cochran, *The American Business System* (Cambridge, Mass.: Harvard University Press, 1957), p. 180.

example, the Delaware and Hudson Canal Company needed an entire
building to house the administrative staff that directed its 4,200 employees.
But the great armies of office workers in manufacturing and trade are the
product of the last 15 or 20 years of managerial rationalization. During
the 1920's and most of the 1930's, about 13 percent of all who were employed in manufacturing were classified as nonproduction workers. In the
late 1930's, the ratio jumped to about 19 percent, where it remained until
after World War II. As recently as 1947, nonproduction workers represented about 17 percent of all manufacturing employment; today, 30 percent are nonproduction workers. Office workers have multiplied from 8 1/2
percent of the working population in 1910 to over 25 percent today.

THE SECURITIES MARKETS AND THE
COLLECTIVE OWNERSHIP OF BUSINESS

Big business is a collective institution in all its aspects—its management, its direction, and its ownership. As early as 1926, John Maynard
Keynes pointed to "the tendency of big enterprise to socialize itself by
management's tendency to consider the general stability and reputation of
the firm more than maximizing profit." But the movement in the direction
of collectivism was more apparent in the ownership than in the management of big business.

Big business was made possible only by the appearance of something
new in capital institutions, that is, a broad and open securities market.
In the transition to big business, ownership passed from a handful of
partners to a much larger number of widely scattered stockholders. This
occurred in railroads in the 1850's, but it was not until the 1890's that it
took place in industrial firms. Between 1898 and 1902, the New York
Stock Exchange welcomed an array of corporate giants, including United
States Steel, International Harvester, American Can, American Car and
Foundry, and United Fruit.

There were many reasons for this important institutional change. Big
business on a broad scale could exist only under conditions of diverse
ownership, and this could be accomplished only by inviting "the public"
in. Investment bankers, who were now playing a major role in business,
naturally used the milieu with which they were familiar: the stock exchanges and the securities markets. Savers, who had previously invested
their surplus in real estate, railroads, and government securities, welcomed
an opportunity to diversify their investments through stock ownership.
Finally, the industrialists, despite the suspicious hostility that some of them
evinced towards bankers and securities markets, had much to gain by "going public."

There was only one industrial stock listed on the New York Exchange in 1885, but listings and activity picked up rapidly thereafter. The first million-share day came toward the end of 1886. The first three-million-share day came fifteen years later. But it was not until June 1928 that five million shares were traded in a single day. Sixteen million shares changed hands on Black Thursday 1929, a record that was not surpassed until 1968. Then, on June 13, volume reached an all time high of 21,351,000 shares which in turn was surpassed by 31,730,000 shares on August 16, 1971.

Total annual activity passed 1.1 billion shares in 1929, a figure that was not equalled until 1963. Yet, clearly, more and more people were buying equities. There were only 200 companies listed on the New York Exchange in 1907, over 800 in 1929, and over 1,250 in the late 1960's. It was estimated that 3 million people owned listed securities in the early twentieth century. By 1929, it had climbed to 10 million, and it doubled again by the late 1960's.

Yet big business firms were drifting away from dependence on the securities markets. The two most important sources of capital funds for the country's nonfinancial corporations in the twentieth century were the sale of securities and internal financing (depreciation allowances and retained earnings). It appears from existing data that the latter supplied 55 percent of gross capital needs in 1901–12, 60 percent in 1913–22, and 66 percent in 1957–1965. The ratio was much higher in manufacturing where internal financing covered 80 percent of gross capital outlays in the 1960's. The trend away from security-financing was well illustrated by the major steel companies. In the first twenty years of the 1900's, they financed 55 percent of their property acquisitions by the sale of bonds and common and preferred stock. Around the middle of the century, securities paid for less than 25 percent.

The extensive practice of using retained earnings to finance investment spending had the advantage of eliminating the question of where the funds were coming from. It also made business less dependent on the money-market managers—the commercial and investment bankers whose ideas were often opposed to those of the business managers. But it also had the disadvantage of reducing capital mobility by excluding corporate saving from the pool of capital available to new enterprises or to would-be entrepreneurs with ideas but no ready cash.

But whether retained earnings were on net balance advantageous or disadvantageous from the social point of view, they did tend to enhance the value of existing equities. For this reason, among many others, the rate of return (including capital gains) on the common stocks traded on the New York Exchange was better than the rate obtained by any other form of investment.

In 1913, there were 101 industrial stocks listed on the Exchange.[6] An

[6]Only seven more than in 1907.

investment of $10,000 in each costing $1,014,855 would have been worth $20.4 million fifty years later, a return of 6 3/4 percent a year. Yet of the 101, 9 were a total loss and 22 were selling below their prices in 1913. In other words, roughly 30 percent were failures, but the other 70 percent were very successful. Consider that a $1,000 investment in Corn Products Refining would have been worth $103,000 fifty years later. The same amount in American Can would be worth $313,000. Twenty shares of Ingersoll Rand, costing $52 a share, would total 3,801 shares today with the price per share slightly less than it was in 1913.

A much more ambitious study covering the years 1926–60, found that the rate of return on all common stocks listed on the New York Stock Exchange varied from 6.84 to 9.01 percent, depending on the investor's tax bracket. But buying stocks was not a one-way street to riches. Some stocks did phenomenally well; others did phenomenally poorly; and over time, stocks fluctuated, to use J. Pierpont Morgan's frequently quoted phrase. Between 1900 and 1929, the Standard and Poor Index zoomed from 60 to 260 and then fell back to 70 from where it again soared to almost 1,000. The rate of return on all common stocks from 1926 to 1932 was minus 16.49 percent and from 1929–1932, minus 48.36 percent. The Dow Jones industrial average dropped 90 percent between 1929 and 1932, 30 percent in the late 1960's, almost 30 percent in 1962, 25 percent in 1966, and 35 percent between 1968 and 1970. In the first 31 months of World War II, the market fell by 40 percent. It did equally poorly in World War I, giving some concrete evidence that war is not good for business.

Table 10   Index of Common Stock Prices, 1900–1970 (1941–43 = 10)

Year	Total 500 Stocks	Industrials
1900	6.15	3.38
1904	7.05	2.92
1916	9.47	6.62
1918	7.54	5.57
1921	6.86	5.07
1929	26.02	21.35
1932	6.93	5.37
1939	12.06	11.77
1943	11.50	11.49
1949	15.23	15.00
1960	55.85	59.43
1968	98.70	107.49
1970	83.22	91.29

Source: Standard and Poor's.

TABLE 11   Assets of Selected Financial Intermediaries as a Percent of Assets of All
Private Intermediaries

	1900	1929	1939	1950	1969
Commercial banks	59.0	60.7	55.1	57.3	46.1
Mutual savings banks	21.8	9.1	10.0	7.6	6.4
Savings and loan	3.8	6.8	4.5	5.7	13.9
Life insurance cos.	10.2	16.0	24.3	21.6	17.0
Other insurance cos.	5.2	4.3	4.1	4.5	4.3
Non-insured pension funds	—	0.4	1.0	2.2	7.5
Investment cos.	—	2.7	1.0	1.1	4.8

Prices of individual stocks also ranged from dismal lows to breath-taking highs. In 1907, Allis-Chalmers ranged from $27 to $4, A.T. & T. from $186 to $88, Westinghouse from $233 to $32, and U.S. Steel from $55 to $8. Again in the 1929–32 debacle, Radio Corporation ranged from $574 to $12, U.S. Steel from $366 to $30, and A.T. & T. from $310 to $70.

Changes in the financial behavior of big business had wide ramifications on financial intermediaries as well as on the securities markets. In the first half of the century, corporations relied more on internal than on external sources of funds. They tended to hold large amounts of cash and government securities and avoided debt. Capital outlays were held within the limits set by the size of retained earnings and depreciation allowances. This conservative behavior was initially a function of the enhanced importance of finance capitalists, for bankers tended to avoid risk and to emphasize caution. Later, the harrowing experiences of the great depression convinced many business leaders that their belief in conservative financial behavior had been a stroke of great wisdom.

The long period of prosperity that set in after mid-century and the boom of the 1960's changed financial behavior materially. Instead of anticipating the inevitability of a business depression sometime in the future, businessmen looked forward to uninterrupted prosperity and a continuous inflationary spiral. Investment spending began to outpace cash flow. Corporate liquidity, that is, the ratio of cash and governments to total liabilities, fell sharply.[7] Financial officers went back into the capital markets to borrow heavily through the use of commercial paper, convertible and other bonds, and term loans, in addition to selling preferred stock.

In the New Era, securities markets, investment banking and commercial-bank business loans soared both absolutely and relatively.[8] But so did contributions to noninsured pension funds and purchases of shares in

[7]In 1945, 50 percent; in 1962, 20 percent; and in 1968, 13 percent.
[8]Commercial loans represented 13 percent of commercial-bank assets in 1950, 20 percent in 1970.

investment companies, so that the commercial bank proportion of the assets of financial institutions continued to decline.

THE CORPORATION PROBLEM

The continuous growth of the giant corporation and the separation of ownership from control produced the so-called "corporation problem," which encompassed the subsidiary problems of efficiency, bureaucracy, and legitimacy.

It is not easy to generalize about whether the separation of ownership and control and the ascendancy of the professional manager advanced or retarded efficiency in the conduct of business. From the economic theorist's view, the most efficient businessman is the one who maximizes profits. Such a businessman needs extraordinary clairvoyance to see the present, the past, and the future. But even if he possessed such wisdom as would put Solomon to shame, it is far from certain that the objective of maximizing profit would produce the most efficient business enterprise. There is another equally important objective—that of perpetuating the organization. Judged by this goal, the most successful entrepreneur is the one who can keep his company growing in an effective way. This is, of course, much vaguer than the goal of maximizing profit. But the true ideal is the executive who can maximize profits while at the same time maintaining and strengthening the organization by adopting his strategy and behavior to the changing environment and to the changing constraints imposed by the other power groups in society—labor and government, for example.

BUREAUCRACY IN THE LARGE CORPORATION

The old-style entrepreneur was invariably pictured as having a one-track mind centered on money and profit. In theory at least, the professional manager was more sophisticated than the classical entrepreneur and was therefore thought to be better equipped to see the long term than his predecessor.[9] It seemed logical, therefore, to conclude that the division of managerial responsibility and the greater degree of specialization of recent decades made business enterprise more rational and more efficient, leading to a more effective use of economic resources. Experts helped to make the decisions in each field. Research became more scientific, more a matter of routine than of vision.

[9]He was in the words of Arthur H. Cole, "the cognitive, sophisticated entrepreneur" who knew a lot about his own business and about business in general.

Like most theoretical propositions, there was much that was wrong with this analysis. The stereotyped old-style entrepreneur with his preoccupation with profits and profits alone was a myth. The owner entrepreneur or the manager with a large personal stake in his company was interested in much more than profit. Similarly, the theoretical professional manager was often a far cry from reality.

In reality and by necessity, the modern corporation became a bureaucratic structure. For splitting down complicated decisions, creating intricate organization charts, cataloging office workers as staff or line, sorting the staff into departments, and creating a profusion of written documents and memoranda meant routine and systematic administration, and systematized administration is the essence of bureaucracy.

It is a well-known axiom that bureaucracy deadens initiative and deemphasizes risk. The bureaucrat's job, as Max Weber long since pointed out, is a permanent career for which he has been specifically trained. Ideally, he is appointed to his job by some superior authority. Normally, he has life tenure, which is supposed to ensure an objective discharge of specific duties. Finally, he receives a regular salary determined by his rank and length of service. Bureaucracy emphasized stability and security, thereby weakening the old business incentives. The career executive in the large corporation, the indictment ran, was less flexible than the "socially irresponsible captain of industry" of a century ago. Alfred P. Sloan, who was a large stockholder as well as president of General Motors, recognized the nature of the problem when he said:

> In practically all of our activities, we seem to suffer from the inertia resulting from our great size. . . . I cannot help but feel that General Motors missed a lot. . . . Sometimes I must be forced to the conclusion that General Motors is so large, its inertia so great, that it is impossible for us to be real leaders.[10]

But bureaucracy was inevitable in large-scale business, for the giant corporation could not possibly operate without systematic, routine administration, and systematic, routine administration, to repeat, is the essence of bureaucracy.

In many respects, the problems of managing big business were the same as the problems of managing big government, big labor, big education, or big anything. Many members of the managerial group adopted the same psychology and the same working plan held by the typical civil service employee. Admittedly, the effects of the opiate of bureaucracy were most prominent in the lower echelons; but even among top executives,

---

[10]Quoted in House Committee on the Judiciary, *Study of Monopoly Power*, Part 2-B, 1949, p. 1214.

there was a tendency to avoid risk and to seek stability. In the early 1900's, the enervating effects of bureaucracy and the seemingly pleasant rewards of large-scale enterprise for the top echelons were being pointed out in the large insurance companies. Some directors asked of their employees nothing more than devotion to duty, loyalty, and cooperation in an organizational structure that had little interest in playing the game of profit-maximizing. For many employees, the preservation of the job became the chief goal. As Adam Smith thought in 1776, so Charles Perkins, the railroad entrepreneur, thought one hundred years later, "The average man will not work as closely for the company as he will for himself." The ideal was to become an anonymous cog in an enormous machine. Initiative was repressed, because "going out on a limb" might imperil the security of the jobholder. In the middle 1920's, an executive of a utility trade association viewed the entrepreneurial world from the depth of discouragement:

> We are raising a lot of thoroughly drilled 'yes ma'ams' in the big corporations, who have no minds of their own; no opinions. As soon as the old individualists die, and there are not so many of them left, I think the corporations will have a lot of trouble in getting good executives. After a man has served 20 or 30 years in one of these monstrous corporations, he is not liable to have much of a mind of his own.[11]

As with any blanket indictment, there were important exceptions to the bureaucratic bill of particulars. Business bureaucracy differed in one most important respect from other bureaucracies: the criteria of success or failure were much clearer; they appeared in the profit or loss that showed up on the income statement. And this elemental difference vitiated much of the criticism deduced from the assumption of unqualified bureaucracy. The career executive may have been much less flexible than the old-time entrepreneur, but there is little evidence to support the notion. Actually, it was the new-style businessman who carried through diversification and decentralization, the major change in business enterprise in the twentieth century. The empire-building owner-entrepreneur was either unwilling or incapable of coping with the problem or adjusting to the changes it necessitated.

Somewhat inconsistently, critics argued that losses were less effective in discouraging mistakes in the twentieth century than in the nineteenth century. The members of the new managerial class had relatively little stake in the business they operated.[12] They therefore did not have to pay

---

[11]Carl D. Thompson, *Confessions of the Power Trust* (New York: E. P. Dutton & Co., Inc., 1932), p. 14.

[12]Actually, they had a much larger stake than contemporary opinion allotted to them. Managerial ownership was small as a percent of total outstanding stock. But to the manager himself, his stock holdings were substantial.

for their own mistakes with their own money. But this too was probably less than true. When told that a person is less likely to be cautious with someone else's money than with his own, Lammot du Pont replied, "No, that's not the point. The danger is that he'll spend it with too much caution."

Because managers had little share in the business, it was argued that profits had lost most of their effectiveness in stirring entrepreneurs to ever-greater heights. But neither the older nor the newer entrepreneur worked for money alone. When Alfred P. Sloan said in 1938, "Making money ceased to interest me years ago. It's the job that counts," he was reiterating what John D. Rockefeller and Andrew Carnegie had said somewhat differently a generation before.

Similarly, the large corporation was criticized because it was "run by committees." But as Arjay Miller, one-time president of Ford, said:[13]

> Large business organizations are not typically run by committees, with a "tyranny of the majority." Rather, the committee meeting serves as an opportunity for discussion, with a hearing for all sides, and with specialists having a chance to comment from their particular vantages. But the decision making rests with the executive, and there is plenty of room for strong executives and strong minds at all levels of corporate organization. Top management cannot afford the luxury of employees who agree with the prevailing philosophy simply because it prevails. . . .

Generalizations on what made the businessman run are more dangerous than most generalizations; but, when all is said and done, the contribution of business to the economy rested more on the managerial ability of individual businessmen than on the size, the legal structure, or the bureaucratic nature of the business organization. Some businesmen had the ability to make successful adjustments; others did not.

Those who viewed the situation with alarm were on much safer ground in insisting that the separation of ownership and control tended to weaken the businessman's position in American society. As the process of running a business became more routine, it seemed to the general public that making business decisions required no unusual effort or ability. It appeared so easy that it came to be accepted as part of ordinary day-to-day existence. The businessman began to lose his glamor; society was no longer impressed by him but began to take him for granted. Professor Schumpeter recognized this as threatening the whole structure of capitalist society when he wrote,

> Success no longer carries that connotation of individual achievement which would raise not only the man but also his group into a durable position of social leadership. . . . Since capitalist enterprise, by its very

[13]Quoted in the *Wall Street Journal*, December 1, 1965.

achievements, tends to automatize progress, we conclude that it tends to make itself superfluous—to break to pieces under the pressure of its own success.[14]

THE CORPORATE EXECUTIVE'S LEGITIMACY

One way of meeting the disadvantages presented by bureaucracy was to encourage incentives by giving the managers a higher stake in sales, earnings, and profits. In 1929, 38 out of 100 large companies paid salaries only; 62 paid salaries and bonuses. The depression temporarily discouraged bonus and so-called incentive payments, but the idea came back strongly with the renewal of prosperity. Stock options now account for one-third to one-half of executive compensation.

Top executives earned $70,000 in 1929, $40,000 in 1932, and $50,000 in 1936.[15] Annual after-tax income in the late 1950's averaged $129,000. Salary and bonus made up 52 percent of this; stock options accounted for another 27 percent; pensions, for 13 percent; and profit sharing for the remaining 8 percent.[16]

Executive compensation in the United States has, like wages and salaries in general, always been higher than in other countries. It has been estimated that American executives earn four times as much as English executives after taxes. American companies in Britain earn much more than British companies.[17] This has naturally led to the conclusion that higher compensation is the incentive that is responsible for higher earnings. But much too much can be read into this. It does not necessarily follow that the most successful companies have the highest-paid executives. Nor does it follow that generous stock options have produced stellar performances in terms of sales and earnings. Some companies with poor earnings records paid their executives better than did some companies with excellent records, and more generous bonuses and stock options were not always followed by more impressive sales and higher earnings.

The frequent disparity between executive compensation and company performance is part of the so-called problem of legitimacy. Unlike the problems of efficiency and bureaucracy, legitimacy is more a sociological problem than an economic one. Moreover, it is not really a business problem, but a charge, an accusation. Critics insist that the modern corporate

[14]Joseph A. Schumpeter, *Capitalism, Socialism, and Democracy* (New York: Harper & Row, Publishers, 1947), pp. 133–34.

[15]Median salary and bonus for 100 top executives.

[16]John Calhoun Baker, *Executive Salaries and Bonus Plans* (New York: McGraw-Hill Book Company, 1938); Wilbur G. Lewellen, "Executives Lose Out, Even with Options," *Harvard Business Review*, January-February 1968.

[17]26 percent compared to 16.5 percent.

executive has no legitimacy because he is not really elected or appointed by anyone. He is not really responsible to anyone, and his objectives are not clear. It is freely implied that since the nineteenth-century entrepreneur owned his own business, the question of legitimacy did not arise.

The indictment portrays twentieth-century management as a self-perpetuating, bureaucratic oligarchy. This stereotype of the free-wheeling, omnipotent business executive is simplistically overdrawn. He may not own his own business, and there may be less constraints on him than on his predecessor. Certainly, he is freer from the owner's control, but he is less free from other constraints on his behavior. These are exerted not only by competitors, customers, and rival products, but also by labor unions, public opinion, the government, and by the ambitions of other members of the intra-corporate hierarchy.

14

PROFITS, PRICES, AND LABOR IN THE TWENTIETH CENTURY

The problems that we have just discussed—the corrosive effects of bureaucracy and the irresponsibility of illegitimacy—did not excite the businessman nearly so much as they excited critics and observers who were outside the business group.

Businessmen were still much more concerned with the problems that had always concerned them—making a profit, meeting competition, raising capital, dealing with labor, and finding markets. To be sure, the relative importance and dimensions of these problems had changed, but in their general nature and their significance to the entrepreneur, they were the same problems that the colonial businessman had faced.

BUSINESS PROFITS AND PERFORMANCE

As we have said before, data on profits are among the least adequate statistics available to the business historian. What we have is a biased sample. In addition, businessmen have tended to keep poor accounts and to publish misleading information. In the early part of the century, this tendency arose out of an infatuation with secrecy. Consider the 1901 balance sheet of the American Sugar Refining Company, a corporation with over 10,000 stockholders.[1] (Balance sheet shown on page 279.)

Much information is available on profits for more recent years. We have statistics on unincorporated business income as well as on corporate profits. But again, they leave much to be desired. The unincorporated

---

[1]William Z. Ripley, *Main Street and Wall Street* (Boston: Little, Brown & Company, 1927), p. 158.

Assets		Liabilities	
Real estate and machinery	$ 34,328,664	Capital	$ 88,280,370
Cash and debts receivable	36,862,702	Debts	24,364,027
Sugar, raw, refined, etc.	12,248,640	Reserves	9,907,491
Investments in other companies	39,111,883		
	$122,551,889		$122,551,889

income figures are not much more than calculated guesses; economists still lack a clear definition of profits; and the intricacies of depreciation are a tribute to the genius of the accountant and the tax attorney. Indeed, as we have said before, the complexities of accounting have increased at a faster pace than the complexities of the world at large. Yet, what data we have are far better than what were available for the nineteenth century.

From these data, at least one conclusion can be safely drawn: profits have been extremely volatile. At any time in American history, a person who staked his all in a business venture had a remote possibility of striking it rich, a somewhat better opportunity of making a fair living, and a strong probability of losing everything. Risks were great, losses were heavy, and failures were frequent, but profits were sometimes large, and there was no discernible tendency for them to equalize among industries or among the firms in any individual industry.

In the twentieth century, corporate profits ranged from a loss of $2.3 billion in 1932 to a high of over $92 billion in 1968.[2] Unincorporated income, which appears to have exceeded corporate income until late in the 1920s, varied from $3 billion to almost $50 billion. However, if the effect of the business cycle is partially eliminated by averaging profits for decades, the range is much less erratic, especially if profits are calculated as a percentage of national income. From 1870 to 1960, corporate profits plus unincorporated income varied from an annual average of a little less than 35 percent of national income in the decade 1910 to 1919 to a little less than 20 percent in the depressed 1930's. The average for the whole period was 25.7 percent, with five decades above the average and five below it.[3]

Business failures averaged 85 per 10,000 listed concerns in the early 1900's. Between 1923 and 1929, the ratio climbed to 102, and in the depression it reached 154 per 10,000 in 1932. During World War II, it sank as low as 4 per 10,000. After the war, the rate of failure began to climb once again, averaging 42 per 10,000 in the 1950's and 55 per 10,000 in the 1960's.

[2]Approximately $50 billion after taxes.
[3]D. Gale Johnson, "The Functional Distribution of Income in the United States, 1850–1952," *Review of Economics and Statistics*, Vol. XXVI (1954); *Historical Statistics; Statistical Abstract*.

TABLE 12   Corporate Profits and Unincorporated Business Income 1909–1970 (billions of dollars)

Year	National Income	Corporate Before Tax	Profits After Tax	Unincorporated
1909	$ 28.7	$ 2.1	n.a.	$ 6.3[a]
1914	33.9	1.9	n.a.	7.1[a]
1920	69.5	3.9	n.a.	13.3[a]
1929	86.8	9.9	8.6	8.8
1932	42.8	−2.3	−2.7	3.0
1946	181.9	24.6	15.5	21.6
1950	241.1	42.6	24.9	24.0
1955	331.0	48.6	27.0	30.3
1960	414.5	49.7	26.7	35.2
1969	769.5	91.2	48.5	50.5
1970	800.1	81.3	43.8	51.4

[a] Includes agriculture.
Source: Department of Commerce.

The median age of all operating businesses is less than 10 years, which is just about the same as it has always been. Liquidation, however, has not occurred with the same frequency in all businesses. Its incidence has been extraordinarily high in retail trade and relatively low in wholesaling and finance. Three-fourths of all wholesale firms, but only three-fifths in retailing, survive their first year. Surprising as it may seem, efforts to protect the small independent operator by attacking his large competitor seem to have had just the opposite effect. Small retailers seem to have thrived best in competition with chain stores.

Was the difference in performance a function of the size of the company? Did the economies of scale make big business more profitable, or did the bureaucratic malaise of the large company give the biggest profits to small business? The question is still being debated.

Some studies correlating profits with the size of business go back as far as 1910. An investigation of profits as a percent of permanent investment in the period 1910–1929 concluded that small companies (under $2 million) had by far the best rate of return, 11.6 percent. Large companies ($50–100 million) came in second best with 9.8 percent, and giant companies were close behind at 9.5 percent. Medium-size companies made the poorest showing (8.8 percent). But the TNEC in 1940 announced that in most industries, the medium-sized company had the highest profit. A study by the Twentieth Century Fund in 1937 found that the larger the firm, the more rigid and stable its earnings. Small business, that is, companies with less than $50,000 capital, made much larger profits in prosperity but suffered greater losses in depression.

More recent statistical compilations, based on much broader divisions of the business universe, concluded that big business consistently earned a higher rate of return than small business. In the prosperous first quarter of 1957, for example, companies with over $100 million in assets earned 24.5 percent on stockholders' equity, whereas companies whose assets were less than $1 million earned 15.6 percent. In the first quarter of the 1961 recession, the largest companies made 14.1 percent and the smallest, 6.3 percent.

Theoretically, of course, big business should show higher profits, because big business means concentration, and concentration means weak competition. "Numerous studies," said the Council of Economic Advisers in 1969, "have shown a significant relationship between high concentration and high profit rates—an indication of weak competitive pressures." But the correlation between high profits and bigness and high concentration may also be evidence that big companies may sometimes be more efficient. A study by the National Industrial Conference Board found that in 23 industries that were characterized by concentration, productivity was higher than the general average; in 14 others it was lower. As Edith Penrose has said:[4]

> At the present time at least it cannot be said that the large firms in the economy are unable effectively to compete with smaller firms nor that they tend to break up because of bureaucratic inefficiency and sheer inability of management to handle unwieldy size. On the contrary, the big firms appear extremely successful and there is no evidence at all that they are managed inefficiently when enough time has been given them to make the adjustments and adaptations of their administrative framework appropriate to increasing size.

PRICING POLICIES

Profits have naturally enough always been closely associated with prices and price-making. In the twentieth century, competition and the market structure underwent a gradual change that made price-making different from what it had been in the previous generation.

---

[4]H. B. Summers, "A Comparison of the Rates of Earning of Large-Scale and Small-Scale Industries," *Quarterly Journal of Economics*, Vol. XLVII (1932); TNEC, Monograph No. 13, *The Relative Efficiency of Large, Medium-Sized, and Small Business* (1940); *How Profitable is Big Business?* (New York: Twentieth Century Fund, 1937); William L. Crumm, *Corporate Size and Earning Power* (Cambridge, Mass.: Harvard University Press, 1939); House Committee of the Judiciary, Study of Monopoly Power, Part 2B, 1949; FTC-SEC, *Quarterly Finance Reports for Manufacturing Corporations*, Betty Bock and Jack Farkas, *Concentration and Productivity* (New York: National Industrial Conference Board, 1969); Edith Penrose, *The Theory of the Growth of the Firm* (New York: John Wiley and Sons, 1959.)

In the nineteenth century, consumer perishables and producers' durables dominated manufacturing. In the twentieth century, consumer durables achieved an equal prominence. New products followed each other in rapid succession, and production was so large that in a surprisingly short time what had been a novelty became a commonplace. With the maturation of his product, the manufacturer's problem changed from producing for a virgin market to marketing for a replacement market. In the virgin market, price elasticity was the crucial consideration. In the replacement market, it was income elasticity. To be sure, price competition continued to be of first importance in some areas, especially in retailing. But in most business, price ceased to be the chief means of competition. Instead, product differentiation, service, and other forms of nonprice competition advanced to chief importance. In short, competitive practice became a mixture of price competition, the hallmark of pure competition, and product differentiation, the essence of imperfect or monopolistic competition. The kind of competition practiced in the petroleum industry came to be typical of most of the business world. Refiners competed with each other (1) through nonprice activities, such as advertising, games, and other persuasive efforts designed to manipulate demand, (2) by product rivalry and service competition, (3) by offering selective price concessions, and (4) by direct price concessions.

The denigration of price competition certainly did not break the hearts of the business community. As Adam Smith long since noted, businessmen chafed under a system in which price was paramount, and they tried at every opportunity to free themselves from its bonds. Attracting customers by slogans and gimmicks was not easy, but it was far less painful than the easier road of attracting customers by emphasizing low prices.

Under conditions of imperfect competition where the purchaser could postpone buying a product, manufacturers regarded price-cutting as ineffective if not suicidal. Under such circumstances, the practice was to cut production more drastically than price. Those who did cut prices suffered the hostility of the majority. But this had always been the case. In the 1890's, for example, the price leader in the carpet industry operated at full capacity regardless of demand. He disposed of his surplus by auction to the chagrin of his competitors, one of whom said, "There is no way of accounting for the action. . . . They are running full force at prices which are below the cost of production. It seems to me that a conservative management would require a limitation on production."[5]

During the gloomy 1930's when demand fell abysmally, the tendency to cut production more than prices reached an extreme that critics of business regarded as scandalous. Industrial prices dropped by 25 percent,

[5]John S. Ewing and Nancy P. Norton, *Broadlooms and Businessmen* (Cambridge, Mass.: Harvard University Press, 1955), p. 95.

but industrial production was cut in half. At the end of 1930, U.S. Steel raised prices by $1.00 a ton, and it was not until October 1932 that it made its first reduction in rail prices since 1922.

PRICE-CUTTING DURING THE DEPRESSION

Price-cutters were especially unpopular during the depression. Trade associations and small businesses were not above using force and sabotage to bring recalcitrant sellers into line. A retail trade association in Milwaukee instructed its members: "If you have to use the blockade method, be sure that it is friendly and peaceful . . . block the driveways for a short time only—but during the busiest part of the day."[6] Other forms of coercion were also used. Gasoline hoses were cut; milk pasteurization plants were bombed; and trucks were overturned.

Among big businesses, the attitude toward prices took strange forms. James T. Farrell of United States Steel lectured the Iron and Steel Institute: "The main trouble with the steel industry is that certain conditions exist . . . and I refer to price cutting. . . . By what manner of means do people get it into their heads that if production goes down, they must sell cheap? It is rising prices that stimulate buying and consumption and a return to prosperous times." The chief culprit was said to be Ernest T. Weir of the Weirton and the National Steel Company, who also headed the labor unions' list of personae non grata. Yet Weir insisted in testimony before a Senate committee that prices should be lowered in prosperity and raised in depression.[7] There were, it was plain, all sorts of ways of cutting prices. Neither National Steel nor other steel producers made any public announcement of price cuts in the first years of the depression. To all intents, their prices were in 1932 what they had been in 1929. But this was unreal. By under-the-table arrangements, rebates, extra services and other devices, manufacturers were selling at much lower prices in 1932 than in 1929.

Although almost everyone was cutting prices in subtle fashion and by subterfuge, no one enjoyed it. The more articulate opponents of what supply and demand was dictating eagerly took their cause to the government and urged it to do something to end "unfair competition" and to "stabilize prices." As we have seen, the federal government responded by passing the National Industrial Recovery Act of 1933 with its "codes of fair competition," the Miller-Tydings Amendment (1937), which was sup-

---

[6]*TNEC Hearings*, Part 16, p 9309.

[7]Herman E. Krooss, *Executive Opinion: What Business Leaders Said and Thought About Economic Issues, 1920–1960* (Garden City, N.Y.: Doubleday & Company, Inc., 1970), pp. 323, 325.

posed to exempt fair trade prices from the antitrust acts, and the Robinson-Patman Act (1936), which outlawed price discrimination.

Businessmen reacted to these legislative attempts to govern the market economy in their usual diverse fashion. First of all, there were those who were in industries whose nature led them to believe that the demand for their product was inelastic—textile manufacturers, retailers, steel men, and so forth. Most of them were obsessed by the specter of overproduction and longed for the apparent advantages of a "planned society" with its "fair competition" and its "stabilized prices." In the opposite camp were the producers who were not overly concerned with price elasticity—automobile producers and machine tool makers, for example. They tended to emphasize productivity and rejected policies that stemmed from overproduction theories.

PRICE THEORY AND THE BUSINESSMAN

Businessmen, except for a few, have never had sophisticated theories about how prices are determined. The complicated theories spun by academicians and displayed in classroom models have mystified and astonished most businessmen.

In economic theory, prices are set at the point where marginal cost and marginal revenue are equal, for that is the point where profits will be maximized. But most of what is written on the theory of competition is written by economists with little interest in the intricacies of actual competitive problems. Whether the entrepreneur's cardinal objective was to maximize profits is still a moot question, but desire did not by any means insure the realization of maximum profits. No businessman, no matter how perspicacious, could measure precisely marginal demand. Moreover, his competitors or some competing good loomed as a constant threat. Pricing decisions, therefore, were based on the industry's market structure, the company's position in the industry, and management's philosophy and outlook.

There was nothing new about this; it had always been the case. In Standard Oil, for example, John D. Rockefeller always advocated a large volume of business at a narrow profit margin. When trade fell off, Standard Oil reduced its prices. Rockefeller then urged further price cuts to increase business even if it meant wiping out all profit. His objective was a policy that would give Standard "the largest percentage of the business." Some of his colleagues, on the other hand, wanted to charge all that the traffic would bear. Still others supported a price policy under which "outside interests might perhaps keep moving, but not derive sufficient comfort to induce increased construction."[8]

---

[8]Ralph W. and Muriel E. Hidy, *Pioneering in Big Business* (New York: Harper & Row, 1955), pp. 117–18.

Having no price policy to which all could agree, businessmen often followed the leader, a practice that is often regarded as sinister, immoral, and socially irresponsible. The implication is that the price leader could dictate a price that all competitors had to follow. This has not been the case. To be sure, in setting prices, there must be a leader; some producer must make the first move. But there is no guarantee that other producers will go along with what the price leader does.

Except for utilities whose prices are regulated, a producer is justified in getting as high a price as he can. This does not mean, however, that he *can* get whatever he pleases. Competitors may view the market differently. Consumers may stop buying, or use less, or take their business to a competitor. Price leadership was one practical way by which a producer could travel through the murky labyrinths of price-making. As the Supreme Court liked to put the matter in the days before the 1930's: "The fact that competitors may, in the exercise of their own judgment, follow the prices of another manufacturer does not establish any suppression of competition or show any sinister domination."[9]

LABOR PROBLEMS AND POLICIES

Of all the problems and policies that perennially confronted business, those that involved labor underwent the most change in the twentieth century.

In the nineteenth century, labor was in short supply. At that time businessmen were primarily concerned with bringing together machines and equipment and developing new sources of power. This was no longer true in the twentieth century. The mechanization of industry had long since been accomplished, and the dynamo and the internal combustion engine had answered the question of from where the power was coming. Machines would be improved, more machines and more dynamos would be built, but the businessman could now concentrate more of his attention on management and marketing.

The transformation of the occupational structure of the labor force demonstrated that labor was no longer in such short supply. It also illustrated the rapid changes that business was making in its use of manpower. Between 1900 and 1970, the labor force multiplied not quite 3 times; the number of clerical workers multiplied almost 15 times; the number of professionals 9 times, and the managers almost 5 times. The country was assuredly becoming a white-collar economy. The proportion of skilled and semiskilled workers in the labor force increased somewhat more than the

[9]Ralph Cassady, Jr., *Price Making and Price Behavior in the Petroleum Industry* (New Haven, Conn.: Yale University Press, 1954), p. 105.

increase in the total labor force, but there were fewer unskilled workers in 1970 than in 1900. (See Table 13.)

TABLE 13   Occupational Makeup of the Labor Force, 1900–1969

	1900	1969	Increase 1900 = 100
Professional	1.2	10.8	900
Managers, officials and proprietors	1.7	8.0	470
Clerical	0.9	13.4	1460
Sales	1.3	4.7	360
Skilled	3.1	10.2	330
Semiskilled	3.7	14.4	390
Unskilled	3.6	3.7	100
Service	2.6	9.5	370
Farm	10.9	3.3	30
Total	**29.0**	**77.9**	**270**

Source: *Historical Statistics;* Department of Labor, Bureau of Labor Statistics, *Employment and Earnings.*

Despite the dilution of the industrial labor force, wages and salaries rose much faster than they had ever risen before. Primarily because of extraordinary gains in productivity, real earnings rose at a rate of 3.5 percent a year after 1929; they had risen 2 percent annually between 1913 and 1929 and 1.3 percent between 1890 and 1913.

In 1900, at least two-thirds of adult males earned less than $600 a year. In the late 1960's, median wages for a skilled worker were $7,500; for semi-skilled, $5,500; and for laborers, $5,330. The median wage for professionals was slightly under $10,000 and for clerical workers, $6,800. Between 1900 and 1968, the median wage for clerical, skilled, and unskilled workers had increased more than tenfold.

THE THEORY OF WAGES

The frustrations that businessmen had run into in trying to find a satisfactory theory of prices were only matched by the frustrations of wage theory.

In the early part of the century, businessmen still believed in a kind of wages fund theory. There was only so much on hand to pay labor. If one got more than his share, someone would have to take less. As John Stuart Mill had once explained, if two workers ran after one employer, wages would go down, but if two employers ran after one worker, wages would go up. Since wages were fixed by the iron laws of economics, neither labor unions nor government could affect them. The difference of opinion between union leaders and businessmen was sharply outlined in an exchange during the 1902 coal strike between John Mitchell and George Baer, the president of the Reading Company, who had a penchant for coining oft-quoted and exceedingly unfortunate phrases. Mitchell offered to submit the miners' demands to arbitration. "If," he offered, "they decide that the average annual wages received by anthracite mine workers are sufficient to enable them to live, maintain, and educate their families in a manner conformable to established American standards . . . we agree to withdraw our claims." To which Baer replied "Anthracite mining is a business and not a religious, sentimental, or academic pursuit."

Baer was right, but there were few who had the stomach to agree with him. Businessmen might still believe in the iron laws of economics, but it was the better part of discretion not to emphasize them. By the 1920's, therefore, a new explanation of wages appeared. This was a melange in which the ingredients were the cost of living, the necessity for a "fair wage," and the desirability of high wages. It became fashionable to assert that high wages were necessary to absorb the enormous production of the country's factories, stores, and farms. Cynics ridiculed the doctrine as a piece of naive hypocrisy. They insisted that when businessmen spoke about the necessity of paying high wages, they really were talking not about what *they* should do, but about what *their competitors* should do. But if this was the case, it was self-defeating, for in setting wage rates, companies tended to follow the leader just as they did in setting prices. Standard Oil, for example, as big as it was, "believed in paying as much as competitors did."

Just as in the nineteenth century, businessmen before the late 1920's paid little attention to productivity in explaining wages. This was surprising, for the principles of scientific management with their emphasis on productivity were clearly elucidated and well publicized in the early 1900's. But it took businessmen just as long as it took most groups to give a sympathetic hearing to new ideas. Even those who were sitting on top of the scientific management experiments were oblivious of what was going on. Charles M. Schwab, for example, remained cool for years to the new departure, but it was in the Bethlehem plant that Frederick W. Taylor first performed his experiments with his man Friday, Schmidt, the ingot mover. What made the matter more mystifying was that Schwab was a production man.

Some businessmen were explaining the importance of productivity in the late 1920's, but it was not until the 1930's that businessmen as a group put more emphasis on the importance of productivity. The high wage doctrine that seemed relatively harmless in the years of prosperity had a hollow ring in the depression. Then too, it had never satisfactorily explained the relationship between prices and wages or, more fundamentally, why wages were what wages were. In relating wages to productivity, businessmen found a much more satisfactory explanation, and they continued to stress that explanation long after the depression was over.

BUSINESS AND ORGANIZED LABOR

As Selig Perlman once so aptly remarked, the essence of labor unionism is that it is an attack on the absolute rights of private property. Businessmen thoroughly understood this although they never said so in so many words.

In the late nineteenth century and early 1900's, business' labor policy combined stern and uncompromising opposition to unions with welfare capitalism and industrial democracy. The opposition to outside unions expressed itself chiefly through organizations such as the National Founders Association, the Anti-Boycott League, the National Association of Manufacturers, the Citizens Industrial Association, and the National Metal Trades Association.

The first employers' organization on a national scale was the Stove Founders National Defense Association (1886). Its purpose was "the unification of its members for protection and defense against unjust, unlawful, and unwarranted demands of labor."

The National Association of Manufacturers, founded in 1895, was in its first seven years a lobbying organization for high tariffs. In 1903, a group of professional anti-unionists took over control and held it until after World War I. David Parry, who became head of the Association, summed up its union views succinctly, "We are not opposed to good unionism. The American brand is unAmerican, illegal, and indecent." The NAM had more specific objections to unionism, objections that were shared by the majority of businessmen. Management was convinced that independent labor unions would usurp the prerogatives of management by limiting the right to hire and fire, by opposing the introduction of machinery, by restricting apprenticeship, and by instituting the closed shop. Businessmen also objected to the use of the boycott, and to jurisdictional and sympathy strikes.

Through their organizations, the employers ruthlessly attacked the unions. They fought the unions in the courts and infiltrated their membership with labor spies. They used the black list,[10] and instituted the yellowdog[11] contract. They resorted to lockouts, hired strike breakers, and

---

[10] A list of union organizers and participants circulated among employers.
[11] An agreement under which an employee promised not to join an outside union.

had private police departments that seemed overly eager to practice violence.

At the same time, employers tried to woo workers away from organizing by offering them fringe benefits and closer participation in the company. These welfare devices and the industrial democracy that joined them somewhat later may have been part of big business' answer to the loss of personal relations. They were also part of the reaction to some of the violent confrontations between labor and management. For example, following the "Ludlow Massacre" that accompanied the struggle at the Colorado Fuel and Iron Company, John D. Rockefeller, Jr., instituted a comprehensive welfare capitalism program. Welfare plans and industrial democracy were also, however, devices by which management hoped to thwart the entry and growth of labor unions and to forestall antitrust proceedings. But whatever the motive, welfare programs brought pensions, accident and health insurance, profit sharing, lunch rooms, libraries, rest rooms, athletic fields, factory clubs, and other amenities. The benefits were small and before 1914 they were confined to big business. Small business would have no truck with them, and labor leaders were thoroughly hostile.

The iron fist in the velvet glove seems to have been effective in its primary aim of obstructing outside unions, for the growth of the AFL, which had been spectacular in its early years suddenly stopped. During the first World War it had another burst of growth. But all through the 1920's, its membership fell.

By the 1920's, employers had come to regard labor unions patronizingly, for they had little to fear from them. Management treated labor in much the same way that parents of the 1920's treated their teenage children, and it thought that the relationship left little to be desired. "The capacity of America to progress," said Charles M. Schwab, "is not altogether due to the great economic advantages we enjoy or to the marvellous improvements in machine and technical science. It is, I believe, due in great part to the good will which has come about between labor and capital."[12] The relationship was purely paternalistic. Most employers were willing "to recognize the dignity and status of the worker." They wanted "the closest possible relations between employer and employee." Some even approved of giving the worker "an effective voice in determining jointly with the employer the conditions under which he works." But this was to be a privilege granted by the employer, not a right to be turned over to a labor union. In explaining his company's labor relations, Schwab said, "We discuss matters, but we never vote. I will not permit myself to be in a position of having labor dictate to management."

Labor unions were looked upon as "bad" children. Most of their an-

[12]All the quotations in the remainder of this chapter are from Krooss, *Executive Opinion*, Chap. 10.

tics could be ignored, and if their actions became too obstreperous, they could be resisted as a piece of impertinence on the part of a group that had nothing of advantage to offer to any one. True to the classical view, businessmen did not think that unions could raise labor's real wages; to the contrary, union efforts to raise wages could only result in inflation or unemployment or both. Businessmen of the 1920's never tired of pointing this out. Judge Gary, for example, always argued that labor unions existed either because an employer was foolish enough to recognize them, so that "the men cannot get employment except by joining the unions," or because the workers felt abused. "Make it certain all the time," he advised, "that the men in your employ are treated as well, if not a little better, than other men who are working for people who deal and contract with unions . . . and, so far as you can, cultivate a feeling of friendship, and influence your men to the conclusion that it is for their interests in every respect to be in your employ."

There was a line beyond which it was dangerous for workers to trespass. Management would not tolerate the closed shop and continued to use its trade associations to discourage membership in outside unions. At the same time, more employers pursued welfare plans with greater vigor and offered the workers membership in company unions. Almost 500 companies established company unions between 1919 and 1924. By 1928 over 1.5 million employees were members of company unions.

The AFL, which aside from the railroad brotherhoods was the only important union, protested that the company union was a sham. It was, the AFL charged, nothing but a stooge for management, rubber stamping whatever the bosses did. In many instances, the majority in fact, the charge was undoubtedly true. But it was not so certain that the majority of workers preferred the outside union. During the 1920's, union membership fell from 5 million to 3 million, and the number of work stoppages fell to the lowest since 1885.

By 1929, optimists about management-labor relations had good cause to be optimistic. Business had reached a pinnacle of prestige, the strike wave of the post-armistice years was a matter of unrecollected history; business leaders were throwing bouquets at the hierarchy of the AFL in one of those labor-capital honeymoons that occurred intermittently in industrial relations; and academic economists were announcing a new day of "people's capitalism" in which workers were sharing as never before in the great affluence that had come upon the country.

Harmony came to an abrupt halt when prosperity collapsed in 1929. To be sure, bloody and violent disputes did not accompany the outbreak of the depression, but businessmen lived in anxious fear of the revolutionary potentials of "hard times." When unemployment absorbed as much as 25 percent of the labor force and reached eight digits, such fears did not seem without some foundation in fact. Like other groups of citizens, businessmen did not understand that strikes and industrial unrest occur more frequently in periods of rising and prosperous business than in times of deep depression.

With the depression, public sympathy swung to labor and to the unions that were considered to be the champions of labor's rights. The Federal government shared the sympathy and moved to improve labor's bargaining powers. In the early 1930's, the Norris-LaGuardia Act put an end to the use of injunctions in labor disputes. Then in the early days of the New Deal, Section 7(a) of the NIRA purported to guarantee labor the right to bargain collectively.

Businessmen promptly responded with a more energetic drive to form company unions. Most industry leaders would have nothing to do with "outside" unions. Concentrating on the potential power that the new law gave to these unions, the business attitude was a mixture of fear, suspicion, and hostility, born of a conviction that unions were essentially anti-social and anti-economic. But many businessmen were far more realistic about unions than were the union champions, for they recognized the objectives that union leaders had to pursue. Alfred P. Sloan analyzed these objectives accurately when he said, "It is axiomatic in employer-employee relationships that organized labor, as such, can never be satisfied. It cannot afford to be satisfied, for being dissatisfied is the very foundation of its continued existence." And Henry S. Dennison, one of the most "liberal" of businessmen, regarded trade unionism with the same scepticism: "Much as I look forward to and favor the wider range of classical unionism in this country, I cannot overlook the flat fact that it is not unionism but the abilities of union leaders which determines whether unionism shall be of net service or disservice to workers and to the country."

Business opposition to outside unions and labor's opportunities under the NIRA set in motion a multitude of strikes and court cases, all of which convinced Congress that something more should be done for labor's bargaining power. In 1935, Congress, therefore, passed the Wagner Act, which was designed to guarantee labor's right to bargain collectively without outside interference.

Businessmen objected to the Wagner Act because it placed no restrictions on labor. In addition, they viewed it as unconstitutional and unfair in that it deprived minorities of their rights. They denied that in bargaining an individual had less power than a group. They also insisted that the act would delay recovery and create an unbridgable chasm between labor and capital. The United States Chamber of Commerce believed much as had those who espoused the open-shop in a previous decade: "In the exercise of the right to organize and bargain collectively through representatives of their own choosing, employees should be free from coercion or restraint from any source. There should be no attempt to lessen through legislative restrictions . . . the freedom of employees in determining the form of any organization created voluntarily."

Businessmen never became reconciled to the Wagner Act. Of all the New Deal measures, they found it the most repugnant. They fought against its passage and when that failed, many of them refused at first to abide by the law because of a conviction that it was unconstitutional. Then when the Supreme Court ruled otherwise, business organized a determined campaign to have the act modified or repealed. But until after World War II, all its efforts failed completely. The unpalatable truth was that during the early and mid-thirties, the economic, political, and social balance turned definitely away from business and more to the advantage of labor unions. The great depression, gradual economic recovery, the election of 1936, and the formation of the CIO were all more important than the Wagner Act in adding to the strength that labor acquired in the 1930's. Indeed, it was the change in the economic and political environment and the shift in public opinion induced thereby that made possible the passage and continuation of the Wagner Act.

During the depression, business lost all the reputation and prestige that it had built up in the preceding generation. Whether correctly or not, public opinion held business and its political representative, the Republican Party, responsible for what had happened. The first signs of economic recovery dealt business another blow. The country's slow emergence from the economic abyss enabled labor to regain some of its courage. At the same time public opinion could not forget the unemployment, bankruptcy, and general poverty that the depression had left as its legacy.

When the AFL did not move aggressively enough, a half dozen of the strongest and most influential union leaders broke away and formed the CIO. To cap the remarkable surge of unionism, the Democratic Party, generally regarded as the party of labor, won the 1936 presidential election with an unprecedented 61 percent of the votes.

In the fight against the Wagner Act, management had its doves as well as its hawks. The more "hard-nosed" industrialists, who were especially prominent in steel and motors urged business to draw a specific line and to hold this line without thought of compromise or retreat regardless of union demands, attacks, or pleas. At the height of the conflict with labor, Tom Girdler of Republic Steel said, "Before I sign a CIO contract, I'll go back on the farm and dig potatoes." At a later time, Charles E. Wilson of GM told a Senate committee that he would never sign a contract for a closed shop. "When it gets around to that," he said, "they can make a farmer out of me." But there were many other businessmen who had no desire to go back to the farm. These less determined managers seemed resigned to labor's victory. They did not welcome it, and they did not like it, but they accepted it as an inescapable part of the wave of the future.

Two dramatic events—the GM sitdown strike of 1936–37 and the settlement between the CIO and United States Steel in early 1937—signalled organized labor's overwhelming victory.

The GM strike was the most important labor dispute in American business history. As a result of it, automobile manufacturing quickly changed from a bastion of open-shop anti-unionism to a completely organized industry. In the dispute, there was no doubt that the CIO was breaking the law, in occupying GM's property without GM's consent. But although the sitdown shook public sympathy, it by no means eradicated it. Many people thought that General Motors was only "getting what it deserved," so far had the company's image deteriorated. As Walter Lippmann put it, GM was lacking in industrial politicians, or as Alfred P. Sloan said, "We were largely unprepared for the change in political climate and the growth of unionism that began in 1933."

The GM strike was a dramatic novelty; the Steel settlement was a melodramatic mystery. At the beginning of 1937, every expert on the steel industry, whether he represented management or labor, would have said that the CIO could not gain anything from steel management without a long and probably violent strike. Yet in March, Myron Taylor, chairman of U.S. Steel, and John L. Lewis, head of the CIO, announced that they had reached an understanding. Big Steel agreed to recognize the union as collective bargaining agent and conceded most of the union's demands. Although the two had been meeting frequently for some time, only three people were not astonished by the announcement. The leaders of Little Steel were speechless in surprise and disappointment. But they too, except for E. T. Weir, eventually capitulated, although they did not surrender without a determined and violent struggle.

MANAGEMENT AND THE UNIONS
SINCE WORLD WAR II

Most big businesses had agreed by 1939 to recognize outside unions and negotiate with them about wages, hours, fringe benefits, and other matters. But businessmen, with few exceptions, had entered the marriage reluctantly and unwillingly. And like all unhappy couples, labor and management continued to snarl at one another. Management continued to lobby for the repeal or modification of the Wagner Act, and it continued to look upon the unions with uneasy suspicion.

The war brought a temporary end to the constant bickering, but as soon as the guns stopped firing, the war between business and the unions resumed. However, management's attitude toward labor and the unions was now much different from what had been in vogue in the first half of the century. Business could not ignore or patronize unions as it had done in the 1920's. And paternalism toward workers was certainly a thing of the past. The kind of anti-unionism of the 1930's was also gone. Employers had come to realize that unions were here to stay. They accepted the fact resignedly, just as they had come to accept ulcers, back trouble, and the attaché case as necessary accouterments of their occupation.

In the new atmosphere of wary, distrustful, and sometimes hostile coexistence, the best that management thought it could achieve was an effective means of containing union power. It therefore subtly changed its strategy. In arguing against the unions and in presenting its case to the public, management differed from the past by putting more emphasis on the importance of productivity and much more stress on the monopolistic nature of labor unions.

Business leaders, "liberals" as well as "reactionaries," retailers and bankers as well as steel men and automobile manufacturers, publicized the argument that labor unions were responsible for "cost-push" inflation. All through the 1950's and early 1960's, they charged that wages were rising faster than output per man hour, and that the consequence of this was price inflation with all the tragedy that it brought to the economy in general, to business investment in particular, and to those who were on a fixed income.

What the business world feared was union economic power. In 1946 during a railroad strike, William A. Jackson, president of the U.S. Chamber of Commerce, urged that "new consideration be given to compulsory arbitration" because "today the Lewises, the Murrays, and the Petrillos, and their kind are infinitely more powerful as monopolists, than the capitalists and promoters of yesteryear." Sometime later, George Romney, then of American Motors, quoted "somebody" as having said:

> Today the greatest concentration of political and economic power in the United States of America are not found in the overregulated, over-criticized, overinvestigated, overtaxed business corporations and certainly not in the hagridden, brow-beaten, publicity-fearful managers.
>
> The greatest concentration of political and economic power are found in the underregulated, undercriticized, underinvestigated, tax-exempt and specially privileged labor organizations and in their aggressive publicity seeking and far too often lawless managers.

But management's uneasiness went much further than this. What many business leaders feared was that unions would achieve political power and exercise that power to turn the country sharply in the direction of collectivism. And what was more, many business leaders thought that nothing could be done to prevent this catastrophe. Henry Ford II characterized the merger of the AFL and the CIO that took place in 1955 as "the most aggressive ascendant force in politics . . . a bulwark of an extreme left wing economic viewpoint."

This was a much exaggerated fear. Labor union leaders could not afford to be collectively minded, for they would be the first victims of the liquidation that would inevitably come with the dawn of collective utopia. Similarly, election after election demonstrated that the political power of labor-union leaders was also much exaggerated. As W. G. Caples, president of Inland Steel, once told his colleagues, "Labor unions don't control votes. Studies have shown that inside the shop the worker considers himself a worker, but outside he thinks of himself as a member of the middle class. The pressure of social groups . . . is what determines his vote."

The picture of the union leader as a dictator unaffected by what his members thought or felt was also unreal. Ernest Breech of the Ford Motor Company, disposed of Walter Reuther, the head of the UAW, as a "union leader with monopolistic power who apparently feels he must always be out to get everything he possibly can." But Breech knew that Reuther was not the master of all he surveyed; he too had a problem. "I don't think," said Breech, "most of us can appreciate the tremendous pressures upon a union leader seeking to maintain and increase his position of power. He must constantly defend himself against the natural drives of ambitious and power-hungry rivals to supplant and surpass him. He must constantly try to achieve for his followers greater gains than his rivals." Breech warned his fellow businessmen not to think that they would do any differently. They too, in Reuther's position, would blame all their troubles and the country's troubles as well on the greed and gluttony of industry. They too would find a scapegoat in "administered prices." They too would act "without regard to economic consequences."

Businessmen had much to say about how to solve the problem of recalcitrant unions. Some thought that the problem would go away in the course of simple economics. "Consumer demand," said Herman Steinkraus of Bridgeport Brass and the Chamber of Commerce, "will bring labor peace." Most of his peers were far less sanguine. They saw no possibility that appeasement would bring the labor-union lions to sup with the management lambs. But few businessmen proposed to meet what they considered an unjust and uneconomic labor situation with force. At least, none openly espoused this tactic. As they shrank from this once popular method of meeting the threats of unionism, there seemed to remain only one other alternative. Business turned to Congress and the state legislatures to redress their grievances.

The appeal to law followed two main routes: the amendment or repeal of the Wagner Act and the adoption of state right-to-work laws. The general philosophy followed closely the principles that had been advanced by the veteran anti-union warrior Tom Girdler in 1937: (1) employees should have the free right to bargain collectively without coercion from *any* source, (2) no employee should be forced to pay dues to a union, (3) a secret ballot before a strike, (4) the responsibility of a union in any controversy should be equal to the responsibility of the employer.

Business was asking Congress "to impose responsibilities and penalties upon labor for wrongful conduct, to preserve the right of free speech, to penalize both unions and strikers for felonies or mass picketing." They also proposed the amendment of the anti-trust laws "so that unions and their members would be subject to ordinary criminal law." Most big businessmen agreed fully with Alfred P. Sloan when he said, "Labor has become a monopoly and monopoly leads to dictatorship," and when he recommended subjecting unions to the Sherman Act, outlawing the closed shop, and amending the Wagner Act's "curtailment of free speech."

Business had apparently struck a responsive chord with the public. Congress and President Truman, sensitive to public pressure, initiated measures to reduce labor-union power and to check the wave of strikes that was taking place in the post-war period.

The President in 1946 introduced a bill that among other things would have given the government the power to draft striking workers and send them back to work under the jurisdiction of the armed forces. Meanwhile Rep. Case of South Dakota introduced an anti-strike bill which was designed "to make" both labor and management "responsible." It would have made unions as well as management responsible for breaches of contract. It would also have outlawed secondary boycotts, unionization of foremen, and employer contributions to union-administered welfare funds, and would have provided for fact-finding boards in disputes involving public utilities. Industry was enthusiastically in favor of the bill, but President Truman vetoed it, and Congress was not able to pass it over his veto.

The struggle, however, did not end with the impasse over the Case bill, which industry supported, and the Truman bill, which industry opposed. In 1947, a Republican-controlled Congress passed the Taft-Hartley Act, which sought in the words of one of its authors to make labor as "responsible" in labor-management relations as the Wagner Act had made capital "responsible." Even though labor leaders condemned the new law as "slave legislation," it did not slow down unionization. Nor did it effectively curb business' twin *bête noires* in labor relations—union monopoly power and wage increases in excess of productivity gains.

Business leaders, chagrined because the Taft-Hartley Act did not seem to redress their grievances, abandoned their legislative campaign. To be sure, here and there, a few business leaders could still be heard urging Congress to extend the Sherman Act to cover labor unions. But most businessmen who did anything about legislation to curb union power did it through the executive branch of the federal government and through so-called "right to work" laws on the state level. But even here the campaign's force dwindled, and by the 1960's business was no longer taking any action to curb the unions. It had become reconciled to the fact that it could live with them. Perhaps one reason for this was that, as a survey of executive opinion concluded, only 15 percent of American firms thought that union security clauses had resulted in a further deterioration in labor-management relations.

15

THE AUTOMOBILE INDUSTRY
AS A CASE HISTORY OF
TWENTIETH-CENTURY
BUSINESS

Of all the industries in twentieth-century America, the automobile industry best illustrates what we have been talking about—the growth of big business, its problems, and its impact on the general economy and on society.[1]

The motor industry began in the 1890's, but it did not achieve any importance until after 1900. As late as 1904, this country produced only 22,000 cars. But thereafter, progress was rapid, and by the early 1920's, automobile manufacturing was the largest manufacturing industry in the world. By the 1960's, the industry had long since become one of so-called imperfect competition, with three companies handling well over 90 percent of total American production. But this statistic, like most statistics, needs some qualification, for no company even today makes everything that goes into an auto or truck. General Motors, by far the biggest producer, buys from 50,000 different firms. The whole industry includes over 800,000 businesses involved in manufacture, distribution, and service. Nearly 13 million people or one out of six in the labor force are employed in producing, selling, servicing, and operating motor vehicles.

Cars and trucks absorb 60 percent of rubber production, 50 percent of lead, 35 percent of zinc, and 20 percent of steel. In the 1960's, it took 80 billion gallons of gasoline to enable drivers to drive 800 billion miles a

[1]There is an immense and valuable literature on the automobile industry. Especially valuable are Alfred D. Chandler, Jr., ed. *Giant Enterprise* (New York: Harcourt, Brace & World, Inc., 1964); John B. Rae, *The American Automobile* (Chicago: The University of Chicago Press, 1965); Alfred P. Sloan, Jr., *My Years with General Motors* (New York: Doubleday & Co., 1964); Allan Nevins, *Ford* 3 volumes (New York: Charles Scribner's Sons, 1954, 1957, 1963).

year. By then, too, government—city, state, and federal—had helped the industry along by constructing 4 million miles of highways.

In its early years, the automobile business closely resembled Professor Gras' petty capitalism. Later, Henry Ford typified industrial capitalism. Still later, the giant automobile companies, especially General Motors and Ford, illustrated Professor Chandler's thesis that structure must change to fit changes in strategy, and decentralization must accompany diversification.

For convenience, the growth of the automobile industry can be divided into three periods: (1) the pioneer phase from about 1893 to about 1900, when the problems of production and finance overshadowed all others; (2) the expansion of mass production from approximately 1900 to around 1925, when the major problems shifted from production and finance to management and marketing; and (3) the era of maturity from about 1925 to the present when unions and ecology entered the list of crucial problems.

During the pioneer period, the automobile was hand-produced for a localized market. This was a stage analogous to "household industry," the putting-out system, or petty capitalism. Entrepreneurs were not determined businessmen, but mechanics like the Duryea Brothers and the Appersons, or refugees from other businesses who treated the automobile more as a hobby than as a promising business. In the latter group were Pope, an eminently successful bicycle manufacturer; Winton, an able engineer; Steinway, the piano maker; Haynes, who had done well in the gas business; Packard, a successful manufacturer of electric cables; and Buick, who had invented a process for installing bathroom fixtures. In these early years, each manufacturer had to answer such questions as whether to produce a gasoline, steam, or electric car; whether to aim for the luxury market or the mass market; what to make in one's own plant and what to buy from parts makers; and how best to allocate one's capital. None of these questions was easy, and because they were so difficult, most of the early makers failed.

Those who placed their faith in electric vehicles failed because electricity was impractical, requiring constant battery recharging. Steam-propelled vehicles also failed because steam was dangerous, requiring a boiler and a fire. In addition, steam had the disadvantages of requiring expert mechanical attention and a constant supply of good water. But most of the early experimenters with gasoline-driven automobiles also disappeared quickly. Some, like the Duryea Brothers, who made the first American automobile in 1893, did not have the vision or the ability to adapt themselves to the needs of a new and different industry. Others, like Winton, failed because they lost interest as soon as a project appeared to be on its way to success. But these were only two examples out of the vast number of the industry's failures. After all, over the course of the automobile's history, over 3,000 different makes of cars and trucks have been manufactured by 1,500 different producers. Less than a dozen of these firms survive. There were 40 different makes in 1926. Since then 134 new ones entered and 55 left the industry. Of the 19 still being made, only 4 go back to 1904. Pioneering led more often to failure than to success, and technological innovation did not necessarily guarantee a brilliant future. The Duesenberg was the first to use hydraulic and four-wheel brakes; the Wills-St. Clair was the first to use molybdenum steel, and the Stutz was the pioneer in the use of safety glass. All were superlative cars for their day, but all failed. The most common reasons why success eluded most of the early companies were the failure to allocate capital efficiently and the incorrect diagnosis of the nature of automobile demand.

Because the early automobile business was nothing more than an assembling process, little capital was required to enter it. Nevertheless, it was not easy to raise even this small amount. As in other infant industries, savings did not flow readily into automobile assembly, nor was capital readily withdrawn from other businesses to be invested in the pioneer automobile industry. Early entrepreneurs financed their enterprises by borrowing from commercial banks and relying on dealers, and the problem of raising capital continued to plague automobile makers all through the stage of initial mass production. Automobile securities were not distributed publicly until General Motors offered some five-year notes in 1910.

In addition to raising the initial funds, there was the more important question of how to allocate them, and here, as in all machine industries, the tendency was to yield to the temptation of expanding technology too rapidly. The consequence was that all of the early firms suffered from a lack of liquidity, and when demand turned down as it did occasionally, most went bankrupt. Even those who survived—Ford, General Motors, Willys, and Packard—missed disaster by the thinnest of margins.

THE BEGINNINGS OF MASS PRODUCTION

Ransom E. Olds was the first to attempt to manufacture rather than build automobiles. He owned a machine shop in which he built gasoline engines. Being an expert workman, he constructed a gasoline-driven automobile, and in 1897, with the financial assistance of local bankers, he began to produce a few automobiles in Lansing, Michigan.

Olds had visions of mass production. He believed that the principles used in manufacturing carriages could be adapted to the automobile. This meant buying the parts in quantity and assembling them. But Lansing could not supply the labor, the money, or the housing for the large-scale project that Olds had in mind, and his motor vehicle company failed. He then contemplated opening a plant in Newark, New Jersey, but eastern capitalists considered his ideas impractical, and they rejected his request for a loan. However, he succeeded in enlisting the help of a Detroit capitalist, S. L. Smith, who wanted to set his sons up in business. In 1899, Olds opened in Detroit with a capital of $200,000. Smith put in $199,600 and took 95 percent of the stock.

The first Olds factory turned out a complicated car whose mechanism was not only too far ahead of its day but whose price, $1,250, was also too high. After one year, Olds moved back to Lansing, and in 1901 he began to produce a $650 Oldsmobile on a mass basis, buying the parts in quantity and assembling them on an embryonic assembly line. Olds was an immensely important pioneer, for he was the first in the industry to use division of labor, the first to use the moving assembly line, and the first to bring the materials to the worker instead of the worker to the materials.

With his improved processes, Olds sold 5,000 cars in 1904 and paid 105 percent in dividends in three years. But at this point, he and Smith broke up their partnership. Olds wanted to continue to build cheap cars; Smith wanted something more distinguished and more expensive.

THE SUCCESS OF THE FORD MOTOR COMPANY

Olds was the pioneer in introducing mass-production methods, but Henry Ford carried mass production much further. Ford did not originate standardization and the assembly line. Indeed, Ford did not originate any of the things he is popularly supposed to have originated. His strength lay in his intuitive confidence that the future lay in a cheap car for a mass market. He believed the automobile to be price-elastic, that is, that reducing the price would result in a more than proportionate increase in sales. Technologically, his great contributions were (1) the emphasis he placed on an expert combination of accuracy, including standardization, continuity, the moving assembly line, and speed, and (2) careful timing of manufacture, material handling, and assembly.

Like most successful business geniuses, Ford was a complicated personality. According to Allan Nevins, who wrote the most definitive biography, he "was on the whole an attractive figure. Complex, wayward, mercurial, with a streak of meanness engendered by his hard early life, and prejudices that arose from ignorance, he could in spite of his glaring faults be called an idealist." But according to Charles Sorensen, who was associated with Ford for forty years, he was "petty, ignorant, jealous, desirous of running a one-man show, devious, insincere, inconsistent, malicious, and friendless."[2]

[2]Allan Nevins, *Ford: Decline and Rebirth* (New York: Charles Scribner's Sons, 1963), p. 270; Charles E. Sorensen, *My Forty Years with Ford* (New York: W. W. Norton, Inc., 1956), p. 3.

No one in business has gone downhill in esteem so much after death as Ford. During his lifetime he was hailed as a great patriot, a benefactor of mankind, and the greatest industrialist the country had ever produced. When he died, he was extolled as "the embodiment of America in the era of the industrial revolution." Less than ten years later, two professors wrote an article for a popular magazine in which they claimed that in addition to being a poor excuse for a human being, he was an inept businessman.

The subject of this diversity of opinion was born in 1863 on his parents' farm in what has since become part of Detroit. His was not a rags to riches story, for he was never poor in the true sense. Although his boyhood was not spent in luxury, Henry grew up in comfortable and pleasant surroundings amidst a large family and many friends.

Early in life he showed an intense interest in mechanical things and an equally intense disinterest in the chores he was expected to do as he was growing up on the farm. Although he attended the rudimentary Scotch Settlement School and the Miller School until he was sixteen, he showed no particular academic interests except for arithmetic in which he did well.

Ford went to work in 1879 and in the next seven years he had more jobs than anyone would care to catalogue. Then in 1886 he went back to the farm. His father gave him 40 acres of timberland on which he did a little farming, operated a sawmill, did repairs, and experimented with engines and machines.

The call of mechanics and machinery was too great to keep Ford on the farm for any great length of time. In 1891 he accepted a position as night engineer at the Edison Illuminating Company (later the Detroit Edison Company) at $45 a month. He was evidently competent at the job for his salary rose, and he became chief engineer at $100 a month. He had a small workshop at the back of his rented house and here he experimented with motors. With the help of fellow employees at the Edison plant, he laboriously built his first automobile. When it was finished in June 1896, it turned out to be too large to get through the door of the shop. Ford impatiently broke down enough of the brick wall to allow the car to emerge, and the first Ford made a short but successful run.

Having developed a basic model, Ford now undertook to strengthen the vehicle. He added sturdier wheels, a new metal steering mechanism, and a seat with metal railing. When completed, it was sold for $200 and Ford began to build a second car.

With the help of William F. Murphy, a wealthy lumber dealer, and three other financial backers, and mechanical assistance from several helpers, Ford, in August 1899, formed the Detroit Automobile Company with more than a dozen stockholders contributing $15,000. Ford received stock in the company but paid no money. At the same time he resigned from the Edison Company and devoted his time to automotive work.

This first venture lasted less than a year. Deliveries of supplies ran late, the labor force was inexperienced, and there were constant findings of shortcomings in design. In November 1900 the company surrendered its charter and went out of business.

Ford now turned to racing cars. On October 10, 1901 he achieved his first victory, defeating Alexander Winton in a ten-mile run at Grosse Point. A month later the Henry Ford Company was organized, with Ford being given $10,000 in stock and the title of engineer. Total paid-in capital was $30,500. While the financial backers fumed and fretted, Ford continued to build racing cars rather than a commercial model. Finally, in March 1902 the stockholders dismissed Ford, and turned the company over to Henry M. Leland, who changed its name to the Cadillac Automobile Company.

Ford had, therefore, already failed twice when in 1903, he formed the Ford Motor Company with the help of Malcolmson, a coal dealer of some means. The enterprise was capitalized at $100,000, but only $28,000 was paid in immediately in cash; $14,000 more was paid in 1904. Ford never again raised new money, but financed all future expansion through retained earnings.

At first, the company was an assembler, not a producer. It bought chassis for $250, bodies for $52, cushions for $16, wheels for $26, and tires for $40. A dozen workers, at $1.50 a day, put these parts together, and the assembled parts were sold for $850, yielding a profit of $246.

But Ford had other ambitions. He also had in the words of a not altogether friendly associate, "a supernormal perceptive faculty." In 1903, he told John W. Anderson, the lawyer who drew up the company's incorporation papers, "The way to make automobiles is to make one automobile like another automobile, to make them all alike . . . just like one pin is like another pin, or one match is like another match."

By 1908, most automobile manufacturers were tending toward high-priced cars. Ford, going against prevailing opinion, determined to produce low-priced cars in immense volume. As he put it, "From the day the first motor car appeared, it had to me appeared to be a necessity." "We were going to build one model . . . the chassis would be exactly the same for all cars, and I remarked, 'Any customer can have a car painted any color he wants so long as it is black.' I cannot say that anyone agreed with me." He bought out his more recalcitrant partners and began to manufacture the Model-T, a standardized product "for the great multitude." Ford's objective was a car with a price "so low that no man making a good salary will be unable to own one—and enjoy with his family the blessings of hours of pleasure in God's great open spaces." The general attitude among his competitors and among those who commented about the automobile business was, "If Ford does this, he will be out of business in six months."

His critics were of course wrong. Instead of going out of business, Ford quickly achieved first position in automobile manufacture. But he also did not fully recognize what he was doing. Despite his "supernormal perceptive faculty," he did not foresee the irony of the automobile. Neither he nor anyone else foresaw that it would become the most potent mankiller and the most thorough air polluter ever invented by man. What he did see was a car well within the reach of the pocketbooks of America's middle class.

Such a car could not be achieved without considerable technological innovation. Even before the Model-T, Ford had begun to proceed along the road toward a completely standardized product. In 1906 he hired Walter E. Flanders, one of Frederick W. Taylor's students, to increase production to 10,000 cars a year. But the real breakthrough came with the construction of the plant at Highland Park, which opened in 1910. Here the construction of an automobile was laid out as a line production system. That is to say, the machines and workers were placed in sequence, so that the materials involved in assembling *any part* of an automobile would move *without interruption* along a line of production. Before the Highland Park plant fully achieved what it was set up to do, the Ford chassis was assembled in one location. First the front and rear axles were laid on the floor, then the frame was assembled with the axles, and so forth. At the same time, at another place, the magneto was being put together. What assembly line procedure there was in this production process consisted of adding the individual parts to the chassis. As Ford described the process, "In our first assembling, we simply started to put a car together at a spot on the floor and workmen brought to it the parts as they were needed in exactly the same way that one builds a house. . . . The first step forward came when we began taking the work to the men instead of the men to the work—as Olds has done."

Full operation of the Highland Park plant was not accomplished overnight. Indeed, it took three years. Progress began with the assembling of the flywheel magneto. Two technicians, C. W. Avery and William Klann, took over from the meat-packing industry the idea of a moving conveyor. In 1913, they applied the principle to the job of assembling a flywheel magneto. Previously, the whole job had taken one workman twenty minutes. By splitting the job into twenty-nine different operations and putting it on a mechanical conveyor, Avery and Klann cut production time to a little over thirteen minutes. Experiments with the height of the conveyor soon cut the time to five minutes.

The next step was to assemble a chassis on a moving line. In the late summer of 1913, Avery and Klann began experimenting with this task. Assemblers worked on a chassis as it was dragged across the floor by a windlass. This took five hours and fifty minutes. But then a mechanized overhead conveyor belt replaced the windlass. With constant time-and-motion studies and adjustments in the speed and height of the belt, assembly was repeatedly improved so that by April 1914 assembly time was cut from the original twelve and a half hours to an hour and a half.

The new method of production required complete standardization, new machines, and an adaptable labor force. The Ford organization was fully capable of producing all of these things. In the early years it, therefore, completely dominated the industry. But there were rivals, the chief of whom was William C. Durant, a person different in every way from Ford.

DURANT AND GENERAL MOTORS

Durant was warm, outgoing, and thoroughly likable. He was born in 1860, the grandson of the governor of Michigan. He started in the carriage business in 1885 and quickly built a thoroughly integrated organization. By 1904, he was a wealthy and highly successful man. By then, too, Buick, another Flint, Michigan enterprise, was in great trouble. In that year, it sold only 28 cars. At the request of the citizens of Flint, Durant took over the company and immediately installed the methods that had proved so successful in the Durant-Dort carriage firm. He began to acquire sources of supply, persuading Charles S. Mott to move his Weston-Mott axle and wheel company from upstate New York to Flint, and Albert Champion to bring his spark plug company to Michigan. He set up distributorships in rural areas and his own retail offices in the big cities. Once again, his methods proved successful. By 1908, Buick was the largest company, producing 8,847 cars. Ford was second with 6,181, and Cadillac third at 2,380.

In 1908, Durant, who believed in expansion, more expansion, and still more expansion, attempted to consolidate Ford, Maxwell-Briscoe, Reo, and Buick. He failed because he could not raise the small amount of cash ($1.5–2 million) that was needed. Instead, he put together Buick, Cadillac, Oldsmobile, Oakland, and McLaughlin Motor Co. of Canada in an enterprise named General Motors Corporation capitalized at $10 million, mostly on paper. Durant continued to expand, but in 1910 automobile sales failed to rise as phenomenally as before, and General Motors faced a liquidity crisis. Unable to meet his demand obligations, Durant borrowed from a syndicate of bankers headed by Lee-Higginson and J. & W. Seligman. In exchange for $12,750,000 in cash, GM gave the syndicate $15 million in 6 percent notes plus 60,000 shares of preferred and common stock. Durant also agreed to turn the management over to a voting trust. James Jackson Storrow, senior partner of Lee-Higginson, became chairman of the Finance Committee. Charles W. Nash, head of Buick, became president, and Walter P. Chrysler succeeded him at Buick. Storrow was chief executive officer and he tried to form a workable organization, but he did not succeed, chiefly because of the lack of cooperation from the division heads, Chrysler, Leland, and others, whose individualism had been encouraged under Durant.

In 1915, Durant came back to General Motors. With the help of the Du Ponts, he first gained control of the Chevrolet Motor Co. Then he used Chevrolet to acquire the controlling interest in GM. The Du Ponts had invested almost $50 million in the company, and in the takeover, they appointed four directors, including Pierre du Pont, J. Amory Haskell, and John J. Raskob.

Durant again embarked ambitiously on an expansion program. Among others, he bought Frigidaire, sending the company on its way to diversification. He also bought various parts makers. In 1916 he combined these with what GM already had in a new subsidiary called United Motors. The new company was headed by Alfred P. Sloan, who had been part owner of one of the purchased parts makers, Hyatt Roller Bearing.

Once again, the business cycle caught up with Durant's failure to provide reserves for the inevitable period of dull business. At the end of World War I, demand dropped dramatically. In October 1920, General Motors had difficulty in meeting its payroll. Once again, Durant departed, this time at the request of the Du Ponts and the House of Morgan. Pierre du Pont assumed the role of chief executive and Sloan became operations vice-president and then succeeded du Pont in 1923. From the early twenties, therefore, Sloan was the chief but by no means the only decision maker in GM. As we shall see, his executive ability had much to do with GM's ultimate spectacular success. In personality and background, Sloan was much different from Durant and Ford. Born in New Haven, Connecticut in 1875, Sloan like Durant came from a well-to-do family. Following graduation from MIT, he entered the family business and was already wealthy when he came to General Motors. Unlike Durant and Ford, he seemed to have no emotions. He looked at life and its participants in the cold light of reason. He seldom called anyone by his first name. Yet, he got along much better with his associates and dealers than did either Durant or Ford. He even got along with the bankers, whom Ford despised and Durant hated. In another respect he differed from other automobile men. Ford collected antiques. Durant gambled in the stock market. But the only thing that interested Sloan was business—the business of General Motors.

Throughout all this period, Ford prevailed in the intense rivalry between him and Durant and between the Ford Motor Company and General Motors. Ford's strategy of integrating vertically through internal growth paid off better than Durant's strategy of growth through consolidation and merger.

With the help of associates who were extraordinarily able businessmen, mechanics, and engineers, like James Couzens, who managed the office; Childe Harold Wills, the brilliant designer; Norval A. Hawkins, in advertising and sales; Joseph Galamb, Eugene Farkas, Carl Emde, and John Wandersee in engineering, tool design, and metallurgy; and Pete Martin, Charles Sorensen, and William S. Knudsen, in production, the Ford Company produced 38 percent of all motor vehicles in 1915 and 56 percent in 1921. In 1911, Ford had produced only 20 percent compared to General Motors' 18 percent. But throughout Durant's tenure, Ford widened the gap, for GM accounted for only 11 percent in 1915 and 13 percent in 1921.

Yet, the Ford Company showed some critical weaknesses. Ford insisted upon having his finger in every pie. He had no use for records, refused to admit his own errors, and was skeptical of those who had some knowledge. Ford lavished almost all his love on the Model-T. He had very little left over for the rest of the company. When the Model-A appeared at a later date, he treated it as an unwelcome stepchild. He did make some attempts to diversify both within the auto business and by entering other industries, but these attempts failed, and they always seemed halfhearted. Research was run in an eccentric fashion, and the company's financial policies often resulted in a dangerous shortage of cash. In 1920, for example, he became embroiled in the same kind of liquidity crisis that caused Durant's downfall, but he managed to extricate himself, chiefly by dumping his inventory on his dealers.

Ford was also an erratic administrator. "Mr. Ford," said one employee, "did not believe in administration." He could not get along with either his partners or his associates. In 1919 he solved one of these problems by buying out all his remaining stockholders. He solved the problem of his associates by firing most of them for inadequate reasons. Many of them in turn went on to successful careers in General Motors.

But in a virgin market in which price was very important, Ford did very well, especially because his chief rival had an organization that was even more chaotic. Durant was interested in growth for growth's sake. He had no financial management, no clear lines of authority, no budgeting of appropriations, and no consistent strategy or tactics. He relied on personal loyalty and personal inspiration as he interfered with everyone else's business. Durant's fundamental weaknesses were best illustrated by his dealings with Walter Chrysler. He constantly made decisions about Buick without consulting Chrysler. Finally, in 1920, Chrysler confronted Durant with an ultimatum:[3]

> Billy, for the love of ———, please now, say what your policies are for GM. . . . Leave the operations alone, the building, the buying, the selling, and the men—leave them alone, but say what your policies are. Billy laughed at me. Walt, I believe in changing the policies just as often as my door opens and closes.

[3]Walter P. Chrysler, *The Life of an American Workman* (New York: Dodd, Mead, 1950), p. 148.

THE EMERGENCE OF GENERAL MOTORS

By 1923, it was clear to the farsighted that the heroic age of the automobile business was over. The crucial problems were no longer production and finance but management and marketing. Price was no longer as important as it had been, and the Ford idea of one model in vast volume at lower and lower prices could not continue to dominate. The figures tell the story of how General Motors and eventually Chrysler overtook and passed Ford. In 1923, Ford's share of the market fell to 46 percent while General Motor's share rose to 20 percent. In 1927, Ford reluctantly abandoned the Model-T, and the company's share dwindled to 9 percent. GM took 43 percent, and Chrysler, whose first full year was 1925, had 6 percent. Ford, of course, came back, but its share never again equalled that of General Motors, and in 1936, it was temporarily passed by Chrysler. The obituary on the Ford practices was finally written after Henry's death when the company reorganized along General Motors lines under Ernest Breech, an executive who had been trained in the GM organization.

There were many reasons for GM's rise to a dominating position, but not the least of these was the ability of the company's executives. By the middle 1920's, the nature of the automobile business had changed fundamentally. Twenty years of high-volume production had put an end to the virgin market of the early days. It was now succeeded by a replacement market. Consumers could postpone purchasing a new car; they could make last year's car do for another year. The market underwent further changes as a result of the building up of the used car market and the institution of installment credit. It was now possible to buy a used car that had been in the luxury class at a price equal or below that of a new car in the low-priced field. And by buying on time, one could further reduce the gap between the lesser and the better.

These alterations in the nature of the market meant that the importance of price had diminished as a factor in the sale of new cars. Originally, the demand for automobiles had been price-elastic, that is, price reductions resulted in a more than proportionate increase in total dollar sales. In the early twenties the demand had become income-elastic, that is to say, the sale of automobiles had become a function of consumer income and consumer expectations rather than a function of price.

The industry had reached maturity. It was no longer a growth industry. Its future progress would occur in steps. Like many other phenomena in economic and business history, the automobile began to experience long swings. The industry sold 5.3 million vehicles in 1929. Then came the depression, and it was not until the years after World War II that production and sales took off in a new burst of activity. The 1929 figure was finally surpassed in 1949; and in 1955, dealers sold over 9 million cars and trucks, a record that was not again exceeded until 1963. In 1965, sales reached a record total of over 11 million.

Another sign of maturity was that the industry had become one of imperfect or monopolistic competition. When the automobile business was young, automobile prices fell regardless of what was happening to the general consumer price index. After the mid-1920's, the price of a car showed a much greater upward slope than the so-called cost of living. Between 1925 and 1940, the consumer price index dropped by almost one-third, whereas the price of a best-selling automobile went up 40 percent. In the postwar period, the price of this same automobile rose 50 percent while the general index climbed 25 percent. To be sure, quoted prices on automobiles were not the prices that were actually paid after the higgling and haggling in the actual market. Quoted price, furthermore, made no allowance for quality change. Nevertheless, it was apparent that as the automobile business became older, prices were becoming less important in motivating consumers, whereas subjective considerations, such as quality, style, and status, were becoming more important. Competition had become a struggle between marketing departments, rather than a contest over price. In order to maintain quantity production, it was necessary to emphasize service, design, and other abstractions. And despite what automobile buffs might say, quality did improve. In 1925, the age of an average motor vehicle was 6½ years and its mileage, 25,000; a generation later, the average age had declined slightly, but the average mileage had quadrupled. At the same time, technological development had become more intensive than extensive. Innovations were more refined than fundamental. The emphasis was less on cost reduction than on demand induction through changes in design and improvements in comfort. Faster-drying paints appeared, and consumers were offered a wide choice in colors. The automobile, which once contained less than 100 parts, now contained 8,000. For those who were interested only in driving, there was shatter-proof glass, heaters and air conditioners, balloon tires, automatic transmission, power steering, and power brakes; for the aesthetes, the teardrop body had made the automobile a work of art.

Increasing maturity not only altered the nature of competition; it so enhanced the importance of management and marketing that they supplanted production and finance as the industry's most important functions.

Sloan understood better than anyone else the transformation that was taking place in the automobile business, for he was an executive whereas Durant was a financier, and the other automobile leaders were production men. To Sloan automobiles were a business; to Durant they were a collection of common and preferred stocks; to Ford they were an industry. Ford was obsessed with production to the exclusion of everything else. Durant was hypnotized by growth for growth's sake. The one ran his company as a dictatorship; the other in a condition of near anarchy. In the Ford organization centralization ruled. At the other extreme, General Motors under Durant operated under a quixotic decentralization that approached chaos. Durant's easygoing ways bothered the Du Ponts, but their two representatives on the board could not do much to improve the situation. Raskob was too much like Durant and Haskell was too old.

By temperament and ability, Sloan was ideally suited to following a middle course between Ford's centralization and Durant's decentralization. As soon as he assumed authority, he submitted a plan designed to revise GM's objectives and reorganize its structure and administration. His plan, which was approved in late December 1920, set up a managerial structure that he described as "decentralization under coordinated control." "Lines of authority," he said, "should be clearly defined, but authority itself should be decentralized as much as possible."

Sloan's plan separated basic decision making from administration by setting up a general office or central organization that would coordinate and appraise what was going on in day-to-day business. He enlisted his executives in a real partnership. "Dictatorship," Sloan conceded, "is the most effective way of administration provided the dictator knows the complete answer to all questions. But he never does and he never will." The entrepreneurial decision makers in General Motors were concerned with long-run objectives rather than with day-to-day activities. They were not "hunch players." They approached problems in a systematic, orderly fashion, in "a constant search for the facts . . . and their intelligent unprejudiced analysis." They emphasized forecasting, coordinating production to demand, collecting statistical data, accounting, and long range planning, all to produce a predetermined rate of return on capital. "As I see it," Sloan wrote, "the strategic aim of a business is to earn a return on capital, and if in any particular case the return in the long run is not satisfactory, the deficiency should be corrected or the activity abandoned for a more favorable one."[4]

In the new General Motors structure, Sloan was the innovator in management and Donaldson Brown and John Lee Pratt, two graduates from Hamilton Barksdale's managerial group at DuPont, were the innovators in the use of statistics and accounting.

Ford had nothing but contempt for the new management practiced at General Motors. "The Ford factories and enterprises," he said in 1922, "have no organization, no specific duties attaching to any position, no line of succession or of authority, very few titles, and no conferences." Probably with GM in mind, he wrote:[5]

---

[4]The quotations here are from Alfred P. Sloan, Jr., *My Years with General Motors* (Garden City, N.Y.: Doubleday and Company, 1964) and Ernest Dale, *Great Organizers* (New York: McGraw-Hill Book Company, 1960).

[5]Henry Ford, *My Life and Work* (Garden City, N..Y: Doubleday and Company, Inc., 1922), pp. 91–92.

To my mind, there is no bend of mind that is more dangerous than that which is sometimes described as the "genius for organization." This usually results in the birth of a great big chart; showing, after the fashion of a family tree, how authority ramifies. The tree is heavy with nice round berries, each of which bears the name of a man or an office. Every man has a title and certain duties which are strictly limited by the circumference of his berry. It takes about six weeks for the message of the man living in a berry on the left-hand corner of the chart to reach the President or the Chairman of the Board, and if it ever does reach one of these august officials, it has by that time gathered to itself a pound of criticisms, suggestions, and comments. . . . The buck is passed to and fro and all responsibility is dodged by individuals—following the lazy notion that two heads are better than one.

Ford's comments were a justifiable criticism of the general evils of bureaucracy in the large organization; but as a dismissal of what was happening in the administration of his chief competitor, they were far off the mark. Times had changed, and Ford was very much behind them.

MARKETING AND PRICING

In 1908, a Ford runabout cost $700 and a six-cylinder luxury car, over $2,500. By 1924 the small Ford was down to $260 and the luxury car to $1,700. The quality of the luxury car had also been greatly improved. The self-starter had replaced the crank. It was now possible to buy a closed car. The demountable rim, forced-feed lubrication, the cord tire, the four-wheel brake, and other innovations had been adopted. But price was still paramount, and Ford was unquestionably the price leader.

Ford's marketing policy was the height of simplicity; price was the only consideration. "We do not have to bother about overproduction for some years to come, provided the prices are right," he said in 1922. "It is the refusal of people to buy on account of price that really stimulates real business." Ford would not countenance any other competition but price. "We never make an improvement that renders any previous model obsolete," he boasted. "It is considered good manufacturing practice . . . occasionally to change designs so that old models will become obsolete and new ones will have to be bought. . . . We want to construct some kind of machine that will last forever."[6]

Despite the stress he put on prices, Ford had no price theory, and his explanation of price policies was vague to the point of being nonunderstandable. As he saw it, price reductions were to be made because of economies achieved in manufacturing, not because of public dissatisfaction with the

6*Ibid.*, pp. 148–9.

product. This reasoning might lead one to believe that Ford pricing depended on cost rather than supply and demand. But Ford explicitly denied this. As he explained the company's policy, "we first reduce the price to a point where we believe more sales will result. Then we go ahead and try to make the price. We do not bother about costs. The new price forces the costs down."

Ford cut prices more drastically in recession when demand fell off than in prosperity when demand was high, but he cut prices at all times. He tried to use price reductions as a means of increasing demand and thereby demonstrated that he did not really understand the law of supply and demand. As he began to lose his share of the market in the early 1920's, he failed to realize that his decline was the result of a shift in that most mysterious of all economic variables, consumer demand. He met the problem by cutting prices sharply, but Chevrolet, emphasizing style and engineering, raised its prices and, despite this, continued to gain on Ford.

If Ford's price policy was vague, Durant's was literally nonexistent. During his regime, each division manager determined the prices for the automobiles he was trying to sell. Durant took little interest in the subject.

Marketing and price policy, like so many other things, changed when Sloan and his colleagues took over. In 1920, the sedans in General Motors' list varied in price from $1,375 to $5,690, with most bunched around $2,150. In 1921 the company adopted in principle the objective of "building a car for every purse and purpose." By 1925 it had accomplished this objective. Its automobiles were evenly spaced in price from $525 for the Chevrolet roadster to $4,485 for the Cadillac Imperial.

To achieve GM's marketing objectives required forecasting, selling, and a price theory or formula.

The forecasting program, which began as soon as Donaldson Brown joined the company, had three objectives: to be used as a tool to control current operations, to enable management to measure performance in regard to rate of return, and to act as a guide in price policy. The program was concerned with general economic growth, seasonal variations, the movement of the business cycle, and the general state of competition.

Using the data available from the forecasting program, Donaldson Brown developed a complicated formula for pricing GM cars and trucks. This formula was put into effect in 1925 and with its appearance, pricing became a standard art, for with minor variations, Brown's formula was eventually adopted by all automobile companies.

The objective of price policy was the same as the company's overall objective: to achieve the highest attainable rate of return on capital consistent with a healthy growth of the business. Every year, each division submitted to the executive committee a price study that estimated sales in units and in dollars, and also estimated costs, profits, capital requirements, and return on investment on the basis of standard volume and on the estimated rate of operation. The standard price of an automobile thus came to be that price, which, with the plant operating at standard volume, would produce the adjudged normal rate of return. In any given year, the forecast for actual volume might be above or below standard volume, and prices would be adjusted accordingly. The price of a car thus came to be computed each year on the basis of last year's costs on last year's volume by last year's production methods modified by next year's volume turned out under next year's production methods.

The use of Brown's complicated formula did not simplify price making. Years after the formula was first adopted, Harlow Curtice, then president of GM, explained price making to a Congressional committee. "Pricing," he said, "is like a tripod. It has three legs. In addition to cost, there are the two other legs of market demand and competition. It is no more possible to say that one or another of these factors determines price than it is to assert that one leg rather than either of the other two supports a tripod." Once the three-legged tripod had determined price, the individual manufacturer had to answer the question of how he knew whether or not his unit costs were being kept below the unit price. Curtice explained this as follows:

It is impossible for an automobile manufacturer to forecast his unit costs accurately in relation to the price he has announced. Nor can he keep adjusting his price to costs as they may vary. This would lead to market chaos. Our approach to this cost problem has been the use of the concept of standard volume. Standard volume may be defined as the estimated rate of operations which represents the normal or average annual utilization of a capacity that must be large enough to meet the cyclical and seasonal peaks which are characteristic of the automobile industry. In General Motors this average annual utilization is estimated at 80 percent of capacity. . . . How do we make use of the standard volume concept? First, labor and material costs that are directly applicable to each unit produced are calculated on the basis of current wage rates and material prices. Indirect or overhead costs are then determined on a cost per unit basis by distributing them over the determined standard volume. . . . This method of estimating unit costs on the basis of standard volume gives us a benchmark against which to evaluate our cost-price relationship. . . . It is obvious that if our benchmark shows that costs are high in relation to price, efficiency has been reduced—unless, of course, cost increases represent a general rise in what the industry pays for labor and materials. In the first case, steps must be taken to reduce costs. In the latter case competitive forces will cause prices to rise.[7]

[7]Joint Economic Committee, "Price Development and Economic Stabilization" (1947).

The last mystery in marketing—how to sell the automobile—was solved by two brilliant salesmen, Norval Hawkins, who came to GM from Ford, and Richard R. H. Grant, a graduate of John H. Patterson's noted school for salesmen, the National Cash Register Company.

Grant's contributions to GM from the time he left National Cash Register for Delco Light in 1915 were prodigious. As sales manager for Chevrolet in 1924 and later (1929) as vice-president of General Motors, Grant organized and nursed GM's widespread dealership system with the tactics and principles he had learned under Patterson. He was so successful that William Knudsen, then head of Chevrolet, set his production schedules on the basis of Grant's estimates of future sales. In other words, Knudsen was producing what Grant could sell in contrast to the old system under which Grant would try to sell what Knudsen produced. Marketing had truly come a long way!

PROFITS AND PERFORMANCE

It was possible for an automobile manufacturer to make enormous profits, and some did. It was also possible for an automobile manufacturer to lose immense sums, and some did. Indeed, some did both. Consider the Maxwell-Briscoe Automobile Company. In 1904, a company prospectus proposed to manufacture a touring car, priced at $1,200 to agents and $1,500 retail, and a runabout to sell for $600 and to be sold to agents for $500. For the first year fixed charges were estimated at $68,500 and floating expenses at $162,000.[8] Maxwell estimated that it would cost $636 to assemble a touring car, and $225 for a runabout if two of each were assembled a day. Assuming total production came to 500 touring cars and 1,000 runabouts, total profit would be $326,500 on a capitalization of $375,000. Reality exceeded expectations for Maxwell-Briscoe and for some years, the company made money. But it eventually went out of business and was absorbed by Chrysler.

Ford's success was of course spectacular. In its first 25 years, the company made $900 million. But between 1927 and 1933, Ford lost $131 million. General Motors did better. Its net income after taxes from 1927 through 1933 was $1.2 billion. Eventually, GM earned over $1 billion in one year, and it lost money in only one year in its whole history.

What these examples and others demonstrated was that it was the innovating entrepreneur who made the spectacular profits and the spectacular failures. He who dared and won, won magnificently. He who did not dare

---

[8]This included $60,000 for advertising, $25,000 for "experimental work," and $6,000 for exhibits.

was certain to end in failure, but his failure would come considerably later than for him who dared and lost.

LABOR RELATIONS

The transformation of labor relations in the automobile business encapsulated what happened in business in general.

It is a commonplace that labor policy today is entirely different from what it was forty years ago. Certain features of this transformation should be stressed: the dominance of paternalism in the early years; its rapid disappearance during the depression of the 1930's; the continued progress of mechanization and automation; and the importance of productivity.

All early employers showed a penchant for paternalism. They saw themselves as benevolent fathers with large families, and followed the rule that father knows best. Henry Ford was especially noted for paternalism, and some of his business policies were regarded by his competitors and by the business press as downright suicidal. This was especially true of the famous five-dollar day which Ford instituted in 1914 and which the *Times* labelled "distinctly utopian" and the *Wall Street Journal* disapproved as "unscientific."

Yet, Ford's paternalism was exaggerated, and its "utopianism" was even more exaggerated. Sound business reasoning lay in back of the $5 day, and although Ford exuded an aura of paternalism, no one was doing more to replace man with the machine and no one was doing more to replace the skilled and the unskilled with the semi-skilled.

In 1916, John R. Lee, Ford's personnel manager, explained the rationale behind the $5 day and the shorter working day. According to Lee, the company discovered in 1912 that production could suffer from labor dissatisfaction, fear, sickness, and other human weaknesses. A labor policy was instituted to rectify this. The first step was to cut the working day from ten to nine hours and to raise the rate of pay, so that nine hours would bring 15 percent more than the previous ten hours. They then cut the 69 different rates of wages to 8. The third step came with the institution of a profit-sharing plan that was immediately labeled "the five-dollar day." The lowest wage for an eight-hour day was 34 cents an hour, but the minimum income was 62.5 cents an hour. The difference of 28.5 cents was profit sharing. But not all workers were eligible for profit sharing. "It was clearly foreseen," said Lee, "that $5 a day in the hands of some men would work a tremendous handicap along the paths of rectitude and right living and would make them a menace to society."[9]

[9]John R. Lee, "The So-Called Profit Sharing System in the Ford Plant," *Annals*, Vol. 65 (May 1916).

In following paternalism, the Ford people clearly had in mind reducing costs by increasing man-hour output. Their policy succeeded admirably. The number of plants in the automobile business increased from 178 in 1904 to 2,471 in 1923, when the automobile industry became the largest in the country. The number of man-hours required to produce a car underwent a startling reduction. Based on 1914 equalling 100, productivity increased to 270 in 1923. In 1914 it took 4,664 man-hours in one plant, 1,260 in another, to produce a car. By 1923, it took 813 man-hours in the first plant and 228 in the second. Wages went up commensurately. In 1903, skilled workers received $2.25 and unskilled $1.50 for a ten-hour day. In 1914, about 200 workers in the Ford plant made $7 in an eight-hour day; 1,000 earned $6; and 1,500, $5.

But the increase in pay was obtained at some expense, for there is a price for everything. The price that had to be paid for a higher standard of living was a speedup of the work, systematic discharge of the old, and a turnover rate that was higher than in other industries. During the 1920's, the Ford plant had to hire 53,000 workers to maintain a constant corps of 14,000.

Paternalism was badly damaged by its own inconsistencies. It was completely shattered by the depression of the 1930's. In the slow recovery that occurred in the late 1930's, collective bargaining, with the United Automobile Workers of the CIO as collective bargaining agent, swept aside the few remnants of paternalism that still remained. The triumph of the unions was a galling experience for the automobile manufacturers. They had resisted unionization with all the powers they could muster, and they had failed.

Henceforth, labor-management relations were on a business basis, altogether different from the arrangement in effect in the early 1920's.

THE AUTOMOBILE INDUSTRY'S ECONOMIC
AND SOCIAL IMPACT

No other economic innovation, including the railroad, surpassed the automobile in its effect on economic and social life. The ways in which motor vehicles influenced management, marketing, finance, and labor have already been discussed. But the automobile permeated every aspect of life, not just business and the seven M's of management. It rehabilitated old industries, like the toll road and the roadside inn, and it created wholly new industries and institutions, such as billboard advertising, the gas station, the motel, and the outdoor movies.

In 1904, the industry produced 23,000 vehicles, with value added equal to only $17 million; by 1929 production exceeded 5 million cars with an added value of over $2.5 billion. In 1968 production had risen to 10.7 million vehicles and added value to over $15 billion. Moreover, one business in every six was intimately related to the automobile industry.

Ever since 1920, automobile manufacturing has employed approximately 4 percent of all manufacturing workers; another 10 percent of the nonagricultural labor force were in jobs that the automobile had created. With constant improvements in productivity, money and real wages climbed upward. By 1946, real wages were more than twice what they had been in 1904. By the 1960's, they had increased another 50 percent.

The automobile also made profound changes in where people lived and in how they spent their money. It made possible the drift to suburbia and exurbia and the transmutation of the city into the metropolitan area. Before long, Americans were spending 5 percent of their disposable income for the purchase and maintenance of automobiles, and by the 1960's, almost 10 percent.

Economists were quite sure about the economic benefits that the automobile had brought. Other thinkers who put more emphasis on social factors were not so sanguine. Traditional moral concepts lost their meaning as the automobile became the distinguishing mark of conspicuous consumption. Sociologists were dubious about the effects of the automobile on the discipline of family life. They also decried the effects of automobile production on mental life, for the auto was synonymous with the assembly line process and epitomized the monotony of a machine society. But in time, much of this criticism lost its bite as safety engineers aimed a major share of their criticisms at the industry. Long the seventh most important cause of death, autos killed 25,000 in 1927, 35,000 in 1950, and 55,000 in 1968. But judged by the number of vehicles on the road and the number of miles traveled, the automobile was becoming safer rather than more dangerous. The accident rate per 10,000 vehicles was only 1.7 in 1950 and 1.4 per year in the 1960's. The fatality rate per 100 million miles dropped from 16.3 in 1927 to 7.6 in 1950 and 5.5 in 1968. But in proportion to population, automobile safety was not improving. Motor vehicles killed 22 people out of every 100,000 in 1927, 23 in 1950, and 28 per 100,000 in 1968.

Ecologists also condemned the automobile as a menace to society. They charged that it was the primary cause of air pollution, and they indicted the entire industry for not doing something about it. To some extent the indictments were exaggerated, for the industry had done something about safety and it was doing something about air pollution. To be sure, progress was slow and there was much foot dragging, but it was also true that if the job of improving the environment was to be accomplished, it would be accomplished by government and business, and business would be the chief role-player by far.

16

BUSINESS
AND SOCIETY

In a sense, business is a social institution, and its practitioners, like those in all social institutions, are interrelated with the other groups in society. Businessmen hire workers and workers labor for business. Farmers, in the American culture in contrast to other cultures, are more businessmen than they are tillers of the soil and raisers of livestock. Many professionals—lawyers, accountants, engineers—work for businesses even though they sometimes do not seem to share the interests of businessmen. Politicians, whether statesmen or not, must be interested in how businessmen regard their peers and in turn are regarded by them. And it seems to be part of the duty of the members of the group who for want of a better name are labeled the intellectuals—professors, writers, and journalists—to judge the value and worth of the business world.

Just as all role-players did, businessmen had views on the other groups and these other groups had decided opinions about business and businessmen. These views did not remain fixed over time, but underwent a fundamental metamorphosis, in some cases rapidly and in other cases, gradually. The questions that we will deal with in this section are: What did businessmen think of the other socioeconomic groups? How did the rest of society regard business? And what did businessmen think of themselves?

BUSINESS ATTITUDES TOWARD LABOR
AND VICE VERSA

As we have seen in previous chapters, businessmen's attitudes toward their workers and toward labor unions went through several shattering changes over the course of a century and a half of business history. From the early years and until at least the end of the nineteenth century, most businessmen followed a stern and rigid paternalism in their labor relations. With few exceptions, they abhorred labor unions and did their best to prevent their workers from keeping "bad company." Hours were to be long enough to keep the workers out of mischief. Wages were thought to be set by inviolable economic laws, the chief of which were the law of supply and demand and the wages fund theory. Within the constraints fixed by these laws, management would set wages as a responsible parent determined his children's allowances.

For their part, the older workers were not hostile to paternalism, provided, of course, that the paternalism seemed fair and management seemed kindly disposed, but younger and more restless workers looked with impatience on the whole paternalistic ritual and denounced it as a piece of crude but cunning hypocrisy. Management tried to disregard these troublemakers and insisted that labor-management relations were peaceful and pleasantly satisfactory to all concerned. But this was a proposition that was hardly in tune with the facts. The awful truth was that labor-management relations in the United States were much more violent than they were in any other country.

Yet, businessmen persisted in looking back at the "good old days" through the distorted vision of nostalgia. Long after they had passed into oblivion, M. G. O'Neil of the General Tire Company recalled the last days of paternalism as being especially *gemütlich*: "Many is the time our rubber workers won measures from management. . . . Although the measures cost him money, my father would provide the beer to help the workers celebrate."[1] Charles M. Schwab lapsed into even greater fantasy as he told reporters how he settled the Homestead strike of forty years before: "I said, 'Boys, this won't do. There never was a strike in the world that paid anybody. . . . We must get together, and if you place your confidence in me . . . you will get a square deal.' Well, I settled that strike." When Schwab told that story, the pure paternalism that he expressed had long since expired. It died in the twentieth century as a result of a shift in the nature of the entrepreneur combined with the growth of labor unions, the trials of World War I, and the great depression of the 1930's.

The entrepreneurs of the new century had no sympathy for the naïvete of paternalism. They no longer tried to explain wages in terms of the law of supply and demand. Instead, they put increasing emphasis on productivity as they came to realize that hours of work and productivity had much to do with each other, and that productivity might increase as hours were re-

---

[1] Except where otherwise stated, all quotations in this chapter are taken from Herman E. Krooss, *Executive Opinion: What Business Leaders Said and Thought 1920's–1960's* (Garden City, N.Y.: Doubleday & Company, Inc., 1970).

duced. In any event, what the worker did in his hours away from the job no longer seemed any of his employer's business. The business attitude toward labor unions also changed. To be sure, businessmen continued to be hostile toward unions, but after an unsuccessful and disastrous struggle with the unions during the depressed 1930's, they resigned themselves to accepting union power as an unwelcome but incurable ailment in the body social, economic, and political. Continuing to deny that unions could raise real wages, their only hope was that unions would learn to live responsibly. Most business leaders thought that the most they could expect was what the banker-industrialist, John E. Rovensky, hoped for when he said, "All sound-thinking businessmen today recognize the right of labor to collective bargaining. Unions are an absolute necessity. . . . But what labor needs today is wiser and more far-sighted leadership to avoid making the mistakes employers made when they were in the saddle."

BUSINESSMEN AND GOVERNMENT

The businessman's attitude toward government and those who were involved in politics also underwent a decided transformation largely as a result of the great depression. What finally emerged was much like what emerged in labor-management relations. Political leaders, who had once been in awe of business leaders and business spokesmen, now practiced a studied irreverence. Indeed, some enjoyed tweaking the noses of those who had once been considered their betters. For their part, most businessmen came to realize that government, like the unions, was here to stay.

Although there were many noted exceptions, most businessmen avoided politics, preferring to leave it to the professionals who, they hoped, would conduct government in tune with business interests. Except in times of crisis, that is, in time of war or economic depression, most businessmen were convinced that government was parasitic and served little purpose. Perhaps they would not have agreed altogether with Fred I. Kent, the retired banker, when he wrote, "Government could lapse and if the people were fairly intelligent, and, in general, rightminded, communities could continue—and constructively—provided business did not lapse." But most would have gone almost as far. After all, business and government have always been natural enemies. They have been known to get along, but only when business held the upper hand.

The antagonism that business felt toward government was more a question of power than of economic self-interest. Businessmen liked presidents on the order of McKinley and Coolidge because they knew their place and were willing to follow the leadership of business. It was Coolidge who said, "This is a business country . . . and it wants a business government. I do not mean a government by business nor a government for business, but I do mean a government that will understand business." Other political leaders of the late nineteenth and early twentieth century were altogether sympathetic to business interests, but wanted to deal with them in their own expert fashion without the interference of businessmen. Such, for example, was Boies Penrose, aristocrat and powerful Senator from Pennsylvania, who told a visiting group of prominent Pennsylvania businessmen:

> Gentlemen, I believe in a division of labor in this business of politics. You send us to Congress; we pass laws under the operation of which you make money; you build up great establishments and accumulate wealth, and out of your profits you further contribute to our campaign fund to send us back again to pass more laws to enable you to make more money. It is your duty to help keep us here, and our duty to legislate. You know your end of the game, and not ours, and we know our end of the game, and not yours; and, after you contribute it is your place to go home and keep your mouths shut.[2]

Businessmen liked Coolidge and respected Penrose and until the depression of the 1930's there seemed little doubt but that government officials would do what was right for business. They would cooperate with business, and business would cooperate with them. The arrangement was considered so tight that historians have gone so far as to claim that the Progressive movement, which once was considered so anti-business, was really a concoction of a group of businessmen led by Morgan partner, George W. Perkins.

But this changed. With the depression of the thirties came Franklin D. Roosevelt and the New Deal. At first, driven desperate by the traumatic experiences of the gloomy years, businessmen welcomed Roosevelt, but as the economy began to show some signs of slow recovery, he lost his fascination. For despite all their disclaimers, businessmen were not really ready for any drastic change in economic theory or economic policy; they had no reason to change drastically. Within a year, the fire of enthusiasm that had at first greeted the New Deal died to a thin wisp of smoke. From then through the Kennedy years, the skirmishes between business and government continued, broken only by the peace that ruled during the Eisenhower administration.

The antipathy of business toward government that gradually expanded into apparently irreparable hostility puzzled many commentators who made the mistake of thinking that human behavior was dictated solely or primarily by *economic* self-interest. In 1935, William Allen White summed up this puzzlement in an editorial in his *Emporia Gazette:*

[2] James E. Watson, *As I Knew Them* (Indianapolis, Ind.: Bobbs-Merrill Company, 1926), pp. 54–55.

A curious phenomenon of the last two years is this: as the rich get richer, they have hated Roosevelt more bitterly. In 1933, when he was proposing really basic economic changes, hardly a voice was raised in opposition. Now that profits are jumping ahead and industrial activity is almost at 1929 levels, the rich are hollering their heads off against Roosevelt. The probable explanation . . . now that profits are restored and they have something to lose, they are bitter against all hint of change.

Again in the 1960's, the noted economist Seymour Harris expressed his astonishment at the business reaction to President Kennedy: "President Kennedy," he said, "did much more for business than President Eisenhower ever dared. . . . Businessmen should have revered him. . . . They never had it better."

But the matter was much more complicated than White in the 1930's or Harris in the 1960's made it out to be. The business hostility toward President Roosevelt and President Kennedy was not simply a display of peevishness. What business leaders found repulsive about the New Deal and the Kennedy administration was the philosophy and the individuals who were thought to be responsible for that philosophy. It was not so much the ends that drove men to bitter words; it was the means for achieving the ends.

Businessmen did not have any rapport with the New Deal's Brain Trust or with the New Frontier's intellectuals, and the lack of sympathy was reciprocated. Early in the New Deal, banker Eugene Meyer asserted, "The nation's most immediate danger lies in the inexperience of the young intellectuals who are now directing the policy of the administration." Again in the 1960's a leading manufacturer denied that business was hostile to Washington, but he went on to say, "There are many people in Washington with no business experience who are inclined to do a lot of loose talking. A professor who has never met a payroll can create the wrong impression."

THE BUSINESSMAN AS PAINTED BY HIMSELF
AND BY THE INTELLECTUALS

Businessmen believed they knew more about some things than the intellectuals did. But then, businessmen had always looked upon themselves with more respect than was accorded to them by the intellectuals.

Among businessmen, there was little question but that the American capitalistic system produced maximum freedom and maximum individual welfare. Nor was there much doubt in their minds that they were the chief contributors to the maintenance of the system. Over the course of time, however, self-praising opinions were stated more modestly.

In the mid-nineteenth century, business writers praised the "merchant," while treating other occupations with contempt. Scoville, the author of a garrulous book of business anecdotes,[3] pitied a certain merchant who had "been reduced to the necessity of accepting a clerkship in the State Department," thinking it "about as low and as desperate a position as a man can reach to hold an office in any one of the departments at Washington." Scoville also had his misgivings about the legal profession, which most people regarded with great respect. "Lawyers are respectable," he admitted, "if they conduct their business properly; but in this community [New York] they rarely raise their heads, unless so lucky as to become patronized by merchants."

Even earlier, James Sullivan in his *The Path to Riches* wrote:

> Every member of civil society, has a clear right to gain all the property which vigilance and industry, regulated by the laws of the state, can bestow upon him. Every thing he acquires in this way, advances the interest of the public, and shows him to be deserving of applause. Such a man, is the just man spoken of in the sacred writings. . . . Commerce . . . is the life and support of civilized states; and the great medium of communication between people of different climates. It . . . will finally, form a chain of confidence and friendship through the world.[4]

To be sure, these were the sentiments of business writers, and business writers have always been more brash than the businessmen themselves. But business leaders were also often arrogant and patronizing. "Success in business," observed Cyrus McCormick, at mid-century "is the foundation of *everything*."

Not everyone agreed with McCormick or with the views of the business writers. Emerson, Thoreau, Parker, and other intellectuals had already decried the business world's mores and denounced its materialism. Parker wrote:

> The Hebres devil that so worried Job is gone, so is the brutal devil that awed our fathers. But the devil of the nineteenth century is still extant. He has gone into trade and advertises in the papers. He makes money; the world is poorer by his wealth. He can build a church out of his gains, to have his morality, his christianity, preached in it, and call that the gospel. He sends rum and missionaries to the same barbarians, the one to damn, the other to save, both for his own advantage, for his patron saint is Judas, the first saint who made money out of Christ. He is not forecasting to discern effects in causes, nor skillful to create wealth, only spry in the scramble for what others have made. In politics he wants a government that will ensure his dividends; so asks what is good for him, but ill for the rest. He knows no right only power; no man but self; no God but his calf of gold.

---

[3] Joseph A. Scoville, *The Old Merchants of New York City* (New York, 1862, 1885, 1889). By Walter Barrett [pseud.].

[4] James Sullivan, *The Path to Riches* (Boston: J. Thomas and E. T. Andrews, 1791), p. 8.

Ultra-conservatives also joined in the chorus of business criticism. In the 1870's, William Graham Sumner, a leading exponent of Social Darwinism and laissez faire, did not appear to distrust business in general, but he did distrust big business. "We have got to have a struggle with the great corporations before we get through. . . . We have not yet learned to charter corporations and still exercise the necessary control over them in the public interest." Toward the end of the century, Henry Adams, who thought the twelfth-century man's finest hour, charged that the depression of 1893 was a Wall Street plot, by that "dark, mysterious, crafty, wicked, rapacious, and tyrannical power . . . to rob and oppress and enslave the people."[5]

The early twentieth century began the golden age in the status of business, and in the 1920's, the golden age reached its peak. As William Feather of *Nation's Business* wrote in 1926, "There is no doubt that the American businessman is the foremost hero of the American public today."

For a time during the Progressive Era, business and the business system had been pummeled by criticism. So able had this criticism been that some business leaders had found their own faith considerably shaken. But by the twenties, this had disappeared. By then almost everyone was happy with business. Intellectuals who had always been the first to challenge its hegemony offered little opposition. The anti-business writers had all but disappeared. A few of the academicians and lawyers remained critical, but not bitterly so, and articulate though they were, they were drowned out in the general swell of business adulation. Many of the novelists of the 1920's did throw darts at the business world, but for the most part they were criticizing the whole American culture, not just business. As for the political world, the *Wall Street Journal* summed it up in a 1925 editorial, "Never before, here or anywhere else has a government been so completely fused with business."

Businessmen, although amazed and to some extent awed at the height to which their prestige had climbed, agreed for the most part with the admiration that the public showered on them. They agreed with Paul Mazur of Lehman Brothers when he said, "While industry dominates the thought of America, there need be no fears. It will continue to write the most significant pages of American history."

Things changed with the depression of the 1930's. As unemployment rose and prices fell, the public's attitude toward business changed from extreme to extreme. And as profits declined, business bewilderment increased, and businessmen lost faith in themselves and even in the system in general. Many business leaders confessed that they had no idea of what was going on, and a number, out of desperation or delight, insisted that what the country needed was a Mussolini.

[5]Quoted in Samuel Rezneck, *Business Depressions and Financial Panics* (New York: Greenwood Publishing Corporation, 1968), pp. 137, 177.

But business prestige, if not popularity, and businessmen's confidence in themselves is a function of economic prosperity. This was most clearly evidenced by the rapid rise in the stock of business that occurred when the economy entered another period of strong growth in the years after World War II. By the 1960's, businessmen had recovered much of the ground that they had lost in the 1930's. Said Lynn A. Townsend of Chrysler: "Business is now occupying a higher place of respect and importance in the minds of Americans than it has in many years." To which one could add a postscript by Charles G. Mortimer of General Foods: "This is a business country. Business is what makes the mare go in these United States."

Once again, business was assuming too much. Although a few writers thought that business had more than regained the position of power it had held in the 1920's, business leaders and business spokesmen should not have been under any such delusion. Certainly, businessmen had not regained the veneration they had received in the twenties. There was none of the awe-inspired hero worship that had prevailed in the days of Ford and Gary. Nor was there the bitterness that had prevailed during the depression. The attitude now was one of indifference. A survey of public opinion conducted in the spring of 1966 showed that almost everyone thought that "free enterprise had made the country great." Almost as many thought that when business profited, the country prospered. About three out of four thought that business paid fair wages, but just as many thought that business was a dog-eat-dog proposition, and almost half of those surveyed believed that "most businessmen would do anything for a buck." In short, the public believed that business was a grimy, but necessary, affair.

BUSINESS IDEOLOGY

In addition to including what businessmen thought about the other social blocs and what they thought about businessmen, the subject "business and society" should certainly include the businessman's philosophy and beliefs and his ideas about society and society's problems.

Most of what people think they know about what businessmen think comes not from businessmen themselves, but from business spokesmen—trade association executives, newspaper columnists, free lance writers, and advertising agencies. Businessmen don't say very much for publication, but it is the business of business spokesmen to get something into print. Given this propensity and lack of propensity for articulation, it is easy to jump to the conclusion that trade association thinking constitutes a business ideology. But the truth of the matter is that there has never been any such thing as a business ideology. Webster defines an ideology as "a manner of content of thinking characteristic of a group, an individual, or a culture." At no time has there been a content of thinking, a set of beliefs, or a body of opinion to which all businessmen subscribed. To be sure, there have always been some opinions which the majority of businessmen shared, and it is therefore possible to generalize about modal opinions and how they changed over time. But this is not an ideology, except by the loosest of definitions.

Businessmen differ from each other in too many ways to permit a solid consensus. Businessmen come in all sizes and shapes. There are big businessmen and little businessmen and "liberal" businessmen and "conservative" businessmen. The variety of differences in occupation, in function, in mental capacity, in personality, and in social background made for massive differences in opinions on economic issues as well as on the general philosophy of life. Indeed, the differences in outlook, philosophy, and opinion were greater among business leaders than among most other groups, including farmers, workers, doctors, and teachers.

There are at least half a dozen ways of cataloguing business leaders. They may, of course, be divided according to age, education, and size of business. But their profession or specialty, their type of business, and the ownership stake they held in the firms they managed had more to do with the way they thought about economic matters.

The professions and jobs in which executives spent most of their careers deeply colored their economic philosophy and economic opinions. Lawyers, for example, thought differently about economic issues than did the company heads who came up through the marketing department, finance, or general administration.

Differences also existed between the professional managers and the businessmen who owned their own firms, but these differences were exhibited not so much in what they thought, but in the way they thought and the ways in which they expressed their thoughts. Hired executives had to subordinate themselves to the organization. They had to be more tactful and more literate. They were generalists more often than they were specialists, and they tended to be people-manipulators rather than thing-manipulators. The owner-manager could at the expense of public relations be an intellectual barbarian with poor human relations, because he was directly responsible only to himself.

Just as there were differences between professional managers and owners, so the opinions of bankers and financiers were significantly different from those of their counterparts in manufacturing and retailing. Bankers were more conservative, and much more faithful to orthodox economic theory. They were more loyal to laissez faire and sound money than were the industrialists and merchants.

It must be evident by this time that with all these differences and more in outlook and approach, any conclusions about what businessmen believed should be cautiously stated and carefully qualified. When in this chapter we say that most businessmen shared an opinion, we are stating a belief, not an indisputable fact. And "most" may mean anything from 50 percent to over 90 percent. There is no doubt, for example, that almost all nineteenth-century businessmen believed that the federal government should, except in time of war, always balance its budget. But probably only a bare majority of twentieth-century businessmen hold the same opinion. It should also be remembered that the only businessmen that we can talk about are the business leaders, for business leaders are the only businessmen who provide us with any data, and what they have left us is sparse enough. One final caveat: the scope of businessmen's interests on any economic issue was always limited by what they considered urgent at that time. Frequently, therefore, publicly expressed opinion was the minority opinion, for on any given issue, the majority of businessmen was more silent than vocal.

BUSINESS BELIEFS AND OBJECTIVES IN THE NINETEENTH CENTURY

Parsimony, thrift, prudence, foresight, industry, paternalism, and economic success were the traditional virtues of the nineteenth-century business world, and they were also the traditional virtues of the country at large. But to the first three of these virtues, business leaders gave more lip service than steadfast loyalty. In their private lives, they may have been parsimonious as, for example, Rockefeller was when young, but their business lives were something else again. Risk and daring characterized their strategy. Morgan summed it up when he said, "Show me someone who has never been in debt, and I'll show you someone who has never amounted to anything."

Businessmen's ideas on objectives and motives revealed a similar inconsistency. Most businessmen probably believed that maximizing profits was their most important objective. When business units were small and aggregate profits were low and hard to achieve, businessmen naturally put more emphasis on maximizing profits than they would later when profits were relatively high and easier to come by. But the profit motive was at no time more than part of the entrepreneurs' incentive. They wanted an occupation to enable them to pass the time without suffering the torments of boredom.[6] Ambition, power, and the excitement of playing the game all played an important role in their motivation. What distinguished the great innovators was their individuality, the inventiveness, their enterprise, their determination, and their administrative capacity. The motives that inspired most of them were not particularly admirable. Indeed, they could not be,

---

[6] J. W. Gough, *The Rise of the Entrepreneur* (New York: Schocken Books, 1969), p. 289.

for innovation is by definition a deviation from accepted mores and customary ways of doing things.

And yet, nineteenth-century business leaders had some concept of social responsibility. Admittedly, it was attached to self-interest, and it was a
vaguely defined notion, but anyone's definition of social responsibility was
and is an exercise in vagary. Nineteenth-century businessmen believed that
business was the only creator of wealth, that large profits were proof of a
major contribution to society, that the building of a large enterprise was
a highly moral activity, and that if business prospered, the arts and sciences
would also prosper. But seemingly concrete as they were, all these beliefs
could be expressed in different ways. To Henry O. Havemeyer, the sugar
tycoon, in 1899, "Business is not a philanthropy. . . . I do not care two cents
for your ethics. I don't know enough of them to apply them. . . . It is right
to get all out of a business that you possibly can." George Baer, coal, iron,
and railroad executive, followed the paternalistic route with his oft-quoted
axiom that the rights of the workingman would be taken care of by those
to whom God had given control of the country's properties. But it would be
difficult to determine whether these remarks portrayed the average business
leader's feelings any better than the less often quoted ideas of Abram
Hewitt, the iron master. Hewitt proposed to create an annual fund of
$1 million by a levy of five cents a ton on anthracite coal. The fund would
be spent for schoolhouses, hospitals, and reading rooms to help convert "a
hell upon earth" into a "terrestrial and a Christian paradise."[7]

Businessmen's opinions on such economic problems as the business
cycle, money and credit, laissez faire, government regulation, and fiscal policy were almost as ambivalent as their views on business objectives.

The ambivalence in the business cycle was that prosperity was most
welcome, but it also had most unwelcome results, for to the businessmen
of the nineteenth century recessions and depressions were the inevitable reaction to prosperity. Bad times were the product of the same inherent characteristics of human nature that produced prosperity: a spirit of overtrading, speculation, and extravagance that led to overexpansion and overtrading
in business and an overuse of credit, an oversupply of money, and a temporary overproduction for the economy in general.

Stephen Girard attributed the depression of 1819 to "the great facilities which our Company Chartered Banks have afforded to several of our
merchants, traders, and mechanics, who with their fictitious capital have
acted imprudently."[8] In the depression of 1837, a Business Men's Convention deplored the "recent haste to be rich." It recommended a return to

---

[7]Rezneck, *Business Depressions and Financial Panics*, p. 137.
[8]*Ibid.*, p. 34.

industry and economy. It deplored the "overaction in all departments of business and the rapid growth among all classes of luxurious habits."[9]

In every subsequent depression, 1857, 1873, 1884, and 1893, the prevalent theme was that business had overextended itself and now had to pay the price for its debauch. Although they did not use the modern figures of speech, most businessmen were convinced that dips in the economy were the result of "overheating" and "unsustainable growth." They believed in an escalator theory of the business cycle: what goes up must come down and it must come down as far as it previously went up.

All through the nineteenth century, too, businessmen paid lip service to laissez faire, but ignored and violated it in their behavior. Businessmen regularly insisted that government should let business alone and just as regularly insisted that the government impose tariffs, regulate the railroad industry through the ICC, and subsidize the merchant marine. Along with most of the population, businessmen believed that the government economy was no different from that of an average householder. Like John Doe, it could not spend more than its income without going bankrupt. It was imperative, therefore, that governments balance their budgets and run surpluses to pay off their debts. Yet, businessmen also abhorred taxes, but without taxes budgets could not be balanced. The way out of this dilemma in the nineteenth century as in the twentieth was to support indirect, regressive taxes—tariffs in the nineteenth, sales taxes in the twentieth.

BUSINESS BELIEFS IN THE TWENTIETH CENTURY

Some of the nineteenth-century businessmen's beliefs continued to be held in the twentieth century, but many of them changed fundamentally. By the middle of the 1900's, business leaders' opinions on motives, laissez faire, competition, money and credit, and the business cycle were sharply different from what had been in vogue in the middle 1800's. The change manifested itself as early as the 1890's, but it came into full bloom in the Progressive Era of the early 1900's. Many prominent businessmen led by George Perkins, Morgan partner, and Elbert Gary of U.S. Steel came to the support of a "New Nationalism" that recognized the federal government's importance in the economy and encouraged its intervention. Many business leaders, but by no means all, emphasized cooperation under federal regulation rather than old-style competition. Admittedly, businessmen had never been enamored of competition, but they had always given it oral support. Now, even that had been eliminated.

[9]Harvey J. Wexler, "Business Opinion and Economic Theory," *Explorations in Entrepreneurial History*, Vol. 1, No. 3, March 1949.

By the 1920's when business reached the height of its prestige, business leaders, carried away by their exalted stature, enunciated a set of opinions that were far removed from the objectives and beliefs that had always been considered traditional to the business way of life. It became fashionable to deemphasize the profit motive and to make much of the role of stewardship and the objective of service. Business leaders became convinced that they were participating in a revolution in which progress was taking place along three main lines: they thought that business management was becoming progressively more professional; they believed that there was a vast improvement in the moral tone and ethics of business, and they had no doubt that the motives that guided businessmen and the objectives they wished to attain were much loftier than those that had guided the "Robber Barons" of the nineteenth century.

Commentators on the new ethics believed that businessmen had developed a decided sense of responsibility toward their organization, to its investors, and to its customers, and some sense of responsibility toward employees. But the main achievement of the new ethics was a revised attitude toward competition. "Cooperation rather than competition" became a watchword of the new outlook. Few businessmen were foolhardy enough to criticize competition openly, for competition was one of the sacrosancts in the American value system. Criticism usually took the form of throwing stones at "unfair competition." But what exactly was meant by unfair competition remained a puzzle. It was generally accepted that blatantly acquisitive or predatory practices were "unfair." But many businessmen went beyond this and included sales below cost, use of loss leaders, and attempts to steal customers or employees.

THE DEPRESSION OF THE 1930's

The confidence that businessmen felt in themselves and in the future evaporated in the depression. The prevalent attitude was one of frustration, helplessness, and bewilderment. The executives who had seemed so competent a few years before abandoned most of their prior opinions as they sought to find a way out of the sea of economic confusion into which the depression had thrown them.

For the moment, business forgot its involvement with service and with stewardship as it struggled to maintain a few dollars of profits. In labor relations, businessmen forsook the high-wage doctrine and settled down to do battle with the unions. Self-interest had assumed primary importance as business leaders wrestled with the depression.

Businessmen were far from agreeing about what caused the depression or what could be done to bring prosperity back. Their widely divergent social and economic philosophies resulted in a whole congeries of explanations. In the previous severe depression, that of 1921, these differences in philosophy had been subordinated to a secondary role. At that time the nature of depression seemed clear, and businessmen had no trouble in arriving at a consensus. It was agreed that the war had inflated everything, and all that had to be done to get the economy rolling was to tighten money and deflate prices, wages, and taxes. Such a consensus was impossible in 1930. Prices were not inflated; federal taxes were low; and, if one took expressed opinions seriously, wages were not too high. Given the divergent philosophies, the area of possible agreement was extremely small. Indeed, it was confined to only two aspects of the depression problem. A number of businessmen in all groups put the onus for the depression on the extravagance of the speculative boom. Almost without exception, they believed that no relief was possible unless the federal budget was balanced. Beyond this, each group—bankers, manufacturers, and merchants—framed its own rationale, and within each group, there was a series of variations on the main theme.

With few exceptions, bankers were disciples of classical business cycle theory. They continued to believe that depressions were the inevitable result of the excesses and mistakes of the previous boom. International factors, such as the war debts and tariffs, loomed large in their explanations. But the chief cause of the existing economic debacle was that "the debauch of speculation reached its climax and stopped." According to Melvin Traylor, Chicago banker, "August 1, 1914 was the beginning of the depression. . . . One of the biggest things was a watered state of mind in which we all thought we were richer than we were." Otto H. Kahn of Kuhn, Loeb & Company joined Traylor in thinking that "the prolonged speculative mania" had put "an unbearable strain on credit."

Like the bankers, many industrialists thought that depressions were inevitable. "These disturbances," said L. F. Loree of the Delaware and Hudson Railroad, "have occurred intermittently and usually run three to six years." When the inevitable came, business leaders, in the words of P. W. Litchfield of Goodyear Tire, explained that "the major causes of the depression might properly be lumped together under the embracing title of extravagance." Twenty-five years later, Litchfield still thought: "We had gone through an era of prosperity and with people as optimistic about the morrow as Americans are, many forgot the age-old principles of thrift and saving, were living beyond their means, buying things they did not need."

Most of the thinking that blamed the depression on extravagance and speculation was a repetition of the "unsustainable prosperity" doctrine that had been so popular among bankers during the boom years. This "what goes up must come down" analysis was in back of many of the pleas for thrift that were offered during the early 1930's. It is not easy to explain how serious people could call for less spending at a time when total income had been cut in half, but opinions in praise of thrift were expressed over and over again in letters to the *Times* and in the comments of business and political leaders.

Bankers also took time to reproach the Federal Reserve System because it had followed too easy a money policy in the years before the crash. Albert H. Wiggin of the Chase Bank, for example, thought that "a stiffer policy on rates and a somewhat different open-market policy might have reduced the extremes to which the speculation went." Charles E. Mitchell of the National City thought that the Federal Reserve would have turned to tight money much sooner if it had it to do over again. George Davison of the Central Hanover regarded it as "quite probable" that "if rediscount rates had been raised a little faster and with less talk, it might have checked much speculation," and might have stopped "the inordinate rise of all prices including securities."[10] J. P. Morgan said, "The failure of the Federal Reserve Board to take the necessary measures to control the inflation in time encouraged the speculative frenzy which carried the market quotations out of bounds."

Unlike the bankers, few industrialists and few merchants were infatuated with classical theory. They were in awe of it, for they had been taught that it was the only true economic theory. But they did not understand it, and they did not sympathize with it. The nonfinancial community found it especially difficult to swallow two of the most important planks in orthodox economics: that competition was "good" and that easy money was "bad." Most, but not all, industrialists and most merchants were not at all sure that competition would automatically produce the greatest good for the greatest number. Industrialists argued heatedly for the suspension of the antitrust laws, so that production would be regulated to "meet demand." Merchants, too, talked about overproduction and underconsumption, and some spoke knowingly about oversaving.

Much of the thinking on overproduction was a holdover from the era of prosperity, when it became fashionable to think that production was a solved problem and that distribution—how to sell the goods that the production mill turned out—was now the great puzzle. Some manufacturers and many merchants came to believe that there was an upper limit to human wants. The limit had been reached by miraculous increases in production. Unless production could be curtailed, a perpetual flood of goods would glut the market. In businessmen's eyes, the market place had lost its attractiveness and turned into a place of gloom. Competition, which in prosperity had seemed so barbaric and so tiresome, now appeared to be an albatross that hampered businessmen's efforts to remain solvent. Most of the business

---

[10] All prices did not rise inordinately. The price level was actually lower in 1929 than in 1924.

leaders—conservatives and liberals alike—vied with each other in thinking up plans for eliminating its strangling effects. All the steel leaders and most of the oil producers bemoaned the overproduction caused by competition. Textile manufacturers, retailers, and others who thought that the demand for their product was inelastic talked to each other about unfair competition. The Chamber of Commerce and other business organizations led a movement to relax the antitrust laws in order to permit businessmen to cooperate about prices and production. Only the largest automobile manufacturers, the big bankers, and a few nonconformist retailers objected to the current trend in the direction of a planned society in a mature economy. For their part the bankers continued to warn against easy money, government spending, and inflation.

As the depression deepened, many lost faith in democracy and yearned for a leader, a Mussolini, "who could bring order out of chaos." They welcomed Roosevelt in his first 100 days, but he quickly lost their allegiance as he failed to balance the budget, an objective that most businessmen considered a *sine qua non* for economic recovery.[11] Toward the end of the depression, business and government became involved in a struggle over which group was to control the seats of power. The administration and business each insisted that it was arguing over the way to economic recovery, but in reality the contest was over matters of principle that had little to do with self-interest. Most of the New Dealers had an opportunity to vocalize their antagonism toward business, and they made the most of it by punishing business for its past, present, and future sins. For their part, many businessmen spent their time in worrying over the future of the "American Way of Life" and the "Free Enterprise System," and in expressing their indignation with the uncertainties created by bureaucracy.

WORLD WAR II AND LATER

The wrestling with the Roosevelt administration came to an end at the outbreak of World War II, for it was then that the New Deal died and was quietly buried. It was then too that business began to recover from its bankrupt reputation. Industry performed magnificently as the economy

---

[11]We hasten to reiterate that there were voices that differed articulately and vociferously with what was clearly the majority position on the need for thrift and a balanced budget. Foster and Catchings recommended spending in an article, "Must We Reduce Our Standard of Living?" Marriner S. Eccles, president of the First Security Corporation of Ogden, Utah, and later chairman of the Federal Reserve System, told a Senate committee "Too large a share of income goes into the hands of savers." He scoffed at the worship of a balanced budget. As he explained, "Experience has demonstrated that the budget cannot be balanced in severe depressions. . . . I contend that the volume of government expenditures should be increased in a depression."

burst from the gloomy years of the depression. Between 1939 and 1945, real per capita disposable income rose by almost 50 percent. Business deserved some credit for this and credit was given.

With the end of the war, there emerged a more realistic set of business beliefs than those that had prevailed in the 1920's and 1930's. There was less disparity of opinion in the 1950's than there had been in the 1920's and especially during the 1930's. The spectrum from the most conservative to the most liberal had narrowed. The strategy and tactics, the structure and organization of business also changed greatly, but not so much the objectives. It was no longer fashionable to downgrade the profit motive, but on the other hand, there was no headlong flight from the concept of service, as it had been called in the 1920's. In the years after World War II, most businessmen—bankers, manufacturers, retailers, and those in transportation —sought an equilibrium between profits and that elusive, undefinable something known as social responsibility. Only a minority—those who were the products of the 1920's—persisted in taking a wary view of the profit motive. An even smaller minority regarded the objective of social responsibility as a pious ambiguity.

This is not to say, however, that this minority inexorably followed its own self-interest measured in dollars and cents. Businessmen have probably never done so, and there were many instances in the fifty years after 1920 when they did not do so. At least one clear lesson emerged from the often petty quarrel between the New Deal and business. That was that most businessmen would strenuously resist behavior and action that threatened to jeopardize their freedom, even though such behavior might be conducive to economic growth and higher profits. "On questions of principle," Thurman Arnold once wrote, "great masses of people will always take sides. Which side they take depends not on self-interest, but on the chance of association of temperament which makes them emotionally responsible to one set of symbols or another."

Critics of business were the first to agree that some major changes had occurred in the business system, but they thought that these changes redounded to society's disadvantage rather than to its advantage. They charged that businessmen were no longer producers, but sellers of goods that no one really wanted. In one of the popular phrases of the day, they had switched from being manipulators of things to being manipulators of people. For their part, businessmen acknowledged that marketing and human relations had become more important than production and finance. The challenge a generation ago, it was said, was mastery over the physical environment; in the modern era, the challenge was mastery over men. Thus, they were not in essential disagreement with this part of the critics' brief, but they couched their agreement in a way that suggested approbation rather than disapproval.

Critics also charged that the separation of ownership from control that characterizes the collective nature of modern business made management a self-perpetuating oligarchy with responsibility to no one and with powers that were not legitimate. Most businessmen did not understand the indictment, and those who did understand it were equally mystified. They insisted that professional management, with or without a large ownership interest, had become a part of modern corporate life like big business and small stockholders. They chose to explain their legitimacy by arguing that professional management acted just as the owner-entrepreneur did, that is, in the best interests of the owners. The great difference was that now the owners were a broad and diverse group, instead of a small and homogeneous one.

Regardless of what the critics said, the mid-century executive had far more hostages to fortune than his predecessors had. He was responsible not only to himself, but to government, labor, the consumer, and sometimes even to the stockholders. He, therefore, had to be more sophisticated and, as the modern word would have it, more knowledgeable than the executive at the beginning of the century. His level of executive education was much higher, and he depended much more on his advisors and his ancillaries to give him their thoughts, which he had to weigh carefully because the necessity of "keeping in touch with the field" was much more intense.[12]

HOW INFLUENTIAL WAS BUSINESS OPINION?

Whatever the extent of the change in business opinion, it was less than that of other groups. Labor union leaders, whether they liked it or not, had to change. Following a conservative line that got them nowhere, they had no power or influence in the 1920's. Their strategy became more adventuresome during the depression. But once they had achieved a more secure place in the sun, they again became steadfast in holding to their opinions. Farmers, having learned that most people found unpalatable the Bryanesque prescription for prosperity through governmental manipulation of the currency and coinage, deemphasized inflation and easy money and adopted a new tactic of having the government restrict production. Academic economic theorists were the most flexible of all, concocting a "new economics" every ten or twenty years.

Businessmen had a much less clear view of their objectives than other groups. Labor union leaders wanted, in the words of Samuel Gompers, "more and more, now and now." Farmers wanted their "fair share of the

[12]One management service estimated that an executive in 1900 could keep informed by reading forty-five minutes a day, but that it took two hours in 1920, three in 1940, and four in 1960.

national income." Politicians wanted to get elected. Academic economists were ostensibly interested in finding out how man could best use his scarce resources for maximum want satisfaction. But businessmen were not sure whether their objective was to maximize profits, or to act as stewards, or to be socially responsible, or to hold the organization together. Other members of society were not nearly so mixed up about business objectives. They knew, whether it was true or not, that businessmen were out to make as much money as possible, or as the economist expresses it, to maximize profits.

The businessman's confusion about his objectives was one reason why business opinion had indifferent influence on society. Most businessmen still believed firmly in the bourgeois values of industry, thrift, profit-making, economic freedom, the superiority of the market place, and law and order. But they were at times just as much confused about the exact meaning of these virtues as they were about their objectives.

During the prosperity years of the 1920's, there is no doubt that most Americans shared business' respect for middle-class values. Just as they had in the nineteenth century, most of the country denounced the radicals and disregarded the conservatives. Whether this was because of business or because of the appeal of middle-class values is another question. But in any event, the depression put the faith to a severe test. It was no longer so plain that industry and thrift paid off. Unemployment made a mockery of economic freedom, and it seemed to more than a handful of Americans that the automatic market place had stripped its gears. Even among businessmen, there was much questioning and back-sliding. Old words lost their meaning as new philosophies came to the fore. Conservatism, which had meant a distrust of change, a belief that when it was not necessary to change, it was necessary not to change, came to mean the philosophy in which businessmen and business spokesmen were assumed to believe. Liberalism, which had meant laissez faire and individualism, came to mean just the opposite. Liberals were now defined to include those who favored more government intervention, those who empathized with labor and warmly supported labor unions, and those who spoke more about the cost of living and overproduction than about scarce resources and productivity.

Once the reality of the depression was accepted, conservatism fell out of fashion and liberalism took its place. A philosophy that appealed to the young usurped the philosophy that still appealed to most of their elders. In the process, business lost most of the influence it had once possessed, and its position of power was assumed by government. In recent years, there has been some return to the older faith. The much discussed "turn to the right" is symptomatic of the renaissance of middle-class ideals. But a full turn to the right does not seem to be in the cards in the near future. The foundations of the conservative structure were too shaken by the trauma of the depression. Business as the chief repository of the old middle-class values, is, therefore, in an ambivalent position. It has regained some of its lost prestige, but judged by the prevalent trends in politics, the course of legislation, the success of the labor unions, and the general indifference to "free enterprise," the majority of business opinion has little influence over general opinion or over the general course of events. Moreover, businessmen have not made an unqualified return to the faith themselves and are therefore hampered in increasing their prestige, for as the late Professor Schumpeter was at great pains to point out, the prestige of American capitalism and the American businessman varies directly with the prestige of middle-class values.

BIBLIOGRAPHY

A NOTE ON SOURCES

It would be impractical, if not impossible, to list a complete bibliography in business history. A selected list of books in business history published in the last decade alone covers four printed pages, single space in fine print. Moreover, a bibliography would not serve the purpose of a guide to further reading. What is more important, there are some excellent bibliographies already in existence. Lorna Daniells, *Studies in Enterprise* (Cambridge, Mass.: Harvard University Press, 1957) was further extended in the summer issues of the *Business History Review*, 1959–62 and the autumn issues, 1963–64. Henrietta Larson, *Guide to Business History* (Cambridge, Mass.: Harvard University Press, 1948) is indispensable. A recent article by Robert W. Lovett, *American Economic and Business History Information Sources* (Detroit, Mich.: Gale Research Company, 1971) and an article by Ralph W. Hidy (Business History Review, Vol. 44, No. 4, Winter 1970) bring the literature up to date.

In this note on sources we have included no references to histories of individual firms, and we have omitted many sources already cited in the footnotes. With due apologies for these omissions we have limited the following to the books and articles that we have found most helpful.

BOOKS

Alasco, Johannes, *Intellectual Capitalism: A Study of Changing Ownership and Control in Modern American Society* (New York: World University Press, 1950).

Allen, Frederick Lewis, *The Great Pierpont Morgan* (New York: Harper & Row, 1949).

Atherton, Lewis E., *The Pioneer Merchant in Mid-America* (Columbia, Mo.: University of Missouri Press, 1939).

————, *The Southern Country Store* (Baton Rouge, La.: Louisiana State University Press, 1949).

Bailyn, Bernard, *The New England Merchants in the Seventeenth Century* (New York: Harper & Row, 1964).

Barger, Harold, *Distribution's Place in the American Economy Since 1869* (Princeton, N.J.: Princeton University Press, 1956).

Baxter, W. T., *The House of Hancock: Business in Boston, 1724–1775* (Cambridge, Mass.: Harvard University Press, 1945).

Bruchey, Stuart W. (ed.), *Robert Oliver, Merchant of Baltimore, 1783–1819* (New York: Harcourt, Brace & World, Inc., 1966).

Chamberlain, John, *The Enterprising Americans: A Business History of the United States* (New York: Harper & Row, 1963).

Chandler, Alfred D., Jr., *Henry Varnum Poor* (Cambridge, Mass.: Harvard University Press, 1956).

————, *Strategy and Structure: Chapters in the History of the Industrial Enterprise* (Cambridge, Mass.: Massachusetts Institute of Technology Press, 1962).

————, (ed.), *Giant Enterprise: Ford, General Motors, and the Automobile Industry* (New York: Harcourt, Brace & World, Inc., 1964).

————, (ed.), *The Railroads: The Nation's First Big Business* (New York: Harcourt, Brace & World, Inc., 1965).

Clark, Victor S., *History of Manufactures in the United States*, 3 vols. (New York: McGraw-Hill Book Company, Inc., 1929).

Cochran, Thomas C., and William Miller, *Age of Enterprise* (New York: The Macmillan Company, 1941).

Cochran, Thomas C., *Railroad Leaders 1845–1890: The Business Mind in Action* (Cambridge, Mass.: Harvard University Press, 1953).

Corey, Lewis, *The House of Morgan* (New York: Grosset and Dunlap, Publishers, 1930).

Davis, Joseph S., *Essays in the Earlier History of American Corporations* (Cambridge, Mass.: Harvard University Press, 1917) .

Dewing, Arthur S., *Corporate Promotions and Reorganizations* (Cambridge, Mass.: Harvard University Press, 1924).

Diamond, Sigmund, *The Reputation of the American Business Man* (Cambridge, Mass.: Harvard University Press, 1955).

Edwards, George W., *The Evolution of Finance Capitalism* (New York: Longmans, Green and Co., 1938).

Edwards, James Don, *History of Public Accounting in the United States* (East Lansing, Mich.: Michigan State University, 1960).

Gras, N. S. B., *Business and Capitalism, an Introduction to Business History* (New York: Appleton-Century-Crofts, Inc., 1939).

————, and Henrietta M. Larson, *Casebook in Business History* (New York: Appleton-Century-Crofts, Inc., 1939).

Greef, Albert O., *The Commercial Paper House in The United States* (Cambridge, Mass.: Harvard University Press, 1938) .

Harrington, Virginia D., *The New York Merchant on the Eve of the Revolution* (New York: Columbia University Press, 1935).

Hedges, James B., *The Browns of Providence Plantations: The Colonial Years* (Cambridge, Mass.: Harvard University Press, 1952).

————, *The Browns of Providence Plantations: The Nineteenth Century* (Providence, R.I.: Brown University Press, 1968).

Holbrook, Stewart H., *The Age of the Moguls* (Garden City, N.Y.: Doubleday and Company, Inc., 1954).

Hughes, J. R. T., *The Vital Few* (Boston: Houghton Mifflin Co., 1966).

Hutchinson, William T., *Cyrus Hall McCormick*, 2 vols. (New York: Appleton-Century-Crofts, 1930, 1935).

Jones, Eliot, *The Trust Problem in the United States* (New York: The Macmillan Company, 1929).

Jones, Fred M., *Middlemen in the Domestic Trade of the United States, 1800–1860* (Urbana, Ill.: University of Illinois, 1937).

Josephson, Matthew, *The Robber Barons* (New York: Harcourt, Brace & World, 1934 and 1962).

Kaplan, A. D. H., *Big Enterprise in a Competitive System* (Washington, D.C.: The Brookings Institution, 1954).

Keller, Morton, *The Life Insurance Enterprise, 1885–1910* (Cambridge, Mass.: Harvard University Press, 1963).

Kirkland, Edward C., *Dream and Thought in the Business Community 1860 to 1890* (Ithaca, N.Y.: Cornell University Press, 1956).

Krooss, Herman E., *Executive Opinion: What Business Leaders Said and Thought, 1920's–1960's* (Garden City, N.Y.: Doubleday and Company, Inc., 1970).

Latham, Earl (ed.), *John D. Rockefeller–Robber Baron or Industrial Statesman* (Boston: D. C. Heath & Company, 1949).

Littleton, A. C., *Accounting Evolution to 1900* (New York: American Institute Publishing Company, 1933).

Lynn, Kenneth, *The Dream of Success* (Boston: Little, Brown & Co., 1955).

McCloskey, R. G., *American Conservatism in the Age of Enterprise* (Cambridge, Mass.: Harvard University Press, 1951).

McGouldrick, Paul F., *New England Textiles in the Nineteenth Century* (Cambridge, Mass., Harvard University Press, 1968).

Miller, William (ed.), *Men in Business: Essays in the History of Entrepreneurship* (Cambridge, Mass.: Harvard University Press, 1952).

Myers, Margaret G., *The New York Money Market* (New York: Columbia University Press, 1931).

Nelson, Raph L., *Merger Movements in American Industry, 1895–1956* (Princeton, N.J.: Princeton University Press, 1959).

Nevins, Allan, *Ford: The Times, The Man, The Company* (New York: Charles Scribner's Sons, 1954).

————, *Ford: Expansion and Challenge* (New York: Charles Scribner's Sons, 1958).

————, and Frank Ernest Hill, *Ford: Decline and Rebirth: 1933–1962* (New York: Charles Scribner's Sons, 1963).

————, *Study in Power: John D. Rockefeller, Industrialist and Philanthropist*, 2 vols. (New York: Charles Scribner's Sons, 1953).

Newcomer, Mabel, *The Big Business Executive* (New York: Columbia University Press, 1955).

Nutter, G. Warren, and Henry Adler Einhorn, *Enterprise Monopoly in the United States: 1899–1958* (New York: Columbia University Press, 1969).

Pierce, Harry H., *Railroads of New York: A Study of Government Aid, 1826–1875* (Cambridge, Mass.: Harvard University Press, 1953).

Pollard, Sidney, *The Genesis of Modern Management* (Cambridge, Mass.: Harvard University Press, 1965).

Porter, Kenneth W., *John Jacob Astor, Business Man* (Cambridge, Mass.: Harvard University Press, 1931).

Redlich, Fritz, *History of American Business Leaders* (Ann Arbor, Mich.: Edward Brothers, 1940–1951).

————, *The Molding of American Banking, Men and Ideas* (New York: Johnson Reprint Co., 1968).

Satterlee, Herbert L., *J. Pierpont Morgan, an Intimate Portrait* (New York: The Macmillan Company, 1939).

Seligman, Ben B., *The Potentates* (New York: The Dial Press, 1970).

Sloan, Alfred P., Jr., *My Years with General Motors* (Garden City, N.Y.: Doubleday & Company, 1964).

Smith, Walter B., and Arthur H. Cole, *Fluctuations in American Business, 1790–1860* (Cambridge, Mass.: Harvard University Press, 1935).

Sobel, Robert, *The Big Board: A History of the New York Stock Market* (New York: The Macmillan Company, 1965).

Sutton, Francis X., and others, *The American Business Creed* (Cambridge, Mass.: Harvard University Press, 1956).

Wall, Joseph Frazier, *Andrew Carnegie* (New York: Oxford University Press, 1970).

Ware, Caroline F., *The Early New England Cotton Manufacture* (Boston: Houghton Mifflin Co., 1931).

Wiebe, Robert H., *Businessmen and Reform* (Cambridge, Mass.: Harvard University Press, 1962).

Wylie, Irwin G., *The Self-Made Man in America: The Myth of Rags to Riches* (Rutgers, N.J.: Rutgers University Press, 1954).

BOOKS OF READINGS

1. Baughman, James P. (ed.), *The History of American Management: Selections from the Business History Review* (Englewood Cliffs, N.J.: Prentice-Hall, Inc., 1969).

2. Coats, A. W., and Ross M. Robertson (eds.), *Essays in American Economic History* (London, Edward Arnold, 1969).

3. Chandler, Alfred D., Jr., Stuart Bruchey, and Louis Galambos (eds.), *The Changing Economic Order* (New York: Harcourt, Brace & World, Inc., 1968).
4. Coben, Stanley, and Forest G. Hill (eds.), *American Economic History: Essays in Interpretation* (Philadelphia: J. B. Lippincott Company, 1966).
5. Cochran, Thomas C., and Thomas Brewer (eds.), *Views of American Economic Growth*, 2 vols. (New York: McGraw-Hill Book Company, 1966).
6. Degler, Carl N. (ed.), *Pivotal Interpretations of American History* (New York: Harper & Row, 1966).
7. Robertson, Ross M., and James L. Pate, *Readings in Economic and Business History* (Boston: Houghton Mifflin Company, 1966).

ARTICLES

AER—American Economic Review

BHR—Business History Review

JEBH—Journal of Economic and Business History

JEH—Journal of Economic History

Bailyn, Bernard, "Communications and Trade: The Atlantic in the Seventeenth Century," *JEH*, Vol. 13 (1953).

Bruchey, Stuart, "Success and Failure Factors: American Merchants in Foreign Trade in the Eighteenth and Early Nineteenth Centuries," *BHR*, Vol. XXXII (1958). Reprinted in 3 above.

Chandler, Alfred D., Jr., "The Beginnings of Big Business in American Industry," *BHR*, Vol. XXXIII (1959). Reprinted in 1, 4, 5, and 6 cited above.

————, "Development, Diversification, and Decentralization," Ralph E. Freeman, *Postwar Economic Trends* (New York: Harper & Row, 1960). Reprinted in 7 above.

————, "Management Decentralization: An Historical Analysis," *BHR*, Vol. XXX (1956). Reprinted in 1 above.

————, "Patterns of American Railroad Finance, 1830–1850," *BHR*, Vol. XXVIII (1954).

————, and Fritz Redlich, "Recent Developments in American Business Administration and Their Conceptualization," *BHR*, Vol. XXV (1961). Reprinted in 4 above.

Cochran, Thomas C., "Role and Sanction in American Entrepreneurial History," *Change and the Entrepreneur* (Cambridge, Mass.: Harvard University Press, 1949).

Cole, Arthur H., "An Approach to the Study of Entrepreneurship," *JEH*, Vol. VI (1946).

————, "The Tempo of Mercantile Life in Colonial America," *BHR*, Vol. XXXIII (1959).

Collins, Norman R., and Lee E. Preston, "The Size Structure of the Largest Industrial Firms, 1909–1958," *AER*, Vol. LI (1961).

Dale, Ernest, and Charles Melog, "Hamilton MacFarland Barksdale and the DuPont Contributions to Systematic Management," *BHR*, Vol. XXXVI (1962).

Davis, Lance E., "The New England Textile Mills and the Capital Markets: A Study of Industrial Borrowing, 1840–1860," *JEH*, Vol. XX (1960). Reprinted in 2 above.

Edelman, Edward, "Thomas Hancock, Colonial Merchant," *JEBH*, Vol. 1 (1928–29). Reprinted in 7 above.

Fabricant, Solomon, "Is Monopoly Increasing?" *JEH*, Vol. XIII (1953).

Gilchrist, David, "Albert Fink and the Pooling System," *BHR*, Vol. XXXIV (1960). Reprinted in 5 above.

Ginger, Ray, "Labor in a Massachusetts Cotton Mill, 1853–60," *BHR*, Vol. XXVIII (1954).

Gras, N. S. B., "Stages in Economic History," *JEBH*, Vol. II (1930).

Gregory, Frances W., and Irene D. Neu, "The American Industrial Elite in the 1870's," *Men in Business* (Cambridge, Mass.: Harvard University Press, 1952).

Jenks, Leland H., "Early History of a Railway Organization," *BHR*, Vol. XXXV (1961).

Lamb, Robert K., "The Entrepreneur and the Community," *Men in Business* (Cambridge, Mass.: Harvard University Press, 1952). Reprinted in 4 above.

Miller, William, "American Historians and Business Elite," *JEH*, Vol. IX (1949).

———, "The Recruitment of the American Business Elite," *Quarterly Journal of Economics*, Vol. LXIV (1950). Reprinted in 7 above.

Mills, C. Wright, "The American Business Elite," *JEH*, Vol. V (1945).

Navin, Thomas R., and Marian V. Sears, "The Rise of the Market for Industrial Securities, 1887–1902, *BHR*, Vol. XXIX (1955).

Rae, John B., "Fabulous Billy Durant," *BHR*, Vol. XXXII (1958).

Sawyer, John E., "The Entrepreneur and the Social Order," *Men in Business* (Cambridge, Mass.: Harvard University Press, 1952).

———, "The Social Basis of the American System of Manufacturing," *JEH*, Vol. XIV (1954). Reprinted in 2 and 4 above.

Schumpeter, Joseph A., "The Creative Response in Economic History," *JEH*, Vol. VII (1947).

Silk, Alvin B., and Louis William Stern, "The Changing Nature of Innovation in Marketing: A Study of Selected Business Leaders, 1852–1958," *BHR*, Vol. XXXVII (1963).

Stigler, George, "Monopoly and Oligopoly by Merger," *AER*, Vol. XL (1950).

Supple, Barry E., "A Business Elite: German-Jewish Financiers in Nineteenth-Century New York," *BHR*, Vol. XXXI (1957).

Index

A. & P. (Great Atlantic and Pacific Tea Company), 226–27, 249
"Accommodation loans," 112–13
Accounting:
  attitudes toward, 126, 147, 188, 206–207, 213, 230, 278
  methods of, 67–68, 141, 157–58, 209, 214, 221, 252, 267, 279, 310, 318
Addyston Pipe and Steel Co., 180
  Supreme Court Case (1899), 186
"Administered prices," 295
Adventurers Company, 23
Advertising, 131, 133, 152, 166, 225, 226, 282
  agencies of, 228, 325
  expenditures for, 229–30, 314n.
  in late 19th century, 149, 154, 223, 227–31
  media of, 228–29, 230
  methods of, 37, 128, 229, 230–31, 316
  in newspapers, 72, 149, 228
Aetna Insurance Company, 235
Agricultural equipment industry, 91, 97–100, 145, 149
  marketing in, 130–31
  technological advances in, 78, 92, 93–94
  vertical integration of, 150
Agriculture (see also Farmers)
  capital needs of, 109
  in colonial period, 22, 24–25, 34–35, 49, 64, 66
  commercial, 109
  credit for, 113–14, 235
  dominance of, 93, 109, 129, 144–45, 244
  fairs, 131, 154
  products of, 24–25, 148, 226, 253
Air pollution, 317
Alcoa case (1945), 260
Aldrich, Nelson, 163
Alger, Horatio (stories), 11, 158
Allen, S. & M., Co., 110
Allis-Chalmers Co., 197, 271
Almy, William, 95, 96
Almy and Brown Co., 92, 95, 105, 107, 129, 150, 177
Aluminum Company of America, 260
Amalgamated Association of Iron and Steel Workers, 207–209
American Brass Association, 177
American Can Company, 191, 268, 270
American Federation of Labor (AFL), 289, 290
  and CIO, 292, 294
American Ice Company, 187
American Immigrant Company, 169
American Iron Association, 177
American Iron Company, 41
American Iron and Steel Association, 172
American Radiator Company, 196, 197
American Society (tariff association), 104
American Sugar Refining Co., 185–86, 189, 191, 193–96 passim, 197, 262, 278
American Telephone and Telegraph (A.T. & T.), 247, 249, 271
American Tobacco Company, 189, 191, 193–94, 197, 230
  Supreme Court case (1911), 255
American Wall Paper Manufacturing Association, 179
Amoskeag Manufacturing Company, 97, 160
Ancillary institutions, 157–58, 188, 267, 335
Anderson, John W., 303
Andrews, Samuel, 213, 214, 217, 219
Anheuser-Busch Co., 149, 152
Anti-Boycott League, 288
Antitrust policies, 183–86, 255–56 (see also Clayton Act; Sherman Act)
  assessment of, 261–62
  attitudes toward, 296, 332
  history of, 256–62, 283-84
  of state governments, 182
  Supreme Court and, 185–86, 254–56, 259–62 (see also Supreme Court decisions)
Apperson family (mechanics), 299
Appleton, Nathan, 96, 108, 111, 130, 163
Appleton Company, 107, 143
Apprenticeship system, 37–38, 57, 67, 70, 138
Arbitration:
  in coal strike (1902), 287
  compulsory, 294
Arbuckle, John, 262
Archbold, John D., 216
Arkwright, Richard, 92
Armaments industry, 91, 92
Armour and Co., 149, 155, 161, 173, 245
Arnold, Aaron, 225
Arnold Constable (store), 225
Artisans:
  in colonial period, 35–38, 62, 64, 65, 70, 112
  and commercial banking, 112
Assembly line, 301, 304–305, 317
Astor, John Jacob, 82, 84, 86, 90
Atchison, Topeka & Santa Fe Railway, 178
Attorney General's National Committee on the Antitrust Laws (1955), 261
Auctions, 86, 129–33, 282
Automation, 78, 315
Automobile industry, 284, 298–317
  diversification in, 253, 306–307
  effects of, 227, 316–17
  finance problems in, 299, 308, 316
  historical development of, 298–300, 333
  labor unions and, 292–94, 315–16
  leaders of (compared), 309–11
  marketing methods in, 130, 150, 311–14, 316 (see also Dealership system)
  maturity of, 309–10
  pricing and profits in, 311–15
Avery, C.W., 304
Ayer, N. W., & Son, 227n., 228, 229

Bache, Perry, Hayes & Sherbrooke, 55
Baer, George, 287, 328
Bailyn, Bernard, 28
Baker, George F., 237, 241
Balance sheets, 246
Balanced budget (see Federal budget, balanced)
Balch, Benjamin, 233
Baldwin, Loammi, 97
Baltimore Company (iron works), 42, 43, 138
Baltimore & Ohio Railroad, 18, 124, 127, 156, 178

345

356

357